CW00818802

BLACK VISIONS OF
THE HOLY LAND

COLUMBIA SERIES ON RELIGION AND POLITICS

COLUMBIA SERIES ON RELIGION AND POLITICS

The Columbia Series on Religion and Politics, edited by Gastón Espinosa (Claremont McKenna College) and Chester Gillis (Georgetown University), addresses the growing demand for scholarship on the intersection of religion and politics in a world in which religion attempts to influence politics and politics regularly must consider the effects of religion. The series examines the influence religion exercises in public life on areas including politics, environmental policy, social policy, law, church-state relations, foreign policy, race, class, gender, and culture. Written by experts in a variety of fields, the series explores the historical and contemporary intersection of religion and politics in the United States and globally.

Terrence L. Johnson, *We Testify with Our Lives: How Religion Transformed Radical Thought from Black Power to Black Lives Matter*

L. Benjamin Rolsky, *The Rise and Fall of the Religious Left: Politics, Television, and Popular Culture in the 1970s and Beyond*

Richard B. Miller, *Terror, Religion, and Liberal Social Criticism*

John M. Owen IV and J. Judd Owen, eds., *Religion, the Enlightenment, and the New Global Order*

Gary Dorrien, *Economy, Difference, Empire: Social Ethics for Social Justice*

Gastón Espinosa, ed., *Religion and the American Presidency: George Washington to George W. Bush with Commentary and Primary Sources*

Mark Hulsether, *Religion, Culture, and Politics in the Twentieth-Century United States*

BLACK VISIONS OF THE HOLY LAND

African American Christian Engagement with Israel and Palestine

ROGER BAUMANN

Columbia University Press

New York

Columbia University Press
Publishers Since 1893
New York   Chichester, West Sussex
cup.columbia.edu

Library of Congress Cataloging-in-Publication Data
Names: Baumann, Roger, 1975- author.
Title: Black Visions of the Holy Land : African American Christian Engagement with
    Israel and Palestine / Roger Baumann.
Other titles: Black visions of the Holy Land
Description: New York : Columbia University Press, [2023] | Series: Columbia series on
    religion and politics | Includes bibliographical references and index.
Identifiers: LCCN 2023042458 | ISBN 9780231198448 (hardback) |
    ISBN 9780231198455 (trade paperback) | ISBN 9780231552639 (ebook)
Subjects: LCSH: African American churches. | African Americans—Religion. | African
    Americans—Relations with Jews. | African Americans—Attitudes. | Public opinion—
    Israel. | Christian Zionism. | United States—Race relations.
Classification: LCC BR563.B53 B38 2023 | DDC 261.7089/96073—dc23/eng/20240116
LC record available at https://lccn.loc.gov/2023042458

Printed and bound by CPI Group (UK) Ltd, Croydon, CR0 4YY

Cover design: Noah Arlow
Cover image: Shutterstock (stained glass)

Contents

Acknowledgments

I n the time I have spent on this project, I have learned over and over that this kind of work depends on the goodwill and guidance of many people. First, I am grateful to the people and the organizations this book is about; they welcomed me into their homes, churches, classes, conferences, and their travels to Palestine and Israel. In most cases, they did not know me when they agreed to talk with me about things that matter deeply to them, and I cannot thank each participant in this research enough for taking that risk. I hope and trust that they recognize themselves in the narrative I tell in this book. They are members, leaders, and constituents of the four organizations that make up the case studies: Christians United for Israel, the International Fellowship of Christians and Jews, the Perfecting Church, and the Samuel DeWitt Proctor Conference. Within these organizations and networks, I am especially grateful to Michael Stevens, Dumisani Washington, Kevin and Angela Brown, Christina King, Glenn Plummer, Taurean Webb, and Waltrina Middleton. These pastors and leaders went out of their way to introduce me to their colleagues, congregants, and constituents; and they invited me into the spaces of their religious communities and their activism. They helped me understand and tell the story of African American Christian engagement with Israel and Palestine from a wide range of perspectives. The people who opened their lives and experiences to me and became my guides in the world of Black religious politics are too numerous to name here, but I thank each one of them for their generous participation in this project.

I began thinking about this project at Yale University when I had only a handful of questions and curiosities. With patient mentorship and guidance from many friends, colleagues, and teachers, I learned to extend those early questions into a research program and how to share what I found with a wide audience. Philip Gorski, Jonathan Wyrtzen, Frederick Wherry, and Clarence Hardy contributed the most to this experience of learning by doing. I am also indebted to Julia Adams, Elijah Anderson, Ron Eyerman, Marcus Hunter, Matthew Mahler, and Elisabeth Wood for invaluable contributions at formative times in the process. When I think about my time at Yale working on this project, I realize that I learned as much from my many generous colleagues as I did from my dedicated teachers and mentors—especially Elisabeth Becker, Sorcha Brophy, Inkwan Chung, Shai Dromi, Jonathan Endelman, Stephanie Greenlea, Jeff Guhin, John Hartley, Todd Madigan, Billy McMillan, Nick Occhiuto, Gülay Türkmen, Hüseyin Raşit, Celene Reynolds, Sam Stabler, Luke Wagner, and Mustafa Yavas. These colleagues and others introduced me to the world of professional sociology and to a wide network of scholars in many organizations who became central to the development of this project and my professional trajectory. In the context of conferences and workshops, many people provided incisive and invaluable feedback on parts of this work. Beyond Yale, I am especially grateful to guidance from Ruth Braunstein, Candace Lukasik, Brandon Martinez, Damon Mayrl, Daniel Winchester, Richard Wood, Rhys Williams, and Sara Williams. I am also grateful for financial and professional support of the Social Sciences and Humanities Research Council of Canada, the Society for the Scientific Study of Religion, the Louisville Institute, the Institution for Social and Policy Studies, the MacMillan Center for International and Area Studies, and the George M. Camp fund at Yale University.

Finally, capturing my gratitude to my family in a few short lines feels incredibly inadequate. This project represents the outcome of a formative period in my personal and professional life that would not have been possible without them. I have always been surrounded by their unconditional love and support. Foremost from Elizabeth, my wife and partner in everything. Over the course of this decade-long project, she was a full-time clinical psychologist and, at every point, my most important editor, advisor, and supporter. When I was off doing fieldwork, whether for days or weeks at a time, she held things together for our family while simultaneously building a successful career as a therapist. She is all I could have ever asked for in a partner and more. My parents—Esther and John—provided me with a loving example from a young age of how to take a leap of faith and courageously follow an uncharted and uncertain path in life. And for the past twenty-five years, Wolfgang has been a constant source of help and support. My sisters—Andrea and Kelly—have always been the most important extension of the circle of love and support that began with our parents. More recently, my in-laws—Pat, Sharon, Cecilia, John, and Anna—have similarly provided unconditional love and support. Finally, always at the front of my thoughts are my children—John, Chloe, and Andrew—all were born during the course of this project, and each one has stretched my heart and mind immeasurably. They are the reason behind everything I do, and this book is for them.

BLACK VISIONS OF

THE HOLY LAND

Introduction

(BLACK) CHRISTIANS UNITED FOR ISRAEL?

On a Sunday night in March 2012, the three-thousand-seat sanctuary of the First Cathedral in Bloomfield, Connecticut, was filled to near capacity. The First Cathedral is an African American megachurch in the suburbs of Hartford, Connecticut. The church sits on a forty-acre property at an intersection where two of the other three corners are occupied by smaller Black churches. Before it became the First Cathedral at its current location, the congregation had existed at two previous sites in North Hartford with the name the First Baptist Church. Claiming eleven thousand members, the First Cathedral is one of the largest Black megachurches in the northeastern United States. On many typical Sunday mornings when I attended, the large sanctuary was dominated by Black church-goers, with just a handful of white and Hispanic faces among the worshipers. But on this night in March 2012, white attendees outnumbered Black attendees for a special "Night to Honor Israel" event. It had been advertised as "an evening of solidarity and celebration with the Connecticut Christian and Jewish communities." The First Cathedral gospel recording artist J. J. Hariston[1] and the Youthful Praise choir blended original contemporary gospels songs such as "Lord You're Mighty" and "Great Expectations" with Hebrew Jewish folk music such as "Hevenu Shalom Aleichim" and "Hava Nagila." Christian worshipers stood with Jewish guests, many clapping or waving their hands in the air to the music.

Throughout the evening, the First Cathedral's senior pastor, Archbishop LeRoy Bailey Jr., welcomed a series of guest speakers to the stage, including then U.S. senator and former vice presidential candidate Joseph Lieberman. "We have Abraham as our father and the land of Israel as our home," Bailey proclaimed to the mix of Jewish and Christian audience members in his introductory remarks. He concluded, specifically addressing the Jewish guests in attendance, "God bless you tonight. God secure you tonight. God secure Israel. You are where you belong. We pray for the peace of Jerusalem. We pray for the peace of Israel!"

The evening's keynote speaker was Pastor John Hagee, the conservative pastor and mainstay of national evangelical television and radio broadcasting. Hagee came to prominence among American evangelicals after building a successful Pentecostal megachurch and media ministry based in San Antonio, Texas. He has made a career of preaching based on interpreting Bible prophecies in anticipation of Earth's "end-times," as well as championing familiar conservative theological and political positions including condemning abortion, criticizing action against climate change as a conspiracy, and arguing for defunding the United Nations. Since 2006 he has become more widely known among evangelicals as the founder and chairperson of Christians United for Israel (CUFI), the Night to Honor Israel's sponsoring organization. CUFI describes itself as the largest pro-Israel organization in the United States, claiming more than eight million members.[2]

At the First Cathedral, Hagee spoke to some of his longtime core issues such as defunding the United Nations. He also criticized then president Barack Obama, insisting that he stop pressuring Israel to compromise with Palestinians and arguing in favor of turning his foreign policy attention to preventing Iran from acquiring nuclear weapons. "America is now in a major crisis," Hagee said. "The major crisis is the nuclear threat of Iran and a global war with a radical Islamic dictator who believes he has a mandate from God to kill Christians and Jews." "If a line has to be drawn, draw a line around both Christians and Jews," he exhorted. "We are one. We are united. We are spiritual brothers based upon the Torah of God." Further warning against radical Islam, Hagee argued: "Adolph Hitler wrote *Mein Kampf*, which means 'my struggle.' The word *jihad* also means 'my struggle.' The struggle of the Third Reich and the struggle of radical Islam is one and the same."

This kind of rhetoric, although familiar in conservative white evangelical circles in the United States, is not typically associated with African American Christianity. When we think of Black churches in the United States and how they relate to politics, iconic civil rights images and the speeches of the Reverend Martin Luther King Jr. are more likely to come to mind than the image of African American churchgoers standing with American Jews, waving

Israeli and American flags together in political solidarity with the State of Israel. What should we make of this interracial, interfaith "Night to Honor Israel" event in Connecticut? Was this an exceptional, one-off event, or was it part of something bigger?

I began to get an answer the following year when I attended a Bible study in the basement of a small congregation of the Black Pentecostal Church of God in Christ (COGIC) denomination in New Haven, Connecticut. On that Wednesday evening, the hosting minister turned the Bible study over to another COGIC pastor visiting from North Carolina for a thematic study called "Standing with Israel." Before the event began, I met a group of three African American women who had come for the Bible study. The youngest was a recent college graduate who had majored in political science and Judaic studies. She told me that she had attended CUFI's annual summit in Washington, DC, the previous year as a student delegate and was currently trying to start a student chapter of CUFI at the University of Connecticut. She was attending the Bible study with her mother and her mother's friend. As we were talking, the host pastor called the group together. He described meeting the visiting speaker at another COGIC event and said he had been impressed with him and his ministry. He also mentioned that he listens to Pastor John Hagee's sermons on Sunday mornings before preaching at his own church. The visiting pastor introduced himself as Michael Stevens, the African American Outreach Coordinator for CUFI. Stevens had also been at the Hartford Night to Honor Israel and had spoken briefly there, introducing another Black CUFI student activist.

At this Bible study, Stevens talked about how his travels to Israel had opened his eyes to the importance of the State of Israel. He described visiting soldiers in the Israeli military near the border with Lebanon and coming to realize that they were not only protecting Israel "in this jihadist world" but were also protecting America. "If the first goal of jihad is to eliminate Israel, the second goal is to wipe out the U.S.," he said. Next, Stevens put a quote from Martin Luther King Jr. on the projection screen: "Peace for Israel means security, and we must stand with all our might to protect her right to exist." Stevens then went on to talk about President Obama's recent visit to Israel, inserting a caveat that CUFI is not a "political organization." Stevens said conservative African American Christians like him are in a unique position because they are proud of President Obama, but they are also unhappy with his position on same-sex marriage and his policies toward Israel. As examples of these policies, Stevens cited the president's "embrace of Muslims" in his well-known 2009 speech on U.S.-Muslim relations delivered in Cairo, as well as what he described as Obama's "snubbing" of Israeli Prime Minister Benjamin Netanyahu in Washington, DC. Stevens then pivoted to the Bible and reiterated that CUFI is not a partisan or political organization but that it is a *Christian* organization. He said, "Everything CUFI does is based on the word of God." He went on to tell the story of how he had come to take on the role of African American Outreach Coordinator for CUFI—an overwhelmingly white organization—and how he came to spend much of his time traveling around the United States and the world teaching Black pastors and churchgoers about the importance of supporting the State of Israel. He emphasized, "God will bless us if we bless the Jewish people." Stevens also had with him copies of his book, *We Too Stand: A Call for the African-American Church to Support the Jewish State*, recently released with a major evangelical publisher.[3]

This was the first of nine events over the next year at which I watched Stevens speak to Black church audiences. These events ranged from pastors' briefings involving about a dozen Black clergy to another Night to Honor Israel at Stevens's home congregation in Charlotte, North Carolina, where more than five hundred members and guests gathered for another Israel-focused interfaith celebration similar to the one held at the First Cathedral in Connecticut. Again, John Hagee was the Charlotte event's keynote speaker. What motivated me to follow Stevens around the East Coast that year, as he carried out African American outreach on behalf of John Hagee and CUFI, were questions about the extent of the appeal of Christian Zionism within Black congregations in the United States.[4] I also wondered why a popular pastor with an established and growing congregation in North Carolina would spend so much of his time doing outreach for a largely white pro-Israel advocacy organization. Through this fieldwork within the Christian Zionist world of CUFI, and eventually a similar investigation of other cases of African American Christian engagement with the issue of Israel and Palestine, I would come to learn many things about the state of Black religious politics in the United States, including how and why Christian Zionism had become a priority for some Black pastors and congregations. I also learned how other, radically different visions of Black religious politics were propelling forms of religious political engagement in the Middle East on very different terms than certain Black churches' alliance with CUFI.[5]

OCCUPIED PALESTINE: HOW SHOULD
THE BLACK CHURCH RESPOND?

On a cold and rainy Monday morning in November 2014, I joined another group
of African American Christians concerned with Palestine and Israel. At the
Howard University School of Divinity in Washington, DC, Dean Alton Pollard
welcomed a group of about a hundred students, scholars, pastors, and activists to
a gathering in the school's chapel entitled "Occupied Palestine: How Should the
Black Church Respond?" "If theological education is not about justice," Pollard
said from the chapel's pulpit, "it is wasting its time." As Pollard continued, he
explained why he thought that, for many in attendance, the question of Israel
and Palestine might seem far removed from more immediate concerns: "We prepare, with bated breath, for the verdict that will come out of Ferguson," Pollard
said, anticipating the upcoming news from Ferguson, Missouri, about the possible indictment of the police officer who had killed Michael Brown, an unarmed
Black teenager, on a residential street just three months earlier. Just a week later,
the St. Louis County prosecutor announced the decision of a grand jury of nine
white and three Black members to bring no charges against the officer. The
announcement set off a new wave of protests against racism and police brutality
in Ferguson and around the United States.

"We prepare," Pollard continued to the audience gathered at Howard, "knowing that there are occupying forces [in Ferguson]. We also recognize that the occupying forces that continue to be in the Middle East and in much of our world—in
the name of power—[are] something that we, who are people of faith, will continue to address." Dr. Iva Carruthers, another convener of the meeting, also gave
introductory remarks on behalf of the organization she leads, the Samuel DeWitt
Proctor Conference (SDPC or "the Proctor Conference"). The Proctor Conference is a network of progressive African American faith leaders that Carruthers
explained to the Howard audience were defined by a vision of education, advocacy, and activism. On the question of a response to the plight of Palestinians, she
emphasized: "For us, it is not a question of *if* the Black Church should respond,
but indeed *how* the Black Church should respond."

I learned more about the Proctor Conference and their engagement with the
Palestinian cause in February 2016 at the organization's annual clergy and lay
leadership conference in Houston, Texas. The theme of that year's conference

was "Look Around: The Cries Will Be Heard." These "cries" were communicated in a montage of striking images on the cover of the program and on the event stage. They included a Black protestor being arrested by three white police officers in riot gear; Black protestors carrying a sign decrying environmental toxins; a Black protestor on a bicycle raising a fist to a line of riot police behind heavy shields; a "Hands Up, Don't Shoot" sign; and portraits of Trayvon Martin and Michael Brown. Setting the agenda for the meeting, Proctor Conference cochair Reverend Frederick Haynes identified the organization's approach to those cries in one word—*activism*. According to Haynes, the Houston conference was "not just a feel-good gathering, but a *movement*." He exhorted the more than five hundred clergy and lay leaders in attendance to "put on our prophetic eyeglasses and tune our ears to the cries."

Among these images of "cries" that the Proctor Conference identified as needing to be heard and responded to was a photo of a Palestinian funeral procession with a large group of marchers carrying the body of a woman wrapped in a Palestinian flag. In her review of the SDPC's 2015 activities, General Secretary Iva Carruthers, who had helped lead the "Occupied Palestine: How Should the Black Church Respond?" event at Howard, explained the relationship between African Americans fighting for racial justice in the United States and the Palestinian cause. She highlighted two leadership delegations that had gone to Palestine and Israel and announced the upcoming launch of curriculum intended as a congregational resource to help Black churches "as they become more aware of the Palestinian crisis and begin to take action on behalf of Palestinian freedom and justice."[6] Carruthers also described a gathering just a few months earlier in which SDPC leaders met with Palestinian activists to "discuss the evolving faces of racial caste and white supremacy that operate in both Palestine-Israel and the United States."[7]

Later that evening, at the opening worship service of the four-day conference, Pittsburgh hip-hop artist and activist Jasiri X was the first of many plenary speakers to bring up Palestine. Describing his 2014 trip to the region, he said:

> One of the realest things somebody said to me in Palestine . . . was [from] a professor at a university in Palestine. He said, "You know why you should care about what's happening in Palestine and why the hood should care?" He said, "Because the policing that you see here is coming to a hood near you." And eight months later—August of 2014—I had to go through a checkpoint to get into Ferguson, Missouri.

The next morning, Taurean Webb, a Chicago-based activist and scholar-in-residence at the Proctor Conference spoke to a workshop audience and told his story of traveling to Israel and Palestine:

> Imagine this, imagine this with me: You are on your way back to the States from a work trip abroad. The region that you're coming from is an active war zone. And the persons with whom you've been sitting, working, journeying are living under a full military occupation, which is illegal under the standards of international law. . . . Because of how you are profiled—in a racially supremacist military state—the movement in space is very heavily policed and surveilled. Because of how you're profiled, you and your cab driver are stopped in the middle of the road by armed military soldiers. They tell you to get out and they grill you on why you were there, what you were doing while you were there, how long you were there, who you were with. All on site, on the spot, at gunpoint. This was my experience coming from the occupied territories of the West Bank, flying out of Israel, coming back to Chicago.

The following evening, the main conference hall was full to hear a sermon from Reverend Neichelle Guidry, a preacher from Chicago. Her sermon was preceded by a responsive litany called "A Litany for Children Hurling Stones," invoking the iconic Palestinian protest tactic of throwing stones at armed Israeli military personnel, which became a symbol of the First Palestinian Intifada in 1987. Following the litany, Reverend Guidry began to preach about "the significance of throwing a stone":

> About two months ago, around the onset of Advent, the Proctor Conference sponsored a sojourn of an intergenerational delegation of clergy and activists to Palestine. To be very clear, let me say upfront that, no, we did not go to Palestine on some traditional Christian pilgrimage. Rather, we were sent to survey the land, to open our eyes and our ears and to see the struggle of our Brown brothers and sisters in and through the Holy City of Jerusalem and throughout the West Bank. Through the force of our visits to Palestinian villages, refugee camps, and homes, I was baptized by fire into a deep melancholic aching of awakeness of the global oppression of Black and Brown bodies. And into a greater understanding of the interconnectedness of our stories and our struggles.

Throughout the four-day conference—in workshops, plenary sessions, break-out conversations, and personal interactions—many others echoed the importance of understanding the interconnectedness of African American and Palestinian struggles. The issue of Palestine was presented alongside racial justice issues in the United States such as education inequality, poverty, mass incarceration, youth incarceration, environmental protection, and police militarization.

COMPETING VISIONS FOR AFRICAN AMERICAN CHRISTIAN SOLIDARITY IN ISRAEL AND PALESTINE

The Palestine-focused activism of the Proctor Conference stands in sharp contrast to the Christian Zionism of CUFI. Both are movements that operate within religious contexts and carry strong political implications. Specifically, they both focus on drawing African American clergy and church members into the issue of Israel and Palestine—one on the side of the State of Israel, the other on the side of Palestinians. Among scholars of Black churches in the United States, attention to political engagement has tended to focus on domestic protest and electoral politics. But the issue of Palestine and Israel takes Black church politics beyond the domestic arena and into a broader global context. In light of this phenomenon, this book raises the following question: Why would African American Christians get involved—and even take sides—with regard to Israel and Palestine when they typically focus their attention on local and domestic issues, if they venture into politics at all?

I consider this question through a comparison of CUFI and the Proctor Conference along with two other case studies. Taken together, these four cases show a wide range of Black Christian responses to Palestine and Israel in religious and political terms. They also get at broader questions about what Black churches are; how they understand their political role and social significance; and how race, religion, and politics converge in both competing and complementary ways.

The third case in this comparison is a Jewish Israeli nonprofit organization, the International Fellowship of Christians and Jews (IFCJ or "the Fellowship"), which raises money primarily from American Christians for philanthropic projects in Israel and to support diaspora Jews making *aliyah* (i.e., immigrating) to Israel. Like CUFI, the Fellowship has, in recent years, launched an African American outreach program that it considers to be a more "faith-based" alternative to what it sees as CUFI's more overtly political activism. The fourth case is The Perfecting Church (TPC), a large, predominantly African American independent evangelical congregation in the south New Jersey suburbs of Philadelphia. TPC is part of a larger (not majority African American) network of evangelical pastors and congregations led by Pastor Bob Roberts, out of his Northwood church in Dallas-Fort Worth, Texas. Since 2010, TPC's senior pastor, Kevin Brown, has led small delegations of his church members to the West Bank to work with Palestinians on issues ranging from religious peacebuilding, to social work, sports, and the arts. They call this cross-cultural work within Palestinian civil society "glocal engagement"—bridging the "global" and the "local" as sites for church engagement and activity.

All four cases are examples of engagement with the issue of Israel and Palestine within Black churches in the United States. Although they diverge significantly in their hermeneutics, public theologies, and modes of political engagement, the Black church leaders and laypeople in all of these groups concern themselves with understanding the ethical, religious, and political implications of their Christian faith in the context of the global issue of Israel and Palestine. Furthermore, they all have something to say about how African American Christians should respond to that issue. Far from operating in isolated social spaces, I suggest that the groups and networks of churches profiled in this account occupy a shared religious social space. Within this space they offer competing claims about how African American Christians should respond to the issue of Palestine and Israel as a group with an ostensible shared history, identity, and culture. Scholars of African American religion have often talked about this distinctive yet diversified social space, giving it the label "the Black Church."[8] But the notion that there is such a thing as *the* Black church is contested, even as many of the African American Christians mentioned in this book assume and profess its existence. At the same time, they offer competing normative accounts of what "the Black Church" is, where it came from, and where it should focus its attention when it comes to social and political action.

I contend that the central question of why and how some Black churches take an interest in Israel and Palestine opens further implications for how we should understand Black religious politics; the social significance of Black churches in the United States more broadly; and the ways race, religion, and politics converge in transnational engagement with the issue of Palestine and Israel. In taking up these questions, I suggest that African American Christian engagement with Israel and Palestine is an instructive case for understanding Black religious politics more broadly as a contest over the character and purpose of "the Black Church." I argue that attention to African American Christian engagement with Israel and Palestine reveals competing priorities about appropriate Black church identities, each of which is sustained by particular narratives and memories, and each of which leads to the development of particular solidarities.

RACE, RELIGION, AND POLITICS IN ISRAEL AND PALESTINE: WHY BLACK CHURCHES?

As new movements for racial justice are gaining increasing attention in the United States, these movements are also appealing to global solidarities. With respect to Israel and Palestine, for example, contemporary Christian Zionist political support for the State of Israel has extended from its roots in American and British Protestantism to include branches around the globe—from Kenya to South Korea and Singapore to the Navajo Nation Territory.[9] When the Movement for Black Lives—a coalition of groups across the United States working on racial justice issues, including Black Lives Matter—released its policy platform in August of 2016, one of the most controversial parts of that platform was its criticism of the State of Israel as "a state that practices systematic discrimination and has maintained a military occupation of Palestine for decades."[10] The policy platform positioned divestment from the State of Israel side by side with priorities for investment in African American communities aimed at achieving higher levels of Black political power and community control. These examples suggest emerging global solidarities with Israelis and Palestinians in racial, religious, and political terms.

Attention to the roles that race, religion, and politics play in Palestine and Israel varies with the overall framework and context of multiple approaches to understanding the contemporary significance of that transnational issue. In some popular accounts, it is a relatively recent political conflict over territory emerging out of a reconfiguration of regional powers and nation-states in the Middle East in the twentieth century. Other accounts frame the issue as a contemporary battleground for an intractable centuries-old religious conflict between Islam as a global force and guardians of Western "Judeo-Christianity" who stand guard against its global domination. The former approach tends to deemphasize both religion and race, whereas the latter attends to religion in an imprecise and detached way with little recognition of racial factors. Both of these common framings largely miss the extent to which global solidarities in overlapping racial and religious terms are increasingly salient in views on Palestine and Israel.

Most attention to the contemporary transnational significance of Israel and Palestine focuses on global solidarities in *political* terms with religious inputs or antecedents—with attention to Zionism as a Jewish political movement and to the international Boycott, Divestment, and Sanctions (BDS) movement on behalf of Palestinians, for example. Less attention has been given to global solidarities in religious or racial terms. Exceptions to this include the recent renewal of scholarly and popular engagement with long-standing and emerging examples of Black-Palestinian transnational solidarity. For scholars of Black-Palestinian solidarity, the qualifier *renewal* is key because of the historical roots of this transnational movement in the early decades of the twentieth century.[11] Much of this recent attention to Black-Palestinian transnational solidarity came out of connections forged among activists and scholars engaged with the Palestinian cause and African American movements for racial justice who, in the summer of 2014, drew parallels between the concurrent police occupation of Ferguson, Missouri, and the sustained Israeli bombing of Gaza in Operation Protective Edge.

In terms of the transnational significance of American religion in Palestine and Israel, scholarly attention to evangelical interest in Israel (under the rubric of Christian Zionism) has been long-standing. This phenomenon came into increased prominence with the Trump administration's recognition of Jerusalem as the capital of the State of Israel, which has been widely cast as a reward for the conservative evangelical elements of the Republican base of voters that helped propel him into office.[12] As the racially charged debate over whether the State of Israel practices apartheid today looms large, I suggest it can only be understood at the intersection of race, religion, and politics, which requires particular attention beyond the world of white American evangelicalism and specifically on transnational solidarity-building across racial and religious lines. Within this imperative I consider American Christian Zionism beyond its white majority, specifically focusing on minority racial and ethnic religious spaces where Christian Zionists seek to build a more diversified base of support. I also include African American Christian critics of Zionism, who find common cause with Palestinians in a racialized global political struggle understood in prophetic religious terms.

With a direct examination of intersections of race, religion, and politics, one of my goals is to open important modes of analysis of the transnational significance of race, with particular attention to the global political spaces in which new solidarities in Israel and Palestine are being created and debated. In examining how some Black churches successfully galvanize their congregants to focus on the politics of the Middle East, I consider how these kinds of global solidarities are sustained in the context of Black churches. I show how some pastors and other leaders construct congregational identities that are concerned with the politics of Palestine and Israel by grafting certain aspects of African American history, identity, and culture onto narratives about solidarities with Israelis and Palestinians, reframing in global terms the appropriate religious responses to pressing issues of racial injustice that have been widely and publicly debated in American religious social spaces and in the public sphere more broadly. I suggest that Israel and Palestine can only be understood with attention to politics, religion, and race in equal measure. I also suggest rethinking what African American churches are, how they engage in politics, and how that engagement happens in the context of contentious global political issues. This introduction lays the groundwork for these discussions: I begin by unpacking questions about what Black churches are and how they relate to politics. I then summarize my central argument—that Black religious politics is best understood as a contested social space in which competing visions of the identity and mission of "the Black Church" are advanced.

WHAT IS "THE BLACK CHURCH"?

The first question to ask in approaching Black religious politics as a contested social space is, *What are Black churches?* I begin by briefly looking at various ways this question has been approached by a range of scholars and other observers of and participants in Black religious life in the United States, including those with a stake in the question itself.[13] The first step is to ask: *How do we know what we know about African American religious history and Black churches?* For a long time, Black religion was, at best, largely viewed through the lens of white religion in America, or it was ignored as unimportant vis-à-vis white religion. Eddie Glaude calls this condition of African American religious life an existence "under captured conditions."[14] What was required even to be able to talk about the distinctiveness of Black religion, then, is what religious historian Albert Raboteau called "an act of recovery."[15] Writing in the late 1970s—a moment when a range of scholarship on African and African American experiences began to acknowledge Black people as agents, not spectators, in history—Raboteau took up the historical task of recovering Black voices, especially through examining slaves' narratives.[16] For him, this revealed a previously "invisible institution" of Black religion.[17]

This was an important turning point, but not the beginning of scholarly analyses of Black religion in the United States from Black perspectives, which traces further back to the work of early African American sociologists and anthropologists W. E. B. Du Bois, Charles Johnson, E. Franklin Frazier, Zora Neale Hurston, Horace Cayton, St. Clair Drake, and Arthur Fauset, among others.[18] Working in diverse institutional contexts and with various methodological presuppositions about where and how to study Black religion, these scholars analyzed Black churches in rural and urban contexts, applying sociological and anthropological methods to the study of Black religious life. Scholarly debates emerged on questions of whether early expressions of African American Christianity were in continuity with an African cultural legacy (as argued by Melvin Herskovitz, for example) or whether that culture had been effectively wiped out by the process of enslavement (as argued by Fauset and Frazier). Scholars were also divided on questions of the extent to which white racism shaped African American religious identities (exemplified in Myrdal's debates with Drake and Cayton). On these early generations of scholarly interest in African American religious communities, historian Barbara Savage notes that perhaps the most enduring legacy of their work is the idea that there is such a thing as "the Black Church" and that it ought to be investigated as such.[19]

Although W. E. B. Du Bois had been writing on "the Negro Church" since the turn of the twentieth century, perhaps the most influential example of the trend in analyses of African American religious life in the first half of the twentieth century to accept the notion of "the Black Church" as an object of analysis is E. Franklin Frazier's *The Negro Church in America*, which was published posthumously in 1963 and based on a series of lectures Frazier gave a decade earlier. For Frazier, after the Civil War African American churches became something new, called "the Negro church," which he described as "a nation within a nation,"[20] that is, a space for social advancement, political agency, and economic opportunity in a hostile white-dominated world. According to Frazier, during the early decades immediately following the Civil War and emancipation, Black churches were places of racial uplift. This general characterization influenced later analyses of the changing social role of Black churches over the course of the twentieth century, focusing in particular on questions of whether "the Negro church" should be seen as fostering or hindering social engagement in political protest. On this question, Gayraud Wilmore notes that the general orientation Frazier described of "the Negro church" as a place for social advancement did not last. Wilmore describes the decades leading up to the 1950s and the high point of civil rights activism as a period of "deradicalization" within Black churches, when racial uplift became more inward-focused for Black churches, privileging self-help over protest.[21] For other observers of Black religious spaces, this led to questions of whether the Black church should be thought of as having a social and political stance of *resistance* or *accommodation*, of political *activism* or *quietism*, of outward-focused *protest* or inward-focused self-help and community *uplift*.

In more religious terms, this divide has been described as Black churches embracing either a *this-worldly* or *other-worldly* orientation, a *prophetic* versus *priestly* character, or an *accommodationist* versus *resistance* stance on political questions.[22] These have been durable typologies, within which some scholars have argued for the idea that Black churches have, by and large, retreated from politics and this-worldly concerns in favor of attending exclusively to the spiritual and religious needs of their communities.[23] Others, however, have seen Black churches as eminently social institutions, deeply connected to various secular aspects of community life, including politics.[24]

Scholarly conceptions of Black religious institutions changed with the social, political, and cultural upheaval of the 1950s and 1960s. In one of the first analyses of American Black churches in the wake of that civil rights era, C. Eric Lincoln proclaimed Frazier's "Negro Church" to have experienced a death and rebirth:

> It died an agonized death in the harsh turmoil which tried the faith so rigorously in the decade of the "Savage Sixties." . . . With sadness and reluctance, trepidation and confidence, the Negro Church accepted death in order to be reborn. Out of the ashes of its funeral pyre there sprang the bold, strident, self-conscious phoenix that is the contemporary Black Church.[25]

This pronouncement about the centrality of the civil rights movement to understanding Black religion in America has been widely influential. Many analyses of African American Christianity following Lincoln have come through this lens and with the primacy of the civil rights legacy built in to it. In this context, various frameworks have been advanced to deal with and add nuance to bina-ries such as *resistance* versus *accommodation* or *priestly* versus *prophetic*. One of the earliest and most wide-ranging studies to deal with the social, political, and theological landscape of Black Protestantism in America in the wake of the civil rights moment ending in the 1970s is C. Eric Lincoln and Lawrence Mamiya's book, *The Black Church in the African American Experience.* In it, they not only offer a methodological defense for using "the Black Church" as an analytic sociological category but also what they describe as a *dialectical model* for analyzing the range of political outlooks, theological orientations, and organizational forms found across the diversity of American Black churches.[26]

This dialectical approach has been influential for scholars of Black religion trying to account for the diversity of Black religious expressions while, at the same time, holding onto the overarching category of "the Black Church." Refining and building on the dialectical model, others have called for approaches to understanding the diversity of Black churches using *dialogical* models or a series of *continua*.[27] However, some recent scholarship—particularly that of Savage—has called into question the appropriateness of continuing to use an overarching label for "the Black Church." Savage challenges the fundamental fusion of African American religion and politics as a product of looking at Black religion primarily through the lens of the civil rights movement. Taking the civil rights lens as par-adigmatic, she argues, obscures important debates about relationships between religion and politics in African American religious spaces.[28]

Black Churches and Black Church Studies

Even early social scientific studies of African American religious communities had prescriptive elements that took them out of the realm of ostensibly dispas-sionate, scientific inquiry into what Black churches *are* and into that of having something to say about what Black churches *ought to be*. For example, scholars like Du Bois, Fauset, and Woodson not only described what Black churches were and what their leaders and members did but also evaluated those positions, suggest-ing appropriate orientations toward political and social issues.[29] In many ways, the question of what Black churches are has always been accompanied by ques-tions about what they should be. In describing the death of "the Negro Church" and its rebirth as "the Black Church," Lincoln added, "for the first time the Black Church has the available intellectual resources to engage in a serious theological debate, *and to construct for itself a theology consistent with its needs.*"[30] Around the same time that Lincoln made this pronouncement about the rebirth of "the Black Church" and its new constructive project, a multidisciplinary field of academic study was taking shape that would come to be known as "Black Church Studies."

The first academic Black Church Studies program was founded at Colgate Rochester Crozer Divinity School in Rochester, New York, in November 1969. Since its inception, Black Church Studies, as a discipline, has been "concerned not only with the study and description of the Black Church as a religious phenomenon but also with using what is gleaned from the research to strengthen the Church as it meets contemporary challenges in and beyond the Black community."[31] If the line between the description of what Black churches are and what they ought to be was blurred in the earliest studies of African American religion (like those of Du Bois, Fauset, Woodson, and others), such overlapping concerns are particularly conspicuous in the field of Black Church Studies, where many engage the discipline as both scholars and practitioners. The study of Black churches has always been subject to intense debates about the salient histories, defining identities, social significance, and political priorities of an ostensible American institution called "the Black Church." In this mode, Raphael Warnock, U.S. senator from Georgia and the current pastor of Martin Luther King Jr.'s historic home congregation in Atlanta, Ebenezer Baptist Church, describes "the Black Church" as being of a "divided mind," searching for its purpose and relevance today.[32] Similarly, Joseph Sorett highlights the "multivocality" behind the often assumed monolithic "the Black Church."[33] The notions of a divided mind and multivocality capture both the diversity of Black churches and the salience of the overarching category "the Black Church," which Savage and others have rightly pointed out implies a homogeneity that, at times, masks the fact of deep and persistent diversity.

"The Black Church" in This Book

The fundamental diversity of Black churches is one of three key insights from studies of Black churches and African American religious experiences that I draw on in this book. Whether described in terms of dialectics, dialogue, continua, or a divided mind, this study of African American Christian engagement with Israel and Palestine builds on the core insight that Black churches are, in fact, incredibly diverse and varied. At the same time, I recognize that "the Black Church" is a salient category that animates the life of Black religious communities, including the ones I analyze here. I treat "the Black Church" as a real object because it is real in the social world that I encountered in the field. But, critically, I also argue that "the Black Church" is a *contested* object. Everywhere I went in my research, I heard talk of "the Black Church"—in terms of its history, identity, and proper position vis-à-vis political issues. The event described at Howard University entitled "Occupied Palestine: How Should the Black Church Respond?" is one example. In the world of African American Christian Zionism, I encountered similarly positioned manifestos, purporting to definitively identify and speak to "the Black Church," such as *We Too Stand* and *Zionism and the Black Church: Why Standing with Israel Will Be a Defining Issue of Christians of Color in the 21st Century.*[34] I suggest that there is, indeed, such a thing as "the Black Church" and that it is a contested category that carries weight in African American religious, social, and political spaces.

A second related fundamental insight I draw is that Black churches exist not in isolation but rather in an interactive social environment. Sociologist Omar McRoberts has shown this cogently in his work on urban religious diversity.[35] McRoberts suggests attention to Black churches as what the sociologist Nancy Ammerman calls "particularistic spaces of sociability," which exist within a religious *ecology* characterized by a demand-driven religious market.[36] Within the diverse and interactive network spaces of Black churches, McRoberts takes a cultural approach to understanding how "symbols are arranged and presented in ways that motivate human action, inspire emotion, give order to existence and, for the believer, constitute realities in themselves."[37] Others, too, have noted the central place of Black church culture, its contested nature, and its importance for studying African American religious life.[38] In this book, I focus on Black church culture as built around competing conceptions of group history, identity, memory, and tradition. Key here is the notion that, as the historian of Black religion Judith Weisenfeld has emphasized, religious and racial identities are categorically fused for African Americans. Underscoring this fundamental link, she suggests paying attention to "religio-racial" as a category of identity.[39] In considering the political issue of Israel and Palestine, I suggest that religio-racial identity is similarly fused with political identity in ways that provoke African American clergy and activists to think about solidarity in different ways—ranging from resisting imperial domination to bolstering global coalitions in the so-called War on Terror.

I also follow recent scholarship that has broadened not only *how* we look at Black religious life in America but also *where* we look. Going beyond the foundational paradigm of attending to Black churches in terms of their (largely male) leadership, their largest organizations, and historic denominations, in this study I follow the work of scholars who have looked at other, less widely appreciated Black religious spaces—such as the everyday lives of the women who make up the majority of Black church attendees, the media spaces of televangelism (which have come to include online communication beyond traditional broadcast television), as well as the emerging physical worship spaces of Black megachurches.[40]

In focusing on the contested meanings of history and identity within the culture of Black churches, I pay attention to these kinds of spaces and places that are necessary for understanding intersections of race, religion, and politics in the context of Black churches—on the issue of Palestine and Israel and many others. I have found that pastors and leaders play an important role in directing Black church interest around Palestine and Israel, but I also learned much from their churchgoers and lay leaders in my fieldwork. Their experiences and reflections taught me how questions about the significance of the issue of Israel and Palestine works itself into the everyday lived experiences of religious people whose vocation is something other than professional Christian ministry. I learned about why and how, for example, school teachers, nurses, social workers, students, and entrepreneurs (among many others) developed an interest in the issue of Palestine and Israel, and how they make sense of the religious, racial, and political stakes of that issue in their own lives and through their own experiences.

Finally, acknowledging the importance of looking at understudied religious spaces within African American Christianity, my research on Israel and Palestine has led me to pay particular attention to the role pastors play in shaping church culture, identifying issues of importance for their congregants, and deploying particular cultural narratives and traditions to steer those congregants into specific kinds of reflection and action on those issues. In tracing development of the prosperity gospel—a popular religious movement that cuts across denominational, racial, and class lines with a message that God intends to bless his followers in terms of wealth, health, and "victory"—Kate Bowler notes that pastors act as "prophets and visionaries" who forge paths to be followed by their congregants, identifying issues of concern, including a range of spiritual, financial, social, and political priorities.[41] Key to pastors inhabiting these roles of prophet and visionary are their personal biographies, which they use as narrative glue to frame issues of concern and draw their followers into those issues. Followers, here, include not only congregants but also other pastors. Bowler highlights the role of formal and informal fellowships (or networks) of pastors and leaders across traditional denominations as organizing structures within the American religious landscape. Denominations remain important organizing bodies in Black religious spaces, but pastoral fellowships and transdenominational networks have emerged as important sites of what Bowler calls "theological cross-pollination."[42] In the world of Black church engagement with Israel and Palestine, this kind of cross-pollination drives much of the outreach and activism focused on recruiting African American Christians to consider Israel and Palestine as an area of concern—either as Christian Zionists or in solidarity with Palestinians.[43] I pay particular attention to the ways pastors work within various social spaces—pastoral fellowships and networks, nonprofit philanthropic organizations, political lobbying groups, and also traditional denominations and conferences—to advance outreach efforts and activism on behalf of the State of Israel or Palestinians. These contexts include predominantly African American spaces—such as the historically Black denomination Church of God in Christ and Black Baptist conventions—as well as predominantly white spaces where Black pastors and leaders work together with white leaders to advance shared goals. Finally, I draw on the work of the political scientist Michael Leo Owens on the role of pastors; his study of African American church partnerships with government considers Black church political engagement beyond protest and electoral politics, emphasizing the ways African American pastors act as *brokers* in their communities. For Owens, brokerage describes the way pastors act as intermediaries between their congregations and broader issues of concern.[44]

To summarize, the approach I take to African American Christian engagement with Palestine and Israel is motivated by three core insights: (1) the diversity of Black churches is coupled with the continued salience of the normative, ostensibly unifying, and contested category of "the Black Church"; (2) Black churches, their pastors, and members must be seen as operating within interactive social environments; and (3) African American pastors act as role models and brokers in their communities and within traditional and nontraditional religious networks. Taking these insights together, I argue that to understand how and why some Black churches get involved in pro-Israel or Palestinian solidarity activism requires a *relational* understanding of Black churches as religious, social, and political spaces. I explain this relational approach in the following section.

BLACK RELIGIOUS POLITICS AS A FIELD OF CONTESTATION

It is necessary at the outset to sketch the sociological framework within which I make the argument about Black religious politics. This section summarizes this framework before I outline the path forward in the following chapters. To explore questions about why some Black churches engage the issue of Israel and Palestine and, within this engagement, why such a range of theological and political orientations exist, I draw on the work of sociologists who have argued for a *relational* approach to investigating social questions and explaining social problems. Summarizing this approach and its attention to the social world in relational terms, Pierpaolo Donati suggests that "the very stuff of sociology . . . is made up first of all of social relations."[45] Within this outlook, primary attention is given to processes of dynamic interaction among social actors. In this vein, Mustafa Emirbayer describes the key insight of this approach as its capacity to view social reality in "dynamic, continuous, and processual terms."[46] Specifically, I develop an account of the diversity of Black religious politics and the position-taking within Black churches on Israel and Palestine using the relational concept of *social fields*, as developed by the French social theorist Pierre Bourdieu. Bourdieu's relational sociology emphasizes that the objects of interest in social analysis must be seen in context and as part of a larger whole.[47] Here, the meaningfulness of social objects, as the sociologist John Mohr puts it, "is determined not by the characteristic properties, attributes, or essences of the thing itself, but rather with reference to the field of objects, practices, or activities within which they are embedded."[48] Mohr draws attention to Bourdieu's key analytical concept of a social field. This concept, along with others that Bourdieu uses in his relational sociological approach, provide a powerful theoretical tool kit for developing a relational outlook on Black religious politics through the lens of Palestine and Israel.

I suggest that the concept of social fields provides a way forward in addressing the paradox of Black religious politics in the United States and its global implications for Israel and Palestine. That paradox is the tension previously discussed between, on one hand, the strong evidence for a recognition of deep diversity and, on the other hand, the persistence of the overarching and contested, normative, and ostensibly unifying category of "the Black Church" in African American religious spaces. I pay attention to how social meanings are always embedded in the real world and are not abstract or detached concepts that exist "out there" somewhere. In other words, the meaning of "the Black Church" is embedded in the lived world of Black religion, where it is tested and contested.

This testing and contesting account of Black religion gets at questions such as the "true nature and mission" of the Black church. Is that true nature best expressed in attending to the spiritual needs of its members, offering salvation and the promise of heaven after death? Or is the true nature and mission of the Black church more this-worldly and working toward the possibility of improving the everyday lives of marginalized people? On Israel and Palestine, these questions follow: Is the calling of "the Black Church" to politically support the State of Israel and its policies? Or is it to stand in solidarity with Palestinians, who accuse Israel of racist policies and discrimination?

Ultimately, my analysis uses engagement with Palestine and Israel to approach broader questions about what I call the *field of Black religious politics*.[49] To construct the field of Black religious politics through attention to Israel and Palestine, I focus primarily on the culture of Black churches and how meaning-laden notions of African American identity, memory, narrative, and solidarity animate contests and challenges over the professed character and qualities of "the Black Church." These cultural dispositions relate not only to kinds of *action* but also to the *positions* of actors within the field. In other words, how the African American Christians I study think about the sources of Black church identity, the particular memories and narratives that sustain those notions of collective identity, and the related possibilities for solidarities across racial, religious, and political lines all contribute to the topography of the field of Black religious politics. The four cases of African American Christian engagement with Israel and Palestine in this book represent different dispositions and positions within Black churches—in part, what Pierre Bourdieu called *habitus*.[50] I show these dispositions through how they are expressed vis-à-vis orientations toward Palestine and Israel, but they also relate to broader orientations toward larger religious-political questions.

For example, the African American outreach coordinator for the IFCJ told me:

One of the entryways that the International Fellowship has [is] coming from a place of faith and shared values, coming from work that's the same kind of interest that the African American community and the African American church has been advocates of. . . . Clothing people, feeding people, helping people to have shelter, bringing people from war-torn countries to a place of safety—all of those things are open doors of the African American community. It's the work that the African American community does here in the United States.

Here, the core identity of Black churches is expressed in terms of a disposition toward acts of charity—helping the hungry, the needy, and the dispossessed. A number of pastors explained this to me as focusing on "the least of these," in reference to Jesus's call in the gospels to serve those most in need. This philanthropic impetus toward charity finds expression in Black-Jewish partnerships, as the same Fellowship coordinator explained:

> I think that the historical relationship between the Black and Jewish community was one of the most successful, phenomenal, impactful partnerships in the history of America. . . . The two main characters of the [civil rights] movement were the Black and Jewish communities.

A pastor in the Proctor Conference network expressed the African American religious impetus differently, describing her goals in leading Bible studies with her congregants:

> The whole notion, for me, in teaching [the Bible] is trying to open their eyes to the fact that you have been for years reading your Bible through the eyes of the oppressor. I want to open this up to you so that you begin to read scripture through the eyes of the oppressed. . . . And now we are looking at those texts [and] they don't tie up into a nice neat bow. What do I do with a God who now could possibly look like, or *be*, the God of ethnic cleansing? When I read Deuteronomy and I see this God—that is the loving compassionate God of the New Testament—I see [him] over here in the Old Testament telling God's people go and wipe this town out, kill everybody in it—men, women, children, it doesn't matter, kill them all and then take the plunder for yourselves. What do I do with that as a Christian? Because when you start to talk about those texts and then you take them right to [the present] and say, "Hey, guess what? This is what is going on right now in Palestine, on the Gaza Strip."

This echoes Reverend Neichelle Guidry's preaching, described previously, which framed her encounter with Palestinians as prompting an "awakeness of the global oppression of Black and Brown bodies [and] a greater understanding of the interconnectedness of our stories and our struggles."

On one hand, the articulation of a Black church identity based on charitable work finds expression in partnerships with Jewish communities in the United

States and in Israel as the foundation for a Black-Jewish pro-Israel alliance. The appropriate solidarity accompanying this Black church cultural disposition is Black-Jewish solidarity across racial and religious lines, where African Americans can most identify with Jews based on a common history of discrimination, dispossession, and enslavement. This also invokes the centrality of the biblical Exodus narrative for the African American experience.[51] But how this is deployed varies among African American Christians. For pro-Israel African American Christian Zionists, the nation of Israel in the Bible corresponds directly to the State of Israel today, and the appropriate solidarity is a Black-Jewish solidarity to strengthen the State of Israel in the face of its many claimed enemies. On the other hand, reading the Bible "through the eyes of the oppressed" can lead to what Reverend Guidry calls "the problem of the flipped script." This flipped script upends the identification of Jews and the State of Israel as the group most like African Americans and most in need of solidarity from Black Christians. "It seems to me," said Guidry in the same sermon, "that the young David—the same one with the five stones—has now become the giant machine of an occupier." The question for African American Christians, then, is *who needs defending* in Israel and Palestine? Is it the Jewish State of Israel, or is it the Palestinians in their struggle against and within that state?

Ultimately, the question of what "the Black Church" is and how its identity relates to Palestine and Israel is a question of solidarity. And solidarity depends on identity, which, in turn, requires sustaining narratives and traditions. A tradition, suggests the sociologist Philip Gorski, represents "a culture that is self-conscious of its past." "To be part of a tradition," Gorski notes, "is to know certain stories, read certain books, admire certain people, and care about certain things."[52] In the context of Black churches and elsewhere, the concept of tradition is dynamic and contested. This creates the possibility for everything from ideas to people to movements and historical moments to be subject to appropriation and reappropriation—constantly negotiating a core shared identity as a point of reference for political engagement. I suggest that this narrative plays an important role in guiding the dispositions of actors in the field of Black religious politics—in their claims-making and position-taking.

Throughout this book I consider the relationship between narrative and identity. Narrative has often been thought of as a combination of beliefs, principles, and ideology. But my focus is on looking at some of the ways different African American stories sustain particular notions of Black church identity, conceptually linking narrative and identity in the context of studying Black religious politics as a social field. In looking through that particular lens at Israel and Palestine, I argue that the field of Black religious politics becomes visible as a site of contestation in which different conceptions of Black church identity, accompanying narratives, and sustaining traditions are entangled and tested. This book is about the very entangled social world that is Black religious politics. Perhaps because no political issue is as polarizing and entangled as Israel and Palestine, I suggest that the insights to be gained from looking at the overlap of race, religion, and politics around that issue are instructive for constructing and analyzing Black religious politics as a field of contestation more broadly.

Finally, in delineating the field of Black religious politics in the United States along these lines, I also consider how these religious and political orientations in the field correspond to *global* religious politics in racialized terms. In other words, I consider what kinds of solidarities are opened up (or precluded) when these modes of Black church political engagement extend beyond local and domestic concerns into global political issues such as those of Israel and Palestine. I argue that engagement with Israel and Palestine is partially shaped by domestic priorities for religious social engagement, but also that global engagement involves the creation of competing dispositions of *global* Black religious political identity. Engagement with Palestine and Israel, as a global issue, provokes novel reworkings of African American identity in contemporary global politics. Although the field of Black religious politics in the United States is somewhat autonomous in how it is constructed and how it works to shape social action, the field is expanded in global terms via engagement with Israel and Palestine, suggesting that the national field is always partially defined in relation to questions of global consciousness. Throughout this book, I show how engagement with Israel and Palestine, as a transnational issue, provokes novel reworkings of African American identity in contemporary global political contexts.

PLAN OF THE BOOK

Chapters 1 and 2 situate my four comparative cases in this configuration of race, religion, and politics in Palestine and Israel, building on the snapshots provided here. Chapter 1 introduces the two Christian Zionist cases, and chapter 2 attends similarly to the two Palestine-focused cases. This overview helps lay the foundation for understanding the field of Black religious politics through the issue of Israel and Palestine. These chapters also provide an introduction to the historical context and key cultural components informing each case—in terms of identity, narrative, tradition, and solidarities—that animate these cases and orient them toward Palestine and Israel in competing ways. For each case, I ask: Who are they? Where do they come from? What is their understanding of Black churches and what they should be doing? Why does Israel and Palestine matter to them? And what is their call to action for African American Christians?

Chapter 3 is the first of three thematic chapters that, together, build an analytical case for understanding Black religious politics as a field of contestation through attention to examples of engagement with the issue of Israel and Palestine. Within their communities, I argue that pastors act variously as brokers and mobilizers who direct the interests of others to particular issues of concern. In this context, chapter 3 explores the dynamics between pastors and their congregants, investigating how church members affect pastoral leadership and brokerage on the issue of Israel and Palestine. I also describe the context of networks (or fellowships) of pastors—on local, national, and global levels—which sometimes transcend traditional models of congregation-level Black church leadership. I show how these social spaces shape engagement with Palestine and Israel, ultimately arguing that this is exemplary of the dynamics of contestation within the field of Black religious politics in the United States more broadly. Finally, chapter 3 emphasizes the significance of personal pastoral narratives as the context for the contestation of Black religious politics.

Chapter 4 explores the significance of African American travel to Israel and Palestine. It shows how the land is an important site of formation on the issue of Palestine and Israel as well as the setting of important debates about competing notions of what "the Black Church" should be doing. Beginning with traditional notions of pilgrimage—which are inescapable in evaluating the religious and political significance of travel to the so-called Holy Land—I argue that politics loom large on even ostensibly "spiritual" visits to the region. I show how traditional concepts of pilgrimage—as spiritual or religious travel—are insufficient for analyzing contemporary African American experiences in the land. This chapter demonstrates how different modes of Black religious politics—emerging from positions within the national field—are translated into the global field of Black religious politics. It describes formative experiences in the land in cultural terms, with attention to how this contributes to explaining these trips as a microcosm of the contestation of Black religious politics in a less familiar setting.

Chapter 5 returns to the task of constructing the field of Black religious politics in the United States most directly. It draws on insights from relational sociology and Bourdieusian field theory to make the case that African American Christianity is best understood as a field of contestation between competing claims to what "the Black Church" is and what it ought to be doing. Building on the cultural analysis of African American churches previously developed, chapter 5 shows how actors across my four case studies variously make claims to the character and mission of "the Black Church," how these claims are in play regarding Israel and Palestine, and how the national and global fields of Black religious politics are connected.

The conclusion brings together the strains of analysis presented and explores what the case of U.S. Black church engagement with Palestine and Israel tells us more broadly about Black religious politics. I examine how new movements for racial justice in the United States—such as the Movement for Black Lives—relate to Black churches as traditional organizers of African American political life. The conclusion also discusses the significance of the fact that the newest generation of antiracism activists is increasingly secular and is organizing outside of the purview of Black religious institutions. I further evaluate the implications of this shift, given the widespread appreciation of the role African American churches played in the paradigmatic mid-twentieth-century civil rights era. Last, looking beyond this project, the conclusion shows how evidence from my fieldwork in the United States, Israel, and Palestine is indicative of broader changes in the relationship between American Black churches and the direction of contemporary race-focused political activism.

CHAPTER 1

Standing with Israel

African American Christian Zionism

CHRISTIAN ZIONISM AND ITS AFRICAN AMERICAN PROPONENTS

Much of the scholarly, journalistic, and popular attention to American Protestant Christian interest in the politics of the Middle East has focused on the decades since 9/11 and the advent of the global "War on Terror." However, America's political engagement with Palestine and Israel and in the Middle East more broadly also have deeper roots that have been analyzed in terms of overlapping theological, entertainment, media, and foreign policy concerns.[1] The last several decades have seen a sharp increase in books, articles, and media coverage devoted to U.S. engagement with the Middle East and to the related phenomenon of *Christian Zionism*—a term now widely used to describe Christian support for the State of Israel based on overlapping religious and political motivations. Its widespread use notwithstanding, Christian Zionism is a controversial term that escapes easy definition: a label worn proudly among proponents and a term of aspersion for critics. Because "support" and even "Israel" are sometimes vague and contested terms, a more precise definition is necessary at the outset. Robert O. Smith defines Christian Zionism as "political action, informed by specifically Christian commitments, to promote or preserve Jewish control over the geographic area now comprising Israel and Palestine."[2] Two aspects of this definition are critical. First, that Christian Zionism is always, on some level, *political*. Second, it is at least partially driven by ideological, moral, and ethical convictions related to specific Christian religious beliefs about the Bible, about the status of Jews as God's chosen people, and about the land of Israel as the Jewish promised land. In other words, Christian Zionism, in its many forms, is never an expressly pragmatic *realpolitik* position—it carries moral and ideological premises. Smith and other religious historians trace the roots of political Christian Zionism to nineteenth-century British and American Protestant movements. They have also focused on locating the deeper roots of contemporary Christian Zionism within Reformation-era Protestant beliefs about biblical Israel; the emergence of dispensationalism as a source for not only theological but also political thinking about Israel; and the subsequent transplanting and thriving of dispensationalist theology within American evangelicalism.[3] The relatively recent surge in interest in Christian Zionism as a political force, however, has largely tracked with political developments in the Middle East following the 1948 founding of the State of Israel and the 1967 Six-Day War, which produced strong feelings among many American evangelicals that Bible prophecy was "unfolding before their eyes" in geopolitics.[4] The ascendant political influence of the Christian right in U.S. electoral politics, beginning in the 1970s and intensifying throughout the 1980s, brought Christian Zionism into far greater relevance politically than it had been in any earlier period. In their contemporary form, the political causes of Christian Zionism have been shaped and advanced most significantly in organizations led by prominent American evangelical televangelists—such as John Hagee's Christians United for Israel (CUFI) and the late Jerry Falwell's Moral Majority.[5]

Given the divisive and politically polarized nature between Israel and Palestine, it is not surprising that treatments of Christian Zionism (in academic and popular works) include many apologetic defenses of the movement's goals and polemical works critiquing it.[6] Within this broad range of work on Christian Zionism as a religious and a political phenomenon, most attention has been given to the white American evangelicals who make up the movement's base of core adherents.[7]

The following sections trace a necessarily brief path to understanding African American Christian Zionism through the story of Black-Jewish relations in the United States, with attention to cultural and political reference points for the emergence of a distinctly African American expression of Christian Zionism, albeit one that emerged within the predominantly white Christian Zionist movement through the work of some of its largest organizations. Here, and in chapter 2, I outline some of the theological and spiritual antecedents in African American religion that inform Black church outlooks on Israel, Palestine, and the Middle East.[8] The antecedents in this chapter are the foundations of African American Christian Zionism; in chapter 2, I shift to discussing theological and political precursors to African American Christian solidarity with Palestinians. Following this attention to the contexts out of which this book's Christian Zionist case studies emerge, I expand my overview of African American outreach programs within Christians United for Israel and the International Fellowship of Christians and Jews (IFCJ).

BLACK-JEWISH RELATIONS AND THE CONTESTED LEGACY OF THE CIVIL RIGHTS MOVEMENT

The history of Black-Jewish relations in the United States is a persistent point of reference for African American Christian Zionists because contemporary political orientations to Palestine and Israel correspond to different takes on the ostensible lessons of the U.S. civil rights movement. African American Christian Zionists tend to speak of the 1950s and 1960s as a high point of Black-Jewish solidarity that made the successes of the civil rights movement possible. Several iconic images represent this foundational solidarity. One example is Martin Luther King Jr. marching arm in arm with Rabbi Abraham Joshua Heschel. Another is the FBI missing persons poster showing three murdered activists from the Mississippi Freedom Summer of 1964—James Chaney, a local Black civil rights activist, with Andrew Goodman and Michael Schwerner, two white Jewish activists from New York. The three young men—all in their early twenties—were murdered while working together to register Black voters in Mississippi in the summer of 1964. For some African American Christian Zionists, Heschel marching with King and Jewish participation in the Mississippi Freedom Summer represent key moments from a halcyon period of Black-Jewish cooperation in the United States, but this gave way to division and discord from the late 1960s into the 1990s. In the recollections of African Christian Zionists, these positive images of Black-Jewish solidarity were overshadowed by back-and-forth accusations of anti-Black racism from African Americans and Black anti-Semitism from American Jews. As later sections in this chapter on the cases of CUFI and the IFCJ show, interpreting the civil rights legacy is an important cultural driver of African American Christian Zionism, and Black-Jewish solidarity within that movement is foundational to political solidarity with the State of Israel. But the legacy of the civil rights movement is contested, and most of the salient figures, moments, and memories of that movement are debated, especially when drawing lessons for Israel and Palestine.[9]

The history of Black-Jewish relations in the United States began as early as the seventeenth century, which saw the arrival of Africans to the "New World" as slaves and Jews as settlers. The period that African American Christian Zionists primarily draw on for inspiration, however, is found much later, in the mid- to late-twentieth century. At that time, large numbers of African Americans had migrated to the North to escape the racial terrorism of the Jim Crow South, and Eastern European Jews had also immigrated to the same northern cities, seeking an escape from anti-Semitism in Europe. The journalist Jonathan Kaufman refers to the cities of the North as "the testing ground, and then the battle ground" for Black-Jewish relations in the twentieth century.[10] Despite decades of economic tensions between African Americans and Jews in northern U.S. cities, Jews were significantly involved (in terms of direct participation and the contribution of funds) in Martin Luther King's Southern Christian Leadership Conference (SCLC), the National Association for the Advancement of Colored People (NAACP), the Student Nonviolent Coordinating Committee (SNCC), and the Congress of Racial Equality (CORE).[11] Cooperation of the early 1960s notwithstanding, growing anger among residents of Black ghettos in northern cities increasingly shaped the trajectories of the civil rights movement in the late 1960s and beyond; Black Nationalism and Black Power movements were gaining influence, and uprisings were on the rise, beginning in the summer of 1964. Furthermore, the demographics of many long-standing Jewish neighborhoods in northern cities were changing as Jews moved out and African Americans moved in, creating another point of tension between the two communities.[12]

As the tone of civil rights activism became more militant in the later part of the 1960s, the support of many of the movement's Jewish allies began to wane. This is perhaps best exemplified in the influential essay by the conservative Jewish American pundit Norman Podhoretz, "My Negro Problem—And Ours," in which he decried "Negro anti-Semitism" and warned that the direction of African American political activism was running against the interests of Jewish Americans.[13] At the same time, grassroots support for alternatives to the nonviolent approach of King and the SCLC began to grow. Proponents of more militant Black Consciousness and Black Nationalist movements in the late 1960s were less satisfied with only challenging discrimination in the laws of the Jim Crow South, which was the focus of the movement up to that point. Spurred by leaders Malcolm X and Stokely Carmichael (who later changed his name to Kwame Ture), Black radicals sought a broader course aimed at addressing racial oppression on a larger, even global, scale. As Black civil rights activists global-ized their concerns, several issues contributed to shifting Black-Jewish relations, including the Vietnam War and apartheid in South Africa. But the question of Zionism emerged as the most central point of tension between Black radicals and American Jews. In introducing the Palestine-focused cases in this book, chapter 2 describes the emergence of this more global racial consciousness—including Palestinian solidarity—among some more radical Black activists.

AFRICAN AMERICAN RELIGIOUS IDENTIFICATION WITH ISRAEL AND JUDAISM

Understanding contemporary African American Christian Zionism also requires turning briefly from the contested legacy of the civil rights movement to religious and theological factors that help situate Israel in the African American political imagination. Here, I look beyond Black attitudes toward Israel as a nation-state post-1948 and consider some of the ways African Americans—especially African American Christians—have understood and interacted with Jewish beliefs, iden-tity, and religious history more generally. To consider only the recent politi-cal and social aspects of relations between African Americans and Jews in the United States would ignore these important religious dimensions. The religious historian Yvonne Chireau identifies two strains of African American religious identification with Judaism that have shaped Black-Jewish relations.[14] For some African Americans, the connection with Judaism and Israel is allegorical or metaphorical and is based on identifying with the Israel of the Bible and the narrative of biblical Judaism. For others, the connection is more literal, and a physical descent or membership in the Jewish community is claimed. Thus it is important to distinguish between African American groups who identify *with* the Jewish biblical narrative of Israel and those who identify *as* Jews, Hebrews, or Israelites. The Christian Zionist cases studies in this book fall firmly in the for-mer category—African American Christians who identify with Jews and Judaism without claiming that identity for themselves.

Within this metaphorical strain of African American identification with Israel, the Exodus narrative of Jewish emancipation from Egyptian slavery takes primacy of place. In the Exodus story, African Americans lift up parallel Black experiences of bondage, exile, persecution and redemption, and diaspora,

providing a similar kind of social cohesion and a sense of a shared history as
the biblical liberation narrative does for Jews. As Chireau emphasizes, these narratives became cultural frameworks on which Black people began to construct
collective identities.[15] The cultural transmission of biblical emancipation narratives happened through many paths, notably in the form of Black slave spirituals,
where identification of the biblical Exodus with the plight of African slaves is
a common theme. One example among many is the well-known spiritual "Go
Down, Moses":

> When Israel was in Egypt land, Let my people go;
> Oppressed so hard they could not stand, Let my people go;
> Go down, Moses, Way down in Egypt's land;
> Tell ole Pharaoh, Let my people go.

Across time and space, the Exodus narrative provided a point of connection with
the Israelites of the Bible, whom God delivered from bondage and oppression.
Albert Raboteau, a historian of American slavery, emphasizes the particular
salience of the Exodus narrative for African Americans as a point of contrast
with the dominant outlook among white American Christians. From the earliest
days of colonization, Raboteau points out, white Christians had also understood
their journey to America as an Exodus from bondage to a "New Israel" as a promised land "flowing with milk and honey." Accordingly, from the English Puritans
on, white Protestant settlers consistently saw themselves in metaphorical identification with the Israelites of the Bible as the New Israel.[16]

Some African Americans have gone beyond this kind of a metaphorical association with Israel to see themselves not just *like* Jews but rather *as* Jews. This represents the second and more literal strain of African American identification with
Israel and Judaism. Informed by the late nineteenth- and early twentieth-century
movement of Ethiopianism, which expanded the biblical concept of *chosenness* to
Black Africans, some African Americans began to see themselves as Black Jews,
Black Israelites, or Black Hebrews.[17] Under such identities, they extended the
metaphor of association *with* Judaism to inclusion *within* Judaism. Furthermore,
some Black Hebrew Israelites claimed an even stronger racial identification with
Judaism that went beyond identifying as a Black group that should be recognized
among other descendants of biblical Hebrews and cast themselves as their *true*
descendants. In this more extreme identification with Israel, some Black Hebrew

Israelites and related movements have viewed modern day Jewish Israelis (and non-Black Jews more widely) as colonizers of Jewish identity itself. The rise of African American religious communities who identified as the true descendants of the biblical Jews in this way generally coincided with the Great Migration. Urban life in the cities of the North provided a context for this kind of religious identity formation because interaction with Jewish communities happened on a level not experienced in the South.[18] Among the most notable early leaders of the Black Jews in the first half of the twentieth century was the founder of the Beth B'nai Abraham congregation in Harlem, Rabbi Arnold Josiah Ford, an associate of Black Nationalist and Pan-Africanist Marcus Garvey. Another group that has established a Black Jewish identity, the Black Hebrew Israelites, occupies a prominent place in Black-Jewish relations because of their migration from Chicago to the State of Israel where they continue to live. Drawing on notions of Black Jewish identity articulated by the Black Jews of Harlem and other Black Jewish movements of the early twentieth century, the Black Hebrew Israelite movement formed in Chicago in the early 1960s under the leadership of Ben Carter (also known as Ben Ammi). An increasing number of Black Hebrew Israelites later developed a desire to flee America, which they viewed as "Babylon"—a place of destruction and oppression. Driven by a Return-to-Africa ideology, members of the group initially settled in Liberia in 1967 and eventually Israel in 1969. The community in Israel, established by Ben Ammi as the Black Hebrew Israelite Nation, has grown since its founding to include more than 3,000 members living in the town of Dimona, in Israel's Negev region.[19]

With an eclectic system of religious beliefs and practices combining West African, African American, and Jewish elements, the Black Hebrew Israelites and other related groups of Black Jews are outside the mainstream of African American Christian views on Israel. Their exodus from urban America to the promised land of Israel, like their association with Judaism in general, is of a more literal kind. African American Christian Zionists tend to find this literal identification with Israel and Judaism a step too far, going beyond religious, racial, and national solidarity into the realm of identity misappropriation. On the other hand, among African American Christian Palestinian solidarity activists, there is a certain amount of concern about the treatment of the Black Hebrew Israelites within the State of Israel, alongside other Black African migrants and Ethiopian Jews. Although Black Israelite religions are beyond the scope of this book and not represented in its case studies, it is important to note their significance in overlapping discourses about racial identities, religious beliefs, and national political movements (including Zionism) in the American religious landscape in the second half of the nineteenth century and the first half of the twentieth century. As Jacob Dorman's history of the rise of Black Israelite religions in America shows, Black Israelite movements were not marginal expressions of overlapping racial and religious identities, nor were they isolated movements. They were, rather, deeply connected to other religious and political movements ranging from Pentecostal Christianity to African American Islam to the Black Nationalist movement.[20] The significance of Black Hebrew Israelite movements to African American religious formation related to the meaning of Judaism, Jewish identity, and the land of Israel also extends beyond these communities specifically, including Black American Muslim expressions of Black Nationalism and white Protestant Christian racial classification hierarchies.[21]

Like the normative category of "the Black Church," these histories of Black religious politics and trajectories of racial and religious identity formation in the United States are contested at every point among the African American Christians in this study. With this in mind, and in light of the broad context for understanding the significance of Israel and Judaism in African American religious history, I now turn to two cases of African American Christian Zionism in two predominantly white organizations: Christians United for Israel and the International Fellowship of Christians and Jews. I show how actors within these groups work with and within this context in their position-taking on Israel and Palestine and how they promote engagement with that issue in Black churches by contesting the history, identity, and mission of "the Black Church."

FOR ZION'S SAKE: CHRISTIANS UNITED FOR ISRAEL

A Night to Honor Israel in South New Jersey

On a Sunday night in the fall of 2013, in the South New Jersey suburbs near Philadelphia, African American Christians representing several local congregations gathered together and welcomed guests from the local Jewish community to a special "Night to Honor Israel" event. Like the Night to Honor Israel in Connecticut (described in the introduction), this event was put on by Christians United for Israel to bring together local Jewish groups and Christians in political solidarity with the State of Israel. The event was hosted at the campus of the

Impacting Your World Christian Center (IYWCC), a 3,000-member, predominantly African American, multisite church with meeting sites in Philadelphia, Pennsylvania, and Cherry Hill, New Jersey. As attendees began to arrive, Black church members mingled with Jewish guests in the lobby of the building, which was once a synagogue. Several local Jewish guests recalled attending services at the synagogue before it became IYWCC in 2009. Inside the sanctuary, a music video from Israel's Ministry of Foreign Affairs played on the large projection screen, depicting a montage of the country's accomplishments as a nation since its founding. On the wall underneath the screen was a large, stylized Jewish menorah, a vestige of the building's many years as a Jewish place of worship, with a sign below reading, "Jesus is Lord."

The event began when the church band took the stage to lead a medley of gospel and contemporary Christian worship songs. The congregation—predominantly African American but with a noticeable number of older white Jewish guests—stood as the music began. Most people were clapping and singing along. After several songs, IYWCC's senior pastor, Ray Barnard, took the stage to welcome the attendees: "Tonight we are here to honor Israel," he declared, adding that the evening would be a reflection on "the reason why Israel is the apple of God's eye." His words were met with applause and shouts of "Amen!" Barnard went on to tell his story of how he came to realize the importance of standing with and supporting Israel. He spoke about his Baptist upbringing and the reverence for the "things of God" that it instilled in him. He also recalled taking a trip to Israel, which he describes as making the Bible "come alive" for him. "If you've ever been there," he continued, "it's a beautiful place—it's breathtaking in fact." To this he added, "there's a lot of military presence there—they fight for their freedom every day." He ended his opening remarks by saying, "as Christians, we take every opportunity that we have lifting up that Star of David and praying for our Jewish brothers and sisters, because we all really find our origin from the same family—we come from the same root. And so, we will always stand with Israel."

Barnard then introduced another local pastor and the coorganizer of the Night to Honor Israel, Pastor Jonathan Leath, who took the pulpit and outlined three reasons he supports Israel. First, he cited a "clear mandate in scripture to stand with Israel," quoting Psalm 122:6: "Pray for the Peace of Jerusalem; they shall prosper that love thee." "I love prosperity," he added, "so I understand how I get prosperity by praying for the peace of Jerusalem." Second, he emphasized that God's covenant with the Jewish people is still intact. Finally, he said, "I just wanna be blessed. Genesis 12 verse 3 says, 'I will bless them that bless thee and curse those that curse thee.'"

The keynote speaker at the Impacting Your World Night to Honor Israel was Pastor Michael Stevens. Stevens worked for CUFI as one of the key proponents of the Christian Zionist movement in Black churches from 2008 until 2015. In addition, Stevens leads a large Charlotte, North Carolina, congregation in the historically Black Church of God in Christ (COGIC) denomination. In 2010, he became CUFI's African American outreach coordinator, having worked with the organization as a state outreach director for North Carolina since 2008. In addition to his full-time role as the pastor of his congregation, Stevens traveled extensively as CUFI's African American outreach coordinator, holding pro-Israel events in Black churches across the United States and around the world. At the Night to Honor Israel in New Jersey, Stevens told the interfaith audience how he had come to work with CUFI. He described sitting alone at home in 2007 in a time of personal prayer. "I'm reading Genesis, chapter 12," he said. "And it was an epiphany moment. I sat there reading my Bible, and I heard the Lord say, 'I want you and I want your church to be a blessing to Israel, to be a blessing to the Jewish people.'"

Stevens went on to recount how he had taken that message to his congregation the following Sunday morning. "I told my entire church, 'you know what, God spoke to my heart and he wants us . . . to be a blessing to the Jewish people.'" Stevens's story of sensing God leading him and his congregation into involvement in pro-Israel activism continued with him attending COGIC's annual Holy Convocation meeting in Memphis, Tennessee, the following month. "[I'm] right there sitting next to Bishop Blake, our presiding bishop," he told the Cherry Hill audience. "And lo and behold, who walks through the door? Pastor John Hagee. Now you gotta understand . . . there's 30,000 [COGIC] African Americans in Memphis Tennessee during convocation. Wasn't two Caucasians in the congregation." Stevens took this encounter with Hagee as "a divine appointment"–a timely and God-ordained opportunity to act on the imperative that he felt a month earlier to "bless the Jewish people." He described the meeting and Hagee asking him to help expand the reach of his new organization, CUFI, which was founded the previous year in 2006. "Needless to say, it was more than just a coincidence, or happenstance," Stevens recalled. "It was a miracle. It was an absolute divine moment." He went on to describe a series of events that established his relationship with CUFI, including Hagee visiting his church in North Carolina

for its first Night to Honor Israel and participating in a CUFI leadership delegation to Israel. Of that trip, Stevens recounted:

> We're at the home of the president of Israel [and] I said, "Pastor Hagee, there's
> a whole lot of African Americans back in the States—somebody's grandma,
> somebody's bishop, somebody's reverend, somebody's mother. They shared
> with us, as African Americans, be kind to Jews, pray for Israel, bless [Israel]. . . .
> It is embedded in us as Christians, particularly in the Black community, to be
> kind towards Jews."

So, in 2008, Michael Stevens joined the leadership of CUFI with a specific mandate to expand the diversity of the predominantly white organization through
outreach to African American churches.

John Hagee and Christians United for Israel

CUFI's founding in 2006 was conceived broadly by John Hagee and his partners as a theological and political Christian force for pro-Israel advocacy work.
That year, Hagee invited 400 evangelical Christian leaders to his Cornerstone
Church in San Antonio, Texas, to what he described as a meeting with a "one-
item agenda"—"create a national grassroots Christian Zionist organization that
would unite millions of evangelicals to stand up and speak up for Israel."[22] Hagee
is most widely known within evangelical and charismatic Christian circles for
hosting popular national Pentecostal televangelism and radio ministries. He has
been a household name for many American evangelicals since at least the 1990s,
recognized for his preaching and publishing on topics related to understanding the end-times and interpreting Bible prophecies. Outside of evangelical circles, he is known for his controversial endorsement of Senator John McCain
in the 2008 U.S. presidential election. McCain quickly rejected the endorsement when critics labeled Hagee anti-Catholic based on his teaching and writing. The author of more than twenty books, Hagee's early publishing included
provocative titles, such as *The Beginning of the End*, *Final Dawn Over Jerusalem*,
and *From Daniel to Doomsday: The Countdown Has Begun*, that were all 1990s best-
sellers in the popular evangelical Bible prophecy genre. The State of Israel and
Jewish-Christian relations have also been prominent topics in Hagee's body of
work. In the world of Christian Zionism, Hagee is widely quoted describing his

first trip to Israel in 1978, saying, "I went to Israel as a tourist and came home a Zionist!" Connecting this personal and political awakening to a broader significance of Israel in his ministry and activism, Hagee explained, "I have traveled the world, but as I walked the cobblestone streets of the Holy City, I knew I was home! My roots were there! I felt a very special presence in that sacred city that changed my life forever."[23]

In retelling the story of the origins of his personal investment in Christian Zionism, as he often does in front of CUFI audiences and through various media, Hagee describes the genesis of the Night to Honor Israel in 1981. When the Israeli military carried out airstrikes on an Iraqi nuclear reactor near Baghdad, Hagee was shocked that the attack was criticized by the United States, the United Nations, and in the media. "I personally felt that Israel had done the peace-loving world a favor by stopping the construction of a nuclear reactor that most assuredly would have been used for the production of nuclear bombs in the Middle East. . . . It was a preemptive strike that spared the world from Saddam Hussein's madness," Hagee recalled. Motivated to act, he asked himself: "How can we publicly express our support for Israel in such a way where the press will send a message to our Jewish friends that we support Israel's courage to defend themselves?" The product of Hagee's initial outreach to local San Antonio rabbis and the Jewish Federation was the first ever Night to Honor Israel, which took place in September 1981 despite an anonymous bomb threat the venue received. Of that night, Hagee recalled: "A bomb never exploded in the auditorium . . . yet there was an explosion in our hearts. We knew that we had done something that was near the heart of God the Father. As we walked off the stage, I said to [my wife], 'We need to do this again!'" The Night to Honor Israel format, as a Jewish-Christian interfaith event in political support of the State of Israel, became a staple in Hagee's organization of the Christian Zionist movement and the hallmark of CUFI's work since its 2006 founding.[24]

In 2012, when I began my fieldwork on CUFI's African American outreach efforts, an event flier described CUFI as "the largest pro-Israel organization in the United States with over 900,000 members and one of the leading Christian grassroots movements in the world." By 2018, when I concluded my fieldwork, the organization claimed more than five million members.[25] But who and what does this growing group represent? What congregations, denominations, organizations, and associations make up this membership of five million Christians Zionists under CUFI's banner? What are the racial, ethnic, class, and age characteristics of CUFI's supporters? I had these questions in mind when I attended CUFI's annual summit in Washington, DC, in July 2013. As I walked through the busy halls of the Washington Convention Center, I saw mostly white attendees over the age of fifty. Similarly, a scan of John Hagee's Cornerstone Church audience on a typical television broadcast reveals an overwhelmingly white congregation. How, then, did Nights to Honor Israel come to take place in a number of African American congregations around the United States—like those of Michael Stevens's University City Church of God in Christ, Ray Barnard's Impacting Your World Christian Center, or LeRoy Bailey's First Cathedral? What accounts for these Black church-based events, racial and geographic outliers among CUFI's hundreds of events each year, generally concentrated in the southern United States—the so-called Bible Belt—where white conservative evangelical Protestantism remains a potent force in religion and politics?

Michael Stevens: Launching CUFI's Black Church Outreach

CUFI's efforts to recruit African American church leaders and members to their religious-political engagement on behalf of the State of Israel initially centered around Michael Stevens in his role as the organization's first African American outreach coordinator, a position he held from 2010 to 2015. The plan to hold a Night to Honor Israel at Impacting Your World Christian Center originated when local pastors gathered at the church for a CUFI African American pastors briefing six months earlier, led by Stevens. About forty African Americans, mostly pastors and other church leaders, filled a large conference room on the campus of Impacting Your World. Besides me, the only other white attendee was a representative of the Jewish Community Relations Council of Southern New Jersey, an organization that has partnered with CUFI in the area. It was Tuesday, April 16, the day after the 2013 Boston Marathon bombing. Stevens stood in front of the group of Black pastors and began the seminar saying, "We are reeling from terrorism and tragedy today." He continued by noting that the hardest part of his job as a CUFI coordinator is the task of connecting African American and Jewish communities, who, he said, "have had ups and downs in their relationship." As Stevens often put it in his sermons and presentations on Israel, he was tasked with "connecting the dots" between African Americans and Jews. Although he talked about it less explicitly, he also had the job of connecting African Americans with CUFI as an organization, overcoming the perception that it is only for white conservative Republicans like its founder, John Hagee. Many (especially theologically conservative) African American Christians share an affinity for the State of Israel on biblical grounds, but they share few other concerns with CUFI's base of predominantly white, politically conservative, evangelical Republicans. In approaching this divide, Stevens presented reasons for African American Christians to get involved in pro-Israel activism that overlap with white evangelical support for Israel. For example, like the host pastors of the Night to Honor Israel in New Jersey, Stevens emphasized to this group of New Jersey pastors a biblical mandate to bless Israel with the expectation that God's blessings will follow. He told the story of how he became involved with CUFI, a story that he would tell again at the New Jersey Night to Honor Israel six months later. Stevens emphasizes a biblical mandate to bless Israel, with the expectation that God's blessings will follow. "I believe God spoke to my heart with a revelation, and I'll tell you my story based on Genesis 12," he told the pastors gathered for the seminar. He then read a passage from the Book of Genesis in which God commands Abraham and promises to bless him and his descendants: "Go from your country, your people and your father's household to the land I will show you. I will make you into a great nation, and I will bless you; I will make your name great, and you will be a blessing. I will bless those who bless you, and whoever curses you I will curse; and all peoples on earth will be blessed through you." In reading this passage from Genesis 12:1–3, Stevens said he felt God was telling him, "I want to bless you, and I want to bless your church." "I want my church to be blessed, and I want to be blessed," Stevens explained, "so I took this scripture verbatim at its word." Stevens also articulated a broad sense of spiritual connection between Christians and Jews:

> We owe a debt of gratitude to the Jewish people for giving us the patriarchs. . . . If it hadn't been for the Jewish community, we wouldn't have our prophets. If it wasn't for the Jewish community, we wouldn't have our Messiah. You know, because last time I checked, Jesus was Jewish. He's still Jewish today. And when you go to heaven, guess what, he's gonna be Jewish when you go to heaven and meet him. So, it would behoove [us] to not only love a Jewish Messiah, but make sure we love our Jewish brothers and our Jewish sisters.

Here, Stevens's rationale for Black church engagement on the issue of supporting the State of Israel largely overlaps with that of white American evangelicals who similarly cite Genesis 12 as a motivation to "bless Israel" with the expectation that they will receive God's blessings in return, and who also emphasize the "Judeo-Christian" connection linking the United States (as an ostensibly Christian country) and the State of Israel as a Jewish state. "But," Stevens continued, "Israel is not on the top-ten list of most Black pastors." He explained the reason for this as the fact that most Black pastors are busy dealing with local issues in their communities and congregations. "So why should Black Christians stand with Israel?" he asked. His seminar presentation outlined four categories of motivations for African American Christians: moral, spiritual, theological, and biblical. Across these categories, he sometimes appealed widely to what he states are universal Christian imperatives, and at times he appealed to the particularity of his Black church audience that day.

In making his case to Black clergy about why they should get involved in pro-Israel activism, Stevens articulated reasons that overlap with the concerns of the white American evangelicals that make up the majority of CUFI's base of support. But he also brought together a narrative about why Black Christians, in particular, should care about Israel. "Here's what Dr. King said," he added, pivoting to the uniqueness of the Black church on the issue of Israel. Paraphrasing Martin Luther King Jr., he said: "The church must be reminded that it is not the master or the servant of the state, but rather the conscience of the state. It must be the guide and the critic of the state, and never its tool. If the church does not recapture its prophetic zeal, it will become an irrelevant social club without moral or spiritual authority." "We are called to be reflective theologians," Stevens explained. "We are called to be contemplative critics. We are called to be monitors of our community." Here and elsewhere, Stevens emphasized a unique solidarity between African Americans and Jews. In *We Too Stand: A Call for the African-American Church to Support the Jewish State*, Stevens writes: "I believe there is no other entity on earth that can most identify itself as a people with the Jews than the African American church. The African American church carries both a prophetic zeal and a historic resolve to boldly stand against injustices and unrighteousness in the world."[26] With the group of Black clergy and lay church leaders in Cherry Hill, New Jersey—and in the ten similar events across five states where I observed Stevens teaching and preaching on the topic of Israel—he expanded this point of connection between African American Christians and Jews by highlighting similarities and points of potential solidarity between the two groups. These include similarities between the transatlantic slave trade and the Holocaust; a shared tendency to seek meaning in suffering by turning to religion; parallels between the African American experience in the South and anti-Semitic pogroms in Europe; and the participation of American Jews in the civil rights movement.

At the Cherry Hill pastors' briefing seminar, Stevens closed with several appeals. He invited the pastors present to join him on a tour of Israel. CUFI pastors' trips to Israel "have gone phenomenally well," he said. "And pastors only pay $500 for the whole trip." "They've gone so well that they are looking to give us another seven trips this year." He also called attention to CUFI's college campus outreach, *CUFI on Campus*, with its then 130 chapters across the country. He encouraged the pastors to recruit college students in their congregations to attend CUFI's annual Washington, DC, Summit, all expenses paid. To give the pastors a sense of what the climate on college campuses was like with respect to pro-Israel advocacy work, Stevens introduced a YouTube video on the question of Israeli apartheid. "College campuses are ground zero for anti-Semitism, ground zero for all of the Muslims and Israel haters who are standing against Israel," he cautioned. "They use South Africa as a backdrop, and they're trying to convince America and us in the West that Israel is an apartheid state," he added.

Dumisani Washington: CUFI's "Black Militant Voice"

I was first introduced to Dumisani Washington by Michael Stevens, who facilitated our meeting at CUFI's annual summit in Washington, DC. At that time, Washington was not formally affiliated with CUFI, but he had been invited to conduct a student seminar at the conference after participating in a CUFI-sponsored tour of Israel for African American pastors that was led by Stevens in 2012. The trip was Washington's first visit to the country after many years of pro-Israel advocacy work and Israel-focused Christian ministry. Until that time, his activism had mainly been in partnerships with Jewish pro-Israel organizations in his home state of California—StandWithUs and the Jewish Federation. We met in the busy lobby of the convention center, where he was surrounded by a group of young people, including some of the few college-age attendees of color in the overwhelmingly white gathering of more than 5,000, that skewed much older than the student cohort. Washington had just given a student seminar on the topic of race, Israel, and Palestine, and several of the attendees sought him out to continue the conversation. They had questions about the significance of race in Israel and Palestine. Washington has a magnetic personality, and it was easy to see why CUFI's students gravitate toward him. He speaks confidently and authoritatively about questions related to Israel and racial identity. I sat with Washington while he carried on several conversations with people he knew and others who were meeting him for the first time. We eventually moved to a nearby hotel lobby where we spoke over coffee.

The senior pastor of the Congregation of Zion church in Stockton, California, Washington is a conservatory-trained musician and former director of a music academy. He was born in Little Rock, Arkansas, where his mother was a seamstress and his father a janitor. His father's father was a share cropper. "We learned about Jim Crow at the kitchen table and at my mom's sewing table," he said. "There wasn't a pity party about being an African American," he added, describing the sense of pride his parents passed on to him. He also described being raised in a Black Baptist church that emphasized a strong connection between African American Christians and Israel. Washington further described the Congregation of Zion church where he is the pastor as "a Hebrew roots congregation." He explained that this means it is a Christian church that focuses on the "Hebrew roots" of the Christian faith. He went through a list of things that make the church more like a Jewish congregation than a typical Christian one: they worship on the Saturday Sabbath as opposed to Sunday; they celebrate Passover instead of Easter; and they embrace the Christian Old and New Testaments but emphasize a "Torah perspective." "Our concept and belief is that Jesus was a Jewish rabbi who came to teach the Torah in a revolutionary way," he explained. "We don't do Christmas," he added. Hearing him describe the Congregation of Zion, I better understood what Michael Stevens meant when he first qualified Washington's approach to pro-Israel activism as "more messianic."[27] Washington is not a Messianic Jew, but he described founding the Congregation of Zion as having come out of many years of participation in messianic congregations. In the early 1990s, he and his wife, Valerie, moved their family from the West Coast to Fairfax County, Virginia, for a position in church music ministry. While there, they began to play for a messianic congregation. He described that context as his first serious introduction to the Hebrew roots of the Christian faith. But in recalling the development of his religious outlook, he also pointed to earlier formative memories of becoming aware of the State of Israel's efforts to bring Ethiopian Jews to Israel in the 1980s. "I always had questions about Israel stuff," he said. Describing his initial encounter with messianic congregations, he added, "the whole messianic thing was weird to me because I grew up very Baptist, so I didn't see this convergence. So I thought the people were strange and weird, and they were nice but just weird. But after I was there for a few years, I started to enjoy it." Washington described his role at the CUFI Summit conference as being the same role he has with other pro-Israel organizations. "I speak to college campus kids, particularly kids of color, about the importance of standing with Israel," he said.

He elaborated on what he sees as his primary task of explaining to students of color the historical connection between African Americans and the State of Israel. Like Michael Stevens, he emphasized the integral role of Black-Jewish partnerships in the historic U.S. civil rights movement—a relationship he believes has been undermined and attacked since that time. "That [Black-Jewish] bond was attacked by Israel's enemies," he said. He named a list of these historical enemies: Saudi Arabia, Egypt, Jordan, Syria, the Soviet Union. He then described a concerted effort in the late 1960s and the 1970s to frame the Arab-Israeli conflict in racial terms—"terms that were particularly pointed toward Black people . . . terms like *Jim Crow segregation*, *apartheid*, *colonialism*. Those are negative images for us, and so if I don't have any more information other than you just feeding it to me, my sense of morality is going to cause me to stand against whoever you say is doing that." He mimicked his critics saying, "Oh look, the Jewish people they're doing segregation [in Israel]." Then responding, "Not true!" "Apartheid?—Not true."

He elaborated on his attention to undermining the argument that the State of Israel's treatment of Palestinians is akin to apartheid South Africa's policies of racial segregation and discrimination: "I have South African friends who are offended when the Arab Muslim community says that Israel's practicing apartheid. When you have Arab Muslim members of the parliament, Ethiopian Israeli members of the parliament, that didn't happen. There's an Arab Muslim supreme court justice in Israel. . . . That's not apartheid, not even close to it." Washington went on to shift to a critique of Palestinian leaders, past and present—such as Yasser Arafat and the current leaders of Hamas—as oppressors of their own people. He also called out pro-Palestinian groups such as the Council on American-Islamic Relations (CAIR) and Students for Justice in Palestine (SJP) for what he described as their hypocrisy on race issues. He pointed out how these groups had joined Black organizations in calling for an investigation in the killing of Trayvon Martin in 2012. "If they cared about Black people, if they cared about Trayvon Martin, why do they condone the slavery that's going on," he challenged, raising allegations of human trafficking in Saudi Arabia.

At the time of our 2013 meeting at the CUFI Summit, Dumisani Washington was also in the process of founding a new organization called the Institute for Black Solidarity with Israel (IBSI, "Ib-see"). IBSI focuses on highlighting positive Israel-Africa relations, including Israel's humanitarian work in Black African communities. The organization also emphasizes Israel as a country with a vibrant multiethnic identity, in contrast to what Washington described as the horrible human rights record of Palestinians. After our initial meeting, I continued to follow Washington's work with CUFI and other pro-Israel organizations. Over the following year, through 2013 and 2014, he continued to operate as a sort of pro-Israel free agent, contributing an African American perspective and voice to Jewish Zionist organizations such as StandWithUs, the American Israel Public Affairs Committee (AIPAC), Hillel International, the Zionist Organization of America, and Jews Indigenous to the Middle East and North Africa (JIMENA). By 2014, Michael Stevens was planning to leave his role as African American outreach coordinator with CUFI, and Washington joined the organization formally as its new diversity outreach coordinator in September of that year.

Washington said that the inspiration and the impetus for the work he does through CUFI and IBSI came from his discovery of an organization founded in 1975 called Black Americans to Support Israel Committee (BASIC).[28] "When I found out about BASIC," he told an audience of college students in Rochester, New York, "I literally sat down in front of my computer screen and began to cry." He described the organization as having been founded in response to the increasing efforts to criticize Zionism as a form of racism, which culminated in United Nations General Assembly Resolution 3379, adopted on November 10, 1975. The resolution declared that "Zionism is a form of racism and racial discrimination." Although many civil rights leaders were siding with Palestinians, Washington recalled how reassuring it was for him to learn that some African Americans rejected that notion. Because of BASIC, he said, "I know that the Black leaders did not just sit down for that." Of the mounting criticism of Zionism at that time, Washington argued, "Israel's enemies decided to do politically what they couldn't do on the battlefield. They turned to propaganda." When he talked about BASIC, Washington showed a picture from the 1963 civil rights March on Washington, with BASIC founders A. Philip Randolph and Bayard Rustin standing with Martin Luther King Jr. Washington explains the pro-Israel, pro-Zionist message of BASIC as the natural outworking of the broader civil rights legacy. Indeed, BASIC's founders cited the Black-Jewish civil rights partnerships among the impetus for the organization's work. News coverage of the 1975 launch of BASIC quoted Randolph explaining, "Jewish Americans supported us, marched with us and died for the cause of racial freedom." Randolph added, "Black people cannot turn their backs on a friend."[29] In 1975 BASIC also responded publicly to United Nations General Assembly Resolution 3379, which labeled Zionism as a form of racism and racial discrimination. The new organization ran a full-page ad in the Sunday *New York Times*, on November 23, 1975, which began with a quote from Rustin: "Zionism is not racism, but the legitimate expression of the Jewish people's self determination. . . . From our 400 year experience with slavery, segregation, and discrimination we know that Zionism is not racism." The statement was cosigned by A. Philip Randolph and more than 200 other prominent African Americans, including other civil rights icons Ralph Abernathy, Coretta Scott King, Rosa Parks, and Wyatt Tee Walker. BASIC's founding and articulation of support for the State of Israel came at a time when African Americans were increasingly polarized on the global implications of the American civil rights movement in the context of decolonization around the globe.[30]

Inspired by BASIC's emphasis on Black-Jewish solidarity in the United States and its advocacy work on behalf of the State of Israel, Washington initially sought to organize his race-focused pro-Israel outreach work under the BASIC name. He approached several surviving signers of the 1975 *New York Times* ad to enlist their support in reviving the organization. From some he got no response at all. From others he got initial support and interest, which weakened considerably when they realized that Washington worked with CUFI (although he was not part of the organization's staff at that time). As Washington described it, for them an affiliation with CUFI—a white, conservative, largely Republican organization—was a barrier to their endorsement or participation in the new proposed revival of BASIC. Washington was dejected but pressed forward under the IBSI name, choosing "Institute" as a nod to the A. Philip Randolph Institute. He chose CUFI as an organization to work for, in spite of the barriers its image presented for many African Americans. "I like John Hagee," Washington told me. "Do I agree with [him on] everything politically? No, but I'm a big boy. We always don't agree." "The important thing is Israel and advocacy and reaching out to the African American community." For Washington, "diversity outreach" is important because it adds visible racial and ethnic diversity to CUFI's mostly white membership. For Washington, this also includes diversity of messaging and tone. He described his relationship with CUFI as a very good marriage: "IBSI had a messaging that CUFI didn't have, but CUFI had the vehicle [with its millions of members and its resources]." By late 2014, Washington had begun integrating IBSI's race-focused, pro-Israel messaging with CUFI's well-established outreach apparatus, bringing what he called "a Black militant voice" to CUFI's array of leaders, speakers, and outreach staff. But Washington said of his typical confrontational style:

> I had to taper some stuff down. [I] couldn't really call people *punk asses* and stuff like that. Couldn't really do that and be the *Christians* United for Israel. . . . But what they [CUFI] were drawn to was the diversity of the message and also a little bit of the attitude that was there too. I mean the righteous indignation—"How dare you use terms like that [apartheid, Jim Crow, etc.]! That's not true!" In a race society, a white guy can't say some of the things I can say.

Washington described IBSI's messaging as a pushback against critics of Christian Zionism who cast the movement as primarily driven by theologies emphasizing Israel's role in Bible prophecy and the end-times. With its increasing attention to organizing students on college campuses, for example, CUFI has shifted the focus of Christian Zionist discourse onto political issues as it downplays controversial but long-standing Christian eschatological and theological motivations for supporting the State of Israel. The kinds of biblical arguments Michael Stevens offers to Black pastors and churchgoers are still the foundation of CUFI's Christian Zionism, but they are increasingly less part of its public advocacy work. Washington described Christian Zionist college students equipped with nothing other than biblical and theological rationales for supporting the State of Israel as unprepared to win the campus debate on Israel and Palestine:

> And so, the kids stand there talking about "bless those who bless you"—you look like an idiot. You're sitting there quoting scriptures, and they're asking you do you care about these people that are dying? And you don't have any information. All you have is the scripture. Now they're attacking your faith. Now you look like a stupid Christian, a stupid Zionist.

Washington described IBSI's messaging on race, Black-Jewish solidarity, and the apartheid question as a pushback against this problem. For him, students trained for pro-Israel activism in political terms are able to speak to relevant social justice issues. They are "armed with real time knowledge about what's going on," he said. And they are effective in taking on the question of Israeli apartheid—"especially if they're Black," he added.

A 2016 CUFI email reported on these efforts to take on the Boycott, Divestment, and Sanctions (BDS) movement on college campuses and to combat the Israeli apartheid narrative:

> There is an evil lie circulating in America and around the world—the lie that Israel is a racist, apartheid state like South Africa used to be. This apartheid myth fuels the BDS movement to boycott Israel, and we are using every available tool to destroy that myth and expose people to the diversity and freedom that characterizes Israel.[31]

CUFI sees colleges as "ground zero" for the debate about Israel and apartheid. In response, Washington and his colleagues developed a "BDS task force" that trains college students to fight BDS efforts on their campuses. The work of the task force also included hosting screenings of a short film featuring Black South African Christian Zionists, who challenge the comparison between Israel's treatment of Palestinians and the treatment of Black South Africans under white apartheid rule.[32]

In addition to CUFI's organizational outreach to Black churches and Black Christian college students, Washington is active on social media, speaking to contemporary race politics—especially the emergence of the Black Lives Matter movement. He is an outspoken critic of Black Lives Matter (BLM), especially for their support of the Palestinian cause. He described the attention BLM and the broader Movement for Black Lives (M4BL) have given to the issue of Israel and Palestine as "cognitive dissonance," criticizing those groups for singling out the State of Israel and ignoring human rights abuses and the treatment of Black people in other countries. In 2017, he wrote on Facebook, "Black Lives Matter is and always has been a sham (the moment they entered the Israeli-Arab discussion and ignored Nigeria, Chad, Cameroon, Kenya, Sudan . . . they showed their true Islamic colors)." In another post, he called the movement "a George Soros funded proxy war against Israel."

Alongside the kinds of campus initiatives focusing on race and politics that Washington helps to lead, CUFI's messaging is broadly political, and its calls to action to its members are similarly politically oriented. A sample of their regular "action alert" emails provides a sense of the political nature of their engagement regarding Palestine and Israel:

- "Action Alert: President Obama is killing serious action on Iran. Don't let him!" (January 30, 2014)
- "Action Alert: Ask Congress to Vote Against the Iran Deal!" (July 20, 2015)
- "Help cut UN funding!" (December 30, 2016)
- "Action Alert: E-mail your senators to demand that they reject the UN's attack on Israel" (January 10, 2017)
- "Action Alert: Ask President Trump to Move Our Embassy to Jerusalem!" (May 16, 2017)
- "Ask Your Senators to Support Mike Pompeo for Secretary of State" (April 18, 2018)

Through its political agenda, CUFI aims to shape U.S.-Israel relations broadly. On the last day of its annual Summit in Washington, DC, CUFI staff take conference attendees to the offices of their congressional representatives with a list of pro-Israel talking points. Lobbying Congress and training college students to talk about their support for Israel in political, race-focused terms are two ways the organization advances its mission to "act as a defensive shield against anti-Israel lies, boycotts, bad theology, and political threats that seek to delegitimize Israel's existence and weaken the close relationship between Israel and the United States."[33]

LIFTING UP THE "SOFTER SIDE" OF ISRAEL: THE INTERNATIONAL FELLOWSHIP OF CHRISTIANS AND JEWS

On the Sunday before Martin Luther King Jr. Day in 2016, Russell Street Missionary Baptist Church—a one-hundred-year-old congregation in Detroit's North End neighborhood, on the border with the city of Hamtramck—held an event celebrating King's legacy. Countless African American churches around the United States were also commemorating Dr. King that day, but this event had the distinction of being cosponsored by a Jewish congregation—Adat Shalom Synagogue. Russell

Street's congregation is predominantly Black, but the majority of attendees at this gathering of close to 400 were white. Adat Shalom is located twenty miles north-west of downtown Detroit, in the affluent suburb of Farmington Hills, but its members could easily get to Russell Street by car on Michigan Highway 10. Many Russell Street members had a harder time getting to the event, even from nearby neighborhoods. A church member told me that the local bus no longer serviced the church area on Sundays because of cutbacks, making it difficult for locals without a car to get there—especially in the fifteen-degree mid-January weather.

The afternoon event opened with a welcome from Mark Jacobs, the Michigan director of African American outreach for the American Israel Public Affairs Committee (AIPAC)—the Washington, DC–based pro-Israel lobbying group. Jacobs is white, with graying hair, and stylish dark glasses frames. Like all of the other leaders on stage, he wore a suit and tie. In introducing the event entitled "Building Bridges Together: An Afternoon of Song and Inspiration," Jacobs gave credit to Russell Street's Black senior pastor, Reverend Deedee Coleman, saying that she is "a woman of action" who "embodies everything Martin Luther King stood for in terms of building bridges." Next Rabbi Rachel Shere of Adat Shalom, in her introductory remarks, described inequality in America using Martin Luther King Jr.'s phrase, "a frustrating and bewildering wilderness." "If we have learned one thing," she said, "it is that the only way out of it is together—praying, singing, working hand in hand together."

Following an opening prayer came performances of three national anthems. The audience was asked to stand for the singing of "The Star-Spangled Banner," "Hatikvah" (the national anthem of the State of Israel), and "Lift Every Voice and Sing" (the Black national anthem). In turn, the audience and the dignitaries on stage stood facing each of the three flags on the Russell Street stage—the American flag, the Israeli flag, and the Christian flag (an ecumenical flag used mainly by Protestants meant to represent all of Christendom, featuring a white field with a red Latin cross inside a blue canton). When Coleman took the pulpit, she announced proudly: "We are the most pro-Israel church in the city of Detroit!" And in taking an offering for building and repairing bomb shelters in Israel, she exhorted:

> [We] talk about Israel, preach about Israel—every Sunday we do it. But it's time to do something. It's time to do something. . . . There is something about this day of Martin Luther King Jr. . . . because Dr. King was also pro-Israel, and he wasn't shy about it. Dr. King said, "Peace for Israel means security, and that security must be a reality."

In addition to the two local congregations, the event was sponsored by the International Fellowship of Christians and Jews (IFCJ). Rabbi Yechiel Eckstein, the founder of the IFCJ and its president until his death in 2019, flew in from Israel for the event. Eckstein was introduced to the audience as "the world's leading Jewish authority on evangelical Christians." It's a title that Eckstein might dismiss as too grandiose, given his unassuming personality, but it is a label that has stuck. His biographer called Eckstein "the Rabbi Who Loved Evangelicals" and someone who does not look the part of a rabbi—"broad-shouldered and big-boned . . . built more like a retired NFL quarterback."[34] Eckstein's unpretentious style notwithstanding, he has a strong stage presence. Cementing his credentials as a rabbi to evangelicals, Eckstein used the Russell Street pulpit to preach a sermon from the Christian New Testament, invoking the words of Jesus in the Gospels and the Apostle Paul's letter to the Romans. He used Paul's language to describe Gentile Christians as "grafted in" to the root of the nation of Israel. He then connected this to Martin Luther King's message of equality, continuing to describe Jews and Christians as two branches of the same root. "We are one!" he shouted. And he concluded his remarks saying, "I'm sure Martin Luther King's soul is smiling on us today." Eckstein also used his time to commend another Detroit-area African American pastor at the gathering, Glenn Plummer, for his longtime partnership with the Fellowship. He described traveling with Plummer to Ethiopia to accompany a group of Ethiopian Jews making *aliyah* (immigrating) to Israel. Finally, having brought his acoustic guitar with him from Israel, Eckstein led the audience in singing the Jewish biblical folk song "How Good and How Pleasant It Is for Brethren to Dwell Together," in English and Hebrew. He said he sang this song in the 1970s, when he recorded a folk music album in Israel. The interfaith celebration closed with more singing. This time the song was the civil rights protest anthem, "We Shall Overcome." Leaders on the stage—Black and white, Jewish and Christian—linked arms. Following suit, attendees in the pews held hands and swayed to the hopeful music. Following the service, everyone was invited to stay for an AIPAC-sponsored reception. In the church's basement, attendees mingled over plates of cake, and Eckstein posed for photographs with attendees.

Although the event at Russell Street Missionary Baptist Church had many contributing sponsors—from AIPAC to Adat Shalom Synagogue—the primary underlying impetus for the event was Reverend Coleman's long-standing work with the IFCJ. In Detroit that weekend, I met her and many others responsible for the IFCJ's pro-Israel outreach efforts among African American Christians.

In fact, several of the key pastors in that initiative are based out of the Detroit area—pastors Edward L. Branch of New Third Hope Baptist Church, Bishop P. A. Brooks of New St. Paul Tabernacle Church of God in Christ, and Glenn Plummer. All of these leaders had been instrumental in helping the Fellowship develop an outreach program to Black churches, and now IFCJ was working to extend its networks in U.S. Black churches to include new denominations. In September of 2014, the IFCJ formed an advisory board to develop a curriculum to nurture African American Christians into faith-based pro-Israel advocacy. Through the networking efforts of that advisory board, Eckstein and the Fellowship participated in a number of national convention meetings of major Black denominations in the United States over the next several years—the Church of God in Christ (COGIC), the National Baptist Convention of America (NBCA), and the Progressive National Baptist Convention (PNBC). The culmination of the outreach program was a series of Fellowship-sponsored leadership delegations sent to Israel. It was on these trips to Israel, and in their broader outreach efforts in Black churches, that the Fellowship cultivated its particular form of Christian Zionism based on the model developed and tested over many years by Eckstein.

Yechiel Eckstein: The Bridge Builder

Given the long history of animosity between Christians and Jews and the apprehension many Jews have of Christian proselytizing, it is remarkable that an Orthodox Jewish rabbi stood on the stage of a Black Baptist church in Detroit and preached a sermon from the New Testament. But as "the Rabbi Who Loved Evangelicals," Eckstein brought decades of interfaith work to his 2016 sermon at Russell Street Missionary Baptist Church. The son of an Orthodox rabbi in a long line of Jewish leaders and scholars, Eckstein followed in his father's footsteps, attending rabbinical school at the Orthodox Yeshiva University in New York.[35] After completing his studies in the late 1970s, Eckstein began working for a local office of the Jewish Anti-Defamation League (ADL) in Chicago. Eckstein left the ADL in 1983 to found his own organization, the Holyland Fellowship of Christians and Jews. This organization, which would eventually become the IFCJ, was started to foster a nascent Judeo-Christian alliance that included conservative evangelicals who had an affinity for the State of Israel as God's chosen "holy land" and for Jews as his chosen people. In his early work, Eckstein found that many of these American evangelicals knew few actual Jewish people and had meaningful relationships with even fewer, if any. Eckstein built his organization on this potential partnership between Jews and Christians and faced a great deal of backlash from the Orthodox Jewish community, who were generally wary because of the reputation evangelical Christians have among Jews for proselytizing. Undeterred, Eckstein forged relationships with evangelical pastors who had, in many cases, never met a rabbi or even a Jewish person. In the context of these relationships, Eckstein "found himself moved by their sincerity, their religious passion, and their unconditional love for God, Israel, and the Jewish people."[36] He saw this sincerity as an opening for building metaphorical bridges between evangelicals and Jews across the United States and, eventually, the world. Eckstein found a high level of unqualified political support for the State of Israel among many American evangelicals, but the largest divide to be bridged between them and the Jewish community was on the question of proselytizing. Driven by the "Great Commission" of the New Testament to seek converts and to make Christian disciples out of nonbelievers, evangelical Christians are known for an often uncompromising missionary stance. Faced with this seemingly immoveable obstacle to sincere and effective Jewish-Christian pro-Israel advocacy including evangelicals, Eckstein came up with a semantic "synthesis principle" that distinguished between *proselytizing*, on one hand, and *witnessing*, on the other. For Eckstein, proselytizing includes coercion, and specifically targeting Jews for conversion. Witnessing embraces a broader, more abstract freedom to share one's faith in the context of everyday experiences and relationships. "Until I came up with the synthesis principle," explained Eckstein in his biography, "evangelicals (and other Christians) related to Jews through missionary activity. They had no other avenue. The novelty of what I did was to give Christians a tangible, meaningful, and orthodox way to deal with Jews without trying to convert them. They could make that contact by supporting Israel and the Jewish people."[37]

When I traveled to Israel with an IFCJ-sponsored leadership delegation from the Black National Baptist Convention of America denomination, each participant was asked before the trip to affirm a "statement of religious respect" that drew on this long-practiced principle developed by Eckstein in his work with American evangelical Christians. The statement read, in part:

From the beginning, The Fellowship has promoted understanding, sensitivity, and respect between Christians and Jews, so decorum dictates that such difference be respected. While it is acceptable to ask questions about a person's

faith and background, we ask that you not promote your own beliefs without personal invitation. Although many of us are passionate about our faith
(which may be the very reason you will be touring the Holy Land), we ask that
you make this concession to ensure a harmonious, shared tour experience.

Many of his Jewish colleagues and partners could not get past the view of
evangelicals as bent on Jewish conversion and motivated by apocalyptic, Bible
prophecy-driven, end-times scenarios playing out in the Middle East through
Jewish conversion to Christianity, but Eckstein exhibited a remarkable level of
patience with his evangelical connections, seeking to teach them how to better
relate to Jewish communities. For example, when then president of the Southern
Baptist Convention, Bailey Smith, made a public speech in 1980 calling Jewish
prayer a form of blasphemy, Eckstein saw it charitably as a "teachable moment."
He encouraged the Anti-Defamation League to invite Smith and a group of
Southern Baptist leaders on an "educational mission" to Israel. The trip included
a meeting with Israel's prime minister, Menachem Begin, who greeted the group
warmly. They also visited Israel's *Yad Vashem* Holocaust memorial. Helping to
facilitate this delegation was an early bridge-building experience for Eckstein.
Throughout the 1980s, as the public profile of many conservative American
evangelicals rose within the Moral Majority movement and the broader political
ascent of the Christian right, Eckstein continued to engage high-profile American evangelicals, attempting to forge a stable pro-Israel alliance with them. In
a 1983 public meeting with the evangelical leader and founder of Campus Cru-
sade for Christ, Bill Bright, Eckstein put his synthesis principle to the test again,
engaging with Christian theology and prefiguring his preaching from the New
Testament in the Russell Street pulpit. To Bright, Eckstein said, "If I understand
your theology, your Great Commission is not to convert people to Christ. It is
to introduce them to the love of God through Christ. But it is God through the
Holy Spirit who either does or does not bring about the conversion. And if God
is sovereign, he can be trusted. He will do whatever he does in his own time,
right?"[38] Bright conceded the point, and this distinction became a stable bridge
between American evangelicals and Jews on the issue of supporting the State of
Israel—one by which evangelicals could "rationalize their commitment to the
Great Commission without antagonizing American Jews."[39] Eckstein founded
the IFCJ based on this initial success at building bridges between American evangelicals and Jews. Through the work of the Fellowship, he continued to build
relationships with high-profile evangelical leaders Pat Robertson, Jerry Falwell,

John Hagee, Hal Lindsey, James Dobson, Jack Hayford, and Billy Graham. After more than three decades in existence, in 2017 the IFCJ was raising more than $140 million annually from its 1.6 million Christian donors, totaling more than $1.5 billion since its inception.[40]

Glenn Plummer and Kristina King: Coming from a Place of Faith

The roots of the Fellowship's outreach to African American Christians began with Pastor Glenn Plummer of Detroit, whom Eckstein commended from the Russell Street pulpit at the Martin Luther King Jr. Day event. Plummer is the pastor of multiple Detroit-area congregations and the owner of several Christian television stations. Born in Brooklyn, Plummer describes his upbringing as cross-cultural, based on having lived with his family in Europe, Libya, and Mississippi, as well as attending college in Michigan's Upper Peninsula. In 2002, Plummer became the first African American chairman and CEO of the National Religious Broadcasters (NRB), an international association of evangelical Christian broadcasters, founded in 1944 to advance their interests in radio broadcasting. It operates as the de facto trade association representing evangelical Christian broadcasters in the United States and around the world, across television, radio, and online media platforms. As chairman and CEO, Plummer became the first Black spokesperson for an organization he described as predominantly white, conservative, evangelical, pro-Israel, and Republican.

The State of Israel's Ministry of Tourism has been a longtime partner of the NRB and presents an annual award at its convention. In 2005, Plummer received this Israeli "ambassador of tourism" award at the NRB convention in Anaheim, California. In that context, Plummer gave a keynote address to the mostly white audience of 1,500 evangelical broadcasting industry representatives on the parallel experiences of Black Americans, Israelis, and American Jews. After the speech, he was approach by several members of the Israeli Knesset (parliament) in attendance, who invited him to speak at the Knesset in Israel. He accepted the invitation and spoke in Israel just two months later, after which he began to think more about the relationship between African Americans and the State of Israel and what he might do to secure and advance that partnership.

Plummer took the idea of founding an organization focused on African Americans and Israel to Eckstein and the IFCJ. Although Plummer had an interest in founding such an organization, given his broadcasting work commitments he did not have the time required to get a new organization off the ground.

For that responsibility, he turned to Kristina King, whom he knew as someone with experience working with Detroit pastors and their churches on marketing and business sponsorship initiatives. "I didn't have a lot of time to give to it personally," Plummer recalled in telling me about his relationship with the Fellowship. "I was pastoring, I was in broadcasting, I owned a number of television stations. I was on the air every day hosting live television programs. . . . And so that's why I hired Kristina to make it happen. I was the president; she was the executive director." Plummer shared with Kristina King the vision he had for strengthening Black-Jewish relations and his thoughts about potential paths for partnerships between Black churches and the State of Israel. Led by Plummer, operated by King, and funded by Eckstein and the Fellowship, the organization launched in 2007 as the Fellowship of Israel and Black America (FIBA, "fee-bah"). Plummer gave King a budget and a research mandate to produce a white paper outlining what the organization could look like and how it could reach Black churches in the United States with a pro-Israel message. This was the first time King became involved with any work regarding Israel. Her entry to the project was research-focused. "I started to study the historical relationship between the Black and Jewish communities," she said, going on to list historical points of contact and cooperation between Black and Jewish communities in the United States: "The founding of the NAACP, the Urban League, the Jewish involvement in the civil rights movement." King described the personal impact of her preliminary research for FIBA:

> As I began to study that history, it just created an overwhelming gratitude towards the Jewish people for me. And I realized . . . their contribution to my personal life, that my life would have been different had the civil rights movement not happened. I wouldn't have gone to the colleges I went to or been able to work at the places that I've worked at. And so, for me, my experience in researching and coming to understand that history created an incredible gratitude for the Jewish people.

FIBA lasted for several years before dissolving. Plummer continued to partner with other pro-Israel organizations, such as the American Israel Public Affairs Committee (AIPAC) and the Fellowship, but Plummer again felt that he could not give the time required to sustain FIBA while simultaneously running his religious broadcasting organizations and his congregations. At the same time, AIPAC was beginning an outreach program targeting American Christians (especially evangelicals) and Hispanic American communities. Plummer facilitated an organizational transition for King to launch AIPAC's outreach to African Americans, including in Black churches. She went on to work for AIPAC for seven years in African American outreach in their political organizing and lobbying structure.

Although the politically focused pro-Israel advocacy work was exhilarating, King began to feel a disconnect from the more spiritual and religious outlook on Israel that she had developed as the director of FIBA:

> It was fascinating to work from a political place. It was fascinating to see how the democratic process in America works, to interact with foreign policy, and to actually see the role, the amazing role that America plays with Israel, and the incredible relationship that those two countries have that most of us just have no idea. . . . But for me, my journey into support for Israel came from a place of faith, and my passion comes from a place of faith.

The spiritual connection with the State of Israel appealed more to King personally as an African American Christian. The most natural connection between Black churches in the United States and the State of Israel, for her, was *faith*. So King turned to Eckstein as someone she believed could develop that faith-based connection with Black churches. Black churches, she contended, would better respond to the teachings of a rabbi such as Eckstein than to the political operatives of groups like AIPAC. Of Eckstein, she said, "Every great rabbi is a teacher and a father. And so, I would call him my rabbi. I look at him as a teacher. I look at him as a father." Based on this relationship, she believed that a Jewish organization like IFCJ, with its religious-oriented message, could generate more support for the State of Israel within Black churches in the United States. King also believed that the point of entry into Black churches could be the historical relationship between African Americans and American Jews, then further drawing on Black Christian resonance with the biblical narrative of Jewish emancipation.

For African American Christians, King explained that support for Israel and knowledge about Israel both begin from a place of faith, from "a biblical place"—not from a political place. She also emphasized how this approach differs from that of Christians United for Israel, which has to overcome what she called "a great gulf in our American culture between the white and Black Christian churches." "There's no warm, fuzzy history between . . . the Black and white communities," she added, emphasizing her skepticism about the potential for CUFI to lead Black churches into support for Israel. CUFI, in her view, is limited to reaching Black Christians in predominantly white religious spaces. "From most African American perspectives," King said, "we see [CUFI] as a right-wing Republican organization. And so even though we may want to support Israel, other places of disagreement would be hard for most African Americans."

Spearheaded by King and other longtime IFCJ partners and advisors including Glenn Plummer, the Fellowship launched a Black church outreach initiative in 2014, which King left AIPAC to lead. They began their work by forming an advisory committee that could facilitate relationships with some of the major Black denominations in the United States. That committee included Kenneth Ulmer, a Baptist pastor of a Pentecostalism-influenced megachurch in Los Angeles; Carroll Baltimore, then president of Martin Luther King Jr.'s Progressive National Baptist Convention (PNBC); Edward Branch of the National Baptist Convention, USA (NBC USA); Deedee Coleman, pastor of Russell Street Missionary Baptist Church in Detroit; and Glenn Plummer, who, after spending most of his career as a pastor of nondenominational churches, by 2014 had joined the Black Pentecostal Church of God in Christ (COGIC) denomination as its "Ambassador to Israel." With this African American advisory committee of experienced and well-connected Black church leaders, the IFCJ began meeting with the leaders of major Black denominations and attending their annual conventions. Eckstein spoke as an invited guest at several of these national meetings. The IFCJ's Black church outreach efforts focused on five Black denominations in particular: the NBC USA, the NBCA, the PNBC, COGIC, and the Global United Fellowship, a recently formed Black Pentecostal denomination. IFCJ outreach within these denominations focused on teaching the Jewish roots of Christianity and the history of Black-Jewish partnerships in the United States, ultimately aimed at building solidarity with the modern State of Israel.

For King, Eckstein was a rabbi working in the tradition of Rabbi Abraham Joshua Heschel, who marched with Martin Luther King Jr. in the civil rights movement. She described Eckstein as "a rabbi who studied and shares the values of Rabbi Abraham Joshua Heschel or Rabbi Joachim Prinz—people who were staunch supporters of the civil rights movement and of the African American community." "And certainly," she added, "Rabbi Eckstein . . . has been a supporter of the rights of all people, human rights supporter, supporter of social justice, and coming from a place of faith." Again, she emphasized pro-Israel advocacy "coming from a place of faith" as distinct from what she sees as the more political leanings of CUFI and AIPAC. For King, this distinction opens the possibility for an alternative, less political approach to pro-Israel outreach among African American Christians for the Fellowship. That approach emphasizes philanthropic and charitable work in Israel, based on the Fellowship's broader model of giving evangelical Christians a nonproselytizing "mission" in Israel. King described this philanthropic model as one with significant potential for reaching Black churches:

> One of the entryways that the International Fellowship has, coming from a place of faith and shared values, coming from work that's the same kind of interests that the African American community and the African American church has been advocates of. . . . Clothing people, feeding people, helping people to have shelter, bringing people from war-torn countries to a place of safety—all of those things open doors with the African American community. It's the work that the African American community does here in the United States. And so, it's like a love fest when you see that same work in Israel.

Deploying this strategy of African American church outreach based on historic Black-Jewish partnerships as a pathway to philanthropic work in Israel begins with Black church leaders, like those on the IFCJ advisory committee, who operate in the same kind of teaching and pastoral role that looks to the example of Yechiel Eckstein.

Deedee Coleman: Lifting Up the Softer Side of Israel

Deedee Coleman is a native of New Orleans. She has lived in Detroit for more than thirty years and has spent more than half of those years as a pastor. In a 2011 interview with a Jewish publication, Coleman described being raised with a strong religious sense of the importance of honoring Israel and the Jewish people:

> I am an African American Baptist female preacher whose origin comes from a deep-rooted spiritual truth and faith that Israel is the Holy Land of this world and its people are the chosen of God. I grew up respecting Israel and the Jewish people; it was something my mother taught us from a young age. From birth on, I was taught that God has a special blessing for those of us that protect and pray for Israel.[41]

Apart from her pro-Israel advocacy work, Coleman is involved in church-based prison ministry as well as prisoner reentry and community reintegration work. Her involvement in building support for the State of Israel in African American churches began in 2007 when she was invited to participate in an AIPAC-led delegation to Israel. Since then, she has taken part in or helped to lead more than ten trips to Israel, including with the Congressional Black Caucus and with other groups of government personnel and pastors. Reflecting on her first trip to Israel, Coleman said, "ever since that time, I've been working with the Jewish community on a different level." That work has included local involvement with the Jewish community in the Detroit suburb of Oak Park where she lives. It has also included joining the AIPAC Speakers Bureau and working for the IFCJ as a consultant. On the differences in her roles with AIPAC and the Fellowship, Coleman noted, "AIPAC gives me the political forum. . . . But the Fellowship gives me the social service connection to the Jewish people." Like Plummer, one of her first exposures to the work of IFCJ in Israel was accompanying a Fellowship-sponsored aliyah mission that brought 450 Ethiopian Jews to Israel. She described coming back from that trip impressed by the work of the Fellowship and further motivated to educate the African American community on "why it is a necessity, according to the Word, that we obey God's commandment in helping the Jewish people to keep them protected and safe." "With the Fellowship," she said, "I am lifting up the softer side of Israel. It's not all about the war. It's about people trying to live. It's about children being traumatized. It's about a country striving and wanting to be alive like everybody else." The "softer side" here refers to the social services and philanthropic work of the Fellowship that Coleman, King, and others distinguish from the more politicized work of AIPAC and CUFI.

On another trip to Israel with Eckstein and the Fellowship, Coleman encountered a need that she and her congregation in Detroit have focused on, the same one she took up an offering for at the 2106 MLK event—building and repairing Jewish bomb shelters. She described Eckstein taking her to a community that lacked adequate bomb shelters to which they could evacuate when sirens warned of possible Hamas rocket attacks from Gaza or other sources of threat. "We visited one of the bomb shelters, and the bomb shelter needed repair," she said. "Immediately when I got home, I talked to my church and said that this would be something that we need to do." The message she delivered to her congregation was: "If there is a need in Israel, and we can fulfill it and fix it, then that's exactly what we are going to do." The imperative was not obvious to everyone at Russell Street Missionary Baptist Church. Some asked how, specifically, they were going to raise the money. Others questioned whether they ought to focus on meeting the needs of the church's own members. Coleman persisted and raised nearly $7,000 in one collection.

Criticism came from outside the church membership too, including questions about why the congregation chose to help build a bomb shelter in Israel at the perceived expense of meeting more immediate local needs in the neighborhoods surrounding the church, which include large communities of Arab Muslim refugees from the Middle East. When a highway billboard went up near the church building reading "Discover Jesus in the Qur'an," Coleman took it as a challenge (and a distraction) to her congregation. She distributed a printed bulletin to her members emphasizing that Jesus was a Jew, not a Muslim. She also began to receive phone calls asking whether the church might help the local Muslim community in the same way that they were working with the Jewish community. In defense of the calling she felt to specifically direct the church's resources to supporting projects in Israel, Coleman said, "We are a *missionary* Baptist church. And if we can build a water well in Africa to save lives, then we can build a bomb shelter in Israel to save lives."

Edward Branch: On the Frontlines of Faith

Another member of the Fellowship's African American outreach advisory committee, Edward Branch has worked closely with the organization to recruit African American clergy to the pro-Israel cause, invoking the civil rights legacy. When I met Branch in his office at Third New Hope Baptist Church in northwest Detroit, he told me how he had become inspired to study the relationship between African Americans and Jews during the civil rights movement, and how he came to understand Jewish support for civil rights as a current debt owed by African Americans to the State of Israel and the Jewish people. For him, interest in the State of Israel and connecting with Jewish communities begins with the Bible. "You cannot, as a Christian, stand and preach and know nothing about Israel," he said. Branch first traveled to Israel in the 1980s with a group of pastors and describes the spiritual significance of visiting Israel as "the Holy Land." "Getting to see the place and experience the land of the Bible is just phenomenal," he said. He also emphasized the importance of seeing "the connection between the lands of the Bible and the people who occupy that land [today]."

Branch met King at an AIPAC presentation for Detroit area pastors, where he became more involved in pro-Israel advocacy work. He later participated in an AIPAC-sponsored trip for Black pastors at the invitation of King in 2013, when she was doing African American outreach for the organization. Branch attended AIPAC meetings, including in Washington, DC, but he also described being ambivalent about AIPAC's politics—specifically citing the organization's strong opposition to President Barak Obama's diplomacy efforts with Iran and what Branch perceived as a one-sided treatment of the issue of Israel and Palestine as troubling issues for him. When King left AIPAC to work with the IFCJ, she brought Branch on as an advisor and outreach leader. After meeting Eckstein and connecting with the work of the Fellowship, Branch began leading clergy teaching sessions and other seminars on the historic relationship between African Americans and Jews. In this he joined Kenneth Ulmer as a teacher and seminar leader working for the Fellowship. Through this role of leading seminars aimed at building support for the work of the Fellowship among African American Christians, Branch began to focus his attention on the civil rights era as a model for Black-Jewish relations. "I looked into Dr. King and his relationship with the Jewish community and the words that he had to say about our Jewish brothers and sisters," he said. "[Dr. King] became the model for [us as African Americans], so that we too could stand alongside those who stood alongside us during the movement."

Branch develops these ideas about the civil rights legacy in an IFCJ-distributed resource entitled "On the Frontlines of Faith: The Historical and Spiritual Bonds Between African-Americans and Jews," cowritten with Yechiel Eckstein. The forty-four-page booklet is a general primer for Black audiences on the civil rights movement, with an emphasis on white (especially Jewish) participation as being key to the movement's success. "If anyone were to ask the question, 'Where was the Jewish community during the Civil Right Movement?,' [sic]" writes Branch in the booklet, "the response would come loud and clear, 'They were on the frontlines of faith.'"[42] Establishing American Jews as frontline partners with African Americans in the civil rights struggle, Branch outlines Jewish contributions to the founding of major civil rights organizations, the Mississippi Freedom Summer project, and iconic civil rights marches. Branch quotes a 1965 interview with Martin Luther King Jr. emphasizing this point:

> How could there be anti-Semitism among Negroes when our Jewish friends have demonstrated their commitment to the principle of tolerance and brotherhood not only in the form of sizable contributions, but in many other tangible ways, and often at great personal sacrifice? Can we ever express our appreciation to the rabbis who chose to give moral witness with us?[43]

In the booklet, Branch also describes his 2013 AIPAC-led trip to Israel with a group of Black Baptist leaders, setting up the political situation of the State of Israel today as parallel to that of African Americans in the United States:

> [We] traveled to Israel to see firsthand the conditions of threat facing our Jewish brothers and sisters on a daily basis. While there, we visited Sderot, the town nearest the Gaza Strip, only to realize that the citizens of this small community live every day under the threat of missiles fired from so close that every home is required to have a bomb shelter. Being less than a mile away from Gaza, they have only a matter of seconds from the sound of a siren to find safety. At the northernmost border with Lebanon, we could easily see that Israeli homes were within striking distance from the wire fence that separated their borders. In a thousand ways, the history of African-Americans and that of the Jews parallel. Hardly anything in life ties people closer together than the pain of a common struggle.[44]

In the "Frontlines of Faith" booklet, Eckstein underscores this linkage between the political struggles of Jews and African Americans: "Dr. King is rightfully known for his pivotal role in the Civil Rights Movement in the U.S. What is less known—but well worth remembering—is that Dr. King saw a clear parallel between the struggle of his own people for equality and the struggle of another group familiar with oppression: the Jewish people."[45]

Is the Fellowship Apolitical?

The use of the civil rights movement to inspire African American Christian solidarity with the State of Israel mirrors African American outreach efforts used by CUFI. But the IFCJ provides a less overtly politicized path to supporting Israel compared to CUFI or AIPAC. The Fellowship does not take its supporters to lobby lawmakers on Capitol Hill, for example. Branch described feeling more comfortable with the Fellowship's approach to fostering Christian support for the State of Israel, compared with more plainly politicized outreach, especially in terms of supporting philanthropic projects in Israel and Jewish immigration initiatives:

> I think with the International Fellowship of Christians and Jews that speaks more to who I am and to the kind of ministry that I believe God has given

more for me. I think it reaches more people. I think it's more about how to help folks, how to service those Jews who are in need and those who are outside of the homeland and desire to get back there.

Within the Fellowship's philanthropic model, funds raised from American Christians provide material support for nonpolitical charitable projects such as orphanages and food pantries. However, they also fund bomb shelters, premilitary academies for Israeli youth, services for active duty Israel Defense Forces (IDF) soldiers and veterans, and Jewish immigration to Israel—all of which carry political implications. In chapter 3, I more closely analyze how politics underlie philanthropic emphases on IFCJ-led delegations for African American Christians by looking at the tensions African American Christians experience between religious/ spiritual emphases on guided "Holy Land" trips and simultaneous introductions to the politics of the region. It is worth noting here, however, looking more broadly at the work of the Fellowship, that other politically charged initiatives of the Fellowship complicate the notion that it focuses exclusively on religious, spiritual, or "faith-based" advocacy work. In 2014, the Fellowship launched a program called "Stand for Israel" alongside existing initiatives to provide charity to poor Jews in Israel and around the world and to help Jews make aliyah. The Fellowship describes the Stand for Israel program as "mobilizing Christian support for Israel" that "aims to engage people both spiritually and politically on behalf of Israel and the Jewish people."[46] The Stand for Israel blog, hosted on IFCJ's main website, features regular posts on political topics including the Israeli military, terrorism, Iran, Syria, the Boycott Divestment and Sanctions movement, ISIS, U.S.-Israel relations, Hamas, the Palestinian Authority, and the United Nations. On these and other issues, IFCJ mobilizes political support for the State of Israel among American Christians. The Fellowship's philanthropic appeals to African Americans and other Christians are part of a larger mobilization effort that includes politically oriented activism in the scope of its outreach—even when it more overtly eschews political approaches to building Christian support for Israel as a Jewish state.

In January 2018, U.S. Vice President Mike Pence—an evangelical Christian and an avowed Christian Zionist, who has spoken in front of AIPAC and CUFI gatherings—visited the State of Israel and reiterated the U.S.-Israel political alliance in no uncertain terms, saying, "We stand with Israel because your cause is our cause, your values are our values, and your fight is our fight."[47] Later that year, the United States officially opened its new embassy in Jerusalem amid ongoing controversy about the political significance of the move. The embassy opening marked a high point for the American evangelical Christian Zionist cause. Furthermore, it was widely cast as a quid pro quo arrangement with the conservative evangelical elements of the Republican base of voters who helped propel Donald Trump into office in 2016. On the occasion of Pence's visit to Israel, Eckstein took stock of the state of the impact of pro-Israel Jewish-Christian alliances on American foreign policy, saying, "Now, you have a situation where all the stars are aligned beautifully. You have evangelicals in the White House, you have Trump who is susceptible to their influence and their constituency, you have a right-wing prime minister in government in Israel, and everything is good."[48]

The Fellowship's African American advisory council has also publicly engaged politics on questions of racial identity in Israel and Palestine. Responding to the release of the policy platform of the Movement for Black Lives in 2016, IFCJ's African American advisors and leaders issued a press release condemning the movement for what they labeled its "anti-Israel stance." The statement began: "*The Fellowship* advisors and African-American leaders—while applauding the overall Movement for Black Lives (M4BL) agenda—criticized the Israel-related portion of its policy platform labeling Israel as an 'apartheid state' and accusing it of genocide." It continued:

> It was a vitriolic attack against Israel laced with misinformation and anti-Semitism and an agenda that is not embraced by the broader African-American community. . . . The anti-Semitism and misinformation found in this small segment is so misleading that it makes an experienced leader question the entire document and thus the intentions of the organization.[49]

The statement also reaffirmed the strength of the U.S.-Israel relationship, praised the State of Israel for pursuing peace with Palestinians, and refuted the claim that Israel is an "apartheid state," emphasizing the inclusion of Arab Palestinians as full citizens of Israel. In closing, IFCJ reemphasized the civil rights legacy of Black-Jewish partnerships; the statement connected this partnership and its implications to the State of Israel: "The Jewish community has been an ally of Black America, most significantly during the civil rights movement and even today. Together these two communities have been the conscience of America leading the fight for human and civil rights for decades. Jews have been our reliable friends, just like Israel."

COMPARING CHRISTIANS UNITED FOR ISRAEL AND THE INTERNATIONAL FELLOWSHIP OF CHRISTIANS AND JEWS

Christians United for Israel and the International Fellowship of Christians and Jews represent two prominent cases of Christian Zionist outreach in American Black churches in recent years. These organizations are similar in that they both deploy and recruit Black clergy within the structure of primarily white organizations. They are also similar in the extent to which each organization articulates primarily spiritual, religious, or "biblical" motivations for supporting (or "blessing") the State of Israel and Jews more broadly, while simultaneously engaging in more overtly political advocacy work. Another important similarity across CUFI and IFCJ is the primacy that Black clergy in both African American outreach programs give to narratives of Black-Jewish cooperation within the civil rights era of the 1950s and early 1960s. Finally, both of these groups work within an interpretive framework that emphasizes a continuity between the Israel of the Bible and the modern State of Israel as a political entity. Furthermore, within the rhetoric of CUFI's and IFCJ's African American outreach work, the State of Israel, Jews, and Judaism are essentially conterminous and used interchangeably—to bless "the Jewish people" is to "support the State of Israel."

As described in the introduction, a goal of this book is to highlight the relationship between narrative and identity, where particular narratives (including beliefs, principles, and ideology) sustain particular notions of Black church identity and corresponding calls to action. Thus these two features of African American Christian Zionist groups—a narrative privileging Black-Jewish civil rights partnerships and a biblical hermeneutic that equates the Israel of the Bible, the modern State of Israel, and Jews/Judaism broadly—represent clear cases of position-taking on the identity and mission of "the Black Church." These are important axes of the kind of contestation over that identity and mission that this book is about (table 1.1). The next chapter contrasts these two cases of African American Christian Zionism with two cases of African American Christian attention to Palestine. The juxtaposition of these cases—including their divergent hermeneutics, public theologies, and modes of political engagement—sets up the central argument of the book about the contested nature of Black religious politics.

TABLE 1.1 Black church culture in CUFI and IFCJ

Case	Key leaders in this study	Key themes	Hermeneutics	Public theologies	Modes of public engagement	Significance of race in Palestine and Israel
Christians United for Israel (CUFI)	• John Hagee • Michael Stevens • Dumisani Washington	Stand with Israel	"I will bless those who bless you and curse those who curse you." "For Zion's sake, I will not be silent."	Christian support for the State of Israel as a "biblical issue" The United States and Israel as a Judeo-Christian partnership against "radical Islamic terrorism"	Campus activism Lobbying U.S. Congress Clergy education	African Americans owe a debt to the State of Israel because of American Jewish support for Black civil rights.
International Fellowship of Christians and Jews (IFCJ)	• Yechiel Eckstein • Glenn Plummer • Kristina King • Deedee Coleman	Building bridges between Christians and Jews	"Comfort ye my people." IS 40:1	"Lifting up the softer side of Israel" (Clothing people, feeding people, helping people to have shelter, bringing people from war-torn countries to a place of safety)	Clergy education Charitable work, social services Interfaith collaboration	Identification with the State of Israel is based on shared histories of oppression.

CHAPTER 2

Journeys to Justice

African American Christian Palestinian Solidarity

THE CIVIL RIGHTS MOVEMENT AND THE QUESTION OF PALESTINE

In chapter 1, I described the contested history of Black-Jewish relations in the United States, with attention to how African American Christian Zionists point to the early civil rights era of the 1950s and the early 1960s as a halcyon period of Black-Jewish cooperation that enabled the success of the movement. For African American Christian Zionists, like those affiliated with Christians United for Israel and the International Fellowship of Christians and Jews, the early partnerships of that ostensible golden age of Black-Jewish relations gave way to a period of breakdown between the once-partnered minority groups. As I also noted in chapter 1, African American Christian Zionists lament the later part of the 1960s, which saw the rise to prominence of new civil rights leaders articulating alternative strategies for organizations such as the Student Nonviolent Coordinating Committee (SNCC), which increasingly put them at odds with Martin Luther King's Southern Christian Leadership Conference (SCLC). Drawing on deep traditions of transnational Black Consciousness, Pan-Africanism, and Black Nationalism, some of these emerging leaders explicitly globalized the aims of the U.S. civil rights struggle, finding common cause with Third World liberationist movements fighting against colonialism and racial oppression on a global scale. In this context, attention to Israel and Palestine rose among African Americans, in part because of the prominence of global political issues in the headlines. But the historian Michael Fischbach argues that the level of attention to Palestine and Israel among both militant and mainstream Black activists in the United States in the 1960s and 1970s is better explained in terms of the deep resonance with competing notions of how to understand Black identity and Black politics in the American context. Fischbach notes, "black arguments over whether to support Israel or the Palestinians mirrored much deeper intrablack debates about race, identity, and political action in the 1960s and 1970s and ended up symbiotically affecting both them and people in the faraway Middle East."[1]

This chapter begins with a partial historical account of developments beginning in the late 1960s to provide context for the two cases of African American Christian identification and solidarity-building with Palestinians. I focus primarily on Black traditions and discourses linking politics, theology, and identity from the civil rights era forward. It is important to note, however, that these traditions have deep roots in earlier expressions of global Black church activism, Pan-Africanism, and Black internationalism. In the late nineteenth century, Black clergy—such as Bishop Henry McNeal Turner and the Reverend Alexander Crummell—were promoting African American emigration to Africa and "the regeneration of Africa."[2] African American clergy were also prominent participants in the first five Pan-African Congress meetings during the first half of the twentieth century, which were organized by W. E. B. Du Bois and others.[3] Furthermore, many politically active African American clergy in the pre-civil rights era developed a global racial consciousness through participation in ecumenical religious meetings around the globe. In the case of the Baptist minister, scholar, and activist, Benjamin Mays, this international ecumenical religious activity developed into the kind of theological critique of colonialism and focus on linking the struggles of oppressed people of color on a global level that are recognizable in the Palestine-focused cases in this book.[4] Thus, although African American Christian Zionists saw the rise of African American criticisms of the State of Israel and identification with the Palestinian cause in 1960s and 1970s as an unprecedented development and a break with a dominant (if latent) African American Christian Zionism, attention to the long history of Black church engagement with Pan-Africanism, Black Nationalism, and Black internationalism show how contemporary critiques of the State of Israel and solidarity-building with Palestinians are an extension of a long trajectory of Black church global social justice activism. With this long trajectory in mind, the opening sections of this chapter elaborate on the seminal role of Black church political engagement and the emergence of Black theologies as expressions of this facet of Black church history that animate the Palestine-focused cases in this book.

The rising influence of Black Nationalism and Black Power, and the increasing attention of civil rights leaders to international issues alongside domestic ones in the 1960s, is perhaps best exemplified in the figure of Stokely Carmichael (who later changed his name to Kwame Ture). As a student activist, Carmichael participated in the CORE Freedom Rides of 1961 and later took on the leadership of SNCC, an offshoot of Martin Luther King's SCLC. After leaving SNCC in 1967, Carmichael wrote the influential book *Black Power* and became affiliated with the militant Black Panther Party. He also began to travel extensively abroad—notably to West Africa, Asia, and Cuba—turning his attention to international issues and Third World liberation movements. At the same time, the mainstream of civil rights leadership was beginning to pay more attention to issues abroad and was shifting the style of their critique to include anticolonial vocabularies. For example, by 1966, King was referring to northern ghettos as a "system of internal colonialism," and in 1967 he controversially denounced the war in Vietnam.[5] Carmichael, for his part, began to argue that Black Americans needed to define themselves as a *people* and to understand themselves geopolitically as Black Africans, which significantly alienated many white allies, including American Jews.[6] After the Six-Day War in 1967, Carmichael and SNCC took a firm and persistent stance against the State of Israel and in support of the Palestinians and Israel's neighbor Arab nations.[7] This explicit anti-Zionist Black Nationalist critique of the State of Israel, which also, at times, included anti-Semitic overtones, effectively severed many African American ties with earlier liberal and left-wing Jewish civil rights allies.[8] For Carmichael and other Black Nationalists, understanding African American experiences primarily through the lens of Third World liberation and Pan-Africanism precluded the kind of relationships forged in early twentieth-century, left-wing political circles, organized labor, and in the civil rights movement of the 1950s and early 1960s.[9] Carmichael's and SNCC's intense criticism of the State of Israel and of Zionism established the Palestinian cause and the politics of the Middle East— both viewed increasingly in racial terms among African Americans—as points of cleavage for Black-Jewish relations in America. As the historian Clayborne Carson notes, Carmichael "provided a model for the use of rhetorical racism and anti-Semitism by Black militants to build support among discontented Blacks," prioritizing concerns of racial consciousness, identity, and loyalty over issues of discrimination and employment opportunity.[10]

Throughout the 1970s, as the Black consciousness movement also became increasingly important to the antiapartheid struggle in South Africa, racialized outlooks on the State of Israel and conflicts in the Middle East intensified for more African American leaders. Focusing on Israel's economic and military ties to the apartheid state, in 1978 Jesse Jackson called Israel's trade with South Africa a "declaration of war on Blacks."[11] The following year, Jackson exacerbated the strained relationship between African Americans and Jews by participating in a trip with other Black leaders to meet with Yasser Arafat and the Palestinian Liberation Organization in Lebanon.[12] That same year, two hundred notable African American leaders collectively called on Jewish leaders to put a stop to "support of these repressive regimes" in South Africa and Rhodesia.[13]

Even when African American criticism of Israel was at its most intense, dissenting voices also emerged. For example, Jesse Jackson's rhetoric and actions in the 1970s represented a trend of pointed African American criticism toward the State of Israel, but later his position shifted considerably as he seemingly reversed himself in describing Zionism as a national liberation movement and by conducting a visit to Israel in 1994.[14] Other Black civil rights leaders directly challenged the anti-Zionist narrative of SNCC and other Black Nationalist organizations. For example, in 1975 a group of veteran Black leaders of the civil rights movement founded the Black Americans to Support Israel Committee (BASIC), which challenged the notion that Zionism is a form of racism on par with South African apartheid. As I mention in chapter 1, organizations like BASIC serve as inspiration and as a template for contemporary African American Christian Zionists like Dumisani Washington. This range of historical reactions to Zionism and the politics of Palestine and Israel among African Americans shows that there have long been options with historical precedents for pro-Israel African American Christian Zionists and Palestinian solidarity activists alike when it comes to invoking memories of Black-Jewish relations and global racial solidarities. In this context, pro-Israel Black church leaders who ask their congregations and their peers to take up the cause of supporting Israel face the task of reclaiming not only the ostensible partnership of the earlier civil rights era but also reformulating points of reference for the "Black experience." Because, ultimately, the kind of Third Worldism, Black Nationalism, and anticolonialism that rose sharply among Black activists in the United States in the late 1960s and into the 1970s is largely incompatible with Black-Jewish relationships built on support for the State of Israel, which is seen from those critical perspectives as definitively being part of the First World.

BLACK RELIGION AND THE CIVIL RIGHTS MOVEMENT

The sustained role of Black religion in the civil rights movement is an important part of the story, and it contributes to understanding the African American Christians in this study who focused on Palestinian solidarity. The role of religion in the civil rights movement is debated among scholars and analysts of the movement's successes and failures. The dynamic role of religion in the movement must account for both the role of Black churches (as institutions) and of Black religion more broadly (as a source of African American collective identity and cultural meaning). In many ways, the civil rights movement provided a context for testing long-standing claims about the tendency for Black religion and Black churches to either impel or impede political action and racial empowerment. By any account, only a small percentage of Black churches and Black clergy participated in the movement, but the influence of Black religion (and African American Protestant Christianity in particular) certainly played an important part in the early success of the movement. Martin Luther King's clergy-led Southern Christian Leadership Conference and the early years of the Student Nonviolent Coordinating Committee were based on Christian ideals: the power of Christian love, the "beloved community," redemptive suffering, pacifism, and nonviolence as both a moral obligation and a political strategy. The historian Barbara Savage characterizes the civil rights movement as a "religious rebellion" against "those who rejected ecstatic religion as primitive and antithetical to activism."[15] It is beyond the scope of this chapter to thoroughly evaluate (or even summarize) the debate among historians and scholars of the civil rights movement about the broader relationship between Black religion and Black political activism. I take as my starting point some fundamental impetus within African American Christianity with regard to the direction of the civil rights movement, but it remains important to further examine the specific roles Black churches and Black religion played in the movement over time.[16]

Savage, again, speaks to both of these facets of the movement in identifying southern Black churches as having "provided a common culture and a sanctuary" to the civil rights movement.[17] Social scientists, too, have noted the central role of Black churches in the movement. For example, Aldon Morris, in his account of how Black institutions, organizations, and networks generated and sustained mass protest movements, identifies Black churches as "the organizational hub of black life," acknowledging their centrality to the movement as an autonomous Black-controlled social space.[18] But he also relegates Black religion to the role of supplying enthusiasm and providing a repertoire of songs, prayers, oratory, etc. that were familiar to African Americans. Savage, on the other hand, argues that Black religious faith was a critical fuel for the movement beyond providing a cultural repertoire and forms of expression.[19] She notes, for example, that many students who joined the movement in the 1960s (Black and white, northern and southern) were motivated, on some level, by faith commitments. Ultimately, Savage argues, it was during the civil rights movement that "the perception emerged that black religion and politics were innately compatible and mutually reinforcing."[20] Finally, another parallel between Black religion and Black civil rights activism that Savage underscores is the role of women in the movement. Savage quotes civil rights activist Marian Wright Edelman making this connection: "Women are the backbone of the Black church without whom it would crumble. As in the Civil Rights Movement, Black women in the church are often asked and expected to take a back seat to men who depend on but disempower them."[21]

BLACK LIBERATION THEOLOGY

Christian ideals about the beloved community, redemptive suffering, and pacifism were important foundations for the early work of many civil rights activists (especially in SCLC and SNCC), but the concept of Black Power generally excluded these Christian foundations. The rift between more thoroughly Black Christian roots and its growing Black Power branches was evidenced in the shift in focus to international issues and global racial solidarities and in the ideological foundations of liberative political activism. The divide was not total, however, as a number of African American Christian civil rights leaders worked to bridge competing commitments to Black Power, on one hand, and Christian love and nonviolence, on the other. In doing so, they also attempted to translate the message of Black Power to wider (white) Christian audiences. One example of this effort to avoid a total separation between Black Power and Black Christianity is a 1967 essay by the historian and civil rights activist Vincent Harding in the liberal Christian publication *Christian Century*, entitled "Black Power and the American Christ."[22] The historians Edward Blum and Paul Harvey describe how Harding's essay positions Black Power as an authentically Christian response to

racism by replacing King's notion of "redemptive suffering" with a new emphasis on "redemptive anger" as a Christian theological foundation for civil rights
activism.[23] Blum and Harvey position Harding as heralding the advent of modern
Black Liberation Theology, a distinctly Christian articulation of Black Power in
Christian theological terms. Another example of an early defense of Black Power
ideology in Christian terms came from an ad hoc group of Black clergy, called
the "National Committee of Negro Churchmen," which published a full-page ad
in the July 31, 1966, edition of the *New York Times* headed "Black Power." Gayraud
Wilmore describes the development, publication, and response to the clergy
statement, noting that its theological and political reasoning were considerably
to the left of the majority of middle-class African Americans. The statement's
signers, Wilmore suggests, placed themselves "in unapologetic discontinuity with
the civil rights movement and the liberalistic, reconciliation strategy of King and
the SCLC."[24]

The late 1960s was in many ways the apex of a period of new Black theological reflection, stimulated by efforts to reconcile Black Power and Christian
theology. What emerged from this period of reflection and position-taking was
a movement that Wilmore lauds as a Black theological *renewal* under the banner
of Black Theology or Black Liberation Theology.[25] Anthony B. Pinn underscores
the importance of that period of theological reflection and renewal, describing
how the elaboration and articulation of emerging Black theologies "gave religious
articulation to a synergy between Christian wings of the civil rights movement
and the Black power movement."[26]

James H. Cone was a newly appointed assistant professor at Union Theological Seminary in New York City when his first book, *Black Theology and Black
Power*, was published in 1969. It was the first book-length treatment of Black
Theology, which had previously been debated and defined in various collaborative statements and manifestos.[27] In 1970, Cone followed that work with a second
book, *A Black Theology of Liberation*, which was the first systematic theological
elaboration of liberation theology published in English. Reflecting on the impetus of *Black Theology and Black Power* twenty years later, Cone wrote,

> I could no longer ignore Malcolm [X]'s devastating criticisms of Christian-
> ity, particularly as they were being expressed in the articulate and passion-
> ate voices of Stokely Carmichael, Ron Karenga, the Black Panthers, and
> other young African-American activists. For me, the burning theological

question was, how can I reconcile Christianity and Black Power, Martin Luther King, Jr.'s idea of nonviolence and Malcolm X's "by any means necessary" philosophy?[28]

In the same decade that Harold Cruse was articulating a new Black political identity in Marxist terms, Franz Fanon was conceptualizing Black identity as a theory of decolonization, and Malcolm X was awakening Black self-consciousness in distinctly non-Christian overlapping religious and political terms, the Black Theology of Cone and others challenged the dominant Christian theologies coming out of white seminaries, seeking to "kill gods that do not belong to the Black community."[29] In "killing" the God's of the white theologians, Black Theology emphasizes the particularity of theological reflection and finds God on the side of the marginalized and the oppressed. The resulting image of God, then, is *as Black*. This ontological affirmation follows from the inseparable identification of God with the racially oppressed. In Black Theology, Jesus too takes on racial particularity—he is a Black messiah and a revolutionary against injustice. Finally, within the framework of Black Theology, salvation is understood less in personal terms than in social and political terms, where salvation is equated with liberation.

From its inception as a field of reflection among professional theologians such as James Cone in the late 1960s, Black Theology and Black Liberation Theology continued to develop and take shape over time, often in response to critiques. Wilmore's historical work in *Black Religion and Black Radicalism* argued for a long-standing presence of radical Black Christianity to undergird Black Theology as an emerging theological discourse. Cornel West's Marxist contribution to Black Theology brought class to the forefront, where race had tended to dominate theological concerns. And a number of Black women theologians—Katie Geneva Cannon, Jacquelyn Grant, and Delores Williams—critiqued the gendered assumptions of Black Theology (echoed in the history of Black churches and in Black political movements). Their critiques, under the banner of emerging Womanist Theologies, contributed feminist concerns from Black perspectives to questions of race and power in Black Theology. The Womanist theological critique was also accompanied by pioneering historical work, such as that of Evelyn Brooks Higginbotham, recovering the role of women in Black churches across time.[30]

From this account of Black Liberation Theology and its roots in questions about the relationship between Black religion and Black activism, I turn to the book's two cases of African American Christian solidarity with Palestinians: the Samuel DeWitt Proctor Conference (SDPC, "the Proctor Conference") and The Perfecting Church (TPC). Both engage with Palestine and Israel primarily by connecting African American Christians with Palestinians. The Proctor Conference does so with an explicitly activist orientation to Black religious politics, drawing on traditions in African American Christianity focused on advancing social and racial justice in prophetic and liberationist theological terms. Alternatively, as an independent Black evangelical suburban congregation, The Perfecting Church distances itself from an overtly activist stance in their engagement with Palestinians, preferring to position the church and its members as potential bridge-builders and peacemakers in the region, seeking to emulate Jesus as a servant to all. Across these cases, Black Theology is, at times, more and less explicit. The presumptions of both cases, however, derive from the fundamental impulse of Black Theology that racially specific theological reflection is even possible and that theological clarity and moral force derive, at least in part, from positions of racial exclusion. As with the Christian Zionist cases presented in chapter 1, these examples of African American Christian Palestinian solidarity offer particular visions of "the Black Church" and its potential with regard to Israel and Palestine through an applied vision of Black religious politics.

PALESTINIAN SOLIDARITY THROUGH THE EYES OF THE OPPRESSED: THE SAMUEL DEWITT PROCTOR CONFERENCE

At the Palestine-focused event at Howard University School of Divinity described in the introduction, on the issue of Israel and Palestine the General Secretary of the Proctor Conference, Iva Carruthers, said that "for us, it is not a question of *if* the Black Church should respond, but indeed *how* the Black Church should respond." The answer to this question of how the Proctor Conference should respond to Palestine and Israel lies in the story of how this network, made up primarily of African American clergy and activists, came to include Palestine within its scope of concern. As cochair Frederick Haynes told an SDPC clergy gathering in Houston (also described in the introduction), the organization is broadly driven by a core mission of activism. As a network of progressive faith leaders and congregations, the Proctor Conference works on education, advocacy, and community engagement around social justice work in partnerships within civic, academic, nonprofit, and business communities. The 2016 clergy conference I attended included thematic sessions ranging from police brutality to mass incarceration, economic inequality, and ecological and environmental degradation.

Founded in 2003 with a mandate to "nurture, sustain, and mobilize the African American faith community in collaboration with civic, corporate, and philanthropic leaders to address critical needs of human and social justice within local, national, and global communities," the Proctor Conference is named after the late Reverend Doctor Samuel DeWitt Proctor.[31] A prominent theologian, pastor, preacher, and educator, Proctor was a longtime professor at Rutgers University as well as the pastor of Abyssinian Baptist Church in Harlem, and he bridged the academy and the pulpit throughout his career. He was also a mentor to Martin Luther King Jr. The founding members of the Proctor Conference include Carruthers and Haynes, as well as Reverend Dr. Jeremiah Wright Jr., then senior pastor of Trinity United Church of Christ in Chicago.[32]

The Proctor Conference emphasizes the prophetic tradition of African American Christianity, linking preaching and teaching with social justice activism on behalf of vulnerable and marginalized people in the United States and around the world. The organization is guided by Proctor's words on the prophetic obligation of Christian ministers: "Some pastors have given up on filling the shoes of [biblical prophets like] Amos, Micah, Isaiah, or Jeremiah. . . . God bless those pastors who stand tall and who, in love, tell the truth. They are the watchmen in the tower, the sentinels at the gate who can save us from total pollution."[33] In this tradition, the issue of Palestine is one in which the prophetic concern to maintain a link between African American theology and activism on behalf of the marginalized takes U.S. Black churches beyond local concerns and into a global conversation, linking African American experiences with those of other marginalized and oppressed people around the world.

I learned how the broadening of global concerns within the Procter Conference came to include attention to Palestine at the Howard University event, where I met Bishop Don Williams. When we spoke again after the event, Williams told me the story of his role in bringing the issue of Palestine to the Proctor Conference, which led to the organization eventually including it under the mantle of the kind of prophetic Black Christianity that it advances. Williams is a leader in the Pentecostal United Church of Jesus Christ denomination, and for three decades he has been a director for African American church relations at Bread for the World, an ecumenical American Christian organization and movement focused on ending hunger and poverty around the globe. In 2011, Williams was invited to go to Israel and Palestine by a former colleague who was then working with World Vision, an evangelical Christian humanitarian organization. Williams described the invitation as coming out of nowhere; Israel and Palestine were not at all on his radar, he explained. He was intrigued and interested in going on the trip but was unsure of what to expect. Being familiar with Israel's efforts to recruit pastors into the Zionist cause, he was somewhat apprehensive about the potential politics of the trip. But he trusted his former colleague enough to look further into the opportunity. Describing his background knowledge and framework for thinking about Israel and Palestine at the time, Williams told me: "I was like probably most African American church folks that really had some, I guess, ideological views about Israel. We pretty much identify with the Exodus, and we could identify with the slavery stuff." Out of a sense of caution, Williams wanted to vet the proposed trip and could think of only one friend and colleague whom he believed could weigh in on whether to participate—civil rights icon and strategist to Martin Luther King Jr., Wyatt Tee Walker. Williams described Walker as the first person he knew who had written anything about Palestine from an African American perspective. Walker was among the 200 prominent African American leaders who signed BASIC's 1975 *New York Times* ad in support of the State of Israel. He was later involved in antiapartheid activism in South Africa and became an activist for Palestinian statehood. Williams visited Walker at his home and gave him a copy of the trip itinerary. "He looked at it very, very carefully," Williams recalled. "He really looked at it, took his time. And when he looked up he said, 'This is a good trip. You need to go on it.'"

Having decided to participate, Williams invited other Black pastor friends to accompany him, but only one took up the offer, Leonard Lovett, then the ecumenical officer of the Church of God in Christ (COGIC). They traveled together in March 2011 as the only two African Americans on the delegation of about thirty American Christian leaders from different denominations and groups. The group also included the president of World Vision. In recounting the trip experience, Williams reflected on how he enjoyed the spiritual emphasis on the places of the Bible:

> So, we used this trip to go to various places and we went to a lot of the normal places that you would go to. We went to the Garden of Gethsemane, we looked over the Kidron Valley, and we went to a lot of the different places—to

the Church of the Transfiguration. . . . What we would do is when we would go to a place, we would find scripture that coincided with the place that we had been. And, somebody within the group would read the scripture, and just kind of do a brief reflection on the place and location. So, that was good and I enjoyed that part it.

Alongside appreciation of the spiritual emphasis of the trip, Williams described how unsettling it was to see some of the conditions in which Palestinians lived. "I guess the place where it really started getting heavy for me is when we decided that we would go down to Hebron, to the place where you had the Tomb of the Patriarchs," he said. He then went on to describe the experience of visiting Hebron, where the Israeli military maintains a presence to secure settlements of several hundred Israeli Jews within the center of the city of over 200,000 Palestinians residents:

We saw how controlled it was by the Israeli soldiers. When we got off the bus, it was almost like we got confronted by these soldiers. And they were kind of walking through the crowd and just about knocked me over. And I got a little upset because of initially what I saw. It just didn't sit right with me, what I saw and what I felt. And, then I'm saying, most likely these gentlemen wearing these uniforms and carrying these weapons probably some of my tax payer money is paying for this. I got a little upset by it. And then we started hearing the stories of how the Israeli citizens treated the Palestinians, and we saw the chicken wire over the market where the Israeli citizens there would throw stones and rocks and bottles.

On the last day of their trip, Williams and Lovett got in touch with the son of some old friends of Williams, who was part of an African American gospel choir touring the Palestinian West Bank. The choir had teamed up with a group of Palestinian performers and was putting on a play about Martin Luther King Jr.[34] Williams described getting to spend the day with the group of performers and exchanging stories about their similar experiences as African Americans in the Holy Land and the particular experiences that the theater group had had among Palestinians in the West Bank. "They were confronted with the systemic problems and racism and all the things that the Palestinians were going through," Williams recalled. "And it really upset them quite a bit," he added. Before Williams parted ways with the touring artists, one of the members of the cast suggested that he get in touch with Mark Braverman, a Jewish American psychologist and Palestinian rights activist.

When Williams returned to the United States, he met with Braverman, who told him about the Palestinian solidarity organization that he was helping to found, called Kairos USA. In the course of their conversations, Braverman invited Williams to become a founding board member of the organization. Williams eventually accepted and also began to serve as its director of African American Church Relations. As a Kairos USA board member, Williams traveled to Palestine two more times in 2011. He described coming away from those trips feeling further compelled to share his experiences with other African Americans:

> I saw so many similarities [with Palestinians] about some of the things that we have experienced over the years as African Americans that I could really, really identify with and relate to. So, I felt that if I was going to do this, then I would need to try to find a way to get people to see and experience some of the things that I saw.

Williams later enlisted the help of another friend and colleague in ministry, Jeremiah Wright. Wright met with Braverman and Williams, and they collectively decided to approach the Proctor Conference about the issue of Palestine. As longtime Proctor leaders, Wright and Williams brought the issue to Carruthers. At that time, the Proctor Conference's annual convention was just a month away, and they were not expecting Palestine to be part of the program, but perhaps there would be opportunities to talk about including it in future meetings. However, motivated by the enthusiasm of Williams and Wright, Carruthers made a late addition to the program, inserting a breakout workshop on Palestine. Williams made plans to attend the conference, accompanied by Braverman and the Black South African antiapartheid activist, pastor, and liberation theologian, Allan Boesak. To their surprise, Carruthers made another last-minute decision during the conference to change an existing plenary session to include Braverman and Boesak as speakers. "I have never seen her do this!" Williams said, recalling the sudden opportunity.

That conference began a partnership–shepherded by Williams, Wright, and others–between Kairos USA and the Proctor Conference to promote Black church engagement with Israel and Palestine from a liberation theology and prophetic Black Christian perspective. Reflecting on this relationship in 2015, Williams wrote of his earlier travels to Palestine, which had motivated his work on that issue:

> As a man of African descent and as a fourth generation Pentecostal who lived through the civil rights movement, it was easy for me to see and feel what my Palestinian sisters and brothers are experiencing because I have also experienced being marginalized. Being in that place where the "Prince of Peace" was born and found no peace produced in me a powerful combination of sadness, hurt and anger.

To this, Williams adds:

> When I came back from my two trips to the West Bank, I was asked by many of my friends what it felt like to walk where Jesus walked. I told them it felt good to walk where Jesus walked but it felt even better to walk where Jesus is walking today and that is with those who are undervalued, underestimated and marginalized.[35]

The connection between the Proctor Conference and Palestine that Williams, Wright, Braverman, Carruthers, Boesak, and others have developed draws on a global view of prophetic African American Christianity, in which the liberation theology impetus to side with the marginalized and oppressed becomes an increasingly global religious lens. It also draws on the experience of parallels between life in the United States for African Americans and life in Israel and Palestine for Palestinians.

Based on this imperative, Proctor-affiliated clergy and activists apply theological and political lenses of prophetic religion and liberation theology to engagement with Palestine and Israel in two directions. First, they emphasize awareness-building among Black pastors, aimed at congregational education on Palestine and its parallels with African American concerns. This effort focuses on challenging certain theological and cultural narratives about Israel among African American Christians who Proctor Conference leaders see as obstacles to prophetic engagement on Palestinian solidarity. Second, the Proctor Conference actively works to extend its prophetic mandate beyond traditional Black church congregational contexts and into emerging spaces of race-focused social activism, especially among a younger generation of activists who are increasingly organizing and working independently from Black churches, denominations, and traditional religious organizations. Both of these paths stem from normative positions on what "the Black Church" is and what it ought to be doing in political terms. In calling Black pastors and congregations to rethink their outlook on the Bible, on the State of Israel, and on political solidarities in global terms, members of the Proctor Conference emphasize a historic role for Black churches in the United States as socially relevant and necessarily politically engaged institutions. Recognizing the distance between traditional Black religious spaces and new movements for racial justice under the banner of Black Lives Matter, the Proctor Conference works to align its prophetic religious imperative and its vision for Black churches with these contemporary movements.

Journeys to Justice: Reorienting Black Churches on Israel and Palestine

The Palestine-focused event at Howard University in 2014 was one event that came from the partnership between the Proctor Conference and Kairos USA, fostered by Williams, Wright, and others. The fruits of that partnership have also been advanced and disseminated through workshops at the Proctor Conference's annual clergy and lay leadership conference under the titles "Kairos USA: The Call from Ferguson to Palestine" and "Palestinian Liberation and the Call to African American Churches." The Proctor Conference has published two resources for Black churches under the theme of "Journeys Toward Justice." The first is a congregational study guide meant to serve as a curriculum for a "biblical and social study of the quest for justice by Palestinians in Palestine and Israel, and Black people in America."[36] The second resource is a video recording of a roundtable conversation among Proctor leaders, similarly titled, "Journey to Justice: From Black America to Palestine."[37]

The roundtable conversation was led by Carruthers and includes contributions from two SDPC trustees, Wright and Valerie Bridgeman, who is a Hebrew Bible scholar and dean of the Methodist Theological School in Ohio. The recorded conversation also included Alton Pollard, dean of Howard University School of Divinity and host of the 2014 "Occupied Palestine: How Should the Black Church Respond?" event, as well as the Palestinian Christian human rights attorney Jonathan Kuttab, who is chairman of Bethlehem Bible College and a board member of the Sabeel Ecumenical Liberation Theology Center in

Jerusalem. The panel identifies and challenges the dominant and problematic view of the contemporary State of Israel among Black Christians, equating the Israel of the Bible with the contemporary political State of Israel. In the discussion, Wright contends that, by and large, Black pastors in the United States fail to help Black churches understand the difference between the biblical nation of Israel and the political State of Israel today. "It's an uphill battle," he explains, "because people start talking about Israel that they see on television as if that's the Israel of the Bible." In the roundtable discussion, the panelists explained what they see as an underlying theological problem among some Black Christians—the tendency for Black religion to become corrupted by nationalism, which marginalizes and oppresses people, especially people of color. Challenging the fusion of religion and nationalism in the video, Wright asks rhetorically, "What kind of God you got that would promise you my land?" It is a question that I had seen him ask in several teaching settings at Proctor Conference events, critiquing theologies that privilege one racial, ethnic, or religious group at the expense of others. "Zionism is racist and sees others as nonhuman," Wright concludes, making his point on the panel discussion. Bridgeman pointed to the problem of African American Christians feeling compelled to "find themselves" in the text of the Bible by comparing Black experiences with those of the biblical Israelites. "The Black church needs to disengage itself from seeing itself in the text," she argues. "People are reading themselves into the text so completely that they can't make these separations. . . . Ancient Israel is not political Israel. It just is not."

The alternative to this interpretive approach to the Bible among African American Christians is to read the Bible as a narrative of oppressed people, said Pollard. In the roundtable discussion, Pollard points to the 1985 Kairos Document, produced by South African theologians, calling on Christian churches worldwide to disavow their theological support for the apartheid state. In the prophetic tradition of liberation theology, the document critiqued what it called "state theology" and called for alternative prophetic theologies, emphasizing the need for reconciliation and justice to prevail in the face of apartheid. This kind of theology, suggests Pollard, is what is needed within Black churches as a challenge to the problem of religious nationalism.

On the question of religious responses to apartheid, Wright adds that the Kairos Document "dares to name apartheid a sin, as a heresy." "And we need to start naming Zionism and Christian Zionism as a heresy," he adds. Wright points to the Kairos Palestine document that similarly critiques Christian Zionism as a form of religious nationalism. Inspired by the original 1985 South African Kairos Document, the 2009 Kairos Palestine Document, written by Palestinian Christians, asks Christians around the world to identify the Israeli occupation of Palestine as "a sin against God." The statement continues in liberationist terms: "true Christian theology is a theology of love and solidarity with the oppressed, a call to justice and equality among peoples."[38] Explaining his critique of Christian Zionism in view of the Kairos Palestine document, Wright adds, "A lot of what we're preaching and teaching in terms of Christian Zionism, or Zionism, nationalism— is *racism*." "There is a difference between Judaism and Zionism," he adds.

In part in response to the theological Kairos call from Palestinians, the Proctor Conference has taken up the call to solidarity between Palestinians and African Americans beyond theology and into political terms, highlighting a "shared struggle" between the two groups. For Proctor Conference leaders, like those who participated in the "Journey to Justice" roundtable, the answer to the question of African American-Palestinian solidarity begins with reclaiming what they see as a lost identity and political orientation among Black churches. "Without question," says Pollard in the roundtable discussion, "we need to always go back home to our roots." For Pollard and the other Proctor Conference leaders discussing the question of the Black church's role in responding to Israel and Palestine, this means "reading the Bible through the eyes of the oppressed" and reclaiming a distinctly Black religious identity. "We continue to be mesmerized by both the idea of being American and Christian in uncritical ways," Pollard notes. "[It] obliterates this very notion of being profoundly Black." And this, he argues, is "precisely why so many young people don't have time for our churches, our congregations, our clergy. Because they do not find us speaking out of that radical, rooted, authentic, genuine sense of truth that will invite them to come back home."

Beyond Israel and Palestine, the Proctor Conference is broadly concerned with bridging the gap between Black churches and young contemporary Black activists, who are largely organizing and working outside of traditional Black religious spaces. Carruthers summarizes the purpose of the roundtable conversation on Palestine as being aimed at initiating "a call to the Black church to find and reclaim its voice and identity." All of the panelists emphasize the need to do this while supporting youth activism and attending to issues of racial justice in global terms. "There is a move afoot," says Bridgeman to the rest of the panel. "I am deeply impressed and hopeful because of our young leaders, because they are in fact doing this international global looking at the ways that these problems are global and not local. . . . I like to remind people of my generation and older, there has never been a successful justice movement that was not led by young people."

The imperative for the Proctor Conference on the issue of Israel and Palestine is twofold. One facet of their approach is challenging Christian Zionism and its supporting theologies within traditional Black religious spaces—especially churches. They emphasize the need for reeducation in Black churches, undercutting the theological foundations of Christian Zionist readings of the Bible. They argue that a Christian Zionist reading of the Bible mistakenly upholds a direct linkage between the biblical nation of Israel and the modern State of Israel. This is a problem for them because they view the contemporary State of Israel as a political project founded on racialized policies of exclusion and discrimination. Proctor Conference leaders are particularly concerned about the extent to which this interpretive understanding of the Bible has taken hold among African American Christians based on their identification with Israel through the Exodus narrative and the experience of slavery, dispossession, marginalization, and oppression. In the roundtable discussion, Pollard emphasizes the shift in African American theological education that this diagnosis requires: "We are oftentimes teaching the 'tradition' rather than teaching freedom," he says. "And if we continue to do this, then we should also expect the demise of our churches, the demise of theological education, the demise of the moral fabric of our people and our society." According the Bridgeman, the first step in this process is "people actually reading the Bible." Wright makes the same point in another way: "We need to deconstruct sacred cows," he says, referring to interpretations of the Bible in Black churches that align African American Christians with Christian Zionism.

Reading the Bible Through the Eyes of the Oppressed

Reverend Lora Hargrove was born and raised in Baltimore in what she describes as a middle-class African American family and community. She was raised in a Black Catholic parish but later encountered and became part of Protestant Black Christian traditions. She preached her first sermon at Bethel African Methodist Episcopal Church in Baltimore and later served at Mount Calvary Baptist Church in Rockville, Maryland. She joined Mount Calvary as a ministry intern during her seminary training, was ordained in that church, became an assistant pastor, and eventually, in 2018, its interim senior pastor. As an assistant pastor, Hargrove oversaw Christian education programs in the congregation and various other ministries. Like many clergy in the Proctor Conference, Hargrove's first exposure to Israel and Palestine came at one of the SDPC's annual meetings. "It's a lot of information to take in at a week-long conference," she told me, reflecting on her initial encounter with the Proctor Conference's engagement with Palestinians. "From there," she added, "I did a lot of research based on the recommendations of my father in the ministry, who was Jeremiah Wright." "So I went down that road. . . . I did reading from various perspectives . . . and was deeply troubled and deeply moved and wondering why this was not at the forefront of what we do as the church of the living God. And especially for me I looked at it in terms of issues related to people of color."

In 2014, Wright invited Hargrove to his Trinity United Church of Christ in Chicago for a meeting of African American clergy and community leaders to discuss the issue of Palestine. "He sent out one hundred invitations," Hargrove said of that meeting. "And out of those one hundred letters . . . only thirteen people showed up." Taken aback by the lack of response among Black clergy to Wright's invitation, and motivated to facilitate such a conversation in the Washington, DC, area, Hargrove collaborated with other local clergy to host a similar conversation. Carruthers and other Proctor Conference leaders became involved, and they eventually settled on Howard University as the location. Hargrove saw that event at Howard as an overall success. But she also described the challenges of working across different churches, denominations, and local contexts to convey the importance of an issue that seems distant to many Black clergy in the United States. Speaking about how she has been able to engage African American Christians on the issue of Palestine, Hargrove emphasized the work she has done within her own congregation:

> I began to incorporate this into my Bible study class. I did not start off with
> this issue of Israel and Palestine. I started off from a broader sense just about
> the biblical text and what you understand, what you see about the biblical
> text. Because there are a lot of folks in church that feel like they know the
> Bible. And what I always tell them is there is a difference between knowing
> what you believe and merely believing what you know.

Hargrove's approach to teaching the Bible within her congregation is in line with the imperative articulated by Wright, Bridgeman, Carruthers, Pollard, and other

Proctor Conference leaders. Hargrove's approach follows the path that Proctor leaders outlined in the roundtable discussion—a broad reeducation of African American Christians to provoke them to see the biblical text as connected to issues of oppression. "The whole notion for me in teaching," said Hargrove, "is trying to open their eyes to the fact that you have been, for years, reading your Bible through the eyes of the oppressor." To which she added, "I want to open this up to you so that you begin to read scripture through the eyes of the oppressed." The issue of solidarity between African Americans and Palestinians based on parallel experiences of oppression is rooted in a particular tradition of biblical interpretation. As a result, teaching about Palestine and Israel from a liberation perspective requires a paradigm shift on the Bible as a whole. "It's not just teaching about Israel and Palestine," says Hargrove. "It is about giving a completely different paradigm of how you even approach scripture."

Carolyn is a life-long member of Hargrove's Mount Calvary Baptist Church.[39] She has a PhD in economics and works at a nonpartisan social policy research organization. When I spoke to her, she had been a regular participant in Hargrove's Bible study. In her midthirties, she described herself as one of the younger attendees in the group. Having attended the Bible study for a number of years, she emphasized the same paradigm shift that Hargrove describes as necessary, explaining how studying the Bible with her pastor has shifted her perspective on a number of issues, and how her concerns have been broadened to include attention to the Palestinian cause. Carolyn also described expanding her notion of what liberation means and the idea that "none of us is free until we're all free." Hargrove, she says, "talked about Jesus as a revolutionary, Jesus as a liberator, Jesus as caring about the least of these." "I had thought about that from an African American perspective," she added, "but I guess the teaching has really helped me to enlarge that concept of 'free.' . . . It's not just the Black community." She continued:

I don't think Jesus is happy [or] approves of the treatment of the Palestinians. . . . So it's connecting the Palestinian struggle to the African American Christian struggle in a way that I had not connected it before. Again, the sort of bringing in the apartheid idea. So just the same way that the world eventually—or at least some portion of it—got to the point where we say that's not okay. White South Africans cannot simply try and control the movements and separate the Black South Africans. And if it wasn't acceptable there, it shouldn't be acceptable anywhere—whether it's Israelis doing it to the Palestinians or any other group.

Sandra is another member of Hargrove's Bible study. In her early sixties, she represents the generation of the majority of regular attendees to the study group. Trained as an engineer, Sandra has had a career in telecommunications, commerce compliance, and global trade regulation. Her work took her to the Washington, DC, area a decade ago, and she joined Mount Calvary and began attending the Bible study regularly. Having become interested in Israel and Palestine through the study group, Sandra attended the Proctor-sponsored Howard University event. She described always having wanted to visit "the Holy Land" of Israel on a pilgrimage tour, but Hargrove's Bible class gave her pause. "What they are being exposed to [on trips to Israel] is not the complete accuracy of the story," she explained. "The African American church needs to be made more aware of that before they go on this trip. They really need to understand that whole conflict and what it is about and how the territories are divided, and the differences in how people are treated and see the whole picture."

Given the impact of the sustained, in-depth study of the Bible from a liberation perspective that Hargrove's class represents, the Proctor Conference has invested in expanding the reach of a mode of Bible interpretation that opens up solidarity with Palestinians based on reading the text from the point of view of the oppressed. To that end, in 2016 the Proctor Conference launched an initiative aimed at developing a Bible study curriculum that Black churches could implement to foster such conversations and to build awareness of the Palestinian situation. The curriculum is described this way:

> An educational resource to better equip congregations and religious communities, specifically African American congregations and religious communities, as they seek to become more aware of the justice issues in the Holy Land today and how they parallel African American experience in the United States.[40]

It includes a ten-lesson study plan packaged as a "Black Church Toolkit," which aims to equip African American Christians to "contribute to the education, activism and advocacy work for both the Black and Palestinian justice struggles." Topics include introductions to Black and liberation theologies, the cultural context of the Christian Old Testament scriptures, background on Israel and Palestine, links between Ferguson and Gaza, the experiences of Black Africans in the State of Israel, Islamophobia, intercultural and interracial dialogue, and "global race consciousness." Created in 2016, the curriculum was adopted for congregational use in several churches as a pilot project. These included Saint John's Church (The Beloved Community) in St. Louis, Missouri, and Abyssinian Baptist Church in Harlem, New York.

Palestine, Black Churches, and Black Lives Matter

The second facet of the Proctor Conference's approach to Palestine is supporting youth movements in their activism, such as in Black Lives Matter. At the end of the roundtable conversation, Carruthers reads and affirms an excerpt from a 2015 statement signed by more than a thousand Black activists, scholars, students, and artists:

> We recognize the racism that characterizes Israel's treatment of Palestinians is also directed against others in the region, including intolerance, police brutality, and violence against Israel's African population. Israeli officials call asylum seekers from Sudan and Eritrea "infiltrators" and detain them in the desert, while the state has sterilized Ethiopian Israelis without their knowledge or consent. These issues call for unified action against anti-Blackness, white supremacy, and Zionism.[41]

The affirmation of this statement is part of the Proctor Conference's efforts to connect with the work of young Black activists organizing for racial and social justice outside of traditional Black religious spaces. In branching out from Black churches and their traditional modes of activism in the United States, the Proctor leaders in the roundtable conversation on Palestine also discussed ways that African American Christians can get involved in supporting Palestinians in practical and political terms. They pointed especially to the Boycott, Divestment, and Sanctions (BDS) movement. In several settings, Wright has described the BDS movement to Proctor Conference audiences as a practical way to address the moral and ethical issues in Israel and Palestine. "It is exactly how we fought in the antiapartheid movement, exactly what brought South Africa to its knees," he says.

The leaders—Wright, Carruthers, Bridgeman, and Pollard (who are all over sixty years old)—have laid the groundwork for growing Black church solidarity with Palestinians, but much of the Proctor Conference's outreach on Palestine—both in church-based theological education and in networks of Black youth activism—is being taken up by a younger generation of emerging leaders. On Monday, May 14, 2018, the United States officially opened its new embassy in Jerusalem, relocating it from Tel Aviv.[42] The controversial move and ceremonial opening of the embassy coincided with the seventieth anniversary of the founding of the State of Israel, which Israel celebrates as its Independence Day and Palestinians commemorate as their day of catastrophe (*Nakba*), when hundreds of thousands of Palestinians were displaced and became refugees in the Arab-Israeli conflict of 1948 that culminated in the founding of the State of Israel. In 2018, this juxtaposition of commemorations—one of national founding and one of national catastrophe—also marked the planned culmination of six weeks of protests by Palestinians in Gaza, organized as "the Great March of Return." More than fifty Palestinians in Gaza were killed by Israeli forces that day. In response, the Proctor Conference sent out an email to its members with the subject, "Prayers for Gaza!" As a call for continued solidarity between African Americans and Palestinians, the email read, in part:

> We are asking you to be in prayer for Palestine. We are asking you to speak out against this injustice. We are asking you to remember why we must not stay silent. . . . We are asking you to use your voice in line with Dr. King's proclamation that an injustice anywhere is a threat to justice everywhere, and that silence is compliance. Finally, family, we are asking you to use your voice because the oppression felt between African-descended and Palestinian-descended communities, over generations, intertwines at various intersections of marginalization and there is strength in our unity.[43]

The email also included a juxtaposition of two photos. The first image was an iconic black-and-white photograph from the South African Soweto uprising of 1976, taken by photographer Sam Nzima. The photo depicts two Black men, Mbuyisa Makhubo carrying Hector Pieterson in his arms after Pieterson had been shot by the South African police. The second image, by AFP photographer Mahmud Hams, depicts a visually similar scene, this one in color, in which one unidentified Palestinian man is carrying another away from the front lines of the Gaza clashes after the latter had been shot by Israeli military forces. The email also included a link to a statement on Gaza from Taurean Webb, an academic and a former scholar in residence at the Proctor Conference who has been one of the key proponents of Palestinian solidarity with the SDPC. Webb's story of traveling to Palestine and being interrogated in Israel at the airport on his way home is highlighted in the introduction to this book. Broadly, Webb's work focuses on parallel racial formations of Blackness and Palestinian-ness as a basis for international solidarities against white supremacy in theological terms. Like Neichelle Guidry (whose sermon at a national gathering of Proctor leaders and members on Palestine also appears in the introduction), Webb is part of a younger generation of Proctor-affiliated activists leading the organization's work on Palestine. In his reflection on the Gaza protests and the U.S. embassy opening, Webb wrote:

> The persons massacred today were persons who looked just like all of our sisters and nephews, aunts and uncles, cousins, sons and daughters—with similar sorts of hopes, dreams, fears, goals and aspirations. If you haven't started to think about what sort of world will be inhabited by those who come long after you have left this place, you might want to start. If you think you're exempt, for whatever reason, from the assault of white nationalist supremacy—Black & Brown folk—ya'll better rethink that.[44]

I first met Webb at the Howard University Palestine solidarity event in 2014, where he told me about the Proctor Conference's growing efforts to connect African American and Palestinian concerns in Black churches in the United States. We met several times in Chicago in the following years, where he was completing his PhD. He kept me informed about Proctor Conference efforts to take Black clergy to Israel and Palestine to see the parallels between Black and Palestinian experiences for themselves. During that time, he was also the primary person in the Proctor Conference working on the Palestine-focused Bible study curriculum. The goal of deploying that curriculum was ultimately to foster more of the kinds of conversations about how African American Christians interpret the Bible that Bridgeman, Pollard, and the other senior Proctor Conference leaders articulated in the roundtable conversation.

Another member of the younger generation of activists and leaders working on Palestinian solidarity within the Proctor network is Reverend Waltrina Middleton. I met her when she contributed to a workshop on Palestine at the Proctor Conference 2016 annual meeting in Houston entitled "The Movement for Justice in Palestine." Middleton told me how she had gotten involved with the Proctor Conference as a seminary student in Chicago. At the time, she was impressed by the work the organization was doing in response to hurricanes Katrina and Rita and wanted to be a part of it. As a student in Chicago, where the SDPC offices are located, she reached out to the organization to see what she could do to get involved. "I just caught the bus to their office and knocked on the door," she said. During that time, Middleton was mentored in ministry by Proctor Conference General Secretary Iva Carruthers and Trinity United Church of Christ pastors Otis Moss and Jeremiah Wright. After graduating from seminary, Middleton moved to Cleveland, Ohio, where she founded a group called Cleveland Action, in response to the police killing of twelve-year-old Tamir Rice. She conceived of Cleveland Action as a social justice organization linking local and global activism. In 2014, she was on the front lines of clergy protests in Ferguson, Missouri, including the "Moral Monday" march. Since then she has served as an associate dean of the chapel at Howard University, her alma mater, completed her doctoral studies at Colgate Rochester Crozer Divinity School, and in 2019 became the executive director of the Community Renewal Society. While at Howard University, she led a group of Howard students on a trip to Charlottesville, Virginia, in the wake of the racialized violence that occurred there in the summer of 2017.

Speaking to a room of about fifty mostly Black clergy at the 2016 Proctor Conference, Middleton began:

> Part of my role here is to share the cultural narrative—to tell the story. One of the things that I do in working with other people in the Black Lives Matter movement is to consider myself a keeper of the stories—those that are untold. And I found that there were several similarities in Palestine that are quite similar to what we experience here.

She later told me about her first trip to Israel, a clergy tour sponsored by the Israeli government. She described efforts to introduce the group to Ethiopians in Israel. She also explained her growing sense of unease when some of the Ethiopians she met voiced their experiences of discrimination in Israel, particularly related to being questioned about whether they are *really* Israelis. "Looking at some of the living conditions [of the Ethiopians]," Middleton explained, "I observed what I felt or perceived as racism towards this community. Just some of the living conditions just did not seem comparable to let's say, an American Jew that was resettling there." Summarizing the feelings the encounter produced for her, she emphasized: "You're like, oh my God, this is the *Holy* Land." For her, the kind of discrimination she observed in Israel did not match the image she had of the land of Israel as a holy place.

Middleton also described her second trip to the region with a group of grass-roots organizers, at the invitation of Palestinians. "It's quite interesting to see the stark difference between what you see when you have an invitation to come as a guest of Israel versus a guest of Palestinian people." She described carrying a heavy burden of racial violence on that trip. That burden included several years of intense activism in the United States and the personal tragedy of the murder of her first cousin in the attack in Charleston, South Carolina, at the Emanuel African Methodist Episcopal Church by a white supremacist shooter in 2015. She spoke about the experience of visiting Palestinian refugee camps, seeing the site of Palestinian homes that had been demolished by Israeli forces, hearing stories of women blocked from attending Muslim prayers in Jerusalem, and the psychological impact of Israeli military night raids in Palestinian villages. On the experience of visiting the Aida refugee camp near Bethlehem in the West Bank, she recalled:

> There were no playgrounds, and there wasn't the infrastructure for even a sewage system. . . . I would see the children actually playing on the mounds of garbage that had built up over a period of time. And one thing that struck me the most was one of the young children saying to me, "We have no sky." And I said, "What do you mean by that?" And he said, "Look up." And because of the barricade or the structure that limits the ability to expand and to build, they have to build up, and sometimes over, so that it blocks the view of the sky.

Middleton talked about how the images she came away with from her experience among Palestinians reminded her of her time working as an activist in Ferguson and Cleveland: "The images that we see of people suffering in the Black Lives Matter movement here. The use of tear gas, rubber bullets, even the awards that militarized police receive for their marginalization of the people." She voiced her outrage that an Israeli officer was given a financial reward for his actions while an investigation was taking place over the shooting death of a young Palestinian by the Israeli police officer. It reminded her of how funds were raised on behalf of Ferguson police officer Darren Wilson after his killing of Michael Brown, and how George Zimmerman similarly raised funds after he killed Trayvon Martin. She also expressed her outrage at the statistics of Palestinian casualties at the hands of Israelis during her visit: four Palestinian teenagers killed in less than thirty-nine hours, 500 youth injured, forty shot with live ammunition, 150 with rubber bullets. "It reminded me of Michael Brown and Trayvon Martin," she said. "[They] did not receive medical care but were left to die." Bringing together these experiences, she added:

> There's so many common strains that connect us here in the States to the suffering in the apartheid State of Palestine by Jewish or Israeli occupation. . . . I left understanding that we have a responsibility to share in their struggle. There's the expression that says, "If you've come here to help me, you're wasting your time. But if you come because your struggle is wrapped up in mine, then let us work together." This is our responsibility, this is our call, to share in the work of the effort for freedom and revolution with the Palestinian people.

For Middleton, this effort to link the freedom struggles against suffering and oppression must emphasize the particular contributions of women of color. In 2018, she invited me to participate in a small delegation of activists on a solidarity-building mission to Palestine (see chapter 4). Throughout that trip Middleton highlighted the contributions of women to freedom struggles around the globe—from the "behind-the-scenes" civil rights activist and organizer Ella Baker, to South African political icon Winne Mandela, to the recently murdered South and Central American activists Berta Cáceres of Honduras and Marielle Franco of Brazil. The assassination of Franco happened during our trip to Palestine, adding a sense of immediacy and urgency to the stakes of global solidarities being forged on the trip.

As members of a younger generation of activists and scholars within the Proctor Conference network, Taurean Webb, Waltrina Middleton, and Neichelle Guidry represent Proctor's emphasis on supporting social justice activism in emerging movements like Black Lives Matter. Although many contemporary antiracism and social justice activists in the United States are intentionally organizing outside of traditional religious spaces, the Proctor Conference seeks to keep Black theologies of liberation relevant to emerging movements and contemporary political critiques aimed at achieving racial justice. In the Palestine-focused sermon delivered to the Proctor Conference general assembly (described in the introduction), Guidry talked about sustaining motivations in the struggle against injustice—in Palestine and elsewhere. "We are the people of the living God," she preached. "And as long as God lives we don't stop." Then she asked, "How are you going to resist?" And she answered by paraphrasing the civil rights activist, feminist, and womanist, Audre Lorde: "You cannot dismantle the master's house with the master's tools." "And many times, the master's tools are nonoptions for the oppressed and the occupied population," Guidry explained. The tools of the Proctor Conference, in its engagement with Palestine and across other issues of concern for the organization, come from its leaders and members working within Black churches to develop emancipatory hermeneutical orientations to the Bible as a Christian sacred text oriented toward justice for the oppressed and marginalized. At the same time, they look outside traditional Black church spaces, seeking ways to make the liberative impulses of prophetic Black Christianity accessible to activists, forging new global solidarities in the struggle for racial and economic justice.

"GLOCAL" AMBASSADORS OF RECONCILIATION: THE PERFECTING CHURCH

Pastor Kevin Brown has a calm but commanding presence on the stage of The Perfecting Church (TPC), where he is the founding senior pastor. A former college basketball player, he is tall and wears stylish eyeglasses and fashionable clothes. He studied marketing and accounting in college and planned a career in business. But after joining a small African Methodist Episcopal church—under the leadership of a pastor he describes as scholarly, rigorous, and charismatic—he became drawn to the idea of Christian ministry as a vocation, wanting to "give something back." While working in marketing and sales jobs, he began taking seminary classes at the Philadelphia Center for Urban Theological Studies and other local schools. He eventually went into business for himself with several partners, and for many years Brown's professional and spiritual goals went along side by side—like "two rails," he says. But he eventually felt called by God to full-time church ministry. With his family, he had been attending a growing, independent, charismatic, and predominantly African American congregation in south New Jersey, where he was eventually called to full-time pastoral work. "We changed our lives entirely to move from this two-professional-business-owner lifestyle to become a servant of Christ," he recalled. In that role, Brown began to think more about how he might lead a local church. He described that period in pastoral ministry as one of being supported by a network of prominent charismatic Christian preachers who would visit each other's churches and support each other's ministries. In that context, Brown began to think about starting a new congregation. "The next thing I knew, I was planting a church," he said. "And when I did, my tribe kicked me out. It was not embraced," he added, explaining the resistance he encountered among the leaders of his home church. "There was some fear about it," he continued, telling the story of the painful separation from his church home of nearly eighteen years. "I got kicked out of my tribe and lost a lot of relationships," Brown lamented. "And that's when I met Bob Roberts online."

Bob Roberts and the "Glocal" Church Model

Bob Roberts Jr. is the founder and senior pastor of Northwood Church in Keller, Texas. Roberts has roots in the Southern Baptist Convention—with ministry degrees from the convention's Southwestern Baptist Theological Seminary and evangelical Fuller Seminary—but Northwood Church operates as an independent, nondenominational, evangelical church. In addition to his Texas congregation, Roberts has grown Northwood into a network of more than a hundred churches through his Glocal.net initiative. "Glocal" (global-local) refers to what Roberts describes as a foundational connection between the local activity of churches and their vision for global impact. "We don't get globalization in the West," Roberts said in a 2014 TED Talk–style presentation at a Christian conference.[45] "We think about the exporting of culture. We think about the exporting of economics. But there is something far bigger in the understanding of globalization." Roberts described American Christians as more likely to begin by thinking locally, then acting globally. This is the wrong outlook for American Christians on global issues, he said. "Start with the global and let that inform the local. The global defines the local." In a Glocal church model, "members use their vocations to serve and live out their faith in the global public square." Leaders work "to connect, facilitate, and equip churches to release their members through the domains of society and build relationships with people of other faiths." The "domains of society" are defined as secular areas of potential influence and service within global society—economics, education, art and media, government, medicine, agriculture, technology, and civil society. The potential impact of a

Glocal church outlook, for Roberts, is the convergence of life, ministry, and vocation. In other words, creating what he calls a "bridge between a person's vocation and ministry that spans community development locally and globally."[46]

Part of the signature Glocal focus includes a "multifaith" emphasis, which Roberts defines as "creating relationships that respect the faith of others while not asking them to compromise their own faith."[47] He differentiates this from "interfaith," which is "where some seek to water down the beliefs of all involved to a common level." The multifaith outlook Roberts incorporated in his Glocal church model led him to invite Muslim and Jewish religious leaders to Northwood's stage, a gesture that led to hundreds of his members leaving the church. Among American evangelicals, Roberts has been particularly controversial because of his relationships with Muslims. In 2018, he invited a Muslim scholar from Abu Dhabi to attend the National Prayer Breakfast with him in Washington, DC. At the high-profile Christian-organized religious networking event—a who's who of American evangelicals, many of whom supported the Trump administration's so-called Muslim ban—Roberts raised more than a few eyebrows by attending with a Muslim scholar and a religious authority from the Middle East. Among American evangelicals, Roberts says that Northwood has been called "a Muslim church" and Roberts himself a "closet Muslim."[48]

Further controversy among evangelicals followed for Roberts and Northwood because of his involvement with Palestinians, including bringing aid to Gaza and participating in the Christ at the Checkpoint conference, organized by Palestinian evangelicals to bring attention to the Palestinian cause among their American coreligionists.[49] Explaining his travels to Gaza, Roberts describes the effort as facilitated by British diplomats, funded by Muslim clerics, and focused on taking evangelical doctors to serve the population. In front of an evangelical audience in 2014, he told the story of his first encounter in Gaza. In his disarming Texas drawl, he recalled asking his Gazan Muslim hosts, "How many of you have ever heard of an evangelical?" "Contrary to popular opinion here," he quickly adds, "we're not all terrorists."[50]

The Perfecting Church: A Glocal Congregation

It was Roberts's message about glocal ministry that first attracted Kevin Brown, as he was planning to leave his longtime congregation and thinking about how to found a new church in his hometown. The focus on Palestine came later.

"[Roberts] talked about the church in the way that I believed that it should be and what I saw Jesus doing in the scriptures," Brown told me. "He talked about the church being *glocal*—meaning being global and local. The church exists in a context locally, but it's a part of a body that expands to the entire world." It was that vision that led Brown and his wife, Angela, to found The Perfecting Church. In the first four years, attendance grew to close to 1,000 people meeting on any given Sunday in a state-of-the-art performing arts center in a local high school. The majority of attendees and members—85 percent by Brown's estimation—are African American, but he describes a vision for a multiethnic congregation that "reflects the kingdom of God better" in terms of diversity.

Brown also described another unique aspect of Roberts's glocal model for Christian churches—"pick a hard place in the world," Brown said. "There's 192 nations in the world. Pick a hard place in the world where you're going to do work that you'll totally have to lean on God, because you don't know anything about that context and work there. So we did." The hard place in the world that Brown and TPC picked was Palestine. Within six months of starting the church, Brown was invited by Roberts to attend a global Christian leadership conference in London and to participate in a delegation of pastors going to the West Bank. As Palestine (and particularly the situation of Palestinian Christians) became important to Roberts, he took this group of pastors he was mentoring, including Brown, to Bethlehem for the Christ at the Checkpoint conference in 2012. "I knew nothing about Palestine," Brown said about his initial thoughts on going to the conference. "I was very pro-Israel, only because that's all I knew. That's all I had been exposed to. That was the way the scriptures had been presented to me." But in Palestine, he said, "I found my theology getting challenged." "Because Bob's circle of friends was large and influential," Brown went on, "he had me meeting all these people while we were there. And each of them challenged me: 'Why don't you come back? Why don't you come back with your church? Why don't you come back with a few people?'" Brown initially balked at the idea of returning to Palestine. He recalled thinking, "We're here as tourists, to learn. *Who comes back?*"

Brown also described his initial encounter with Palestinians as directly challenging his pro-Israel theology:

> My world got rocked the first time I went [to Palestine] . . . because I started realizing that the stories I had heard were not just stories, they were people.

And as I met people and saw people firsthand and heard people's stories first-hand, it made me think very deeply about, where did I get this theology from and how true was it?

In getting involved in Palestine, Brown and TPC were stepping into a theological-political powder keg issue among American evangelicals. But Brown states his interest in the region was apolitical. "I didn't want to be a part of the political narrative there," he said. "I wanted to get on the grid of society there and work with the *people*, meet the people, and not just the Palestinians." His desire, he explained, is to connect Palestinians—Muslims and Christians—with Jews: "In no way am I despising Israel, I love Israel, and I love my Jewish brothers and sisters. But I love the Muslim, and I love the Palestinian, and I love the Afghanis, and I love the Pakistanis. . . . And we no longer build our church on speculative theology."

I asked Brown what he meant by "speculative theology." He explained it as "theology that exalts Israel and makes Israel some type of divine nation that has the right, sovereignly, to dehumanize any other nation in the name of God." He went on to criticize Christians who look at the Bible—especially its prophetic literature—in a speculative way that tries to predict the second coming of Jesus and the role of the State of Israel in the equation of what must happen for that to occur. "And it's speculative at best for us to draw a conclusion. . . . So, we don't," he said. "We've left that alone. All I know is Jesus will return, and I'm looking forward to it."

Brown also described Palestine as a place that made him think differently about race in a global context. For him, the racialized experiences of African Americans and Palestinians are one place where the local meets the global for his predominantly Black congregation. He described a convergence of experiences in Bethlehem that provoked his thinking about Palestine as "a hard place" for his particular church to work, given its racial demographics as a Black evangelical church. "In the Palestinians, I literally saw America in the fifties and sixties," he said. He emphasized parallels between African American and Palestinian aspirations: "They had realized what had happened in our country and how we had found our humanity restored, found our opportunity to contribute to society restored. And then seeing a Black man become president, to them, that was the epitome of what could happen to them." As an African American congregation with a glocal outlook, Brown concluded, "I think Jesus is calling us to follow him there."

The Perfecting Church's Glocal Mandate in Palestine

The Perfecting Church's model for engagement in Palestine emphasizes community connectedness. It is the same model Brown emphasizes for The Perfecting Church. He described his previous congregation as one where people from communities all over came to receive teaching and then went home. The difference in TPC's vision, he said, is that it is "very community connected"—referring to social services that the church provides locally. This community connectedness imperative also drives the church's glocal engagement in Palestine. Brown explained:

> When I went, I took a group of nine people the first time. And I took them and said, we're going to use your job to serve people there. So, the first time we went, we had a team of social workers, and they put together a curriculum on grief and anger, and we taught it to a team of social workers over there.

When I first visited TPC in early 2015, Brown had already led a number of small teams of six to eight church members to Bethlehem, in the Palestinian West Bank, on semiannual trips. He had just returned from the church's fifth trip. It had been a few months since we had first met and spoken about what would happen on that trip. Brown greeted me at the foot of the auditorium stage in the busyness of preparations for the Sunday morning service that was about to begin. He began to tell me about some of the trip highlights. The band on stage was practicing for the service, and Brown told me excitedly about the success they had had on this most recent trip to Bethlehem, especially in terms of building relationships. As he had spoken about in our previous meeting, he emphasized that this was part of the ongoing process of connecting his church with communities in Palestine and Israel. He highlighted the experience of visiting a Jewish settlement in the West Bank, where a settler rabbi had invited Palestinians to speak at his home. This, said Brown, was "beginning the work of reconciliation." He also told me about the challenge of traveling to the Middle East during a time when the spread of ISIS in the region was in the forefront of the minds of the church members on the trip and those back home in New Jersey. He also mentioned that a nineteen-year-old Palestinian youth had been killed by the Israeli military in the Bethlehem area during their trip and described the resulting demonstrations in the streets. Brown said, "but it's not like Ferguson." He talked about the anger he saw in Palestine as being similar to that of the Black community of Ferguson,

Missouri, as trauma of the police killing of Michael Brown was still fresh in the minds of many African Americans.

After a few minutes of catching me up on these trip highlights, Brown excused himself to step up on stage and begin the service. The ushers opened the doors of the large auditorium, and people began filling the seats. The band had left the stage, and an African American woman stood in front of the congregation, on the main floor, praying into a handheld microphone. "We thank you for returning the team safely [from Bethlehem]," she said, among other prayers of thanks. The band returned a few minutes later and led the congregation in several contemporary gospel worship songs. Brown's sermon that morning emphasized that "God's intent is that each expression of his church would be a gift to the local community in which it resides, while extending itself beyond what's familiar." He ended with a call for TPC to be "ambassadors of reconciliation"—in their local community and around the world. "An ambassador is someone who represents another country," Brown said. "And the country that we're representing is the Kingdom of Heaven." "I'd like to introduce [you] to a group of glocal ambassadors who can talk to us a little about what that might look like," he continued after his sermon. Eight members of the team who had just returned to New Jersey from Palestine joined him on stage for a conversation about the trip experience. The four men and four women, who were of various ages, took turns sharing highlights from their experiences over the ten-day "glocal engagement trip." The members included a recent college graduate, a public school history teacher, a management consultant, and a retired state insurance regulator. The team talked about the people they had met, the sightseeing they had done, and the engagements they had led. They described how this trip had focused on collaborating with local social workers and running a sports camp for women.

After that Sunday service, I met most of the trip participants and spoke to several of them in the following weeks about their experiences in Palestine and Israel. As plans for the next trip to the West Bank were being finalized, Brown invited me to join that group for what would be the church's sixth trip to the region. In the first planning meeting for the trip I took part in, Brown emphasized the purpose of the trip and how it fit into the church's vision for glocal engagement: "We're not going on a Holy Land tour," he said. "That's not what this is. We're not going as tourists. We're not going as missionaries," he continued. "We're going to engage the domains of society, engaging and being a part of bringing reconciliation between Christians, Muslims, and Jews." Previous groups had focused on education and social work as relevant "domains of society" for engaging with Palestinians, but this group would focus on business development and entrepreneurship. In this meeting and others before the trip, the question of "taking sides" came up frequently. Brown assigned two books by evangelical authors, one on the history and politics of Israel and Palestine and one on Muslim-Christian relations. On the politics of the region, he emphasized, "We are not taking a position. We're taking the same position that Jesus took and that is the cross. We're not picking a side. We wanna love our neighbors."

The trip included Brown and his wife, Angela, three members who had been on earlier trips to Bethlehem, and three new participants. The returning members were all men: an army veteran and entrepreneur with a health, wellness, and athletic training business; a retired insurance regulator who had been on the previous trip; and a union elevator construction worker who was pursuing part-time seminary training in pastoral ministry. The three new participants included one man and two women: a commercial real estate developer working on clean energy initiatives; a leadership development and management trainer; and a financial analyst with experience in telecom and health care. The group's primary focus would be engaging with Palestinians on the topics of entrepreneurship and business development in the context of the parallel challenges that African Americans and Palestinians face in those areas. This happened through seminars at a Palestinian university and at the Bethlehem Chamber of Commerce, and in other smaller ad hoc meetings with Palestinians.

Although focused on engaging "the domains of society," politics and controversial theology came up early and often on the trip. On the day of our arrival, the group met our primary Palestinian contact at Israel's Ben Gurion Airport, and we took a bus ride from Tel Aviv, through Jerusalem, and Bethlehem via an Israeli checkpoint crossing into the West Bank. Not long after crossing into Bethlehem, as we drove toward our Bethlehem hotel, we passed a painted sign on a building wall with an Israeli flag crossed out in a red circle saying "Boycott Israel." My roommate, the real estate developer and clean energy researcher, read the sign out loud with a questioning voice: "Boycott Israel?" That night, in the first of our evening debriefing meetings, Brown warned the group about the "bad theology" of Christian Zionists and "their failure to recognize the personhood of anyone but Jews in this region."

On our second day, we received an introduction to the political geography of the West Bank, driving to meet a Jewish settler who would share a Zionist perspective on the religious significance of the land. As we drove south out of Bethlehem, Brown pointed out the Dheisheh Palestinian refugee camp, prompting a conversation about why many Palestinians are refugees today. He also described the significance of West Bank Areas A, B, and C, representing different levels of Palestinian and Israeli control of the territory. We continued to the area of the Gush Etzion settlement block—a group of Jewish hilltop settlement villages and towns in the hills south of Bethlehem. As we left Bethlehem and the Palestinian controlled Area A, we pulled over and picked up our guide for the day. Shimon boarded the bus and introduced himself. He looked to be in his middle to late thirties, but his wire-rimmed glasses and long tangled beard with some gray in it made him look older at a glance. He was dressed casually in blue jeans and leather sandals. He explained to the group the other details of his appearance with religious significance: the side curls of his unkempt hair, the *tzitzit* (tassels) that hung from the sides of his waist, and his knitted skull cap. He told us about his upbringing in Washington State in a Conservative Jewish synagogue and his decision to immigrate to Israel in 2000. He pointed out that it was a time when the Oslo peace process was breaking down and the Second Intifada was erupting. He also told the group that he lived in the Bat Ayin settlement, which has a reputation as the home of many far right-wing religious Jewish settlers.

Shimon took us on a walking tour of the area, and we could see a vast landscape of the West Bank with views as far as the Mediterranean Sea and the city of Hebron in the distance. His goal for our visit, he said, was to talk about the Jewish connection to the land. "I'll start with the Bible and then get into politics," he explained. "We're gonna go from Abraham to the present." As we walked under the bright midday sun, Shimon's topics ranged from the agricultural cultivation of the land and its connection to Jewish law to the political significance of Areas A, B, and C. My roommate had told me the night before that he was skeptical of feeling any kind of emotional connection to the land. As we walked, however, he came up to me and said, "I feel a connection with the Bible [here]. I didn't think I was gonna feel that."

Taking us back to his personal story, Shimon talked about how he came to feel that Israel was the home of the Jewish people. "For two thousand years," he noted, "Jews have lived everywhere as minority." "Jewish life looks very different when you're the minority," he explained. "For Jews in the land, a key question is: What's the Bible's vision for society? Those questions come up here." He went on to describe how the prophets of the Jewish Bible pointed toward a time of living in the land again. "But," he added, "our prophets didn't mention the Palestinians." Shimon continued to talk about how both Palestinians and Jews are traumatized people, adding, "God has given us the ultimate challenge with the Israeli-Palestinian conflict."

Our walking tour eventually circled back to the intersection where our bus was parked. From there, we drove together with Shimon to a site run by the organization he works for called Roots. The location, sitting at the end of a dirt driveway next to a small supermarket, was a small fenced plot of land. We sat under a makeshift tent next to a small building with a kitchen. There we met Michel, a Palestinian Christian who works with Shimon in the Roots organization. Michel added a Palestinian perspective on the land as he and Shimon took turns telling their personal stories of how the work they do to build bridges between Jews and Arab Palestinians became important to them. The conversation continued over a lunch of rice and lentils, cucumber salad, and roasted chicken.

This visit with Shimon and Michel, on the first full day of the trip, underscored the reconciliation imperative that Brown had spoken about at length before we departed and as we arrived in the West Bank. The emotional and compelling Jewish Zionist narrative Shimon gave over the course of several hours provoked different responses among the African Americans in the group from TPC. When Shimon talked about the origins of the modern Zionist movement coming out of European Jews feeling that they could never be safe or integrated into European society, he said they became increasingly motivated to find a way to have their own land where they would not be the minority or on the margins of society. In response, one of the women in our group, in Israel and Palestine for the first time, said, "Zionism reminds me of Black Wall Street." She explained how Shimon's account of the Jewish understanding of the land was like efforts to establish an alternative economy for African Americans in Tulsa, Oklahoma, in response to racial segregation and discrimination by whites under Jim Crow. The elevator worker from Camden, New Jersey—in the land for his second engagement trip with TPC—made a different point of connection with the locals in a private conversation with me. Talking about his experiences being pulled over by the police and the harassment that he routinely encountered, he said: "I'm mindful when I'm in a neighborhood where there aren't a lot of people who look like me . . . and I'm praying that I won't appear as a threat." He added, "I saw it with our [Arab] bus driver when Shimon got on the bus," noting the parallels between his experiences as a Black man in Camden and how Palestinians have to navigate the Israeli-controlled areas of the West Bank.

Beyond this half day spent with Shimon and the Roots organization, virtually all of the rest of the ten-day trip was spent with Palestinians in and around Bethlehem. But as Brown and TPC still strive to avoid being seen as "taking sides" in Palestine and Israel, even their efforts at connecting with Jewish Israeli communities—especially in West Bank settlements—are not uncontroversial among the Palestinians with whom they have worked over several years to build relationships and trust. Brown told me about an interaction he had during the trip with a Palestinian Christian friend in Bethlehem that he had gotten to know over several visits. When the Palestinian friend found out that The Perfecting Church team had met with a Jewish settler, there was a strong sense of betrayal. Brown said he understood the perception among Palestinians, who might think that the members of TPC are firmly on their side. "It might be like me meeting with the KKK. People [in the U.S.] would say, 'Why are you meeting with them?'" Later, reflecting on this tension, Brown told me:

> I remind people, we're not choosing sides, we're choosing the cross like Jesus did. So it's important to give people both experiences, because I found that we quickly will connect with the underdog. And as much as you thought you would go and relate only to Israel, you go and quickly find yourself, as a Christian, wanting to empathize with the Palestinian. And I said that's not what we're here for; we're here to take up our cross daily, deny ourselves, and follow after Christ.

Throughout the rest of the trip, we spent our time in Palestinian olive groves helping with the harvest, in classes with Palestinian university students, and in business development seminars with local entrepreneurs and people interested in starting their own businesses. We visited a Palestinian orphanage and were invited to a baptism service and celebration by a local Orthodox Christian Palestinian family that TPC members had become connected to over its many visits.

As we spent time among Palestinians in the Bethlehem area, Brown continued to speak to the question of taking sides, as some of the team members expressed feeling the pull toward politics in Israel and Palestine. Brown continued to emphasize his "both sides" approach to glocal engagement when we spoke about the trip after returning to the United States. As I sat with him and his wife, Angela, in the church's offices, he reiterated:

> Much like I've worked on as not choosing a side, I've worked on as not getting politically involved. I know that there are some Christians there that are

doing an incredible job at being politically involved, but I don't think you can do both well. So I think our responsibility is to be involved with people's lives, be involved with the domains of society, and to be present on the street. Some people are lobbying, some people are working with their congress people back home and they're writing letters and doing other incredible things. And that's the unique way that they're called. So I think we're more boots on the street. . . . I don't feel that [politics is] our assignment there.

But the tension between striving for apolitical glocal "community engagement" and the pull toward politics existed even in his own family, he noted. "She's political," he laughed, pointing at Angela sitting next to him, and she jumped in:

I try not to be political. But I absolutely understand that, in doing so, we're choosing a side. And in choosing a side, then you lose the ability to influence the other side. . . . But at the same time, I'm aware that Israel is very skillful and paying churches and pastors to travel to Israel and to indoctrinate them with their propaganda so that they ultimately choose a side.

She continued with a laugh, "I am named after Angela Davis," referring to the Black radical activist. "So I'm ready to put my fist in the air often and tell the world about the injustices that I see." "But," she added, seeming to catch herself, "I have to remind myself not to choose sides—choose the cross." She described her responsibility of sharing her story of overcoming obstacles in life with Palestinian women, and in turn taking their stories and holding them up as parallel examples of resilience. "[Women] hold up families, they hold up societies," she said. "And that has the power to heal whole entire families, nations, communities, the world."

The Browns, along with the congregation they lead, work in Palestine with a tension between the imperative to avoid taking sides and at the same time experience deeply felt connections between their experiences as African Americans and those of the Palestinians they encounter in Bethlehem and throughout the West Bank. But, at times, they also feel a strong connection to the Jewish Zionist narrative and its biblical claims to the land. In spite of this ambivalence and the constant caution against "taking sides," the Browns, with their growing Black congregation, have faced the same kinds of challenges that their mentor, Bob Roberts, does as an American evangelical leader reaching out to Muslims and getting involved in Israel and Palestine. They see it as their role, however, to add a much-needed African American perspective on race that is largely missing from the circles of American evangelicals who engage with Palestinians under a peacebuilding and reconciliation mandate. For example, on the experience of participating in several Christ at the Checkpoint conferences, Brown lamented the lack of participation from Americans who can directly identify with Palestinian experiences of oppression. He described cringing at what some white American evangelicals said at the conference about the need for reconciliation in Israel and Palestine, lacking an experience of marginalization and discrimination. "The voice of the one who hasn't been oppressed doesn't ring true sometimes," he said, pointing out the lack of diversity among some of the partners of Palestinian Christians, especially among white evangelicals.

Since I traveled to the West Bank with TPC in 2015, its leaders and members have continued to develop their approach to working in Palestine as African Americans. In spite of relentlessly resisting "taking sides," they have continued to emphasize connections between African Americans and Palestinians that are based on shared experiences of discrimination. Making this link, Angela Brown told me:

> I thank God for social media, and thank God for what technology has done to connect the world. And so many of our Palestinian friends—when the hashtag #BlackLivesMatter movement happened on Twitter—many of them were responding and felt, again, because of trauma, a sense of connection. Whether it was a policeman in Staten Island or in St. Louis or Cleveland, or if it was the IDF [Israel Defense Forces] in Area B or Area C, that immediately connected people.

She added, "African Americans, through the Black Lives Matter movement, have had an opportunity to demonstrate that Black lives matter around the world." In 2018, she took to Twitter to voice criticism of efforts in the U.S. Congress to advance the Israel Anti-Boycott Act, aimed at punishing activist boycotts of the State of Israel. She also tweeted in disapproval of CNN's firing of the political commentator, Black activist, and professor, Marc Lamont Hill, after he gave a speech at the United Nations criticizing the State of Israel and advocating for a "free Palestine." The Perfecting Church operates in Palestine with a tension between the universalistic ethical imperative to relate to "both sides" and the more particular and recurring experiences of resonance, over years and many visits, of the connections between African Americans and Palestinians. In theological terms, the impetus for TPC's engagement with Palestinians began with notions of reconciliation and peacebuilding, drawing on white evangelical theology more than the kind of marginalized and racially specific theological reflection of Black liberationists. In choosing Palestine as a "hard place" in the world, however, Kevin and Angela Brown, and their African American congregation, face tensions between the universalistic theological impulses of evangelical theologies of reconciliation and the experience of particular solidarities based on shared experiences of marginalization and oppression. The latter draw implicitly on themes in Black Liberation Theology and the possibility for theological reflection as a driver of political action from the margins that liberation theology opens up.

COMPARING THE SAMUEL DEWITT PROCTOR CONFERENCE AND THE PERFECTING CHURCH

In this chapter, I introduced the religious-political outlooks on Israel and Palestine of two groups of African American Christians in detail (table 2.1). The Perfecting Church and the Samuel DeWitt Proctor Conference both focus extensively on identifying with and supporting Palestinians. The Perfecting Church does so by attempting to avoid "taking sides" and downplaying overtly political and activism-oriented elements of their engagement in Palestine, consistently reaffirming their desire to be neutral agents of reconciliation in the land. The Proctor Conference takes a more overtly activist orientation to the issue, unapologetically aligning their organization with Palestinians, whom they see as engaged in a struggle for liberation that not only mirrors but is also linked to the experiences of Black Americans. In relating to Palestinians, both groups look to African American experiences as parallel and similar to those of Palestinians. But Brown and the members of TPC most often talk about Palestinians experiencing something comparable to *past* African American experiences of discrimination—Angela Brown's more political references to Black Lives Matter notwithstanding. On the other hand, Proctor Conference affiliates, who work on solidarity-building with Palestinians, consistently compare *current* parallel experiences linking African Americans with the people of Palestine—including mass

TABLE 2.1 Black church culture in SDPC and TPC

Case	Key leaders in this study	Key themes	Hermeneutics	Public theologies	Modes of public engagement	Significance of race in Palestine and Israel
Samuel DeWitt Proctor Conference (SDPC)	• Iva Carruthers • Jeremiah Wright • Neichelle Guidry • Taurean Webb • Waltrina Middleton	Solidarity with the marginalized and oppressed Intertwined struggles and intersections of marginalization	Reading the Bible through the eyes of the oppressed Walk where Jesus is walking today—"with those who are undervalued, underestimated and marginalized"	Prophetic witness of speaking truth to power Challenging religious nationalism Teaching freedom, not tradition	Clergy training and mobilization Protest and encouraging youth activism Congregational curriculum development	Impetus to confront racialized structures of social and political power. Zionism as racism.
The Perfecting Church (TPC)	• Kevin Brown • Angela Brown • Bob Roberts	Reconciliation Relationship-building	Avoid "speculative theology" Scripture as a template for reconciliation	"Take up our cross daily, deny ourselves, and follow after Christ" Serve as "ambassadors of reconciliation"	"Glocal" engagement in "domains of society" Linking vocation and ministry on a global level	Israel and Palestine reflect American race politics of the 1950s and 1960s.

incarceration, youth incarceration, unequal access to resources, police brutality, militarized policing, and other forms of structural inequality.

The four cases of African American Christian engagement with Israel and Palestine presented in chapters 1 and 2 represent a range of "on-the-ground" theological reflection and related political position-taking. The work of the pastors and church members described in this chapter pushes Black churches variously into partnerships with white Christian Zionists, American Jewish and Israeli Zionists, Palestinian Christians, and Palestinian Muslims. Chapter 3 focuses more specifically on the role of pastors as leaders within these groups, showing how they work as brokers and mobilizers on Israel and Palestine within their congregations, denominations, and other spheres of influence.

"My Pastor Is Where? He's in Israel?!"

Black Pastors as Brokers and Mobilizers

I met Jackie and her daughter Angela at their home church in Charlotte, North Carolina, a few weeks after they returned from a 2014 tour of Israel led by their pastor, Michael Stevens. As the African American outreach coordinator for Christians United for Israel (CUFI) at the time, Stevens organized the trip as a bridge between his congregation and the pro-Israel advocacy work that took him away from his Charlotte home many Sundays out of the year. Led by Stevens and cosponsored by CUFI, the trip opened Stevens's race-focused pro-Israel advocacy work to lay members of Black churches. Many other trips Stevens took to the region were on behalf of CUFI and focused on taking clergy to the Holy Land with the expectation that they would take CUFI's message to their congregations, denominations, and professional clergy networks. But unlike CUFI's highly subsidized trips for pastors, the congregation tour Stevens led cost each participant more than $3,000. Despite the prohibitive cost, Jackie was determined to make it happen, and she wanted to bring her daughter along. Jackie is a retired nurse, and Angela is a community college student who is planning a career in physical therapy. I sat with them in a Sunday school classroom at their University City Church of God in Christ in Charlotte, North Carolina. They spoke about their pastor in glowing terms. "What I uniquely like about him," said Jackie, "is he dreams big." "He doesn't put himself in a box. . . . He thinks outside of the box, and I like that a lot." They both talked about the excitement they felt being part of a growing church that Jackie described as a family.

Stevens described the same Holy Land tour to his congregation as a "bucket list trip"—something each member could check off their personal list of dreams to realize in their lifetime. Jackie immediately felt that she wanted to go when she heard this. She wanted to be part of what the church was doing beyond the city of Charlotte. Jackie also wanted to have a personal experience of the Holy Land, which she had only imagined. She had heard about the Holy Land Experience theme park in Florida but said that did not seem good enough. She laughed as she told me about her thinking on the decision, "No, I don't think so. I think I want to go to the real deal." Angela described her motivations differently. After spending time in and out of the hospital dealing with chronic health issues, she wanted to get back to feeling like herself. She did not feel the same kind of lifelong draw to the Holy Land that her mother described, but she was open to it. When Jackie presented the idea of taking the trip together, Angela's response was, "That must cost a lot of money." After looking into the trip details and seeing pictures of sites they would see together, Angela became convinced. "It was so beautiful there," she explained. "I don't want to be stuck at home doing nothing. I want to go somewhere to, you know, just come alive, [to] just come back to myself."

For both Jackie and Angela, the motivation for joining the tour extended beyond their personal desires to check off an item on a bucket list or to begin feeling more like themselves again. It was also about connecting with a cause that was a major part of their church's identity and their pastor's work, but it was a cause they actually knew little about. Angela had a vague awareness of Stevens traveling frequently to Israel and around the United States, working on Israel-related outreach. "I'm always like, 'where's my pastor, where's my pastor?' And I'm like, 'wait, he's in Israel? [I] wish he'd come back." This outlook on her pastor and his role as she perceived it changed after the trip. "Now, when we finally went with him [to] see what he does there and that people recognize him, that just blew my mind. It took me to another level. . . . It's like people [in Israel] see our church and hear him speak online, and they say, 'Oh, I've heard your ministries for a long time.' They'll say, 'I love you, I love what you do.' And that just amazed me, and I'm glad I was a part of it."

African American pastors like Stevens play an important role in shaping the religious and political concerns of their church members. Without Stevens, Jackie and Angela probably would have known little about the State of Israel other than a vague notion of it being "the land of the Bible"—a place connected to the scriptures they love but very far away from their everyday lives in North Carolina. Or they might have thought of Israel primarily as a site of conflict, violence, and terrorism. Through the work of Stevens and pastors like him, African American Christians are drawn into concerns with which they are unfamiliar. This is true when it comes to Christian Zionism as a political cause and also when understanding the situation of Palestinians. In this chapter, I look at the specific role pastors of Black churches play in shaping and guiding the concerns of their congregants and constituencies as well as how they direct the interests of their fellow Black clergy on engaging in politics and where they should aim their political interests.

WHO ARE BLACK CHURCH PASTORS?

Early scientific social studies of Black churches in the United States were largely concerned with tracing the development of Black religion and its (mostly Christian) institutions from slavery through the Great Migration of African Americans from the rural South to the urban North.[1] For these early researchers of Black religious life, Black churches were "a nation within a nation."[2] Pastors acted as central community pillars, leading Black churches that served as an "all-comprehending institution" that touched every area of the social life of their communities.[3] African American churches were widely understood as places where Black community leaders could operate and exert influence outside of white control.[4]

In these studies, W. E. B. Du Bois, Carter Woodson, Benjamin Mays, Joseph Nicholson, St. Clair Drake, Horace Cayton, and others went beyond descriptions of Black churches and African American religiosity and lamented the unrealized potential of Black churches in spurring social progress.[5] They attributed these failings, in large part, to a lack of education among most clergy, their decentralized authority, and an overemphasis on emotion and spirituality in their ministry. Others critics, such as the journalist Ida B. Wells, were even more forceful in condemning Black clergy, arguing that they were largely corrupt, ignorant, and too timid politically.[6] Within this body of work that spanned the first half of the twentieth century, analysts of Black churches were generally ambivalent about their significance as social institutions, recognizing their potential for affecting social progress and political change but lamenting their failures to live up to that potential. Some, however, such as the anthropologist Zora Neale Hurston, countered these more pessimistic outlooks on African American pastors and their congregations. Through her ethnographic studies of Black religion, she argued that Black churches were not, by and large, failing African Americans, rather they served as social spaces for "Black joy."[7]

Renewed and refocused attention to the social significance of Black churches and Black pastors came following the civil rights movement. The political impact of African American clergy, in the wake of the 1950s and 1960s, was undeniable. Observers of Black religion in America increasingly identified the central role of Black clergy and lay church leadership in the movement's successes. In one of the most comprehensive social studies of U.S. Black churches following the height of the civil rights era, C. Eric Lincoln and Lawrence Mamiya argue that, far from being monolithic, "the Black Church . . . encompasses a continuum of socio-political and theological views and postures."[8] Thus, in the face of evidence of both political activism and quietism in the second half of the twentieth century, scholars began to emphasize the extent to which Black pastors variously inhabit spiritual as well as social leadership roles. These pastors, they suggest, advance a range of priorities across religious and political concerns. In studies of Black churches, pastors were increasingly described as spiritual, cultural, social, and political leaders.[9] Similarly, in *Origins of the Civil Rights Movement*, the sociologist Aldon Morris describes how Black churches operated as an autonomous force and an Indigenous institution during the movement. Black churches, he notes, were "the organizational hub of black life."[10]

The 1980s saw shifts in the political role of Black clergy with Jesse Jackson's presidential campaigns in 1984 and 1988. As Allison Calhoun-Brown shows, "Jackson's candidacy was based on the legitimacy of African American ministers as political leaders and on the centrality of the African American church as a facilitator of popular mobilization in the black community."[11] The Jackson campaign, argues Adolph Reed, was a "reassertion of both ministerial claims to primary black leadership status and notions of the centrality of the church as a political linkage institution and agency for popular mobilization."[12] Continuing to contend for their place as leaders of Black communities, at the end of the twenty-first century, African American pastors tended to embrace politics and to pursue a central role in Black community and political life. They became "enthusiastic about their roles as community leaders," writes the political scientist Eric McDaniel.[13] However, as R. Khari Brown and Ronald E. Brown have shown, African American clergy also tend to pursue "low-cost political activism"—inviting candidates for public office to speak in their churches during elections and generally emphasizing the importance of voting from their pulpits.[14] Far fewer congregations take up more time-consuming political activities that demand significant organizational resources, such as sustained mobilization or activism on political issues.

Furthermore, in recent decades, scholars of Black religion have charted the changing leadership dynamics of Black churches with attention to a "new Great Migration." African American religion changed with the first Great Migration from the rural South to the urban North, and scholars have also traced changes in Black religious life that have accompanied the migration of many major Black churches from urban centers to suburban communities. In the context of a history of urban development and later suburban expansion, Black churches have increasingly become what the sociologist Omar McRoberts calls *particularistic* churches—niche groups where people "sort themselves into religious communities according to a complex bundle of preferences."[15] Suburban Black megachurches have contributed to this development of Black religiosity, especially since the 1980s, with their sprawling church campuses facilitating a wide range of social and religious services.[16]

Some observers of megachurch trends in African American Christianity have pointed to the ways Black pastors have continued to function as key drivers of education and empowerment.[17] Others have emphasized pastors as charismatic marketers of "spiritual commodities" within a marketplace of American commercialized spirituality[18]—what Paula McGee has called the "Wal-Martization" of African American Christianity.[19] As Jonathan Walton asks, how should we understand the fact that eminent African American theologians—such as James Cone and Katie Cannon—are relatively unknown in the pews of Black churches, but the Black religious broadcasters T. D. Jakes and Creflo Dollar are ubiquitous icons of Black popular culture in the United States?[20] Outside of these well-known Black televangelists and in a broader marketplace of Black religiosity, pastors of local churches remain part of a Black ideological elite that spans the political spectrum and anchors Black political culture to moral foundations.[21] But Black clergy also find themselves increasingly in competition with others over the mantle of Black leadership. Black clergy were once what W. E. B. Du Bois called "the most unique personality developed by the Negro on American soil," but to maintain their leadership status in Black communities they have increasingly sought wider social and political avenues for renewed relevance.[22]

WHO ARE BLACK "POLITICAL" PASTORS?

In accounting for the ways Black religion and Black pastors have experienced an evolving social significance across time, political scientists have led the way in studying a certain type of contemporary Black church identified as "political."[23] This recent analysis of what makes some Black churches political has come in the context of debates over time about whether Black churches in the United States are guided primarily by their attention to spiritual concerns or by more mundane and practical social and political realities.[24] Generally concluding that a certain subset of Black churches can be thought of as "political," however, has not always come with a precise definition of what it means for a Black church to be political. For example, studies of political Black churches consider generally how religion "mobilizes African Americans into the political process."[25] And political Black churches have been identified as ones that "actively engage their members in the political process by mobilizing them for political action and providing information about issues and candidates,"[26] "provide an environment where politicization can take place,"[27] or "increase the propensity for voting, campaign activism, and other political participation by members."[28] Such studies of political Black churches tend to focus on participation in electoral politics.[29] Others have addressed the role of Black churches in public life more broadly, looking at electioneering as part of a repertoire for civic engagement that includes electoral politics, protest politics, and community development work.[30] Here, electoral participation is framed as one part of democratic political participation in pursuit of liberation, equality, and justice. Others still have taken an issue-based approach to Black religious politics by looking at how Black churches work on specific issues, such as HIV and AIDS, for example.[31] Some political manifestations of African American Christianity operate within the mainstream of politics, focusing on electoral participation and community development. Others fall under the category of what the sociologist Christian Smith calls "disruptive religion," which tends to challenge the political status quo as opposed to working within it.[32] Some have called this kind of Black religious political engagement in protest movements a "disorderly" mode of political engagement.[33]

BLACK PASTORS AS BROKERS AND MOBILIZERS

In *God and Government in the Ghetto*, the political scientist Michael Leo Owens argues that attention to Black religious participation in electoral politics and protest movements captures only what happens during political campaigns and during sustained movements of organized disruption.[34] Thus it misses much of the day-to-day political engagement in Black churches that happens within policymaking processes. He suggests that attention to collaboration with government is a distinct mode of political engagement for Black churches—the kind of partnerships between churches and government that have become most well-known in recent decades in the context of the "faith-based initiatives" of the George W. Bush administration and the welfare reform projects sponsored by the Clinton administration. Owens refers to the tendency to focus exclusively on electoral and protest politics as a kind of myopia, one that Alison Calhoun-Brown similarly describes as obscuring "other important parts of the political process including agenda setting, interest articulation, policy formation, policy implementation, policy impact, and policy assessment."[35]

This distinction Owens and Calhoun-Brown make is key to understanding engagement with the issue of Israel and Palestine as drawing on divergent notions of Black religious politics. First, it necessarily broadens definitions of political engagement to include Black church-based activities outside the scope of protest mobilization and electoral participation. Second, it pays particular attention to the role of Black clergy as leaders who shape the political trajectories of Black religious politics in congregations, denominations, parachurch organizations, academic institutions, and grassroots organizations. They key clergy role Owens advances is that of pastors as *brokers*, where the primary role clergy play is as intermediaries acting on behalf of others, mediating political interests and priorities on behalf of their congregants. When they act as brokers within their religious communities, Black pastors appoint themselves as agents who "transfer political messages from the masses to the elite and political resources (symbolic and substantive) from the elite to the masses."[36] Brokerage is a form of elite political participation in which pastors represent their members, as opposed to empowering members to represent themselves. This, for Owens, is the opposite of a more grassroots approach to Black religious politics that emphasizes building mass participation through mobilization.

For Owens, it is important to pay attention to the ways some Black churches act politically by partnering with government (at the federal, state, and local levels) to "agree with public agencies on a purpose . . . and act jointly to achieve it."[37] Pastors of Black churches can be political actors heading politically engaged groups, either as *brokers* or as *mobilizers*. Religious political brokerage tends to happen at more elite levels, within networks of religious and political leaders, whereas religious political mobilization is a more grassroots-oriented endeavor.

Generally, Black clergy act as brokers to the extent that they serve as intermediaries on issues of concern, interfacing with actors representing political interests beyond their congregations and communities, mediating political messages, and adapting them to their members. They act as mobilizers to the extent that they work to drive political change through direct action and electoral participation.

BROKERS AND MOBILIZERS ON ISRAEL AND PALESTINE

In this chapter, I use Owens's broker/mobilizer distinction to analyze the various pastoral roles Black clergy play in relation to Israel and Palestine. To understand the Black religious political dynamics of that issue within African American churches requires attention to how Black church leaders take on various (sometimes overlapping) roles as both mobilizers and brokers. This is not to suggest that the broker/mobilizer distinction is a simple dichotomy—the potential for overlap is key because many Black clergy who engage with the religious-political issue of Palestine and Israel operate, to some extent at least, as both mobilizers and brokers. On Israel and Palestine, as on a number of political issues, some Black church leaders primarily play the role of brokers, who operate within elite networks of religious and political actors and institutions to collaborate within and across denominations and congregations. Their engagement with Israel and Palestine is shepherded by organizations that similarly engage Black churches at elite levels. Other Black clergy work primarily as mobilizers, operating at a grassroots level to affect change from the ground up, incorporating Israel and Palestine within a broader set of concerns for grassroots political mobilization.

This chapter highlights the ways the four cases introduced in the first two chapters include dynamics of broker-driven and mobilizer-driven clergy political engagement on the issue of Palestine and Israel. The broader significance of this distinction for the contested identity of "the Black Church" in the United States is then picked up in chapter 5. Here I argue that Black church pastors and leaders who take up pro-Israel political advocacy tend to function more as brokers than mobilizers. Whereas Black clergy focused on Palestinian issues tend to function more as mobilizers than brokers, incorporating the global issue of Palestine into their broader grassroots-oriented activism as a transnational issue linking communities suffering from systems of racial injustice.

BROKERING AFRICAN AMERICAN CHRISTIAN ZIONISM I: CHRISTIANS UNITED FOR ISRAEL

Like American Christian Zionism more broadly, the African American Christian Zionist movement (discussed here in cases of African American Christian outreach in Christians United for Israel [CUFI] and the International Fellowship of Christians and Jews [IFCJ]) has a wide reach in U.S. Black church contexts. By working primarily with influential pastors and denominational leaders, these organizations are able to make the case to many African American Christians for why they should "support Israel"—with their attention, their voices, their votes, and their money. The issue of Israel in African American Christian Zionist circles is presented as a natural area of concern for Black pastors who preach about Israel as the land of the Bible and the people of Israel as God's chosen people.

Jonathan Leath and CUFI

I met Jonathan Leath at a CUFI pastors' briefing with Michael Stevens in Cherry Hill, New Jersey. At that time, he had been actively working to orient his congregation toward the issue of Israel and to broaden that outreach to other local congregations in south New Jersey. Leath was the founding pastor of Destiny Church, a predominantly African American congregation who he hoped would become more multiracial. In 2018, that vision became a reality as the majority-Black Destiny Church merged with a predominantly white congregation to become Converge Church. In 2013, as Leath was becoming more involved with CUFI's outreach to African American Christians, he described his mandate on behalf of Israel as being focused primarily on his own congregation. "My mission," he said, "is to show our church . . . that there is a relationship that we have with the Jewish nation and it's because God cares for them and God's gonna always care for them. . . . When God says, 'I'm gonna bless you,' it's in context with our relationship to our Jewish brothers and sisters. So I'm bridging the gap."

For Leath, "bridging the gap" between African American Christians and Jews through pro-Israel activism parallels Michael Stevens's emphasis on "connecting the dots" for Black Christians on the issue of Israel, and Leath similarly emphasizes that work as being primarily about biblical literacy and education. "My role is to use the Bible to show the correlation between [African Americans and

Jews] and then also find where we can have commonalities." For Leath and other Christian Zionist pastors, the rationale for supporting the State of Israel is simple: "If you love the Bible, then there's no disputing there. If you read some of the scriptures, Israel is right there and there's no way to get around it." Leath pointed out that some of his Black colleagues in ministry criticize the State of Israel on the ground of its treatment of Palestinians. But, returning to the Bible, he said: "There cannot be an argument when it comes to the Bible. And so, I take them back to the Bible."

Leath described CUFI as an organization that helps him bring the issue of supporting the State of Israel to his congregation in a compelling way. "When [CUFI] came along," he said, "I embraced it, and I'm bringing our congregation to it." He described success in his efforts at brokering engagement with Israel within his congregation through CUFI, but he also acknowledged the challenge of advancing pro-Israel advocacy in Black churches more broadly. "The hard part is for pastors of African American congregations to say, 'listen we're gonna support Israel,' when they themselves are struggling and their congregations are struggling." "Some churches," Leath explained, "feel they don't have time to take on anybody else's struggle because they're dealing with our own [struggles]. But little do we know that when we link up to help someone else's struggle, our struggle will be diminished and there may be something that, out of us helping another, we will in turn get blessed." For Leath, getting his fellow pastors to take up the issue of Israel is about positioning pro-Israel work as a path to blessing and relief from community suffering. He credits Stevens as leading the way in this effort to transform more local-oriented Black churches into congregations that can include the far-off issue of Israel and Palestine among their political concerns. "I think Dr. Stevens is doing a great job because people are seeing the embracing of it, they're seeing the benefits of it." Stevens is a pastoral role model for aspiring brokers on the issue of Israel among Black Christians. With his large, growing congregation in Charlotte, North Carolina, Stevens is a model for the kind of blessings in their ministries and personal lives that pastors can expect when they decide to broker Israel-focused political engagement among their members and peers. As Leath said to the audience gathered for the first Cherry Hill Night to Honor Israel, "I just wanna be blessed."

After the New Jersey CUFI Night to Honor Israel in Cherry Hill, which he hosted with Ray Barnard, Leath took stock of what it would take to work within his community to build additional support for CUFI's outreach in Black churches. He concluded that it would have to be a sustained effort within local networks of pastors. "It's helping people become informed," he said, "and it has to take place in one-on-one conversations." Here, pastors like Leath act as brokers on the issue of Christian support for the State of Israel. Unlike Owens's notion of brokers, Christian Zionist Black clergy mediate African American Christian participation in white-led organizations such as CUFI rather than in partnerships with governments on particular policies or projects. Beyond working as a broker for CUFI with his church members, Leath collaborated with Barnard to raise the issue of support for Israel in a regular local African American pastors' roundtable meeting in which they both participated. Leath described his role as counteracting what he called propaganda on the issue of the State of Israel's treatment of Palestinians. For him this meant challenging African American identification with Palestinians in racial terms. "When people look at the skin tone of most of the Israeli people they know, they look white. So it's that whole thing of, oh man, these are just white people, and the Palestinians are dark skinned." Leath described the challenge he faces with some of his fellow Black clergy when it comes to solidarities based on shared experiences of oppression. "A lot of churches are dealing with the oppression issue. We just kind of look at who's hurting. And right now, I tell ya, the Palestinians have a lot of sympathetic people, and they can paint the picture that, hey we're hurting the most." Leath expressed pessimism at the prospects of being able to personally change the views of these pastors, but, he added, "you just hope that they come across something that's gonna enlighten them."

For Leath, the challenge of succeeding as a broker among other Black pastors on support for the State of Israel is also a regional challenge. As a native of North Carolina, now pastoring in New Jersey, Leath described a difference in the openness of Black clergy between the southern and northern United States, mostly based on levels of education:

> I think in the south there's more a willingness to accept anything that is Bible. It's just accepted at face value. . . . You go above the Mason-Dixon line, the thing is, you know it's very educated up here, so education is a real big deal. You can be so educated that you're closed off. . . . I think down South [support for Israel is] just more easily perceived as, hey this is God, this is biblical. Oh, well if it's in the Bible, okay, I believe it. But up here man, you gotta say stuff in the Bible, then you gotta show 'em, you gotta get the historical facts, you gotta get the context, and people just aren't easily accepting of things in the North.

LeRoy Bailey and the First Cathedral

In 2016, I attended a two-day CUFI teaching forum at the First Cathedral Church in the suburbs of Hartford, Connecticut—the same church that hosted the 2012 CUFI Night to Honor Israel event described in the introduction. The First Cathedral's senior pastor, Archbishop LeRoy Bailey Jr., welcomed the CUFI regional outreach coordinator Victor Styrsky as the forum's speaker. Unlike African American CUFI coordinators Stevens and Dumisani Washington, Styrsky is white. But to the mostly Black audience of about a hundred people gathered at the First Cathedral, he emphasized his connection to African American churches in his presentation. His home church in Sacramento, he said, is a Black church with a Black senior pastor. Describing his relationship with his pastor he said, "I took him with me to Israel a number of years ago. It turned him upside down. From that point on, he put an Israeli flag in the sanctuary, and it stays there every day of the year." Styrsky then showed a video clip of him singing in a gospel choir at his home church. As a CUFI outreach coordinator for the Northeast region of the United States, Styrsky speaks in a range of settings, including Black, white, and Hispanic congregations. Of CUFI's pro-Israel outreach work, he told the First Cathedral gathering: "CUFI's got a lot of heart, not a lot of money. So it's a true grassroots, spirit-led, church-driven ministry, and we just love it."

Covering an array of issues during the two-day seminar, Styrsky spoke about "radical Islamic terrorism" as a growing threat to the United States and Israel, anti-Semitism on college campuses, and what he called "the myths of the Israeli-Palestinian conflict." "I will mix the word of God and the world around us," he explained, as he wove together his pro-Israel message including current events, history, and biblical interpretation. He noted the importance of political advocacy work on Capitol Hill as a part of CUFI's mission. As if preempting an aversion to direct political engagement among the attendees, Styrsky said, "I've had pastors say, 'Pastor, the church shouldn't be political.' Now I get whatcha mean on that, yeah absolutely. But Israel's not political, it's *biblical.*"

Throughout the event, Styrsky praised Black church pastors LeRoy Bailey and his sons (who also work as First Cathedral pastors) for their work on behalf of the State of Israel. When Bailey spoke in closing at the end of the first day of the forum, he explained his love for Israel as something he inherited from his father, who was also a preacher. His father, he said, had a close relationship with the Jewish community at a time when Black-Jewish relations were stronger than they are now. Bailey then told a cautionary story to contrast the positive example of his father's regard for and relationship with Jewish communities. "I had a [pastor] friend," he said. "And I couldn't figure out why he had this terrible disposition about the Jews. But when he was speaking about them, I said hmmm, I feel like something's gonna happen to him." Most of the audience nodded their heads, some chuckled, knowingly affirming where they knew the story was heading. "And I want you to know," Bailey continued, saying what the gathering was by then expecting, "He hasn't been the same since. His health has deteriorated, his ministry went sour." "When God says 'I will bless those who bless you and curse those who curse you,' I know exactly what he means."

At this forum and other CUFI events I attended at the First Cathedral, members and lay leaders in the church were joined by guests representing local Jewish and Christian congregations and organizations, and I met a number of other Black pastors who are mentored by Bailey. Ryan Walker was one of those pastors under the leadership of Bailey and his First Cathedral. His ministry is in nearby Springfield, Massachusetts. That ministry, Walker said, is independent in the sense that it is nondenominational like the First Cathedral. But, he explained, it is "under" Bailey and the First Cathedral's leadership. He noted that this meant not only that his church is affiliated with the First Cathedral but also that the pastoral mentoring relationship he has in ministry under Bailey provided accountability. Explaining the importance of pastors like himself having senior mentors with successful ministries and congregations, Walker said, "God has blessed him tremendously. I guess where we're trying to go, he has been there and has proven successful." The mentorship relationship Walker and other pastors have with Bailey also includes participating in First Cathedral's leadership conferences for Black clergy—Churches Covered and Connected in Covenant—that Bailey and the First Cathedral routinely host.

Walker had never traveled to Israel when I met him, but he would love to go, he said. Apart from his affiliation with Bailey and the First Cathedral, Walker was familiar with CUFI because he is a regular watcher of John Hagee's television ministry programs. But actually getting involved with the organization came only as a result of his relationship with Bailey. When CUFI held its 2012 Night to Honor Israel at the First Cathedral, Bailey invited all of his pastoral mentees to attend. "Because of that I signed up with [CUFI] and [began] supporting them also financially," Walker explained. Walker aspires to follow in Bailey's footsteps in church ministry, holding up Bailey and the First Cathedral as a success story.

When Bailey repeatedly quotes God saying in the Bible to the people of Israel, "I will bless those who bless you," he links his success in ministry to his willingness to support the State of Israel in partnership with CUFI.

Inspired by the CUFI events he had attended at the First Cathedral and by Bailey's personal success in ministry, Walker began reaching out to pastors of other churches in the Springfield area. His goal, he said, was to get as many Springfield pastors connected with CUFI as possible, ultimately "helping to see that America continues to stand with Israel." His vision for the potential blessing from God that he expected to stem from working to build support among African American Christians for the State of Israel included personal blessings in his family and ministry, but also national blessings. "I personally believe that one reason for our great success as a country is because of our involvement and love for Israel," Walker explained. "And I strongly believe that with my heart. . . . We live in this country, and we wanna make sure that God's hand and blessings continue on this country." The connection made between personal, family, ministry, and national blessings expected for supporting the State of Israel through partnerships with CUFI was echoed by CUFI-affiliated pastors I met from around the United States. As a pastor of a large congregation, Bailey brokers engagement with pro-Israel activism within his congregation. He also acts as a broker of other Black pastors such as Walker on that issue in his role as a mentor over pastors in New England and around the country.

Brokering "a Seat at the Table"

Among African American CUFI-affiliated pastors, there is an interpretive biblical imperative to support the State of Israel: *God says to bless Israel, so bless Israel.* There is also a prosperity imperative, and pastors of large, successful congregations are held up as models to be emulated in terms of the personal and professional blessings to be expected for supporting Israel in theological and political terms. There is also a status imperative. Here, Owens's brokerage framework for understanding Black clergy political engagement proves valuable in analyzing the role of Black pastors on the issue of Palestine and Israel. Owens notes that explanations for various kinds of political partnerships between government and Black churches involve a combination of opportunity, necessity, and conviction, describing clergy motivations as *political*, *programmatic*, and *professional*. Key to understanding the kinds of political partnerships Black pastors enter into and the ways they choose to act as brokers on particular issues of concern requires attention to how they balance opportunities for engagement with the capacities of their churches.

Beyond this calculation, however, Owens emphasizes that the reputation of clergy in the leadership of Black civil society is also a driving motivation for political engagement as brokers. Throughout the mid-twentieth century, Black clergy in the United States were widely esteemed as political leaders in Black communities—"the natural political leaders and interest brokers in the black community."[38] However, as competition over the leadership mantle of the Black civil sphere increased in the second half of the twentieth century, Black secular elites began to rival pastors in cultural and political influence. Such elites included secular academics, activists, and politicians.[39]

In CUFI's Christian Zionist outreach to African American pastors, recovering the mantle of leadership is a priority that Black CUFI coordinators like Stevens and Washington have advanced. In 2014, I attended a CUFI briefing for African American pastors in a small Black Baptist church in the Bronx's Co-op City housing development. The host church was located in the basement of a larger multipurpose building that had a barber shop, a pharmacy, and a deli on the ground floor. The building was surrounded by several of the many high-rise apartment buildings of Co-op City. The briefing took place in the church's small sanctuary, and the group of about fifty attendees required additional chairs to be brought in as the room became filled over capacity. In a presentation typical of his pro-Israel outreach message, Stevens spoke to the biblical imperative for African American Christians to support Israel. He highlighted the civil rights partnerships of African Americans and Jews as a model for cooperation and as a relationship impelling a moral duty among Black Americans to repay the investment of Jews in Black civil rights progress. He also emphasized the State of Israel as America's best ally in the fight against what he called a "jihadist terrorism tsunami" in the Middle East. Bringing together his case for a moral, religious, and political imperative to "stand with Israel," Stevens appealed to the words of Martin Luther King Jr. as he often did in front of Black Christian audiences. Paraphrasing King's vision for Black churches, as he did at the New Jersey pastors' briefing described in chapter 1, Stevens said:

> The church must be reminded that it is not the master or the servant of the
> state, but rather the conscience of the state. It must be the guide and the

critic of the state, and never the tool of the state. . . . If the church does not recapture its prophetic zeal, it will become an irrelevant social club without moral or spiritual authority.

Stevens explained the significance of this quote with another quote, this one attributed to the white evangelical leadership guru John C. Maxwell. "If you're not at the table, you're on the menu," Stevens said. The audience responded with nods and several "mmm-hmms." Stevens elaborated on his point, focusing specifically on why he believed African Americans needed to take their seat at the table of pro-Israel political advocacy.

I've had a lot of great accomplishments these last several years in this great organization doing what I'm doing for God's kingdom. One of the crowning moments was a few years ago when I sat at the table of Bibi [Benjamin] Netanyahu, the prime minister of Israel . . . I sat at that man's table. But more important than me being at that table, I had eight—not one, not two, but *eight*—African American pastors sitting at the table of the prime minister of Israel. And for twenty-five to thirty minutes we had dialogue . . . [and] there were African American leaders who were not on the menu, they were at the table.

Positioning working on behalf of the State of Israel as a priority to be elevated in Black churches, Stevens continued:

Too long we've made up the choir stands, we've cooked in the kitchen, we've ushered, and we've done security. And I'm not against domestic serving. I believe we're great because we serve. But we haven't had a seat at the table. The table of diplomacy, the table of engineering, administrating, networking, agreement, decision-making. But that day, those African American leaders were at the table.

Anticipating the potential objection that the table of Christian Zionism was not the place for Black church participation, Stevens said:

We don't have a right to criticize Christian Zionism as being white, Republican, and from Texas if we're not willing to come to the table. And you may not make it to his table, but there's a table right here in New York City. There's a table in the state of New York, there's a table on the East Coast. There's got to be a table. Maybe it's on the internet, maybe it's on your website, maybe it's in radio, maybe it's the TV, maybe it's the Sunday School classroom. But we cannot be satisfied with just cooking, cleaning, and singing in the choir stand. We deserve a place at the table of greatness.

The call to the "table of greatness" is one I heard Stevens make to other gatherings of Black clergy and lay church members around the country. In Cherry Hill, New Jersey, he put it this way: "I believe, particularly in the African American community, there is a seat at the table of greatness, particularly as it relates to supporting the Jewish state," leaving no room for doubt about the particular political issue that could translate into greater African American political relevance.

The imperative to take a seat at the table is one CUFI leaders have used to describe African American engagement in politics, more recently in cooperation with the Trump administration, after Stevens left his position as the organization's African American outreach coordinator. On February 1, 2017, Trump met with a group of African American leaders, including several clergy members, for what the White House called a "listening session" to mark the beginning of Black History Month. CUFI diversity outreach coordinator, Dumisani Washington, shared a video of that meeting on Facebook with this description: "President Trump meets with phenomenal Black leaders in all fields at the beginning of Black History month to discuss his administration's work in the Black community." He followed the description with the commentary: "If you're not at the table, you're on the menu."

Through the influence of Black pastors who have worked on full-time pro-Israel outreach such as Stevens and Washington, other pastors including Barnard, Leath, and Walker have taken up the issue of Christian Zionist political activism in their churches and clergy networks. For many CUFI-affiliated pastors, however—even those who travel to Israel on subsidized trips and participate in hosting local events like Nights to Honor Israel—sustaining pro-Israel activism as a broker in Black churches is challenging. The tendency to focus on more local and immediate issues, as Leath has described, affected him also. In 2019, he told me that he had scaled back his involvement with CUFI to focus on establishing his new congregation. During that time, Leath also self-published a book on leadership. Although he said he was aspiring to reengage with CUFI's pro-Israel activism, Leath's punctuated brokerage on the issue of Israel is an example of the kinds of challenges he had described. With extensive resources to take pastors on tours of Israel and to fund local events and provide speakers and teachers, CUFI has worked with many Black clergy to gain a foothold in their congregations. But taking up this kind of political brokerage is intermittent for many Black pastors whose congregants love and support the State of Israel for religious and theological reasons but often share few other political priorities with CUFI's predominantly white and politically conservative ranks.

This call to "take a seat at the table" also stands in sharp contrast to the vision for Black political participation articulated by the leaders of the Samuel DeWitt Proctor Conference. As part of the Palestine-focused "Journeys to Justice" roundtable in 2018, Alton Pollard cautioned against the moral and ethical pitfalls of pursuing relevance and recognition in the way African American Christian Zionist leaders have advocated.

> For any peoples on the face of this earth that have undergone systemic oppression . . . we yearn to be acknowledged, to be recognized as human. And sometimes that takes us to very dangerous places with respect to the biblical text, with respect to the Christian witness. . . . It is the case that we are seeking to be like what we see [in] others without being critical about what is the worst and the best in what that otherness may represent. The exceptionalism that goes with the Zionist traditions—that goes with both Christian and Jewish forms— is something that we've imbibed. We've been intoxicated by it. The idea that we too can be somebody, that we can be recognized. Not giving careful critical attention to the fact that in so doing we are then creating the same kind of negation of other bodies, of other selves, of other peoples that has been perpetrated upon us is something that's terribly wrong and fraught with danger.

The implication, for Pollard, is that "taking a seat at the table," by working with Christian Zionist organizations, is a corruption of an authentic "Christian witness," especially from a Black perspective based in experiences of oppression.

NETWORKS AND NARRATIVES

The case of Christians United for Israel and their outreach into American Black churches is an instructive example for evaluating the kinds of political engagements with Israel and Palestine that are possible or likely among African American Christians, based on the leadership of their pastors. Before looking at brokerage and mobilization in the other case studies, I briefly discuss a perspective that helps make sense of how pastors act variously as brokers and mobilizers—on the issue of Israel and Palestine and more broadly. In their outreach work for CUFI, established Black pastors—Stevens, Washington, Leath, and Bailey—rely on personal and professional *narratives* about themselves and their ministries in the work of brokering Black church political and theological engagement with pro-Israel advocacy. Kate Bowler, in her study of the prosperity of Christian pastors, emphasizes the importance of pastoral biographies and narratives to the ministries of prominent pastors who act as "pastors, prophets, and visionaries" to their congregations.[40] Pastoral biographies, Bowler argues, are a kind of "narrative glue" that hold together a set of priorities in their professional, personal, and political lives. And these narratives fuel the aspirations of other pastors, who aim to have the kind of growing churches, public influence, and financial success that high-profile pastors embody. African American Christian Zionist pastors such as Stevens lead by example in their efforts to establish political support for the State of Israel in Black churches, attributing their success in ministry to God's blessing on them for their commitment to "blessing Israel." Pastors Stevens, Washington, and others act as brokers on the issue of Israel within their congregations, in their denominations, and in less formal networks of affiliation across traditional denominations.[41]

In looking at pastors as brokers and mobilizers on the political issue of Israel and Palestine, it is important to reiterate that Black pastors play different roles in different contexts when they act variously as brokers and mobilizers. Key to the role of the African American pastors as broker is the context of local congregations. Pastors who work as mobilizers, on the other hand, although usually part of (or even leaders of) local congregations, rely more heavily on networks beyond traditional African American denominations (including academic and activist networks). In different social spaces, Black clergy develop various kinds of authority and deploy a range of resources to advance particular religious and political causes. As many scholars of African American Christianity have noted, material resources are key to understanding the political activity of Black churches, whether driven by brokering or mobilizing pastors. Owens calls such resources "tangible, substantive, and physical assets," which include physical spaces, money, membership rolls, and volunteer networks.[42] But Black pastors also deploy cultural resources in their churches to advance political causes.

Among cultural resources, pastoral narratives and their embedded meanings for Black religious and political life in America are central. It is not simply that pastors tell their stories to establish their authority or credibility. Their stories carry deep meanings about key cultural features as shared points of reference within African American Christianity—including Black church identity, notions of calling, collective memory, and how, based on these, the group should be prepared to act. These meanings ultimately constitute visions for what "the Black Church" is and ought to be doing in the United States and in the world. In chapter 5, I consider how the category of "the Black Church" itself is contested in these cultural, identity-focused terms. In this chapter, however, attention to cultural resources—such as personal narratives—and how Black church pastors use them in the service of Israel and Palestine activism helps explain how brokerage and mobilizing efforts around the issue of Palestine and Israel work. Black pastors who take up the issue of Israel and Palestine—both as brokers and mobilizers—do so through the allocation of material resources, but also by deploying ideas, beliefs, values, and solidarities.

In different roles and to different ends, African American pastors who take up pro-Israel or Palestinian-focused activism emphasize different kinds of religious authority in their political engagement. The CUFI pastors discussed here rely heavily on personal charisma and stories of success in ministry as markers of blessing, which other pastors and lay church members strive to emulate and attain. In pursuing blessings for supporting the State of Israel, these pastors emphasize taking a "seat at the table"—"the table of influence" or "the table of greatness." And they use personal narratives to show how God's blessing is real in their lives and can be realized in the lives of others who extend their circle of political concern to include attention to the State of Israel and the Middle East. These prosperity-inflected notions of blessing are not the only culturally salient expressions of African American religiosity that drive engagement with Israel and Palestine, however.

In elaborating other expressions of Black pastoral brokerage and mobilization on that issue in the cases of the International Fellowship of Christians and Jews, the Samuel DeWitt Proctor Conference, and The Perfecting Church, the rest of this chapter looks at alternative approaches pastors take as leaders of Black religious communities. In the case of the IFCJ, African American Christian Zionist pastors emphasize the effects of affirming the State of Israel's significance in terms that focus more on religious authority through reading and preaching the Bible, as well as through establishing pastors as leaders of efforts to provide community services, philanthropy, and charity. This is in contrast to CUFI's prosperity-inflected appeals to Black pastors that focus on blessing as success and influence in Christian ministry and, at a national level, American national prosperity in terms of economic and military hegemony. Among the clergy and lay leaders within the Proctor Conference, there is little talk of blessing when it comes to understanding Palestine and Israel. The narratives of Proctor clergy working on Palestinian solidarity instead focus attention on suffering and paths to solidarity that come from recognizing that African American suffering and Palestinian suffering are connected in a shared global struggle against racism and injustice. The Perfecting Church presents a somewhat hybrid case, in which brokerage and mobilization come together in a single congregation under the leadership of a pastoral couple who use their personal narratives of Christian spiritual growth to impel a church vision for connecting local and global engagement on core issues of concern.

BROKERING AFRICAN AMERICAN CHRISTIAN ZIONISM II: THE INTERNATIONAL FELLOWSHIP OF CHRISTIANS AND JEWS

When the International Fellowship of Christians and Jews launched its outreach program to African American Christians, it began by forming an advisory committee of influential clergy and denominational leaders from several large historically Black Protestant denominations and networks of charismatic Black churches (see chapter 1). The members of the advisory board facilitated IFCJ introductions to denomination and convention heads, which led, in turn, to speaking engagements for the Fellowship's then leader, Rabbi Yechiel Eckstein, to speak at several national meetings of African American denominations and church fellowships. Shepherding these high-level denominational connections were coordinators such as a veteran of the Jewish pro-Israel lobby, Kristina King, and pastors Deedee Coleman and Glenn Plummer, who brokered connections with Black Baptist denominations and the Pentecostal Church of God in Christ (COGIC), respectively. These preliminary connections with the leaders of several key African American denominations led to a series of leadership delegations to Israel from 2015 to 2017. The Fellowship invited denominational heads with whom they had formed relationships to assemble leadership groups of twenty to thirty participants to take part in all expenses paid tours of Israel for their organizations. On these trips, they would focus on outlets for ministry and social services in Israel—what Reverend Coleman calls "the softer side" of Israel.

For King and the Fellowship's African American outreach team, the goal is to educate Black pastors on Israel-related issues so they can incorporate new Israel-centered priorities in their ministries, congregations, and spheres of influence. The point of entry for this work is what King describes as working "from a place of faith." This, for her, is a more theologically oriented approach to pro-Israel activism than the overtly political work she's saw AIPAC and CUFI doing. The faith-based connection the Fellowship aims for relies primarily on giving pastors and Black church leaders the opportunity to visit the State of Israel as "the Holy Land."[43]

King emphasized the significance of taking Black clergy to the Holy Land: "You cannot imagine how much joy it is to take an African American pastor who has been studying the Bible their whole life and never thought that they would ever go to Israel, and then to be able to provide them with that opportunity. And it's a life-changing opportunity." She also underscored the need to begin with Black pastors and to enlist their support in reaching African American communities because of the historically prominent role clergy have played in leading Black communities. Speaking about the civil rights legacy and the social and political advances African Americans achieved during that time, King said, "They did it following a *pastor*," referring to Martin Luther King Jr. "And they did it based on a very long and strong history of Christian values and spirituality," she added. "The Black Church is the most powerful institution that the Black community has," she noted, pointing out that it is Black pastors who control Black churches. "To be able to genuinely engage with the leadership of the Black church is a powerful relationship."

Glenn Plummer similarly described pastors as strategically central to Black church pro-Israel outreach efforts. "True leaders have people following them," he said. "A leader who has nobody following them is just on a walk somewhere." Plummer sees leaders in African American communities as falling into three categories coming out of developments in Black politics in the formative civil rights era: Christian pastors (Martin Luther King Jr., Ralph Abernathy, and Wyatt Tee Walker), Black Muslim leaders (Elijah Muhammad, Malcolm X, and Louis Farrakhan), and secular Black leaders (who Plummer calls "more angry" Black leaders). In describing his outlook on the contemporary landscape of Black political leadership in the United States, Plummer sees little influence of Black Muslim leadership, an expanded political role for secular leaders in government and education, and a persistent and widespread platform for Black pastors in Christian churches and religious networks. Secular leaders in academia and in elected offices often get a lot of attention, Plummer noted. "The cameras gravitate to them." But he argued that African Americans are less likely to follow secular leaders on the issue of Israel. "The greatest bulk of Black folk in America go to church," he said. For this reason, he insisted, pastors are the most natural leaders in Black communities to encourage support for the State of Israel. "And why do their pastors support Israel?" Plummer asked me rhetorically. "Because it's *biblical* and they preach it all the time," he explained. "Pastors preach these dynamic sermons using Moses, Elijah, Joshua. And we go on to all these other prophets of the Old Testament. And these fascinating stories about David and all these people. And so we name our churches after some Israeli biblical site or person or something. And so Black folks who attend churches are naturally pro-Israel." Plummer then described Black pastors as having "the ears and the hearts of the people." In doing pro-Israel outreach work, Plummer relies on his ability to speak the language of pastors in making the case that their affinity for Israel as the land of the Bible should naturally lead them to standing in political solidarity with the State of Israel today. That shared mantle of Black religious leadership, he noted, "makes it much more easy for me to talk to them, to convince them about tying in the current secular Israel and the current modern day Israel to the Israel that they understand from the Bible." Beyond this connection to the State of Israel via the biblical narrative, King described how the next step for affirming and advancing a pro-Israel message in Black churches begins with learning about positive historical examples of Black-Jewish cooperation, and experiencing Israel as the land of the Bible makes an impact on their priorities as religious community leaders: "Pastors, when they study things, it gets in their hearts, and they begin to teach, and they begin to share the message. . . . And I've seen pastors go to Israel, come back, and the message that's churned in their hearts and the passion that's churned in their hearts, that they've then come back to share with their congregation."

Preaching Differently

I traveled to Israel with two groups of African American Christians whose engagement with Israel began with the International Fellowship of Christians and Jews. First, in the spring of 2016, I accompanied a leadership delegation from the National Baptist Convention of America (NBCA), organized by the convention president, Samuel Tolbert, and sponsored and led by the Fellowship. Later that year I joined a Church of God in Christ (COGIC) group, led by Glenn Plummer. The COGIC tour, described as a "mission," aimed to establish a denominational relationship with and a presence within Israel, building on a 2015 COGIC leadership delegation that the Fellowship sponsored and led.

Chapter 4 takes a closer look at the experiences of pastors and lay church members in the land of Palestine and Israel, with attention to the kinds of tensions that emerge on trips that result from competing spiritual, commercial, and political priorities among various trip stakeholders, of which participating pastors are just one. In this chapter, given the Fellowship's emphasis on an ostensibly apolitical and spiritual orientation to supporting the State of Israel cultivated through outreach to pastors, I highlight the ways pastors within the Fellowship's African American outreach efforts describe the religious significance of traveling to Israel and how that experience becomes part of their personal and pastoral narratives. On a personal level, virtually every one of the pastors I traveled with or spoke to about their experiences emphasized some aspect of personal religious growth based on experiencing Israel as the land of the Bible. On a corporate level, these same pastors recognized and affirmed the importance of their having been to Israel and the impact that that experience would have on their congregations, their families, and their wider communities.

In the case of Samuel Tolbert and the NBCA, Coleman contacted him through a relative of hers who knew an NBCA pastor in Tolbert's home state of Louisiana. Coleman is the pastor of Russell Street Missionary Baptist Church in Detroit (see chapter 1). The connection was made and Tolbert and Coleman began discussing ways that the NBCA could partner with the Fellowship. When I asked Tolbert why he wanted to travel to Israel with the Fellowship, he expressed many of the kinds of religious reasons King and Plummer had noted that provide a religious and spiritual point of entry to the concerns of Black clergy. Tolbert pointed to "religious education" as his primary interest in the trip. "I think it will help, even now, my spiritual formation," he said. "And as denominational leader, who recognizes that much of our preaching is centered around that geography, I think it'll just enlighten me more in my preaching and even in my leadership. Because many of the leadership models that we got from Jesus and his disciples took place in that geography."

Tolbert selected pastors and lay leaders to take part in the trip based on their various positions of denominational leadership in key ministries, such as clergy oversight, lay leadership groups, women's ministry, and youth ministry. He specifically invited a number of younger leaders, he said, to provide them with a once in a lifetime experience so that "every time they think about this experience, they have to remember the convention. And also remember the very committed work of the Fellowship in building bridges between people in the Holy Land and, of course in our case, people here in the African American community."

Several of the NBCA pastors Tolbert invited to participate in the Fellowship-led trip echoed his emphasis on the spiritual significance of their travels in Israel. Keith, the pastor of a Virginia NBCA congregation, put it this way:

> I've spent so much of my life preaching and teaching the Bible and talking about Jesus and the different stories of the Bible. And to actually walk and to see the places that I've talked about all my life—that I've spent so much of my life's to work on—and to actually be there and to think about the opportunity to go there. . . . I was really excited about doing that.

Another NBCA pastor from Tennessee similarly described the personal and spiritual significance of traveling with his denominational leadership in Israel: "It makes me look at the New Testament differently in my preparation. To really have an idea from your preaching and your teaching. When you hear the guides, you have that image in your head because preaching is often storytelling as well."

When pastors like these NBCA leaders travel to Israel, their personal story is enlarged, and the religious authority they hold in their communities and congregations is expanded. If preaching is storytelling, pastors who travel to Israel within the Fellowship's African American outreach program get examples of how to convey the significance of their time in the Holy Land. This Tennessee pastor took cues from the storytelling of professional tour guides and incorporated new kinds of stories with new kinds of authority into his personal and professional biography as a minister and as a preacher.

Similarly, on my 2016 trip with the COGIC delegation led by Plummer, pastors and lay members of the denomination learned how the personal experience of the Holy Land could affect their spiritual lives and ministries. Preaching and teaching are common features of American Protestant Christian tours of Israel. Many of the well-traveled sites of Christian religious significance in the

Holy Land have permanent spaces set up for holding religious services. When American Christians visit places associated with the life and ministry of Jesus—the Garden of Gethsemane, the Mount of Olives, the Garden Tomb, or the Mount of Beatitudes—their tour typically includes time spent preaching, praying, singing, or studying the Bible. On pro-Israel Holy Land tours such as the NBCA and COGIC trips, visiting Christians travel with professional Israeli tour guides who generally do not share their religious faith, but they see themselves as ambassadors for the State of Israel and for its Jewish citizens.[44] Pastors acquire powerful personal religious narratives via experiences mediated by these tour guides. The principal trip narrative is the guide's to share because they are largely in control of what is noticed and what goes unnoticed by participants. They are the ones holding the microphone on the tour bus and during site visits. Trained and knowledgeable, they provide the raw materials for making meaning out of the various sites visited.

Israeli guides present narratives framing Israel as the land of the Bible but also as a modern, flourishing state facing extraordinary geopolitical challenges. On the first day of the COGIC trip, the group's guide established a link between a biblical trip narrative and the political story of the modern State of Israel, saying, "We are seeing a modern country but the topography hasn't changed. History is very much part and parcel of our lives here in Israel. You can close your eyes and imagine the places of the Bible." Trip participants generally accepted the tension between sacred and secular emphases throughout the experience. At times, however, the tension between the secular—what was sometimes labeled "educational"— emphases of tour guides and the sacred frameworks of trip participants clashed. COGIC trip leader and pastoral authority for the COGIC group, Glenn Plummer, then on his seventeenth trip to Israel, sometimes flagged a remark by our Jewish tour guide with the caveat: "Historians may say [this], *but the Bible says . . . ,*" offering an alternative narrative explanation. Most of the pastors participating in the COGIC delegation had the opportunity to preach during the trip. After preaching a short sermon and leading a prayer and healing service on Mount Carmel—where the biblical Prophet Elijah is believed to have defeated the prophets of the Canaanite god Baal—one COGIC pastor from Ohio declared, "I came to put my hands on this table where Elijah worked, I came to walk where Jesus walked. . . . When I go home I can preach this thing because I was there."

The emphasis on experiencing the State of Israel as "the land of the Bible" is not only taken up by individual pastors, it is performed and modeled by both experienced Holy Land traveling pastors and pastors visiting the Holy Land for the first time. On the mount of precipice—a mountain just outside the city of Nazareth—Plummer read the relevant account of events from the Gospel of Luke. Describing how Jesus had just returned from his temptation in the wilderness, Plummer explained how Jesus went to the synagogue in Nazareth and read from the scroll of the prophet Isaiah. And how the people of Nazareth, "filled with rage," took him up to the mountain to throw him off. Coming to a rhetorical climax, Plummer emphasized: "*The Bible says* he walked right through the crowd and returned to Capernaum." Another COGIC pastor and first-time visitor standing next to Plummer seamlessly and spontaneously took up the story from there and continued talking about the significance of Jesus returning to his "home base," pointing in the direction of Galilee where the group had just been. Smiling, Plummer and a third COGIC pastor looked at the preacher who had picked up the message from Plummer and remarked, "You're gonna preach different from now on!" Reflecting on this moment later, a female COGIC missionary supervisor talked about the significance of this experience that overflowed from the senior pastors on the trip to the many lay members and leaders present: "We began to just tell the story. And as we told the story, someone else brought another key point in. . . . And so many people were having so many different emotions. Some people were emotional about looking out over the city of Nazareth. This is where *Jesus* looked. You know, to think this is where he was, this is what he said." For African American pastors and lay leaders who travel to the State of Israel with the Fellowship, a faith-based approach to pro-Israel advocacy produces a mutually beneficial relationship between Israeli Jews and visiting African American Christians. Visiting pastors, lay leaders, and church members get an experience of the Holy Land that adds to their personal and professional credibility and authority as Christian ministers.

Yael Eckstein, daughter and successor to Fellowship founder Rabbi Yechiel Eckstein and then the IFCJ's executive vice president, underscored what she saw as a naturally symbiotic relationship between Israeli Jews and African American Christians. On the first day of the NBCA trip, when the leadership delegation went directly from arriving at the airport in Tel Aviv to a Fellowship-sponsored orphanage, she welcomed the visiting Baptist pastors over lunch in the orphanage dining room. She talked about the "special relationship" Jews and African Americans have because of their similar histories of suffering. "I don't have to explain what it means to suffer as the Jews have, because African Americans understand," she said. She went on to talk about how this trip—organized, paid for, and run by the Fellowship—was being provided "without strings attached." She added that the Fellowship does not require visiting pastors to preach a particular sermon or to share a specific message with their congregations. "We just want you to experience Israel and let the experience speak for itself," she explained.

In traveling to the State of Israel, the biographical "narrative glue" that Bowler describes as holding together and driving the personal and professional aspects of Christian ministers includes an authoritative experience in "the land of the Bible," which equips pastors to "preach different" because they have "been there." Having "walked where Jesus walked," they gain a higher level of authority as interpreters of the Bible and as preachers and teachers in their communities. "I put my hands on the alter," one of the COGIC preachers emphasized. The COGIC missionary supervisor, who described how the significance of the moment of preaching and teaching in Nazareth spread throughout the group, also underscored for me later how important the trip was for her and for African Americans like her. She described experiencing Israel for her parents and those who came before her, who never had the opportunity to visit the Holy Land. "They can't even imagine it," she said. "To go that far, to step on the ground that Jesus walked, to see many of the things . . . that we've seen." "Many of us were seeing it and crying, not because we were seeing it but we felt that everybody in us was seeing it."

Throughout trips like the ones in which COGIC and NBCA delegations participated, pastors and other Black church leaders acquire a different kind of experience and authority that enables them to speak about Israel beyond its significance as the land of the Bible. Trips like these move fluidly between ancient sites of biblical significance and sites of modern political significance (see chapter 4). On the same day, a group might visit a military outpost in the Palestinian territories and a Bible site such as the Garden of Gethsemane. For example, on the COGIC trip, the group met with a political group in Israel's Knesset (parliament) and visited the Garden Tomb—believed to be a possible location for the death, burial, and resurrection of Jesus—back to back. As their personal pastoral narrative includes the authority that comes from "walking where Jesus walked," it also includes the authority to speak on the politics of the Middle East. Christian Zionist tours, like those led by the Fellowship, invariably become a fusion of biblical experience and international politics.

As leaders of congregations, Black pastors take this blended religious-political experience of the land of Israel back to their churches and denominations.

Their ability to act as brokers in those religious spaces depends, in large part, on the extent to which the experience becomes part of their narrative in a compelling way. In addition to experiencing the "land of the Bible," they also experience the land of Israel as a modern nation-state, and they are introduced to the politics of the region. Just as their experience of Israel blends religion and politics, their personal pastoral narrative about the spiritual significance of the "land of the Bible" and the political significance of the land of Israel today overlap. The Fellowship provides the opportunity and asks Black clergy to be ambassadors for the State of Israel based on what they have seen, learned, and experienced. This "no strings attached" approach creates the opportunity for a kind of political brokerage that emphasizes Christian charity and philanthropic work. African American outreach leaders such as King see this as a natural point of connection to the work that Black pastors are already doing in their local churches and communities (see chapter 1). The work of the Fellowship gives them an opportunity to extend their sphere of political concern (in philanthropic terms) to the State of Israel, based on an affinity for the land of the Bible and developing a sense of solidarity with Israeli Jews through shared narratives of suffering. Chapter 4 explores how philanthropic work elides religion and politics on some trips to the Holy Land for African American Christians. In this chapter, I now examine two other modes of Black pastoral engagement with Israel and Palestine—mobilization and reconciliation.

MOBILIZING BLACK CHURCH SOLIDARITY WITH PALESTINE: THE SAMUEL DEWITT PROCTOR CONFERENCE

Chapter 2 describes the Palestinian solidarity engagement of the Samuel DeWitt Proctor Conference (SDPC) as part of a broader set of political imperatives in Black churches in the United States. The first of those imperatives is reorienting African American Christians in their understanding of the biblical text. As the Proctor affiliate Lora Hargrove put this imperative to her congregation in the Bible study she leads in her Rockville, Maryland, church: "You have been for years reading your Bible through the eyes of the oppressor. I want to open this up to you so that you begin to read scripture through the eyes of the oppressed." The second imperative for the Proctor Conference is to position Black churches in solidarity with contemporary movements for racial justice—in the United States and around the world—through expressions of prophetic Black Christianity. Neither of these religious imperatives is primarily about Palestine and Israel. Both, however, provide a distinct role for Black clergy in speaking to that issue through the lenses of racial justice and prophetic Black religion. For Hargrove, engaging with Israel and Palestine begins with pastors reframing what the Bible is and what it means for Black Christians. This kind of reframing opens possibilities for political mobilization based on new global solidarities. Focusing on the role of pastors, the following sections show how Proctor-affiliated Black clergy invoke liberation theology as a political mobilizer with implications for Israel and Palestine. Less concerned with brokering organization-level political partnerships, SDPC-affiliated pastors and leaders work broadly to mobilize African American Christians by providing a more activist-oriented and liberationist outlook on politics, creating the opportunity for solidarity with Palestinians based on shared experiences of systems of racial injustice.

Gregory Edwards: The Prophetic Calling of "the Black Church" and the Role of Black Clergy

Gregory Edwards is the senior pastor of Resurrected Life Community Church in Allentown, Pennsylvania. He and several of his church staff attended the Proctor-sponsored event at Howard University entitled "Occupied Palestine: How Should the Black Church Respond?" Edwards learned of the event from his friend and colleague in ministry, Dennis Wiley, a Proctor Conference affiliate and longtime pastor of Covenant Baptist United Church of Christ in Washington, DC, until his retirement in 2017. At Wiley's invitation, Edwards saw an opportunity to expose some of his church staff ministers to what he described as an outlook on Palestine and Israel "outside the realm of a lot of the propaganda and dogma that is lifted up." When I spoke to him after the event, Edwards described how his seminary training (at Drew University and New Brunswick Theological Seminary) had equipped him to lead his congregation (especially its Black members) out of "deeply held, not factual but dogmatic doctrines."

Edwards was raised in the historically Black African Methodist Episcopal denomination. After college, he joined a Baptist congregation in the Black National Baptist Convention. In founding his Resurrected Life Community Church, however, he opted for a nondenominational church identity. The majority of Resurrected Life's membership is African American, although Edwards described the congregation as multiracial and multicultural in terms of its specific racial and ethnic diversity. For Edwards, the issue of Israel and Palestine is broadly significant for Christian churches, but he described a specific need for Black churches to interrogate their outlook on Israel. "Many Black evangelical pastors," he noted, "tend to be very narrowly sighted with Israel . . . their hermeneutic is really based upon a certain understanding of Israel, I think, that ties Israel the state in 1948 to the Israel in the Bible, which of course we know is not the same. But nonetheless, I think that's why many of them are very–almost unanimously–pro-Israel." This critique of the dominant outlook on the Bible and the State of Israel echoes that of the panelists on the Proctor Conference's roundtable discussion on Palestine, described in chapter 2. For Edwards, this biblical hermeneutic is central to the unique identity of "the Black Church" and its sociopolitical roots. Expressions of Christian Zionism in Black churches, suggests Edwards, reflect notions of Black Christian religiosity that ignore the roots of Black churches as prophetic religious institutions. In describing his understanding of the identity and mission of "the Black Church," Edwards invoked the work of pastor and author Raphael Warnock on the identity of "the Black Church."[45] Citing Warnock, he described a tension between "prophetic" and "pietistic" tendencies within African American Christianity. Edwards explained, "There's been this proclivity to freedom that's in our bones. And we've read the biblical text in a prophetic way. And so, until recently, that's truly been kind of our foundation."

The contested nature of competing visions for the history, identity, and mission of "the Black Church" is the central puzzle I take up in chapter 5. In evaluating the specific role of pastors in Israel- and Palestine-focused activism, however, the implications for pastoral leadership roles are important here as well. Warnock, whom Edwards cited in describing his orientation to the issue of Palestine and Israel, sees Black pastors and theologians as having played different parts in the history of African American Christianity and the development of Black churches as social institutions. According to Warnock, Black pastors (even when they engage politically) have tended to emphasize the pietistic side of African American Christianity, "aimed at the freedom of the soul, in this world and the next."[46] Black theologians, however, "have focused primarily on the political side, radical protest aimed at the freedom of the body in this world."[47] This distinction reflects Edwards's priorities in church ministry, which he described as having been nurtured in his academic seminary training. "I think that some of that [seminary experience] has really helped to shape and inform my theology, my thinking, and really the practice of what we do in Allentown."

On African American outlooks on Israel and Palestine, Edwards acknowledges that "there are unquestionable parallels between the struggle of Black Americans and also of the Hebrew people." He qualifies this connection, however, noting that "the Exodus passage has been used for decades—for centuries—to help develop a *prophetic* theology." He described the prophetic impulse as "a way of approaching the biblical texts" but also as "a way of approaching ministry . . . a way of approaching your neighbor and God that sees God very much in the struggle with people who have been dispossessed and marginalized."

Edwards described how this prophetic orientation shapes his church ministry more broadly. For Edwards, conversations in Black religious spaces, like the one at Howard University, emphasize the importance of the prophetic dimensions of Christianity—especially African American Christianity. "I think that what [these kinds of conversations] do is they challenge us locally to think about, ultimately, our practice of ministry." He described this as a needed corrective to what he sees as too much attention exclusively to continuing the priestly ministry of Jesus within Black churches. Linking this prophetic imperative to Israel and Palestine, and drawing on a prophetic interpretation of the Exodus narrative, Edwards said:

> It takes a big stretch to see what's currently happening in the Israel-Palestine conflict and not understand the political . . . and without that critique, I think that folks automatically—specifically the Black church—have been led to be very pro-Israel. And not understanding that the Israel that has emerged now is a Eurocentric Israel that, to a certain extent, has been very discriminatory. Not only to the Palestinians, but even [to] their Ethiopian brothers.

Edwards is a pastor steeped in Black theologies of liberation that emphasize identification with the marginalized and the dispossessed. And this is an approach to the Bible that he links to the Exodus narrative of Jewish emancipation from slavery. Bringing this theological lens to bear on Israel and Palestine—or on politics in general—is a kind of mobilization effort in which pastors like Edwards mobilize ideas about what the Bible says about justice within the political sphere. For Edwards and others, a Black liberationist reading of the Exodus narrative compels solidarity with Palestinians. It also provokes the questioning of what

Edwards described as uncritically held dogmas about the State of Israel. In this, Edwards is not working on brokering any particular organizational political partnership with Israel or Palestine. Like the leaders of the Proctor Conference, in their roundtable discussion on the issue, his pastoral work is more about a mobilization of African American Christians into a broadly liberationist outlook on politics—one that attends closely to racial injustice and discrimination. African American pastors like Edwards and Hargrove, in their capacities as preachers and Bible teachers, work to reclaim what they see as a lost way of reading and understanding the Christian scriptures among people of color. Their mobilization of the specific critiques and hermeneutics of Black theologies work at a fundamental level to shape religio-racial political outlooks among the African American Christians in their congregations.

Lucas Johnson: Linking Struggles

A different pastoral role in the Proctor network is appearing among the younger generation of clergy, for whom political brokerage is even less significant and mobilization even more important. Lucas Johnson was in his early thirties when I met him in 2014, and he is part of the generation of younger clergy and activists who the Proctor Conference supports in new avenues of activism and religious political engagement. Although elders of the Proctor Conference and the civil rights movement may perceive him as part of the youngest generation of new activists, Johnson reminded me that there are many emerging activists who are younger still. These activists in their teens and twenties, Johnson said, need to speak for themselves because they have their own unique perspectives and experiences.

Johnson is an ordained Baptist minister and comes from a family that split its time between primarily white and Black religious congregations as he was growing up. His father had a career in the U.S. Army, and Johnson was raised in Germany, where his father was stationed. In Germany, his family became connected to a group of Southern Baptist missionaries. The family moved to Hinesville, Georgia, when Johnson was eight years old, and they mainly attended white Southern Baptist churches as a family. But Johnson's extended family had roots in Black Baptist churches. His grandfather was a minister in the Progressive National Baptist Convention. Although his family regularly attended a white Southern Baptist church, his upbringing was punctuated by experiences in

Black churches, especially with his grandmother. Of living in these two religious worlds, Johnson said:

> I knew enough to understand that my grandmother's [Black] pastor and the [white] pastor of First Baptist Hinesville were often talking about two different gods. . . . My grandmother's God was much more concerned about justice and what was happening in people's lives. That conversation with God that I experienced in those church services was much more about real life, so to speak. Whereas the God that I learned about in my Southern Baptist experience was much more concerned about sex and who is having what with whom. And much more concerned about heaven and hell and this other world of existence.

Between high school and college, Johnson felt a call to Christian ministry, although he was not sure what kind of pastor he would want to be. He grew up listening to the speeches of Martin Luther King Jr. on the stereo on rainy days at home or on family road trips. He said that this affected his understanding of what a Black preacher should be. "King definitely shaped my image of what it meant to be a preacher more than the people that were pastors around me did. His life and work just resonated with me so profoundly." Johnson pursued a seminary education at Emory School of Theology in Atlanta, already committed to the struggle for racial justice. But "it was very important for me to be secure in my identification in relationship to the Black community and our freedom struggle. I felt that my being queer alienated me from that possibility. I didn't understand how I was going to do it. I didn't think that I could do it."

Unsure of the prospects of living out both his commitment to racial justice work and his sexual identity, Johnson considered law school as an alternative track through which to work on justice issues. In law school, "I could be of service without putting myself in the position of being a moral voice, because I didn't think that my moral voice would be accepted." Being part of the Black LGBTQ+ community in Atlanta helped Johnson come to terms with these concerns and influenced his thinking about a potential trajectory in activism. It was through that community that he became aware of queer writers and activists of color who had been "working in the shadows," as he described it—publicly active but often forced into privacy in their sexual identities. Johnson listed Audre Lorde, James Baldwin, Bayard Rustin, and Joseph Beam as examples of figures who helped him reconcile his commitment to racial justice work and his queer identity. "There was an activist community in Atlanta that really helped me reintegrate myself and helped me understand that there are many of us that are Black and gay, Black and queer." Johnson described coming to understand that "that intersection is not something to run from but something to lean into and embrace, and it should be a very important part of your actions and work."

Johnson's path would take him into NGO work with the International Fellowship of Reconciliation, a Netherlands-based humanitarian and human rights organization that promotes nonviolence and reconciliation. He described the Fellowship of Reconciliation as an organization where he could be "a full person." "I'm not a single issue person," he explained:

> I couldn't work for the uplift of the race while ignoring what's happening to LGBTQ people. And I felt like . . . certain people within the Black church tradition or connected to the Black church tradition were asking for that. Or they were asking for me to not talk about that because it would jeopardize other things. I couldn't do that. There are a lot of problems in the Black gay community, a lot of pain and suffering, in part because of the Black church.

Through his work with the Fellowship of Reconciliation, Johnson was introduced to the historian, civil rights activist, and Martin Luther King Jr.'s biographer, Vincent Harding. After he interviewed Harding for the Fellowship of Reconciliation's magazine, Johnson said, "Doctor Harding immediately embraced me, welcomed me into his life, into his family, into his community. So, for the rest of our relationship, he was 'Uncle Vincent' to me. And I was one of his adopted nephews." It was Harding who asked Johnson to travel with him to Palestine for the first time. The invitation came after the issue of Israel and Palestine had already come to his attention in 2010, when the Fellowship of Reconciliation debated the question of a formal position of Palestinian solidarity at its international council meeting. Reflecting on that debate, Johnson laughed, "I knew then that I was kind of in trouble." He explained, "I kind of sensed then that I needed to know more."

Following that experience, he attended a Fellowship of Reconciliation youth seminar in Berlin, where he met two young Palestinian women. "They were the first to really lay it out in front of me and talk about their experiences." "I committed to them that I would come to Palestine and do more to support them."

After returning home to Atlanta, Johnson told the Fellowship of Reconciliation community that he wanted to say more and do more about what was happening in Palestine. That initiated a year of discussion and learning for the group. "We all felt like it was our moral responsibility to be able to make up our minds about where we stood and what we were going to do," he explained. It was at the end of that year that he got the invitation from Harding to participate in an intergenerational African American delegation to Palestine being organized by the civil rights icon Dorothy Cotton and her human rights leadership institute. The trip included civil rights elders, historians, and other Black academics whom Johnson described as representing different parts of the Black freedom struggle over time. Reflecting on the experience, Johnson recalled, "It changed my whole orientation to the subject. And I could no longer be a passive ally—I had to be an active ally." He described how the several generations of African American religious, political, and intellectual leaders on that trip to Palestine grappled with their shared narratives about Israel, rooted in the Bible, and in the context of the current political climate in the region.

After that first trip in 2012, Palestine became increasingly central to Johnson's work and ministry. In 2014, he led an African Heritage delegation to the region with the Interfaith Peace-Builders organization. In his activism on behalf of Palestine, Johnson represents a different kind of political engagement in Black churches than that of the brokerage model. He operates outside the fixed positions in local congregations, mobilizing African Americans on the issue of Israel and Palestine across a number of religious, academic, and civil society organizations. For Johnson, these have included the Fellowship of Reconciliation, Interfaith Peace-Builders, and the Samuel DeWitt Proctor Conference.

Neichelle Guidry: The Role of the Preacher

Neichelle Guidry is another Proctor-affiliated Black clergywoman leading African American Christians on the political issue of Israel and Palestine outside of a traditional local church ministry. When I met her in 2016 at the Proctor Conference annual meeting (where she preached the Palestine-focused sermon described in the introduction), she was an associate pastor at Trinity United Church of Christ and was completing her PhD at Garrett-Evangelical Theological Seminary. Since then, she has taken up the position of dean of Sisters Chapel at Spelman College, a leading historically Black women's college. Guidry is also the founder of "shepreaches," a nonprofit professional development organization for Black millennial women in ministry. Guidry focuses on young adult and worship ministries at Trinity but told me that recently she had been focusing on building connections between Black millennial clergy and Black millennial activists in Chicago. "The Movement for Black Lives is happening, and a constant refrain and critique is that the Black church is nowhere to be found." "We [Black clergy] are not out there," she explained. "We've created the culture of *you come to us*." She described her work as coalition-building and suggested that Black churches need to take a supporting role: "The church has to do something different. The church has to get into the open. But the problem is that when churches get into the open, they want to co-opt the whole thing." "In this particular movement," she continued, "that's not the role of the Black church. The church is called to a supportive role—to a role of providing sanctuary." Guidry described this imperative for Black churches to stand in solidarity with young Black activists in the Movement for Black Lives as having been sparked by theological and political reflections that came out of her trip to Palestine the previous year. She explained how the trip had raised questions for her about solidarity and what it requires. What are the ethics that guide global relationships rooted in solidarity? she asked. And what kind of theology undergirds solidarity?

Guidry first visited Israel as a seminary student at Yale Divinity School, when she spent a semester at the Hebrew University of Jerusalem. Reflecting on that first visit, she recalled: "I think that there was a lot of care taken to kind of tailor my experience there and to curate it in such a way to where I didn't really get an eye for and the occupation." Guidry described that time in Israel as "a Zionist experience." "I went under the guise of, 'you're Black, we're Jewish, we've all been oppressed.'" Her more recent trip to Palestine in 2015, however, came at the invitation of Taurean Webb, then a fellow PhD candidate at Garrett-Evangelical Theological Seminary and later the director of its Center for the Church and the Black Experience. When she preached to the plenary gathering at the Proctor Conference convention in 2016, Guidry explained her second trip to Israel and Palestine as a baptism experience. "I was baptized by fire into a deep melancholic aching, and I was also baptized by fire into a deeper understanding." She emphasized that there is no easy way to be introduced to the evil of empire and the power discrepancies of the occupation in Palestine. "To see it, and to be with people in that space . . . you're initiated through the grief."

Returning to the imperative of preaching in her ministry, Guidry emphasized that "I'm a preacher. That's my first vocation, even before pastor. I preach." She described preaching as a key medium through which to awaken African American Christians to the imperative of political solidarity and political activism. "As a preacher, part of my call is to be a person who wakes people up." "One of my biggest problems with Black church folk is they are tired and they are sleeping all the time. And *woke* is a popular way of saying you need to be conscious, and you need to be aware and you need to be involved. . . . So one of my calls is to wake up the church." In describing how this awakening and mobilization could happen among African American Christians, Guidry emphasized the importance of narratives. "There's something deeply humanizing about hearing people's stories." And this potential, she continued, is something critical that the Proctor Conference does particularly well—creating spaces for the exchange of knowledge and the exchange of narratives. Returning to the central role of preaching, Guidry explained, "Preaching in the Black church carries its own authority." She continued:

> Israel is paying people thousands of dollars to preach Zionism—*Black* people, *Black* clergy. And they're taking that money! There needs to be a counternarrative coming from the Black pulpit, and it needs to be a woke narrative about what's really happening. . . . I hope to model woke preaching about the issue [of Palestine]. I hope to embody that, because I feel like, just knowing the culture of Black churches around Black preaching, I don't know of any other medium in the lives of Black church people that has that much authority.

Guidry also emphasized the importance of Black clergy making solidarity-building trips to Palestine, like the one she went on with the Proctor Conference—particularly as a counter to more widely available Christian Zionist-funded trips for Black clergy. "As long as Black clergy are being offered thousands of dollars to go to Israel and then come back and preach, there's gotta be a remnant that goes to Palestine and offers a counternarrative. And I think Proctor is making a way for people to do that." Here, the language of a remnant is apt because it gets at the relative resources and reach of the Samuel DeWitt Proctor Conference, the International Fellowship of Christians and Jews, and Christians United for Israel. The latter two have tens of millions of dollars at their disposal from donors large and small, including significant funding from the State of Israel itself.

The Proctor Conference has much smaller resources and thus a less amplified voice within African American Christianity. The call of the Proctor Conference—on the issue of Palestine and on other political issues, including the Movement for Black Lives—is a prophetic call from the margins, not the mainstream of African American Christianity. It is a call that Guidry describes as one that works against apathy, ignorance, and an ingrained loyalty to biblical Israel among Black Christians. For Guidry, these challenges require a clear articulation of the connection between Palestinians and African Americans. "These struggles don't exist in vacuums," she said. "There's actually a lot of interconnection here—and that makes way for buy in."

Glenn Plummer, the Detroit-based Black pastor and point person on building Black church support for the State of Israel through the International Fellowship of Christians and Jews and in the Church of God in Christ, said of Black clergy, "True leaders have people following them." Adding, "A leader who has nobody following them is just on a walk somewhere." His point was that the power to engage African American Christians in political issues lies with pastors of local churches, which fits Owens's model of Black church political activism as brokerage. Black clergy like Johnson and Guidry, who work through a nexus of institutional affiliations not necessarily based out of one local congregation, present another model of driving Black church political engagement. This alternative is more about mobilization than brokerage.

THE AFRICAN AMERICAN PASTOR AS RECONCILER: THE PERFECTING CHURCH

Palestine has been part of The Perfecting Church's ministry since the congregation was eight months old, when the church's founding pastor, Kevin Brown, accompanied his mentor, Bob Roberts, to Palestine. As described in chapter 2, TPC's model for engagement in Palestine and Israel is one of community connectedness, bridging the local and the global in a "glocal" mandate for international solidarity-building and reconciliation. Brown calls his church members who travel to Palestine "ambassadors of reconciliation," who aim to avoid taking sides. Instead, they aspire to "choose the cross"—a way of affirming what Brown describes as a unique mandate in the region as peacemakers and bridge builders between Palestinians and Jewish Israelis.

The vision for a race-conscious engagement with politics founded on reconciliation, which Kevin and Angela Brown preach, teach, and model at The Perfecting Church, is discussed in detail in chapter 5. It is a vision that Kevin Brown outlined in 2015, in the weeks following their return from one of the congregations many delegations to Palestine, in a sermon series entitled "Race, Reconciliation, and the Cross." For Brown and The Perfecting Church, the politics of race are guided by the Christian theological imperative of reconciliation. Confronting racial tension—in south New Jersey or in Palestine—means doing the work of "tearing down barriers" and "building bridges." The purpose of speaking openly about race, for Brown, is to advance the goal of multicultural, multiracial church membership, beginning in their local congregation and then expanding outward into their community and even around the globe. The salience of the idea of race, in this paradigm, is that it comes with strong prejudices that stand in the way of unity within churches. Brown argues that God desires to reflect diversity while maintaining a unity of purpose and common religious identity. Racism is a lens through which individuals see each other that is marred by prejudice. For Brown, the solution to the problem of racism is becoming acutely aware of racial prejudices and how they work so their effects can be mitigated to achieve unity.

In one sense, as the founders and senior pastors of The Perfecting Church, Kevin and Angela Brown act as brokers for their members on the issue of Palestine and Israel. But because the glocal mandate for global engagement is central to the church's founding identity—and because the Browns' choice of Palestine came at the earliest stages of the congregation's growth—their work on Palestine is also a kind of locally focused mobilization. The Perfecting Church represents a hybrid mode of narrative-driven, pastoral-led mobilization on the issue of Israel and Palestine that includes elements of brokerage and mobilization.

Pastoral Narrative in The Perfecting Church

As with the previously discussed cases, The Perfecting Church's engagement with the issue of Israel and Palestine is driven and sustained by personal narratives. "Telling our stories," said Kevin Brown, "moves us past our own values, our own judgments, our own conclusions that we get familiar with in our own home context. But when I come out of my own home context, I see oppression differently. I see the oppressor differently. I see violence differently."

Angela Brown comes from an African American family with a deep sense of its history. She is a member of the Still family, who are descendants of the nineteenth-century brothers William and James Still. William Still, an abolitionist known as "the Father of the Underground Railroad," helped hundreds of slaves escape to freedom. James Still was a self-taught homeopathic physician called "the Black Doctor of the Pines." As a child, Angela recalled gathering in Lawnside, New Jersey, each year for "Still Family Day." She remembers her father and uncle dressing up in period costumes and reenacting the lives of William and James Still. "That was embedded in my upbringing," she said. "That just shaped who I was." She also described other parts of her identity that shape how she thinks about who she is and how she conceives of solidarities in Israel and Palestine, noting in her ancestry a Jewish great grandmother who married a Native American man, for example.

That complex identity shapes how she looks at her church's role among Palestinians and Israelis. About what connects people, she said, "It's not about ethnicity. It really is their experiences. Far too many people have been shaped by trauma and been put in disadvantaged positions." "We have that in common," she explained, noting connections she feels toward both Palestinians and Jewish Israelis. "I was very aware of the role of Jews in the civil rights movement," but, she continued, "they were shaped in an environment similar to what we see Palestinians being shaped in, what we see African Americans [shaped in today]. I think, unfortunately, trauma is what connects us."

When I traveled with The Perfecting Church to Palestine and Israel, Angela Brown experienced a particular point of resonance with a female Palestinian leader with whom we met. When we sat with the mayor of Bethlehem, Vera Baboun, the mayor told the group about having majored in African American studies in college and the inspiration she drew from Black women authors. Brown recalled this resonance with her own experience of finding hope in the works of Black women writers. She described being newly married and dropping out of college, pregnant with her and Kevin's second child. "I was in a really dark, depressed place," she said, "until I started reading Maya Angelou's *I Know Why the Caged Bird Sings*." Brown told me about the impact that had on her, as a young African American woman with one child and another on the way. "I came back to life," she said, telling me the story of how Kevin then went out and bought her every book that Maya Angelou had ever written. "And I consumed all of them," she added.

In Palestine, Angela Brown and Vera Baboun connected, initially over the impact of the work of Maya Angelou on their lives but eventually on broader shared experiences of trauma and injustice. On coming to recognize shared struggles through storytelling and narrative sharing, Angela recalled, "I think that, in and of itself, is healing because you see that we're not the only ones that have gone through this, and we're not the only ones who have come out. There's hope." Angela Brown's personal story and the story of her journey from despair to hope is central to the identity of The Perfecting Church. It is something she shares openly in the church and in her wider work and ministry, including in writing for an audience beyond her church on the topic of women's empowerment. And her story has resonated especially with Palestinian women. Reflecting on points of connection between Palestinians, like Vera Baboun, and African Americans, Angela Brown added, "I also see us being able to stand in the middle. Jews played a very vital role in the civil rights movement because of their experience with the Holocaust. And now, African Americans are being placed in a position really of privilege, where we can go to both sides, where now Palestinians relate to us as African Americans."

There is a persistent tension for The Perfecting Church—beginning with the church's pastors—between their strong identification with Palestinians and their desire to avoid taking sides. On the unique connection between African Americans and Palestinians that Kevin, Angela, and members of their church have felt, Kevin Brown said, "Our presence, physically [in Palestine], is hope because Palestinians watch the African American experience . . . they know about our experiences here in the United States." He has come to see how Palestinians have looked to the racial progress of African Americans as a source of hope. "They've seen African Americans through President Obama's rise to the highest office in the land. So it's incredible hope."

Kevin Brown also described part of their motivation for working in Palestine as wanting to challenge what he sees as the prevailing Christian Zionist assumptions of many African Americans. "More African Americans need to be there because many African Americans are Zionists. And we've inherited that thinking not just from our seminaries but from our spiritual experiences. Our churches have shaped us to be Zionists. And when we get our feet on the ground, I think we'd be shocked how quickly we would relate to the Palestinian rather than the Israeli. . . . Spiritually we'd think we would immediately relate to the Israeli. Now, that can be dangerous. So I've worked on interacting with both sides.

And you might have heard me constantly say Jesus chose the cross, not a side." Summarizing The Perfecting Church's aspiration to bridge "both sides," Brown said, "We want to be ambassadors for Jesus Christ, ministers of reconciliation when we're there."

I had multiple conversations with eleven members of The Perfecting Church who have traveled to Palestine with pastors Kevin and Angela Brown at least once, six of those took part in the trip I joined in 2015. A common thread linking those members, who varied widely in age, occupation, and education, was their affection for their pastors as spiritual leaders and mentors, and their commitment to following the example of not taking sides, even when they felt themselves sympathizing primarily with Palestinians. One twenty-six-year-old woman who traveled to Palestine with the church in 2015 applauded Kevin Brown's vision for global engagement, going beyond the local, "We sometimes lose sight of what's happening in the rest of the world because we're concerned about our own little comfort zone, our own little world. . . . That's why I think The Perfecting Church is so involved with doing work globally, is to make people aware that life isn't just here, in Burlington Township, New Jersey." Another church member in her fifties described Pastor Kevin as being "like a magnet," saying how "he fit the mold" of what she was looking for in a pastor. She explained why she admires her pastor: "What The Perfecting Church is doing is an act of selflessness. They're not just focusing on building numbers, they're focusing on what God feels is important. And it's his people, not just here but abroad." Virtually all of the church members I spoke with expressed some version of this admiration for their pastors and their shared vision for global engagement and the ministry of reconciliation. Some had even followed pastors Kevin and Angela from their previous church ministry when they founded The Perfecting Church, specifically because of that vision.

Although members of The Perfecting Church who visit Palestine aim to walk the path of reconciliation and reject taking sides, many feel the same kind of tension Kevin and Angela Brown describe in wanting to identify more with the plight of Palestinians. "I definitely will say that the lion's share of my opinion was formed on [the Palestinian] side," explained a high school teacher in his fifties. "I definitely developed a sense of empathy, understood exactly what they were going through," he added. Another TPC lay leader and trip coordinator similarly confessed, "I needed help to not take sides. Because I found myself, my heart, hardening to Israel, and it was beginning to harden and I felt it. . . . Because I saw so much of my own people's pain [in the Palestinians]." He described asking for divine intervention to help him not pick sides. Another trip participant, a male pastor in training preparing to lead his own satellite congregation of The Perfecting Church, said he felt that the engagement trip perhaps spent too much time with Palestinians. "I started seeing a lot of our thoughts shifting and solely focusing on the Palestinian struggle." "Why don't we start engaging more Israelis?" he asked. "And not just the ones who feel how we feel but the ones who feel the opposite of what we feel," he continued. "Because in my humble opinion, that's how you start really bridging gaps."

Members of The Perfecting Church follow the lead of their senior pastors, Kevin and Angela Brown, in their vision for glocal church engagement that links the global and the local, and in their specific struggles to transcend their inclination to side with Palestinians in favor of a "both sides" approach, aspiring to be bridge builders and agents of reconciliation. Thus, as pastors, Kevin and Angela Brown act as both brokers and mobilizers, directing the interests and energies of their members but also training them to think in a particular way about race, politics, and theology.

Building on this attention to personal narratives and the roles they play in how African American pastors act as both brokers and mobilizers on the issue of Israel and Palestine, chapter 4 looks more closely at the role of travel to Israel and Palestine in the contestation of Black religious politics. In Israel and Palestine, some African American Christians emphasize "walking where Jesus walked," whereas others prioritize "walking where Jesus is walking now." These mandates in the Holy Land frame Black Christian experiences in ways that connect to broader Black religious-political impulses. For African American Christian Zionists, "walking where Jesus walked" goes along with "preaching where he preached," and both contribute to a kind of pastoral status and authority deployed in brokering Christian Zionism among Black churchgoers. For African American Christians who prioritize engaging with Palestinians, the global racial solidarities opened up and experienced in Palestine are meant to mobilize Black churches in race-focused political engagement more broadly.

CHAPTER 4

Walking in the Footsteps of a Whitewashed Jesus?

I was sitting in a mall food court in the Jerusalem suburb of Mevaseret with two of my fellow travelers on a trip to Israel sponsored by the African American Pentecostal Church of God in Christ (COGIC). One was Lennox, the pastor of an Ohio COGIC congregation in his fifties. When we first met in the baggage claim area at Ben Gurion airport in Tel Aviv, Lennox told me that he did not grow up going to church but had found his way to the Church of God in Christ and full-time ministry after serving in the Marine Corps and attending Ohio State University. Also sitting with us was Ella, in her early sixties and retired from a career as a corrections officer in California. She grew up attending a Baptist church with her family but got involved with COGIC as a teenager. Her husband is a Baptist, and she still maintains ties to her denominational roots but primarily serves as a lay leader helping to facilitate COGIC national meetings. "I've been Bap-COGIC all my life. . . . That's my made-up term," Ella said, laughing as she described her joint affiliation and hybrid identity. Lennox and Ella were among the more outspoken members on the COGIC trip to Israel. Lennox was not shy in speaking his mind about what he thought of our experiences in the Holy Land as they unfolded. Ella has a quick wit and was always ready to keep her fellow travelers, including Lennox, on time and in line.

We were a week into our ten-day tour and had just finished a busy morning schedule that included a stop at a military museum and memorial site for the Israel Defense Forces Armored Corps and a visit to an absorption center for Ethiopian Jewish immigrants to Israel. When I took the empty seat at the table with Lennox and Ella, Lennox was talking about how he felt pressured to donate money that morning when one of the Jewish trip coordinators took up an impromptu collection at the end of the visit to the Ethiopian absorption center.

They brought me up to speed on the conversation: "There's a lot of politicking to the trip with the emphasis on Ethiopians and Black Israelis," said Lennox. "It's overkill now," he added. "We get the message. I've got some Black people at home that need help." Ella was quick to shoot back: "You better get used to it because this is what [this trip] is about. You're gonna keep hearing about it—it's a *mission*." Ella was echoing the trip's promotional materials that promised:

> This is not just a tour, this is a MISSION! The mission will include informative meetings, visits to the community, on-location teachings, fervent services, and amazing praise & worship. Naturally, we will visit all the biblical and historical Christian and Jewish sites. . . . You will experience the Bible come alive before your very eyes!

The mission emphasis of the tour was often repeated by trip leaders and other members as a guiding framework for the experience. But it hardly settled the question of the trip purpose for travelers like Pastor Lennox. Varied goals—from touring, to spiritual experiences, to serving a mission—proved to be difficult for trip leaders to harmonize, as Lennox's reaction suggests. There, in the land of Israel, over a plate of Chinese food, Lennox was trying to make sense of the tensions he had been experiencing over the past week of traveling in the Holy Land with a delegation including lay church members, pastors, and national leaders from his COGIC denomination. When we spoke a few weeks after the trip, he elaborated:

> The whole trip was designed according to Ethiopians. . . . So you have to politic that piece, you have to market that piece. . . . I'm coming to Israel to learn about Israel and that's a good thing, but then I'm also coming because of the Ethiopian part too. But you're making me pay *my* money for *your* politics. . . . I could have done without any of that. . . . I came for Jesus. I came for the Holy Land experience—to see where he walked.

He went on to describe his preferred vision of how this trip could have had a different balance of priorities. The purpose of the trip was an important point of contention for him—after all, he had paid *his* money to be in the Holy Land. What was this trip supposed to be? What was it about? And how did the experience fit with the religious and political sensibilities that participants brought with them from their congregations and communities at home?

This trip was a follow-up "mission" for COGIC, which had been invited the previous year by the International Fellowship of Christians and Jews (IFCJ) to tour Israel on an all-expenses-paid leadership delegation. About twenty COGIC national and international leaders took part in that first trip in 2015. The trip that I shared with Lennox, Ella, and forty other COGIC travelers came a year later, in late summer 2016. Like the 2015 leadership delegation, this trip included a number of denominational leaders and pastors, but it was also opened to lay members of COGIC. The goal, according to the trip's organizer, Glenn Plummer, was to build on the connections made on the IFCJ-led trip, especially connections with the Ethiopian community in Israel. But on this trip, and all of the trips I took to the region across the cases of engagement with Palestine and Israel presented in this book, the ostensible purpose varied greatly depending on who I asked. The purposes of these trips also differed significantly from each other, indicating very different priorities for various stakeholders.

AFRICAN AMERICAN CHRISTIAN TRAVEL TO ISRAEL AND PALESTINE

African American trips to Israel and Palestine often begin at the initiative of sponsoring organizations: the IFCJ, Christians United for Israel (CUFI), The Perfecting Church (TPC), and the Samuel DeWitt Proctor Conference (SDPC). These organizations and their leaders play an important role in shaping trip priorities, narratives, and potential outcomes. But these trips ultimately involve a number of stakeholders, including individual participants, trip coordinators, professional tour guides, lead pastors, supporting staff, and in-country contacts representing NGOs, religious institutions, government agencies, etc.—all of whom bring their own experiences and outlooks on intersections of race, religion, and politics to these trips.

In this chapter, I consider the role of travel to Israel and Palestine across the book's four case studies. I argue that the land is a crucial site of formation for African American Christian positions on the religious and political significance of the Holy Land. But I suggest that it is also a site for the formation of Black religious politics more broadly, where national and local concerns and dispositions are reworked in the global context of a foreign place and in an unfamiliar political landscape. In all four cases, that ostensibly distant context is made to feel closer to home for participants, who often come to see their own experiences as African Americans being relevant to interpreting the politics of the region and their connection to Israelis and Palestinians as a shared struggle.

In the highly politicized Christian Zionist paradigm of CUFI, African American Christians are presented with an image and experience of the State of Israel as a beleaguered democratic state surrounded by threatening antidemocratic forces—most notably the threat of radical Islam and "global jihad." Israel is thus presented—and *experienced*—as America's closest ally and an outpost for democracy on the front lines of the global war on terror. The Samuel DeWitt Proctor Conference, with its network of Black clergy and activists, also takes a more overtly political approach to understanding and experiencing the land. Largely rejecting the notion of a spiritualized pilgrimage or Holy Land tourism, Proctor activists visiting Israel and Palestine tend to focus on the everyday experiences of Palestinians within Israel and the Occupied Palestinian Territories, seeing parallels with African American experiences and those of marginalized peoples of color around the world. The International Fellowship of Christians and Jews and The Perfecting Church take less explicitly political approaches to understanding and experiencing the Holy Land, but politics inevitably creeps into even ostensibly apolitical trips to the region.

In this chapter, I show how the overlapping religious and political orientations of African American Christians represented by these four cases exemplify distinct approaches to Black religious politics, on both national and global levels. Trips to Israel and Palestine, variously conceived and carried out, are sites for connecting national-level and global-level expressions of Black religious political identity and action. In each case, a disposition within the national field of Black religious politics in the United States forms the basis for global-level engagement. But it is important to note that global expressions of various visions of Black religious politics and Black church identity are neither fixed nor predetermined. Instead they emerge from a number of contingencies that arise during the experience of visiting Israel and Palestine—as a material place, as a malleable landscape of cultural meaning, and as a site of embodied experience. In all four cases, the primary tension that shapes how national-level and global-level modes of Black religious politics are formed is the tension between religion and politics. Guided experiences of the land by CUFI and SDPC expressly fuse religion and politics but in very different ways, revealing nearly polar opposite orientations toward Black religious politics in national and global terms. TPC's glocal model for engagement in the land emphasizes a religious imperative for peacebuilding and reconciliation and engages with Palestinian civil society through social work, business development, the arts, and sports. The IFCJ emphasizes Israel as a site for a Christian mission in charitable and philanthropic terms. But as I will show, an alternative notion of "mission" in Israel—as proselytizing and evangelism—is also opened within the Fellowship's African American outreach work.

Across these cases, I argue that trips to Israel and Palestine can be seen as a microcosm of the tensions of Black religious politics in the United States on less familiar terms. The Holy Land is an important site of connection between the national field of Black religious politics and the global field. It is a salient global site in the Black American religious imaginary and a place where the national-global connection is realized and formed. It is also a place where competing dispositions toward Black religious politics are contested—sometimes through a sort of trial and error—as various stakeholders compete to define trip priorities and to impose an overall outlook on Palestine and Israel. These competing priorities and corresponding outlooks sometimes mesh with existing religious-political sensibilities African American Christian travelers bring with them, but sometimes they clash. For African American Christian Zionist visitors to the Holy Land, religious identity tends to be at the forefront of their experience of Israel and Palestine, and racial identity is relegated to a secondary position. The primary lens offered to Black Christian Zionist visitors is a universal Christian experience that transcends race. This opens the possibility of emerging political solidarities based on broader Black-Jewish connections and novel recognitions of racial diversity among Israeli Jews. For some African American Christians more focused on Palestinian solidarity, however, racial identity is prioritized over the traditional religious significance of the Holy Land. For these travelers, the metaphor of an "unholy land" becomes more apt, and traditional notions of religious pilgrimage and accompanying Zionist narratives are cast as "whitewashed" experiences of the land, reflecting the priorities of a whitewashed Jesus. There is a double meaning here, of course. On one hand, African American critics of Christian Zionism see subsidized Holy Land pilgrimage tours as a tool of the State of Israel and its political allies, useful for presenting the land in idealized and sanitized terms that perpetuate the oppression of Palestinians. On the other hand, this critique invokes racial politics, suggesting that an authentically Black experience of Israel and Palestine requires a different kind of engagement in the land—one that shuns the tourist trail and the well-worn pilgrim path.

In the following sections, I consider moments of synthesis between the religious politics of Israelis and Palestinians and those of the African American Christian travelers who come to the land for various reasons and with divergent expectations about what the experience means for them and their communities and churches in the United Sates. I pay particular attention to which narratives about the land and its peoples "stick" with visiting Black church leaders and lay members. In presenting and unpacking these tensions, I include attention to several cultural concepts: embodiment, memory, materiality, and authenticity. Together these concepts structure the experiences of the land for African American Christian visitors and, in turn, shape competing dispositions toward Black religious politics more broadly. First, I briefly outline a range of approaches to studying African American Christian Holy Land travel, beginning with the traditional notion of pilgrimage. I show how the pilgrimage imperative to "walk where Jesus walked" is salient across these cases of African American Christian engagement with Israel and Palestine. I also show how these groups conceive of and organize African American Christian travel in the land and how they transcend this spiritual mode of encountering and experiencing the Holy Land, incorporating other trip priorities stemming from competing visions of Black religious politics.

WHAT ARE THESE TRIPS?

Christian religious pilgrimage to Israel and Palestine has been well documented in historical and contemporary contexts, with Jerusalem notably standing as the first true pilgrimage site within Christendom.[1] Israel and Palestine are "the Holy Land" of not one but three major religions. Pilgrimage to Jerusalem was a part of biblical Judaism at least as early as the First Temple period, and later Christians and Muslims began to travel to Jerusalem for religious reasons. For many centuries, these trips were attainable only for very wealthy and very pious travelers. This changed with the advent of modern secular tourism to the region in sixteenth-century Europe and increased dramatically in the nineteenth century, most notably with the organized tourism to Jerusalem offered by the English travel agency Thomas Cook beginning in 1869.[2] Organized tours became the blueprint for the type of Holy Land tourism that most visitors engage in today, with large groups of all kinds traveling together on a fixed itinerary and led by a professional tour guide. With the advent of such tours, travel to the Holy Land became highly accessible, blurring the line between pilgrimage and tourism—between sacred and secular purposes. Today Christian travel to the region persists in high numbers, with 56 percent of Israel's 3.3 million visitors identifying as Christian pilgrims or tourists in 2014.[3]

WHAT IS PILGRIMAGE?

In seminal anthropological studies of pilgrimage, Victor and Edith Turner portray pilgrimage as a specific kind of religious ritual.[4] They develop an approach to understanding pilgrimage in its institutional form—attending to the structure of values, norms, symbols, customs, roles, and relationships that are manifested in religious pilgrimage—focusing primarily on pilgrimage as a form of religious praxis. Pilgrimages are a type of social process consisting of liminal (or in-between) social relations outside of the bureaucracy and the regularity of mundane social life. These liminal relations are characterized by ambiguity of social positions and a sense of what the Turners call *communitas*—the condition under which particular kinds of homogeneity and comradeship that would be impossible in pilgrims' everyday social contexts are made possible on pilgrimage.[5] The Turners' work on pilgrimage also acknowledges the extent to which modern pilgrimage has become connected to international markets for leisure as a commodity, linking ritual aspects of pilgrimage with modern tourism.[6] Furthermore, anthropologists and scholars of religion have advanced this outlook on pilgrimage, linking it increasingly to the everyday.[7]

In light of this widely recognized complexity, we need to be cautious and avoid taking for granted the meaning of religious travel for participants and assuming a traditional definition of pilgrimage as a social phenomenon. In addition to presenting travel to Israel and Palestine as a site for competing visions of Black religious politics connecting national and global fields, I suggest that attention to African American Christian travel to Israel and Palestine can also advance a richer, more capacious view of pilgrimage. In this approach, pilgrimage is a social site full of incumbent tensions and contestations that make it less divorced from the everyday exigencies of social life than more ritual-focused theories of pilgrimage suggest. Paying attention to how economic, political, organizational, associational, and religious factors all contribute to the pilgrimage or "Holy Land travel" experience is key.[8]

BEYOND PILGRIMAGE

Extending studies of Holy Land pilgrimage beyond attention to ritual, scholars have variously paid attention to the political, touristic, and missionizing ramifications and complexities of religiously motivated travel to the Holy Land. Furthermore, religious travel as "pilgrimage" has increasingly been studied as a phenomenon wielded by political actors competing for recognition and territorial control, especially in Israel and Palestine.[9] A number of recent studies of religious travel have paid increasing attention to how contemporary pilgrimage intersects with tourism, occurring within a market for the production and consumption of symbolic products and experiences of foreign places. For example, Shaul Kelner's study of Jewish birthright tours of Israel suggests that tourism studies can contribute to understanding religiously inspired travel by highlighting the "centrality of symbolic consumption to self and society in market economies."[10] Hillary Kaell, in a study of American Christian Holy Land pilgrims, similarly notes the tension between religion, commercialization, tourism, and the consumption of a "global experience" in the pilgrimage process. Kaell also recognizes the extent to which commodities are present and deeply embedded in religious worlds and in the lived experiences of religious people.[11] Given this overlap between religion and market economies, it is important to note that tourism is not only about consumption but also about symbolic *production*, as government officials, professional tour guides, and a range of other individual and institutional actors mediate the experiences of tourists.[12] The Christian ethicist Sara Williams has also demonstrated the effects of the tension between symbolic production and consumption within Christian trips to Palestine and Israel, going beyond attention to acquiring "global experiences" into an analysis of processes of commodification and consumption of specific moral and ethical narratives. Williams uses the term "journeys to the margins" for such trips, highlighting them as sites of ethical formation and self-making for foreign visitors seeking to encounter and learn from marginalized groups.[13]

For American Protestants, "the Holy Land" (and the broader Levant) has not only been a site of pilgrimage and tourism but also a site for proselytizing—for Muslims as well as non-Protestant Orthodox and Catholic Christians.[14] As evangelization and conversionary missionary activity remains a priority among the international activities of many American evangelical and charismatic Protestant

Christians, the framework of "mission"—whether in philanthropic/humanitarian terms or as religious proselytizing—is also germane to understanding contemporary African American Christian travel to the Holy Land and how experiences of the land shape Black religious politics more broadly. Beyond these religious models for understanding the social significance of pilgrimage, abundant examples of secular pilgrimage suggest that pilgrimage, as a recognizable social form, is more common that we might think. As an analytic device, pilgrimage has been used to study travel to sites of political, artistic, recreational, and personal significance.[15]

Whether describing the transformation of traditional religious pilgrimage sites or wholly new and secular pilgrimage phenomena, some scholars have described this broadening view of the social significance as an ambiguity about what pilgrimage is and how it works.[16] It is precisely this ambiguity about pilgrimage that animates my approach here. Because we can recognize aspects of pilgrimage in even explicitly nonreligious examples of meaningful travel, we should likewise be motivated to consider the extent to which even the most obviously religious examples of pilgrimage travel—like Christian tours of "the Holy Land" of Israel and Palestine—are multifaceted social phenomena and sites of important cultural contestation and formation. Attention to studies of the kind of travel that has traditionally been understood as pilgrimage helps establish the important starting point that travel to Israel and Palestine is informed by more than just spiritual or religious concerns. As sites of contestation and formation on Black religious politics, linking national and global levels of racialized religious politics, the trips described in this chapter (and elsewhere in this book) are examples of contested social spaces—where ostensibly religious or spiritual purposes are in tension with other priorities.

HOLY LAND TRAVEL, CULTURAL PRODUCTION, AND CONTESTED MEANING

As meaning-laden places, pilgrimage destinations in Israel and Palestine are religious landscapes created by spiritual imaginaries. In his work on collective memory, Maurice Halbwachs describes how religious travelers to the Holy Land bring with them an imagined collective memory of the land as they set out on a pilgrimage, even though they may never have been to the Holy Land before.[17] This collective memory becomes overlaid onto the site of pilgrimage, giving meaning to the material place and taking meaning from it. In other words, as the sociologist Vida Bajc puts it, religious travelers to the Holy Land "look for places that will make [their] beliefs come alive."[18] Certain locations and types of experiences come to the forefront to inspire the American Protestant religious imagination and facilitate religious experiences. As pilgrims, the American Christian travelers I studied seek to walk in the footsteps of Jesus and other biblical figures to become more Christ-like in their own lives. As the Turners put it, "Pilgrimage is one way, perhaps the most literal, of imitating the religious founder. By visiting the site believed to be the sites of his life and teaching mission, the pilgrim imagination relives those events."[19] In this mode, Kaell calls contemporary Holy Land pilgrimage "the ultimate mimetic act" and a way for pilgrims to feel like and be construed as good Christians with spiritual expertise and authority.[20]

With their rejection of traditionally venerated Catholic and Orthodox places of worship in the Holy Land and their capacity for embodied spiritual experiences, American Protestant Christians often use Holy Land travel to imagine and enact performatively an embodied religious experience. They link themselves to Bible characters and places through their experiences in "the land of the Bible." In this way, material culture also plays an important role in shaping pilgrimage experiences. In addition to the collective memories American Christians—including African American Christians—carry with them to Israel and Palestine, the meanings and forms of their pilgrimages depend significantly on processes of making sense of "the Holy Land" as a material place. Meaning-making processes related to encounters with and experiences of natural and human material conditions play an important role in shaping what Holy Land travel is for American Christians. A nonmaterial emphasis on the Bible as scripture in the Protestant religious imagination—through its reading, recitation, memorization, and contemplation in prayer—has been pointed out by a number of anthropologists and sociologists of religion.[21] In other words, the Bible—as words, as text—does much to return Protestant Christians to the master story of their religion over and against more material points of reference for collective identity and shared belief. Although it is true that the text, *as text*, has inspired the Protestant religious imagination, the experience of material places and artifacts connected to the Bible are also significant to understanding American Protestant religiosity and how it is connected to economic and political forces. For African American travelers, collective cultural memory also has racial significance in Israel and Palestine because contemporary African American Christian travelers to the Holy Land carry with them collective memories and identifications with the Israel of the Bible and the Exodus narrative in particular.[22] They also sometimes carry more recent legacies of Black-Jewish[23] and Afro-Arab[24] spiritual connections and political solidarities.

Collective memories, material and embodied experiences of the land, and racialized solidarities are contested aspects of contemporary African American Christian travel to Palestine and Israel. Because of this, even the seemingly basic notion of "walking in the footsteps of Jesus" can mean different things to different African American Christian travelers to the Holy Land. For some, well-established pilgrimage sites operating as tourist attractions provide the context for an authentic religious experience of the land—including walking where Jesus (and other biblical figures) are said to have walked, preaching where they preached, and praying where they prayed. For others, an authentic religious experience of the land requires looking elsewhere, away from what is perceived as a well-worn, overly touristic pilgrimage path. For some of the travelers I accompanied, for example, this meant choosing not to offer prayers at the Western Wall of the ancient Jewish temple in Jerusalem, but instead praying at the Israeli West Bank barrier wall (alternatively called "the security wall," "the separation wall," or even "the Apartheid wall," depending on one's perspective) in solidarity with Palestinians. On the surface, this juxtaposition may look like an embrace of pilgrimage in religious and spiritual terms or as a rejection of that outlook. I suggest, however, that both represent distinctly religious outlooks on the Holy Land, conceived in different terms and reflecting different visions of Black religious politics.

Ultimately, I argue that the land is a site of social contestation for African American Christian travelers, where competing collective memories and frameworks for Black religious political engagement contend with each other. On these trips, African American Christians deal with tensions between political activism and quietism in their collective histories and identities. Through these intragroup contestations, intergroup racial solidarities with Israeli Jews or Arab Palestinians become increasingly possible (or impossible) for trip participants. In my fieldwork, these tensions and contestations were most apparent when it came to identifying the purposes of Holy Land trips. As noted previously, I found that participants consistently asked themselves, their leaders, and each other—explicitly and implicitly—What is the purpose of this trip? This persistent question opened a range of notions of what trips *should* be about for the African American Christians with whom I traveled. Were participants there primarily for individual and collective spiritual reasons, or to learn about the history and politics of the region (with some impetus to act politically on that knowledge)? Or were they there on some kind of "mission" of Christian service? Were they tourists, just looking to get away on a vacation? I consistently found tensions expressed between these purposes across different trips with various organizations and within specific trips. Various stakeholders—including pastors, denominational leaders, trip organizers, representatives of sponsoring organizations, professional tour guides, and others—present trip purposes in different terms and to varying effects. At times competing priorities clashed, at other times a level of synthesis was achieved. In all cases, no trip in which I participated could be properly categorized with a single label representing one overarching priority. Some groups did rally remarkably around a single unifying trip purpose, whereas others were more contested and questioned throughout. But all of these trips, to some degree, were contested and multifaceted.

The next two sections outline how—in many ways and across these cases—African American Christian travel to Israel and Palestine invokes traditional notions of pilgrimage around the idea of "walking where Jesus walked." Following this, I take a closer look at travel to Palestine and Israel that shows competing conceptions, enactments, and embodiments of African American religiosity playing out in the Holy Land. For each case, I highlight tensions over appropriate guiding priorities, emphases, and narratives to illustrate how core tensions within trips reflect priorities that derive from competing dispositions of Black religious politics in the United States. In this context, the land of Israel and Palestine can be understood as a global setting in which U.S. Black religious politics are enacted with reference to these existing dispositions. Because the land presents an unfamiliar cultural, political, and material setting—one that is ripe with opportunities for solidarity-building across religious, national, and racial lines—various forms of African American Christian political identity are reformed, expanded, redefined, and redeployed on trips to Israel and Palestine.

WALKING WHERE JESUS WALKED

Religiously motivated Holy Land travel is a personal and community religious experience for travelers who see themselves, in at least some capacity, as pilgrims on a religious trip. For such travelers, this includes experiences of spiritual renewal, healing, personal transformation, "going deeper" in their faith, and becoming equipped to preach or read the Bible differently (see chapter 3). Some form of the religious imperative of "walking where Jesus walked" or related notions of experiencing the Holy Land—like feeling the Bible "come alive"—were nearly ubiquitous among the Black Christians I traveled with on Holy Land trips.

Late into the evening at the end of the first busy day of touring biblical sites, I sat with about twenty members of the COGIC group in a hotel conference room to debrief the day's experiences and to prepare for the rest of the trip. As each person took turns speaking, the significance of walking where Jesus walked came up for most participants. Talking about the Bible "coming alive" for him, one man emphasized, "It's not just words on a page—it's real!" One woman said, "I wanna suck up as much as I can from the spiritual realm while I'm here." Another added, "I'm looking for God to bless me in a big way. I know that my life is gonna change. . . . God is gonna anoint me while I'm here, and I'm gonna leave here with full power."

The significance of being in "the Holy Land" or in "the land of the Bible" was variously expressed by spiritually minded travelers in both general and specific terms. A female physician in her thirties on the same COGIC trip expressed her expectation of spiritual transformation and empowerment in uncertain terms:

> I felt going into the trip that I was expecting a transformation of some kind, I didn't know what kind of transformation, I didn't know what to expect in terms of the details of what that meant but I felt that I was being called at that time as a transformation in my ministry somehow . . . I feel more empowered spiritually.

Similarly, a COGIC music and ministry leader, in Israel for the third time and who had also been part of the 2015 IFCJ-led leadership delegation, described the experience of returning to the Holy Land as one of refueling for ministry:

> For me, it was an opportunity to enrich myself once again . . . to just be in that environment, to let it soak into my spiritual pores, so that I come back and I exude the authentic mindset of God. . . . And so, for me, it's a filling station; it's the ability to learn and to glean so much more than what I know because every time I go, I learn something new. Then I'm able to come back and share that with the constituency that I've been placed over.

Others traveled to the Holy Land in search of specific healing and miracles. One female lay leader in her seventies on the National Baptist Convention of America tour, led by the IFCJ, told me about the most meaningful part of the Holy Land experience for her. She described standing in the Garden of Gethsemane—where Jesus spent his last night before being crucified—praying for her daughter suffering from cancer. "She has been on chemo daily for almost five years now. . . . And I stood there at that garden, and I prayed and asking the Lord that [she would become] cancer free."

The significance of visiting biblical sites can also be about a material and embodied experience that enhances the traveler's religious imagination and ability to identify with biblical figures. On a trip with The Perfecting Church, one woman similarly spoke about how being in places of spiritual significance captured her imagination and her view of the Bible:

> It was amazing to think about. For instance, when we went to Gethsemane and to think that this is the tree that Jesus knelt down and he was praying. And this might be the tree or the area where Peter sliced off the soldier's ear. Would I have been like Peter and sliced off the soldier's ear? . . . It was like the Bible coming alive.

The religious impetus to "walk where Jesus walked" and to pursue an embodied experience of the land of the Bible did not resonate only with those on pro-Israel Christian Zionists tours. Across all four cases in this book, the significance of the land as ostensibly holy was salient. But in some cases it was a point of political critique rather than a basis for personal and embodied spiritual experience.

The pilgrimage experiences of the African American Christians I studied was not limited to trying to experience personal transformation, imitate Christ, or enhance religious imagination, it also includes the impetus to better understand the stories and the message to become better equipped for ministry. This dynamic was often expressed by pastors as learning to "preach differently" in their home churches and ministries. Chapter 3 includes the stories of several pastors who were equipped by their experiences in Israel and encouraged by trip pastoral leaders to "preach differently." When pastors shape their preaching ministry after a spiritual pilgrimage experience of the Holy Land, laypeople feel equipped to "read the word differently." For both pastors and laypeople, there is a strong performative aspect to pilgrimage in the Holy Land when experienced pastors model this kind of preaching and Bible reading to first-time visitors who, in the course of the trip, come to see the potential to elevate their preaching and exposition of the Bible as someone who has "been there." The meaning of the trip becomes embodied, as the act of walking where Jesus and other Bible figures walked enables travelers to imagine themselves in the Bible's stories. The symbolic meaning of the trip is also performed as pastors learn from "preaching where they preached" and touching or seeing the places they inhabited and carry that experience with them to impart to their congregations when they return.

REJECTING AND REFRAMING "WALKING WHERE JESUS WALKED"

Among the clergy and activists of the Proctor Conference network, the spiritual imperative of travel to the so-called Holy Land is reframed. On the second night of the Proctor Conference's annual meeting in 2016, Reverend Neichelle Guidry preached a sermon on her recent experience on a Proctor-sponsored delegation of clergy to Israel and Palestine. She rejected the notion of "walking where Jesus walked," but she did so without ceding the spiritual imperative of the trip:

> No, we did not go to the "Holy Land" to walk in the sanctified footsteps of a whitewashed Jesus and lay our hands on the place where he wept in the Garden of Gethsemane. We did not go under the guise of being good Christian Zionist pilgrims, who unquestioningly sow our dollars into the occupation of people who look just like us. No, we went to see about our people, to learn about what they are facing on a day-to-day basis, and just how they are holding their lives, their families, their spirits, and their humanities together.

Further invoking an alternative religious paradigm for her experience in the land, Guidry explained:

> We were sent to survey the land, to open our eyes and our ears and to see the struggle of our Brown brothers and sisters in and through the Holy City of Jerusalem and throughout the West Bank. Through the force of our visits to Palestinian villages, refugee camps, and homes, I was baptized by fire into a

deep melancholic aching of awakeness of the global oppression of Black and Brown bodies. And into a greater understanding of the interconnectedness of our stories and our struggles.

On several of my trips to the Holy Land with African American Christians, I saw Black participants deeply moved by the experience of being baptized in the waters of the Jordan River, imitating the baptism of Jesus. Here, Guidry invokes a different kind of baptism—a baptism into the mundane realities of Palestinian life under occupation. For her, the connection realized in traveling to the land was not just material or political but spiritual. She later explained to me, "I think it was the similarities not only in the conditions but also in the spirit, right. Like this kind of sense of resistance being the work of the spirit." In describing Palestinian resistance as "the work of the spirit," Guidry holds to a spiritual and religious impetus for her travels in Palestine and Israel, while simultaneously rejecting the typical pilgrimage experience as "whitewashed," and thus not being attuned to the social and political dynamics of race and the suffering of Palestinians.

This echoes the sentiments of Bishop Don Williams, who helped bring the Palestinian issue to the attention of the Proctor Conference and leaders like Guidry. Reflecting on his visits to Palestine, Williams wrote:

> When I came back from my two trips to the West Bank, I was asked by many of my friends what it felt like to walk where Jesus walked. I told them it felt good to walk where Jesus walked but it felt even better to walk where Jesus is walking today and that is with those who are undervalued, underestimated and marginalized.[25]

The trope of "walking where Jesus walked" is not rejected out of hand for African American critics of Christian Zionism. Rather it is reframed to ask, Where is Jesus walking today? This juxtaposition of the spiritually formative embodied experience of being in the land versus a more politicized alternative religious imperative to open one's eyes to the region's injustices does not neatly separate Christian Zionist and Palestinian-focused African American Christian travel to the land. The following sections elaborate on how the organizations and the individuals within each of this book's cases frame travel to the Holy Land. Both Christian Zionist and Palestine-focused trips provide contexts in which tensions between the ostensibly spiritual and the more overtly political purposes play out.

"I WENT THERE A TOURIST AND I THINK I LEFT A ZIONIST": CUFI BRIDGING THE BIBLE AND POLITICS FOR AFRICAN AMERICAN CHRISTIANS

In his tenure as African American outreach coordinator for Christians United for Israel (CUFI), Michael Stevens traveled the United States and the globe, recruiting Black pastors and churchgoers to CUFI's advocacy work on behalf of the State of Israel. In his seminars and sermons in this outreach work, Stevens refers to the moral, spiritual, theological, and biblical reasons Christians—particularly African American Christians—should "stand with Israel." Across these categories, he appeals to a kind of authority that traveling to Israel bestows on pastors. To a gathering of Black pastors in New Jersey he explained:

> I've been to Israel going on nine or ten times now. It's a joy. You'll never preach the same. Not only will you not preach the same but you won't teach the same. You cannot go there, walk at Capernaum, walk where Jesus walked, see where the miracles took place, understand the Mediterranean, the culture, the people. You will not come home and preach and teach the same way.

The starting point for CUFI's outreach is an appeal to the desire of many African American Christians to visit the Holy Land. This appeal carries significant weight for Black pastors and churchgoers (see chapter 3). On CUFI trips to Israel, that desire is met and overlaid with a political narrative about the State of Israel that encompasses perceived threats from its enemies and the necessity for its military and political responses to those threats. The goal is to take Christians who have a baseline affinity for Israel as the land of the Bible and turn them into staunch allies for the State of Israel in political terms. In other words, to make Zionists out of tourists. In a 2018 fund-raising letter, CUFI founder John Hagee and director David Brog emphasized the importance of travel to Israel for the organization's mission of religious and political pro-Israel advocacy:

> Early on, we realized that one thing held more power than anything else to transform a passively pro-Israel or neutral Christian bystander into a passionate Zionist[—]a personal experience with the land and the people of Israel.

These newly energized Zionists then return to their sphere of influence and are compelled by their love of Israel and the Jewish people to take action.[26]

In his Israel-focused speeches and sermons, Hagee often describes his first visit to Israel in 1978 when he "went to Israel as a tourist and came back a Zionist." This is a frequent refrain among CUFI pastors and activists, connecting the religious imperative to visit Israel on a pilgrimage with the political mission of the organization. David Walker, an African American college campus organizer for CUFI, shared a similar story, making the connection between attracting American Christians to pro-Israel advocacy work through Holy Land travel. When he spoke at a college audience "CUFI on Campus" event in Western New York, he said:

> My first trip to Israel . . . that was really where my activism was awakened. I went there a tourist, and I think I left there a Zionist. Because I saw a lot of the interesting sites that really spoke to me, being where Jesus was. . . . Once you go to Israel, it multiplies your faith. Because you see that, this faith that we have, this gospel that we preach is *real*. These figures that we talk about, these heroes that we draw inspiration from; they were real. . . . It made me stronger and have more conviction in what I believe. And it made me more of a Zionist.

Every year CUFI takes hundreds of pastors on what it calls "familiarization trips" to Israel. These pastors travel at CUFI's expense (or are highly subsidized). Thousands of laypeople have traveled on CUFI-sponsored trips too; these participants pay their own way, typically $3,000 to $5,000 for a trip lasting a week to ten days. One of the obligations for participating pastors on a subsidized trip is to organize a CUFI seminar in their home church for other pastors in their local networks—or their "sphere of influence," as Stevens calls it.

In working to turn passively pro-Israel tourists into politically active Christian Zionists, CUFI takes the enthusiasm pastors have for visiting Israel as "the land of the Bible" and translates that into related enthusiasm for supporting the State of Israel politically. One of the ways they accomplish this is by adding sites of political significance to a typical Holy Land itinerary otherwise focused on religious sites. These political tour stops include visits to the Israeli Knesset and meetings and briefings with politicians and activists, and visits to Israeli military bases and absorption centers for Ethiopian Jewish immigrants. In my conversations with pastors and lay church members who traveled on CUFI-sponsored trips to Israel, almost everyone I spoke to shared a story that linked spiritual motivations for traveling with more politically oriented takeaways from the trip experience. When I asked CUFI travelers why they wanted to visit Israel, over and over again they told me it had always been a dream of theirs to visit Israel—to walk where Jesus walked, to see the land of the Bible. They talked about their motivations almost exclusively in religious terms. When I asked them what parts of the trip made the greatest impression on them, however, they tended to talk about political lessons as much as religious takeaways. African American CUFI travelers talked about the spiritual significance of being at the Sea of Galilee where Jesus and his disciples ministered, of visiting the Garden Tomb resurrection site in Jerusalem, and of praying in the Garden of Gethsemane. But, like Walker, they also talked about coming away from the trip with a sense of urgency about Israel's political situation.

A North Carolina Baptist pastor who traveled with Stevens on a subsidized pastors' familiarization trip expressed the double impression the trip made on him: "I wanted to go because it is the Holy Land. I wanted to see the sights that we have read and preached about. . . . [And] I think I have begun to pay a little more attention—closer attention—to some of the struggle that has been taking place . . . [and seeing] how seemingly vulnerable the State of Israel is." Another pastor of a nondenominational African American congregation in Pittsburgh similarly described the same trip in spiritual terms, saying it was an experience on a Christian's "bucket list." In addition to recounting some of the spiritual highlights of the trip, he emphasized the significance of learning about Israel's vulnerability to its neighboring enemies. He described the tour that trip pastors got of a strategic military outpost in northern Israel, where the military tour guide pointed out the proximity of Israel's enemies. Recounting the scene, he told me:

> [Our guide] said "look to your left." And we looked to our left, maybe 300 yards. And he said, "right there, that's one of the enemies.". . . He said, "and off to your right, beyond these trees and the mountains, there's Al Qaeda." You know, so they are surrounded by enemies that are like a stone's throw away. . . . And he showed me a rocket that had exploded. The metal was still on the ground. And it was just amazing to know how close people who really want to do you serious harm live in reference to the nation of Israel.

Lay church members who paid their own way to travel to Israel on CUFI-sponsored trips similarly described being impressed at touring Israeli military installations. A female member of Stevens's church in North Carolina, who traveled with him to Israel, talked about how moved she was:

> When we went to the Lebanese border . . . that was fulfilling. It was a little bit scary. I don't think I want to do that again, but it was very fulfilling because we actually had the chance to converse with [Israeli soldiers]. And just to learn how young they were first of all, but how committed they are at such an early age, simply because of what they believe and their level of dedication to it. . . . That was scary, but I enjoyed meeting the soldiers and just hearing their stories.

This work on trips to Israel to transform African American Christian affinity for Israel as the land of the Bible into a political expression of support for Israel as a Jewish state is a broad strategy among politically active Christian Zionists, and it is not unique to African American constituencies. As I described in chapter 1, much of CUFI's work to recruit African American Christians into the otherwise largely white world of Christian Zionist political activism invokes the U.S. civil rights legacy and Black-Jewish partnerships during that time. This pro-Israel civil rights narrative is also a facet of African American–focused CUFI trips. On the first day of their tour in Israel, after visiting the Israeli military base near the border with Lebanon, Stevens and his congregation traveled to a nearby forest planted in memory of Martin Luther King Jr. and his wife Coretta Scott King. This was a trip highlight for many participants. A female member of the trip recalled the visit proudly and beamed as she opened a photo of her at the tree planting site on her iPad to show me. "I'm going to blow it up, and I'm going to put it on the wall," she said, "since I planted a tree in the Holy Land." As we looked at the photo together, she read the text of the sign she was standing next to in the picture: "Coretta Scott King Forest." Another woman on the trip similarly recounted the impression that the visit to the Coretta Scott King Forest made on her early in the tour: "I had no idea, just how involved [Jews] were with civil rights. That's one thing that I learned. When you think about civil rights, you think about just African Americans, but I really didn't know how many Jewish people stood with African Americans back in the sixties." The intended take away on the trip—as it is in CUFI seminars and outreach events for African

American audiences—is that Jews stood with African Americans during the civil rights struggle, so African Americans need to stand with the State of Israel today.

Another racialized mode of translating a religious affinity for Israel into a political position is through the Ethiopian Jewish community in Israel. CUFI takes African American visitors to absorption centers, where recent immigrants making aliyah from Ethiopia live while they are fostered into life in Israel. In addition to being the land of the Bible, the message to visiting African American Christians is that the modern State of Israel is welcoming to racial minorities. Jackie, the participant in Stevens's trip with his home congregation (see chapter 3), told me about the significance of her of visit with Ethiopian immigrants:

> We saw the children who were in front of older people who were making crafts . . . and we went to the younger people who were just learning how to speak English, and understand Hebrew. It was just wonderful, when you are seeing the big shift and people who are trying to give their all into the community. And that they were helping them with that, and I just thought that was amazing.

Through this kind of work in Israel, CUFI brings together two complementary narratives for African American Christians visiting Israel for the first time. First, that the State of Israel is the historic land of the Bible, where Jesus, the prophets, and apostles lived and breathed. And second, that the State of Israel today is a thriving, diverse democracy in need of protection from enemies who want to destroy it from within and without. By bringing together these two narratives, CUFI works to take African American Christians, who identify with the people and the land of the Bible, and turn them into politically engaged Christian Zionists who also identify with the Jewish inhabitants of the land of Israel today. In CUFI's words, the goal is "to act as a defensive shield against anti-Israel lies, boycotts, bad theology, and political threats that seek to delegitimize Israel's existence and weaken the close relationship between Israel and the United States."[27]

In taking African American pastors and lay churchgoers to Israel, CUFI cultivates a form of Black religious politics largely divorced from contemporary domestic racial politics in the United States. Israel is primarily presented as being important to African American Christians because of its efforts to create a diverse, multiracial democracy in the Middle East. The link to domestic racial politics is historical rather than contemporary—the civil rights struggle is upheld as a model for Black-Jewish solidarity that should lead to pro-Israel political advocacy today. As noted in chapter 1, many African American Christians find little in common with CUFI's majority white ranks—represented by leaders like Hagee—beyond an inclination to think favorably about Israel. However, through formative experiences in the Holy Land, CUFI presents African American Christian travelers with an image of the State of Israel as embattled and in need of American support. It also fulfills the lifelong dreams of many to visit the Holy Land and to "walk where Jesus walked." If African American CUFI travelers do not come back ardent Christian Zionists, they tend at least to carry with them a newfound affinity for Israel as a modern nation, and not just as "the land of the Bible." The longer-term political effects of this approach to Holy Land travel among African Americans is less clear, and this is a subject for chapter 5.

"MISSION IS WHAT WE DO!": THE INTERNATIONAL FELLOWSHIP OF CHRISTIANS AND JEWS AND AFRICAN AMERICAN CHRISTIANS

The International Fellowship of Christians and Jews explicitly works to distance itself from what it sees as CUFI's more overtly political Christian Zionist outreach among African American Christians. Similar to CUFI, however, the Fellowship sees its outreach to African American Christians as an opportunity to combine multiple narratives on the State of Israel. In doing so, they create an alternative vision for Black religious politics on a global level through travel and encounters in Israel. Their outreach work begins with an almost identical fundamental appeal to African American Christians (especially pastors and denominational leaders) to visit the land of the Bible, to see it for themselves, and to "walk where Jesus walked." Kristina King, the Fellowship's director of African American outreach, introduced in chapter 1, is one of the key planners and coordinators for the Fellowship's sponsored tours of Israel for African American church leaders. From 2015 to 2017, the Fellowship organized and led all-expenses-paid leadership delegations to Israel for several African American denominations—including the Church of God in Christ, the National Baptist Convention of America, the Progressive National Baptist Convention, and the Global United Fellowship. "It's a life-changing opportunity," King said, of pastors traveling to Israel. "And to be able to see those biblical sites and then discuss the issues both as people of faith and as people for human rights and social justice issues. . . . It's just unbelievable." The human rights and social justice narrative that the Fellowship combines with the "life-changing" spiritual experience of being in the land of the Bible is based on philanthropic and charitable work. As King described it: "Clothing people, feeding people, helping people to have shelter, bringing people from war-torn countries to a place of safety—all of those things open doors with the African American community. It's the work that the African American community does here in the United States." Beyond the religious impetus of personal and communal spiritual growth through an experience of the Holy Land, the Fellowship's model for African American Christian experiences of Israel is another religious framework—that of *mission*. This was underscored in this chapter's opening scene, when Ella reminds Lennox that the trip they are in the middle of is a *mission* and that he better "get used to it." As a Christian-supported philanthropic organization in Israel, the Fellowship was founded on the idea of building bridges of understanding between Christians and Jews. Within this framework, charitable work in Israel is seen as a natural extension of the social services and support that Black churches provide in their own communities in the United States.

The Fellowship and the National Baptist Convention of America

In 2016, I traveled with a delegation of leaders from the National Baptist Convention of America (NBCA) on an IFCJ-sponsored tour. Alongside visits to Bible sites, our tour included several stops at philanthropic projects supported by the Fellowship and funded through Christian donations. These included a children's home, a premilitary academy for low-income minorities in Israel, an Ethiopian Jewish community center, a military base where soldiers received IFCJ aid, and a "pantry packers" food bank facility. After visiting the food bank, one NBCA pastor said: "What you call 'pantry packers,' we call 'mission'—and mission is what we do!"

NBCA trip delegates consistently affirmed and applauded the IFCJ outreach initiative as a welcome partnership for their convention and their congregations. Several members described it as an extension of their work in the United States and in their other global missions. "Our president is reaching out to form partnerships with other groups . . . to build relationships and spread the mission of the [convention]," said one retired lay leader on the trip. Another pastor said, "That's the focus of our convention—we're a mission-oriented convention."

Still, other leaders emphasized an underlying impetus to support Israel on a theological level. Like the NBCA vice president, Bartholomew Banks, who said:

> We endeavor to find partners who may not necessarily have a 100 percent agreement in "mission." . . . But if we can come together to accomplish certain mutual goals, then that will be helpful to us. . . . With a partnership with the International Fellowship of Christians and Jews, it's possible that we can now include Jews in Israel as part of our foreign mission program, because we can see the benefit of helping those individuals who have come from those scattered places back to their homeland. Because that's part of the "Zionist movement" and that's part of the prophetic plan that we believe to be God's ultimate desire for the nation of Israel. So, from our perspective, it broadens our horizon in terms of our foreign mission efforts.

Like CUFI, the Fellowship's outreach efforts to African American Christians emphasize Israel as a multiracial, inclusive society through encounters with the Ethiopian Jewish community and the State of Israel's efforts to facilitate their immigration and naturalization. For the NBCA delegation, these encounters included a briefing with a government coordinator of the Ethiopian evacuations from Africa during the 1980s and 1990s, a visit to an Ethiopian Jewish community center, a premilitary academy for Ethiopians and other minority Israeli youth, and a visit with Ethiopian border patrol soldiers at their West Bank outpost. The NBCA president, Samuel Tolbert, described becoming aware of the existence of Black Ethiopian Jews and the opportunity it presented for his convention:

> I think many people that were on our team were very interested about Jews being Ethiopian and their being air-lifted back to Israel. I guess mostly, when many African Americans think about Jews, they are not thinking about Ethiopian Jews. And that really, I think, struck a chord in our heart—to know that there are Ethiopian Jews and they are wanting to get home. And that the Fellowship is providing a mechanism for them to do that.

The Fellowship asks participants to sign a "statement of religious respect" before the trip, indicating their understanding that mutual religious respect and cooperation between Christians and Jews requires refraining from promoting one's own religious beliefs, unless personally invited to do so. The NBCA leaders traveled to Israel seeking a "mission" partner on different terms than the joint evangelistic and humanitarian efforts they undertake in other places where they work internationally—such as Africa and Haiti. This, as Reverend Banks noted, broadens the international connections of the conference. Although this nascent NBCA connection to Israel does not fully line up with the evangelistic efforts they sponsor in foreign missions in other parts of the world, it does contribute to advancing the common Christian Zionist imperative and helps fulfill the Bible prophecy by aiding diaspora Jews in returning to their homeland in Israel.

The Fellowship and the Church of God in Christ: Christian Mission Beyond Philanthropy

Denominational leaders from the Church of God in Christ had gone to Israel on a similar Fellowship-sponsored philanthropic mission the year before the NBCA delegation. On that trip, however, Pastor Glenn Plummer—who was then serving in COGIC's World Missions Department as the director of Israel missions and was later appointed its Bishop of Israel—arranged another mission component to the trip outside of the auspices of the Fellowship. When the visiting bishops and other national leaders from COGIC went to Israel for the first time, they spent the tour's Sabbath day with a congregation of Ethiopian Jewish followers of Jesus (or "Ethiopian believers").[28]

While the Jewish tour guides and Fellowship trip coordinators took a day off, the COGIC group traveled to advance a different kind of mission among Ethiopians in Israel, beyond the kind of philanthropic work the Fellowship promotes. Having been in conversation from overseas, and based on their shared racial and spiritual identities and convictions, COGIC leaders officially welcomed five congregations of Ethiopian Jewish believers into the COGIC denomination on that visit.

When I joined the follow-up COGIC trip to Israel the next year, some of those national leaders returned to Israel, but many laypeople also traveled to the Holy Land representing COGIC churches. In fact, the majority of participants on this follow-up mission were lay members of COGIC. Although it built on the previous Fellowship-sponsored delegation, this trip was not sponsored or led by the Fellowship. For some of the returning leaders, this freed the group to focus more directly on their collective interests in the Holy Land. Under the leadership of Plummer, this group was primarily tasked with continuing the outreach efforts to support their Ethiopian Israeli COGIC brothers and sisters, recently incorporated into the denomination. This happened outside of the Fellowship framework and opened new narratives on the role of Ethiopians in Israeli society.

Introducing the group to the issue of Ethiopian believers in Israel during a debriefing meeting at the end of the first full day of the trip, Plummer said, "Ethiopians have been woven into the fabric of what God is doing." He told the story of how the Ethiopian Jews had been brought to Israel as Jewish immigrants, noting that some of those immigrants were already believers in Jesus as Messiah when they arrived in the country. "Is it possible that God could use the Ethiopians to bring greater Israel to salvation?" he asked rhetorically. Plummer acknowledged that Ethiopian believers cannot always be overt about their faith in Israel. But "now is their time to be bold," he added. "We're standing with them." He went on to describe how American Christians are in a position to help these Ethiopian believing communities because of the importance of the U.S.-Israel political relationship and the fact that Israel needs U.S. friendship. "You play a prominent role in the nation of Israel coming to know their savior," he added, in his message to the group. "Helping Ethiopian believers is a way to bless Israel." A COGIC missionary then led the group in prayer: "Our heart's desire is that the Jews would be saved. Our heart's desire is for revival. . . . Have your way in this place."

Although the COGIC trip included transformative spiritual experiences facilitated by tours of biblical sites, participants consistently came back to their "mission" to serve the believing Ethiopian Jews as the guiding focus of the trip. A national music leader on the trip emphasized this: "The mission of the trip, I believe, was to be a blessing to our Ethiopian brothers and sisters . . . to be there, to support them, to let them know that they're not alone." She added, "We have had the opportunity to be a blessing to them—whether it be financially or just lending them support by teaching and training instruction and impartation— that we are actually expanding the kingdom." Talking about her reasons for joining the trip, one COGIC missionary said: "I went, from a missions perspective. My primary purpose, from a missions part, was to be able to meet the Ethiopian Jews." Another COGIC missionary similarly expressed her desire to find more time on the trip to spend with the Ethiopian congregations: "Our purpose here is not really to just see the Holy Land. Our purpose is to be edifying the body of Christ." This mode of Christian mission in Israel departs from the Fellowship framework, guided by its "statement of religious respect." Linking evangelism and humanitarian aid in the broader missions work of COGIC, a missionary supervisor on the trip explained her mission philosophy in the countries she oversees, including India and Ethiopia:

> We bring medical clinics and all those kinds of things . . . and we offer Christ. That's not something that you want? We offer what he represents. And so, we believe that God is love and Jesus is love. And so that's what we believe in doing and we do it regardless. . . . When they see my team coming, they're like, make way for her, because she brings dentists, she brings doctors, she brings nurses, and no one else is doing that. And then they just say, oh, why do you come here? And I said, my Jesus told me to come. And they say, give us this Jesus.

Overall, the COGIC visitors to Israel were mindful of the legal prohibition against proselytizing, and they did not engage in any evangelistic work themselves. Yet they maintained that it was their unique calling to go beyond providing material aid or political support to the State of Israel by supporting their new COGIC congregations with the spiritual, material, and theological resources to "expand God's kingdom" in Israel. This mode of engagement with Israel and Judaism has a long history in the Holy Land (and the broader Levant), which has not only been a site of pilgrimage and tourism for American Protestants but also a long-standing site for proselytizing.[29]

CUFI seeks to transform biblically engaged African American Christians with a love for "the land of the Bible" into politically engaged Christian Zionists, whereas the Fellowship disavows politics as their primary bridge-building focus. In their outreach to African American denominations, the Fellowship favors a more "faith-based" approach under the rubric of philanthropic "mission." Ultimately, however, they walk a similar line between spiritual and political concerns. The NBCA delegation and the COGIC follow-up mission were both consistently presented with narratives about Israel's geopolitical struggles and military defenses similar to those that are central to CUFI trips. This happened through visits to the Knesset, military outposts, war memorials, and briefings with political lobbying groups. Under the rubric of "mission," however, the political impetus for Holy Land travel within the Fellowship's African American outreach work is reframed through primary attention to social services and charity in Israel—what IFCJ advisor Coleman calls "the softer side of Israel."

Although their trips were infused with politics, Fellowship-affiliated visitors from the NBCA and COGIC often expressed hesitancy to engage with aspects of the trip that they found "too political," which was almost universally a negative judgment on certain trip encounters. For example, when political questions and the issue of Palestinians came up on the COGIC trip, Plummer communicated to the group that COGIC's presiding bishop, Charles Blake, had emphasized to him the importance of the trip not being perceived as being against the Palestinians. "We love everyone," Plummer said to the group. "We are the people of God. We represent the kingdom of God. We don't want to get mired in the politics." "But," he added, "it's important that we understand the facts on the ground." "Facts on the ground" came up multiple times on the trip, as Plummer and the group's Jewish guides flirted with political issues in celebrating Israel's military victories, spurning the idea of conceding any part of Jerusalem or the West Bank to the Palestinians, and challenging the notion that the State of Israel's policies toward Palestinians are like those of apartheid in South Africa.

Politics undeniably came to the forefront on several occasions with the COGIC group, however. In a briefing meeting, a representative of the Knesset Christian Allies Caucus spoke about the imperative of "putting biblical support for Israel into political terms" through "faith-based diplomacy." He encouraged promoting anti-Boycott, Divestment, and Sanctions (BDS) legislation in the United States and focused in particular on the political importance of maintaining a unified Jerusalem as the undivided capital of Israel. A petition to that effect was presented to the group, and a number of people signed it. As we left that presentation, one pastor leaned over and said to me, "That seemed like a *political* document to me." When I asked him whether he had signed the petition, he said, "Oh no! I try to stay away from that. I know the leader and others signed it, but I try to stay away from politics." When we arrived back at our hotel, another lay leader on the trip told me, "I thought that was very political. I didn't sign it. I think our covenant [with Israel] is spiritual. . . . I think it's good that they have their land here, but God is going to do what God is going to do, no matter what we do."

The emphasis on mission among some African American Christians highlights the importance of philanthropic work and even religious proselytizing (or "soul winning") in the broader religious outlooks of Christian visitors to the Holy Land. The IFCJ favors a philanthropic view of Christian mission, focused on meeting people's material needs. Out of this comes a vision for Black religious politics focused on providing charity. In Israel, this takes on additional theological significance, ostensibly fulfilling the biblical command to "bless Israel."

For African American Christian groups working closely with the IFCJ, this requires an emphasis on charity and a de-emphasis on proselytizing—two aspects of mission that often go hand-in-hand for them in other parts of the world. For the COGIC initiative in Israel, which grew out of an IFCJ-sponsored delegation, mission focused on evangelism and not just charitable work is reclaimed in working directly with Ethiopian Jewish believers in Israel outside of the auspices of the Fellowship as a sponsoring organization. In all cases, and like a more personal spiritual emphasis, mission often is seen as being at odds with political purposes. Among NBCA and COGIC visitors, I observed a hesitancy to engage with overtly political aspects of trips. For some, this came from a general hesitancy to get involved in politics in favor of a "spiritual covenant" with Israel. For others, it was expressed as a reluctance to broach politics abroad and in an unfamiliar setting. As I show in the last section of this chapter, some pastors are much more comfortable getting involved in politics at home but express reluctance about appearing to "take sides" politically in Israel and Palestine. This is one salient barrier to linking the national- and global-levels of Black religious politics with Israel and Palestine among African American Christians.

"WALK WHERE JESUS IS WALKING TODAY": THE SAMUEL DEWITT PROCTOR CONFERENCE AND PALESTINIAN ACTIVISM

The religious impetus to "walk where Jesus walked" is present, even for activist-minded clergy like those of the Samuel DeWitt Proctor Conference. Bishop Don Williams—whose work to bring the Palestinian situation to the attention of the Proctor Conference is described in chapter 2—told me how much he enjoyed visiting Bible sites: the Garden of Gethsemane, the Sea of Galilee, and the city of Nazareth. These and other Bible places linked to the ministry of Jesus are meaningful sites for religious experiences not only for Christian Zionists but for virtually all African American Christians. "I enjoyed that part of [the trip]," Williams explained, but he followed that with the need to take an alternative religious perspective on travel to Israel and Palestine: "It felt good to walk where Jesus walked, but it felt even better to walk where Jesus is walking today, and that is with those who are undervalued, underestimated, and marginalized."[30] He explained that this path produced strong feelings of a disconnect between the positive experience of visiting places of religious significance and encountering the plight of Palestinians:

> As a man of African descent and as a fourth generation Pentecostal who lived through the civil rights movement, it was easy for me to see and feel what my Palestinian sisters and brothers are experiencing because I have also experienced being marginalized. Being in that place where the "Prince of Peace" was born and found no peace produced in me a powerful combination of sadness, hurt, and anger.[31]

There is a shift away from visiting traditional religious sites to engaging with Palestinians and learning about and from their struggle. When I traveled to Palestine with a group led by the Proctor affiliate Reverend Waltrina Middleton, one Palestinian Christian family we visited expressed this shift in different terms. The family applauded the group's desire to go beyond visiting the "dead stones" of the land (i.e., the many biblical archaeological sites and churches) and to spend time with the "living stones" in the land (i.e., the Palestinian people).[32]

When Guidry preached to a plenary session at the Proctor Conference annual meeting about her travels in Palestine, two other Proctor-affiliated clergy members articulated a similar prophetic Black religious orientation that echoes Williams's impulse to not only "walk where Jesus walked" in the Holy Land but to "walk where Jesus is walking today" among the marginalized and dispossessed people of the land. Reverend Starsky Wilson encouraged Proctor attendees to reject "the religion *about* Jesus" in favor of "the religion *of* Jesus." It is the latter that is the true religion, the religion of *action*, of "praying with your feet," he said. Reverend Traci Blackmon presided over the plenary worship service and applied the same critique to what she described as insufficient action to address the ongoing water crisis in Flint, Michigan. "Sending water to Flint is not justice—it is *charity*," she chided. "So don't celebrate what we're doin' and take your eye off the ball." She went on: "Heads have to roll in Flint. Adjudication is justice. Reparations is justice." Echoing Wilson's language on true religion, Blackmon said: "If the people of God rest on our laurels because we collected some water, then what you have is a ministry *about* Jesus, not the ministry *of* Jesus." For partners of the Proctor Conference network of clergy, activists, and organizations, the proclivity to reject—or at least to go beyond—traditional notions of pilgrimage or walking where Jesus walked is part of a prophetic orientation within Black religious politics that embraces—even requires—activism.

The tendency among visitors to Israel and Palestine affiliated with the Proctor Conference to disparage walking where Jesus walked is not a rejection of spiritual or religious purposes. It is a pursuit of what they see as authentic African American Christianity through the lens of Black Liberation Theology and the prophetic tradition of Black religion. Their critique of that mode of religious encounter comes when it leads to an inability to recognize the political realities of the region, the plight of Palestinians, and the connection between African American and Palestinian experiences. Lucas Johnson, the Proctor-affiliated minister and activist introduced in chapter 3, described his reaction to encountering traditional religious pilgrims and tourists in Israel while taking part in a political fact-finding mission:

> [You're] immediately confronted by these pilgrims that are walking around and having a religious experience. . . . You are just well aware that they have no idea—*have no idea*—what's happening right in front of them. . . . And if it's not for me or someone else telling them to look up at that settlement right there, they wouldn't see it. Well, if they did see it, they wouldn't know what they were looking at.

With this framing, the typical pilgrim experience of the land gets in the way of seeing Israel and Palestine through the lens of justice. Proctor Conference activists engaged with the Palestinian cause are offering a prophetic Black religious voice to counter what they see as a dominant Christian Zionist narrative about Israel that is pervasive in Black churches. Jeremiah Wright, speaking to a Proctor Conference gathering of Black clergy, castigated African American Christian Zionist trips to Israel of the kind CUFI and the IFCJ sponsor:

> They take students from HBCUs [Historically Black Colleges and Universities] and Black congregations—pastors and members—to the State of Israel, so they become the number one Star of David flag wavers for the biggest land grab since we stole this land from the Native Americans. . . . "Don't you wanna see where Jesus was baptized? Don't you wanna be baptized in the Jordan?" . . . They're not gonna show you Gaza. They're not gonna show you the West Bank. They're not gonna show you what's on the other side of the wall—the apartheid wall that they're building. . . . "Come see where Jesus was born" [they say].

Seeing what often is ignored when African American Christians visit Israel and Palestine on "Holy Land" tours or Christian Zionist trips is a driving motivation for Proctor Conference activists to work among Black clergy.

Middleton returned to Palestine many times as an activist after her initial trips (see chapter 2). In 2018, I joined a small group of young Black activists she led on a trip to Palestine. The participants were mostly college students and recent college graduates from Howard University and the Washington, DC, area. Two Native American activists, who called themselves "water protectors," were also part of the group. They had met Middleton at the recent Standing Rock protests against the construction of the Dakota Access Pipeline. They were on the trip to learn about shared struggles linking Native Americans and Palestinians. Under the title Diaspora Dialogues, Middleton described the trip as a "sojourn" and a "global immersion encounter" intended to "help bridge gaps between cultural, spiritual and even intergenerational intersections . . . upholding the core pillars of leadership, education, advocacy, and discourse." Ahead of the trip, Middleton emphasized that the common thread linking participants was the collective work of transforming and exposing injustices, along with personal learning and growth. She charged the group "to simply be a present witness in community." On the first day of the trip, she reiterated the importance of bearing witness, being present, and learning.

In line with the Proctor Conference's efforts to engage contemporary social justice and antiracist activism from a faith-based perspective and against the tide of a secular shift in political civil rights activism in the United States, most of the participants on the trip were either avowedly secular, nominally Christian, or practiced an Indigenous spirituality. Although the trip was thoroughly multifaith (and even secular), under Middleton's leadership it featured distinctly Christian religious characteristics throughout. This was, in part, because of Middleton's Palestinian partner organization for the trip, Sabeel, an ecumenical Palestinian Christian organization that describes its work as being aimed "towards theological liberation through instilling the Christian faith in the daily lives of those who suffer under occupation, violence, injustice, and discrimination."[33] Sabeel's founder and leader, Reverend Naim Ateek, took part in a Proctor Conference workshop with Middleton on the "Movement for Justice in Palestine," and Ateek has been a regular participant in Proctor Conference work on Palestine. Our Sabeel guide, Daoud, a Palestinian Orthodox Christian, emphasized that there are many competing narratives on Israel and Palestine, but none are 100 percent true. He went on to explain that his own perspective was what he had to offer the group. This was the first of many narratives and perspectives on the people and the land from what were consistently described as marginalized perspectives.

Across the ten-day trip, Middleton and her coleader, Daoud, led us on an extensive tour of Palestine, with little time given to traditional locations for tourism or pilgrimage. During our visit to Jerusalem, we passed major religious sites—the Church of the Holy Sepulchre and the Western Wall of the Jewish Temple—but we spent most of our time with members of Jerusalem's Afro-Palestinian community, walking through quiet streets of the Old City that are rarely visited by tourists. Our attention was directed to the homes of families threatened by Jewish Israeli settlements. We also visited a depopulated Palestinian village, a refugee camp, military checkpoints, and the sites of Israeli prisons for Palestinians. Typical tours of Israel focus on spiritual geographies ("the Land of Israel," "the Land of the Bible"), whereas our attention was directed toward the political geography of the land: the location of Jewish settlements in the West Bank, road networks, and the Israeli separation barrier and its implications for the daily lives of Palestinians living in East Jerusalem and the West Bank. In daily meetings and briefings with Palestinian activists, human rights workers, and community organizers, we were presented with narratives about challenges faced by Palestinians due to the unequal distribution of public resources and the impact of Israeli policies on Palestinian communities.

Our first full day of touring was entitled "Occupation on the Ground: An Introduction to the Realities on the Ground." Daoud took us to the Shuafat Refugee Camp in East Jerusalem. We got off the bus at a traffic circle that deadended against the separation wall. In front of us was a large green dumpster with pungent smoke coming from burning trash. As we walked by, Daoud said, "This is what you do with the trash when there's no one to come pick it up." He explained that Shuafat is a neighborhood of the municipality of Jerusalem in East Jerusalem, but its residents are not treated the same as the residents of the neighboring Jewish settlement of Pisgat Ze'ev. The settlement, he reiterated several times, is illegal under international law and according to the United Nations. He described how the residents of Shuafat pay full taxes but receive few public benefits—like water, trash collection, or schools. "The residents of Pisgat Ze'ev," he said, "are subsidized heavily by the state." "There are two things the residents here do get from the Israeli government," he added, "taxes and arrests."

As we entered the camp, Daoud looked back at the group over his shoulder as he passed through the one-way turnstile gate (like exits from the New York subway) that was the only way through a tall wire fence. "Welcome to our neighborhood," he said with a wry smile. As we walked, Daoud explained: "This is not a poor neighborhood. This is a community whose resources are sucked out. These are hard-working people. You see poverty here, but don't see it through the eyes of poverty, see it through the eyes of discrimination." He pointed out how the buildings are built on top of each other, on top of the sidewalks, saying that an earthquake would cause it all to crumble. "About every one hundred years we have an earthquake," he said. "Who knows when it will happen next." Many of the narrow sidewalks were covered over with additional buildings, making them tunnel-like. We passed cars coming and going, parents with children, teenagers on their way home from school. I recalled the story Middleton had told at the Proctor Conference's annual convention about a Palestinian child telling her, "we have no sky." At the end of our time in the Shuafat, we waited for our bus at a point in the camp overlooking the valley next to it and the Pisgat Ze'ev settlement across the way. "What more can I show you?" Daoud asked. "If you don't get it here, what can I show you?"

One of the persistent questions on the trip was the significance of apartheid in the context of Palestine—specifically whether the situation in Israel and Palestine should be compared to the South African system of racial segregation and discrimination. We had a meeting with diplomats in the South African Representative Office in the West Bank capital of Ramallah, including its Head of Mission, Ashraf Suliman. "When you talk about apartheid, everyone turns to South Africa," he told the group over coffee. Broadening the conversation to include American influences, he said, "In the fight against apartheid, South Africans were inspired by American movements for racial justice. That [inspiration] was part of the mass mobilization of our people." "What Palestinians are living in is worse than apartheid," he declared emphatically. Later in the trip, a human rights lawyer echoed this sentiment. "This is not apartheid," he said, speaking of the Palestinian situation. "It's much worse. It's annexation of territory. They [Israel] want to take the territory without the people."

Another recurring theme on the trip was linking the struggles, especially of Palestinians with African Americans and Indigenous peoples around the world. Learning about Israeli military raids and arrests of Palestinian youth in West Bank villages drew comparisons among participants to African American experiences of police harassment, intimidation, incarceration, and racial profiling practices in the United States. In a meeting with Palestinian university students in Ramallah, we learned of the arrest of a student leader on their campus just days before our arrival. They showed us smartphone videos of undercover Israeli forces violently arresting the student in the middle of the busy campus, describing the sense of shock and trauma on their campus. We also heard from an Israeli activist about Israel's training of American police in counterterrorism tactics. She mentioned that a Washington, DC, police chief had called Israel "the Harvard of counterterrorism."[34] In this moment of the conversation, the DC-area students and activists on the trip became especially aware of the link between policing in Israel and in the United States. The point of connection recalled the question Jasiri X—the hip hop artist and activist quoted in in the introduction— was similarly confronted with in Palestine: "You know why you should care about what's happening in Palestine and why the hood should care? Because the policing that you see here is coming to a hood near you."

Conversations like these with Palestinian and Israeli activists about common struggles against oppression prompted ongoing discussions about appropriate strategies for fighting injustice, including debates about the merits of nonviolent forms of resistance. Middleton shared a quote with the group from the Aboriginal artist and activist Lilla Watson: "If you have come to help me, you are wasting time. But if you have come because my liberation is bound with yours, let us work together." Throughout the trip, Middleton led the group through the process of imagining what it would mean for African Americans, Palestinians, and Indigenous peoples to collaborate more actively, recognizing their common political struggles.

For many Proctor Conference affiliates who had experienced Israeli and Jewish narratives of the Holy Land through more traditional Holy Land tours, these initial encounters provoked questions about the situation of Palestinians and the presence of systemic racism and discrimination in Palestine and Israel. Like Middleton, Williams, and Guidry, they experienced the Holy Land first as tourists or spiritual pilgrims, but eventually their lens shifted to activism. This shift is not a rejection of religious motivations for traveling, but it reframes them on different terms, revealing a vision for Black religious politics on a global scale. In a sense, Black religious politics is always global for Proctor activists because they are coming from liberationist theological traditions that emphasize "reading the Bible through the eyes of the oppressed." On the last day of the trip,

Middleton summarized the experience from a Christian leadership perspective, posting this on social media: "Instead of flocking to The Holy Land for a safe, perfectly packaged pilgrimage to see dead stones; more faith communities must come see the suffering of the living stones."

THE PERFECTING CHURCH AND GLOCAL ENGAGEMENT WITH PALESTINE

When The Perfecting Church's senior pastor, Kevin Brown, met with the team who would soon be heading to the West Bank in the fall of 2015, he stated: "We're not going on a Holy Land Tour. That's not what this is. We're not going as tourists. We're not going as missionaries. We're going to engage the domains of society." He went on to talk about engagement with Palestinians and Israelis as an effort to bring reconciliation between Christians, Muslims, and Jews in the land. This included a caution against "taking sides" or getting too involved in politics, an often discussed concern among leaders and members of The Perfecting Church. "We are not taking a position," he explained. "We're taking the same position that Jesus took and that is the cross. We're not picking a side. We wanna love our neighbors." The mission of The Perfecting Church in Palestine is not primarily driven by proselytizing, preaching, or charity. In fact, Brown resisted accepting preaching engagements at Palestinian churches for many years, aiming to keep a low profile while he and his church members made inroads into the Palestinian community. When I traveled with TPC to Bethlehem in 2015, it was the first time in six trips with his members that Brown had agreed to preach a sermon at a Palestinian church.

Like the Baptists and Pentecostals who work with the International Fellowship of Christians and Jews, The Perfecting Church describes a different vision for church engagement in Palestine versus in the United States. Brown explained this with reference to Jesus's command in the New Testament to "be my witnesses" throughout the world: "I think Acts 1:8, when Jesus says, be my witnesses in Jerusalem, Judea, Samaria, and the uttermost parts of the world, each one of those places had a different type of transformation. They all represent something different." Within this mandate, members of The Perfecting Church seek to love their neighbors at home and abroad, but their vision for what this should look like in the context of Palestine and Israel evolved over time. For Brown, once the church became well established in its community, it could branch out from there. He referred to the founding impulse of The Perfecting Church to "pick a hard place in the world" and to work there. Initially, this meant starting a new church in the same state as his previous congregation, then it quickly became a challenge to go abroad with the new church's members. Brown felt compelled to choose Palestine after attending a conference in Bethlehem in 2012 with his mentor in the glocal model of churches, Bob Roberts.

Since then, teams from The Perfecting Church have returned to the West Bank once or twice each year to partner with Palestinians working with trauma counseling, small business development, and caring for orphans. A female college student from TPC who traveled to the West Bank described the importance of going as learners, seeking to connect with people and to contribute when possible. "Too often," she said, "as Christians, we have this tendency to think that we can solve all the world's problems. And that we're going to come over there and preach this gospel and everything is going to change. But we forget that we have to go there and learn and connect and relate. And just see how we can even be used, not even just assume that we have a solution." TPC's glocal engagement work is driven by this commitment to learning, to reconciliation, and to loving neighbors.

On the TPC glocal engagement trip I joined in 2015, six church members joined Kevin and Angela Brown in Bethlehem for the church's sixth trip there following Kevin Brown's first visit to the region in 2012. From the outset of the trip, questions about what it meant for the church to be "engaging" in Israel and Palestine were persistent. What was the place of politics on the trip? How much time should first-time travelers expect to spend touring the holy sites they had imagined visiting all their lives? My roommate on the trip spent many evenings in Bethlehem watching the 1977 Franco Zeffirelli miniseries *Jesus of Nazareth* on his laptop, which he had grown up watching and said had spurred his imagination about the Bible. "I'm a very visual type of person," he said. "So what particularly made [the trip] more enjoyable for me was growing up as a very young kid watching *Jesus of Nazareth*, I would say, a million times." He acknowledged that "we're not going on a Holy Land tour," but experiencing the land of the Bible interested him throughout the trip, as it did for other travelers. Participants realized that they were not on a Holy Land tour and adjusted their expectations accordingly. But first-time visitors, especially, voiced their interest in visiting sites of biblical significance and later voiced their disappointment when some of these sites were taken off the schedule.

Few participants on the TPC trip were focused on politics or building solidarities in political terms, as Proctor Conference travelers do, but the pull to politics was persistent. Upon arrival at the airport in Tel Aviv, a small bus took us to Bethlehem. All of the participants were excited, but travel fatigue took over and many drifted off to sleep. When we approached the Israeli checkpoint at Bethlehem and were questioned by Israeli authorities, the group roused at the change in scenery and upon seeing the imposing barrier. The potential for politics came to life as we continued beyond the checkpoint into the West Bank and to our Bethlehem hotel. One first-time visitor noticed a painted sign on a building wall near our hotel with an Israeli flag crossed out in red saying, "Boycott Israel." He read the sign out loud with a questioning tone in his voice, wondering what he had gotten into.

As The Perfecting Church's leaders, Kevin and Angela Brown recognize the pull toward politics in Israel and Palestine. They see a propensity for African American Christians to be Christian Zionists and recognize a powerful Zionist narrative among African Americans. "We've inherited [Zionist] thinking, not just from our seminaries but from our spiritual experiences," Kevin Brown explained to me. "Our churches have shaped us to be Zionists, and when we get our feet on the ground, I think we'd be shocked [by] how quickly we would relate to the Palestinian rather than the Israeli." Indeed, I saw the church's members relate more easily to Palestinians than to Israelis in the Holy Land. In part this is because we spent most of our time in the West Bank with Palestinians. Among the TPC members with whom I traveled, comparisons between African American and Palestinian experiences were common. "The Palestinians are an oppressed people," explained one female traveler. "They lack the freedom that, let's say, the Israelis have over in Jerusalem. They lack freedom to go, and to come, and to do. And some of their children have never seen the beach because they are not able to freely move about. And so that's very much African American. We were oppressed." While driving through Jerusalem, another female visitor from The Perfecting Church spotted a Palestinian teenager on a bicycle being questioned by an Israeli police officer. "It's just like the States," she said, shaking her head as we drove by. "You can really see the parallels," another woman added.

Given this tendency to identify with Palestinians, Kevin Brown and other leaders at The Perfecting Church consistently emphasize the need for the church not to choose sides. This presents a challenge for leaders and lay members alike, especially once they have begun to identify with Palestinians. One TPC leader studying for ministry and preparing to plant a new church location in Camden, New Jersey, described trying to overcome an anti-Zionist disposition he had come away with from his previous engagement trip. "When I came back, I was very anti-Zionist. . . . And this trip I realized where my mind and heart had went and I noted it needs to shift a little bit. If we're going to fulfill the mission that God has called us here to do, we've got to be pretty much the clean slate. We are not here to pick a side, whatsoever." He later distanced himself from overt political activism even further, saying, "My thing—I'm not an activist. I don't boycott, I don't march, I don't riot, I don't protest." Another repeat visitor and trip leader from The Perfecting Church echoed this sentiment: "I needed help to not take sides. Because I found myself—my heart—hardening to Israel. And it was beginning to harden, and I felt it. And God awakened me to that reality. Because I saw so much of my own people's pain. I saw such a mirror of horrendous acts—dehumanizing events that began to swell inside of me." For Brown and TPC members, not choosing sides goes beyond feeling connected to Palestinians or Israeli Jews. It also means resisting the pull to get involved in politics in Israel and Palestine. "Much like I've worked on not choosing a side, I've worked on not getting politically involved. . . . I don't feel that's our assignment there," Brown said.

My TPC roommate in Palestine wanted to see the land of the Bible he had experienced on film since his childhood. Others, too, wanted to see and experience the Bible sites with which they were so familiar: the Mount of Olives, the Old City of Jerusalem, Nazareth. Despite the strong emphasis on "engagement" over tourism, we did see a few Bible sites. The group did a whirlwind self-guided tour of the Galilee area, and we visited the Garden of Gethsemane in Jerusalem. These experiences were meaningful to trip participants, especially those visiting for the first time. One woman described the significance for her of being in the Garden of Gethsemane: "It was amazing . . . when we went to Gethsemane and to think that this is the tree that Jesus knelt down and he was praying. . . . It was like the Bible coming alive." TPC members shared a desire to experience the land of the Bible and to have it "come alive" for them, much like visitors on pro-Israel trips led by CUFI and the IFCJ. For repeat visitors such as the trip's coordinator who worked closely with Brown on developing the itinerary for this, his third trip, the impulse to visit biblical tourism sites was minimized. "[Through] the tourism, I think we get to be a little bit more detached," he said. And he went on to explain the difference between visiting the "dead stones" of holy sites and the "living stones" of the people of the land:

> I'm allowed to see the dead stones and accept it for what it is, and then interpret on my own its relevance or its significance. So I get to look at this mosque or this stone or whatever, and I get to make it all about me. So it's about me and my experience, so I take a picture with it or whatever. . . . The main difference with the engagements with people . . . is it becomes the exact opposite. So now, it's not about me at all, really. It's about this living stone who has its own experiences.

This echoes the image of "living stones" and "dead stones" that Palestinian Christians employ in appealing to Christians worldwide to consider their political and religious plight in the Holy Land. They represent themselves as the living stones of the land—the beleaguered church in the Holy Land, tracing its roots to the time of Jesus—in juxtaposition to the "dead stones"—the inanimate churches and other relics made from stone that most Western Christians come to see in the Holy Land. The same trip coordinator balked at the commercialization of Holy Land tourism sites: "Everywhere we went [sightseeing] . . . the people that were there experiencing it were mean and nasty. When we went to the Church of Nativity, the people were almost fist-fighting to go in and touch a place where Mary gave birth to Christ. And I'm sitting here, like, I don't understand." Reflecting on visiting the area around the Sea of Galilee, he was critical: "It was so commercialized, it was so capitalism-drawn, it was so about making money."

Even first-time visitors recoiled at what they saw as overly touristic sites. One woman said, "Just how much tourism is around all of the holy sites. . . . I could see where Jesus would come to the temple and just turn all the tables over. He's so frustrated about all the marketing and commercialization that happened that, how holy really is that?" But even as TPC travelers affirmed they were there for Palestinian-focused "engagement" and acknowledged they had not signed up for "a Holy Land tour," some participants challenged those boundaries. When the sightseeing visit to Jerusalem was canceled—except a brief stop at the Garden of Gethsemane on the Mount of Olives—one participant said, "We missed Golgotha and all of those different things. So I think it left me wanting to experience those things as well. Hopefully, if I can go back, I would like to experience those things."

When driving through the Judean Desert as we returned to Bethlehem after visiting another site, another participant added, "We were like right there at the Dead Sea. I was just like why can't we just go down [to see it]?"

RACE, PILGRIMAGE, AND COMPETING NARRATIVES

This chapter describes how African American Christians, sometimes in partnership with predominantly white organizations and institutions, cultivate divergent racialized experiences of Israel and Palestine as an ostensible "Holy Land" or as a problematic "unholy land." These divergent types of experiences are the product both of their domestic outlooks on the intersecting significance of racial, religious, and political identities in the United States and of the uncertainty of the process of negotiating that intersection in an unfamiliar setting, where the meanings of those identities are in flux more than at home.

African American Christians in the four cases represented here brought certain ideas of racial politics and religious imperatives with them. Groups that the Fellowship solicited in its pro-Israel outreach, eschewed politics on the surface but found points of resonance with the political realities of the land and its inhabitants who they encountered along the way. The Samuel DeWitt Proctor Conference and CUFI's African American outreach leaders took the political challenge of the region head on, but in very different ways. CUFI's message to African American Christians began with an appeal to the Bible and presented Israel and Palestine primarily as the "land of the Bible." This was an entry point to the contemporary and historical politics of the region. The goal of CUFI's outreach to African American pastors and laypeople was not for them simply to have a religious experience of the Holy Land but to be able to translate that experience into political action—moving from tourists to Zionists. As CUFI's former executive director stated, "to transform a passively pro-Israel or neutral Christian bystander into a passionate Zionist."[35] The leaders of the Proctor Conference approached the politics of Palestine and Israel more directly and in line with their broader theological commitments to racial justice and interpreting the Bible "through the eyes of the oppressed." Members and affiliates of the Proctor Conference sought out and forged solidarities with Palestinians based on shared experiences of marginalization and injustice. The Perfecting Church was also caught between an ideal apolitical mandate and the reality of the draw political solidarities in the region had on its members, primarily toward Palestinians but also toward Israelis.

Among these cases, the more activist-oriented trips of the Proctor Conference network demonstrate the most cohesive purpose in expressly and openly embracing contemporary racial politics in a global solidarity-building project. But even here, the connection between the African American experience and the Palestinian situation is not obvious, nor are its implications. As one Black activist questioned in Palestine: Why should Black Americans focus on this seventy-year-old problem in Palestine when African Americans have a 500-year-old problem of their own? Neither the salience of race, the social meaning of race, or the specific political implications of these can be taken for granted in evaluating African American Christian engagement with Israel and Palestine. But the range of possibilities evident here helps answer the central question of this chapter: What are these trips?

To the extent that these trips to Palestine and Israel include political questions in racial terms—about identity, solidarity, and action—they show how African American Christian travel to the Holy Land is multifaceted, always including at least some political realities, even when overlaid on ostensibly apolitical religious purposes. And, it must be noted, the political here is not always the secular flipside to a distinctly spiritual core purpose. For African American Christians, politics can be deeply entwined with religion and spirituality.

When politics come to the forefront of these trips, their implications for shaping pilgrimage experiences stand most at odds with the traditional anthropological notion of pilgrimage as a break from the mundane. Indeed, it has been a key insight of scholars of pilgrimage in recent decades that pilgrimage is always inextricably intertwined with political economies in terms of consumer-driven tourism industries, questions of governance, and political fights for recognition. For some of the African American Christians I met and traveled with, politics was at the forefront of their engagement with Israel and Palestine. For more politically minded activist travelers, no liminal experience of communitas or accompanying homogenization of status is possible given the political realities of the region. In this view, the region is not an idealized place outside of normal space and time that connects heaven and earth. For African American Christians who travel to Palestine and Israel as activists, the focus is precisely on the mundane aspects of the lives of Israelis and Palestinians—including travel through military checkpoints and other restrictions on movement, youth incarceration, land seizures, home demolitions, and access to natural resources. Israel and Palestine, for them, is a place where injustice toward Palestinians mirrors the everyday experiences of people of color in the United States.

For African American Christian Zionists, however, the land is a place where Jewish Israelis live under the constant threat of hostile neighboring countries and terrorist networks seeking their destruction. "Pro-Israel" activists combine religious narratives about the State of Israel as the cradle of Judeo-Christian identity with political narratives about the State of Israel's plight in the Middle East, whereas Palestinian-focused Black Christians see the notion of Israel as a "Holy Land" as a distraction at best and a purposeful deception at worst. These Black activists reject the idea of going to Israel and Palestine to "walk where Jesus walked." Instead, they encourage an "awakeness" to the material conditions of Palestinian life. Here, racial identity and race-consciousness come to the forefront; Black Americans and Arab Palestinians are linked in a common anti-colonial struggle against institutionalized forms of racism and discrimination.

Whether oriented toward solidarities with Jewish Israelis or Palestinians, each of these case studies shows how African American trips to Palestine and Israel are multifaceted and unpredictable. On all of my trips to the region with African American Christians, it was difficult to anticipate when and where race would become salient in either religious or political terms, or both. Even when reactions to politics could be expected (at an expressly political site, for example), the outcome of the encounter and the meanings drawn by participants were similarly unpredictable. Important for the purposes of this study, these trips are examples of how the contestation of Black religious politics takes on a different character when it is adjudicated outside of the United States in less familiar physical and political geographies. Attending to the land of Palestine and Israel as a site of formation for American Black religious politics is key to understanding the complexities of these cases and how they represent broader trends in African American Christianity, but a fuller account of where the religious-political-racial orientations of African American Christians represented here come from and how they relate to each other in the social space of African American Christianity is required. This is the task of chapter 5.

The Field of Black Religious Politics

I n my six years of research in the world of African American Christian engagement with Israel and Palestine, and across the four cases analyzed in this book, I consistently heard references to "the Black Church" regarding its history, its identity, and its proper position on a range of political and social issues. When I attended an event for Black clergy, students, and activists sponsored by the Samuel DeWitt Proctor Conference at Howard University entitled "Occupied Palestine: How Should the Black Church Respond?," the Proctor general secretary, Iva Carruthers, stated, "For us, it is not a question of *if* the Black Church should respond, but indeed *how* the Black Church should respond" (see introduction). Among African American Christian Zionists, I similarly found broad appeals to the authority of "the Black Church," including "A Call for the African American Church to Support the Jewish State and Zionism" and "The Black Church: Why Standing with Israel Will Be a Defining Issue of Christians of Color in the 21st Century," from Christians United for Israel African American outreach staff member Michael Stevens and Dumisani Washington, respectively.[1] On the contestation of Black religious politics, I suggest that there is such a thing as "the Black Church" and that it is a debated category that carries weight in African American religious, social, and political spaces. Regarding Palestine and Israel, competing cultural frameworks for "the Black Church" are used to prescribe appropriate religious and political orientations, ranging across the kinds of engagement seen in the four case studies in the preceding chapters. In this chapter, I provide a final comparison of their visions of what "the Black Church" has been, is, and ought to be. Furthermore, in light of those visions of African American Christian collective identity, I elaborate the range of responses among

African American Christians on the question of what "the Black Church" should think and do collectively with respect to Israel and Palestine.

"THE BLACK CHURCH" AS A SOCIAL OBJECT AND A COLLECTIVE IDENTITY

In the introduction, I raised this question: What is "the Black Church"? I explored the ways that both scholars of African American religious life and Black Christians themselves have sought to answer that question and described the ways they have prescribed collective social action corresponding to those definitions. Implicit in that framing of this central question are two premises: (1) although there is disagreement about its specific history, identity, and mission, "the Black Church" exists as a social object, and (2) the work of defining that object has been taken up by both insiders and outsiders to American Black churches. In other words, "the Black Church" (at times expressed in earlier variations as "the Negro Church") is a category that has been used by observers of and participants in Black religious life in the United States for more than a century.

Given this dual use of the term (both within and outside Black churches), my central argument is that "the Black Church" exists as a social object, whose meaning and significance for the overlapping religious, social, and political identities of African American Christians is contested. In sociological terms, these two perspectives on "the Black Church" evoke the distinction between *categories of practice* and *categories of analysis*, as described by the sociologist Rogers Brubaker and the historian Frederick Cooper.[2] Following the work of Pierre Bourdieu, they define categories of practice as "categories of everyday social experience, developed and deployed by ordinary social actors." This is distinguished from categories of analysis, which are "experience-distant categories used by social analysts."[3] One of the important insights for my central argument regarding the contested nature of "the Black Church" is that we can analyze something as a category of practice without treating that category the way some social actors operating within the category itself do—especially when these actors understand the category as fixed, universal, or immutable. That is, we can understand and appreciate how and why different African American Christians invoke the idea of "the

Black Church" without taking those uses for granted.⁴ The academic enterprise of "Black Church Studies" is premised on the overlap and mutual recognition of "the Black Church" both as a category of analysis (for scholars who study Black religious life in the United States) and as a category of practice (for African American Christians), and many scholars within the field are both.

The question of the meaning and social significance of "the Black Church" is a question of identity. Additional insights from Brubaker's work on collective identity will help lay out my framework for comparing competing visions of what that collective identity means for "the Black Church." Brubaker explains collective identity in two related senses:

1.   Collective identity as *groupness*—A sense of belonging and solidarity; produces an "us" vs. "them"; a boundary between insiders and outsiders.
2.   Collective identity as *self-understanding*—"One's sense of what one's group is about, of social location, and of how (given the first two) it is prepared to act."⁵

The second sense of collective identity is important because it includes *action* as a central component, which has strong social and political implications. The category of "the Black Church" is a source of identity and belonging for African American Christians, but it also carries meanings about the church's purpose in the world. "The Black Church" includes a sense of belonging and solidarity, drawing a racial and religious boundary between those who have experienced the particularities of walking through life as African Americans within a particular religious worldview and those who have not followed the same path. It is important, however, to recognize that the church also presents imperatives about how, given that particular identity and experience, members of the group should be prepared to act in the world.

Finally, on collective identity, the cultural role of narrative has been central to my discussion and continues to be important here. Narratives are one of the primary ways group identities are constructed, negotiated, and deployed by their members.⁶ Group narratives offer what the sociologist Ruth Braunstein calls "blueprints" for social action, which enable groups to act in the world based on selected aspects of their collective self-understanding.⁷ In recognizing "the Black Church" as a category of practice, I focus on how African American Christians variously construct versions of group identity around that category. Furthermore, they deploy that identity to propel particular kinds of social and political action—in other words, how they are prepared to act is based on particular notions of what "the Black Church" means. In looking at Black religious politics as a contested social space—or as a field of contestation—I pay particular attention to the ways these visions of Black church identity are multiple, competing, and often mutually exclusive.

BLACK RELIGIOUS POLITICS AS A FIELD OF CONTESTATION

To suggest that Black religious politics is best understood as a field of contestation directly invokes the work of the French sociologist Pierre Bourdieu. For Bourdieu, a social field is "a network, or configuration, of objective relations between positions."[8] It is a relatively stable social context (milieu) in which actors representing various interests interact and relate to one another. As the sociologist Emily Barman put it, a social field is a "domain characterized by its own architecture and a shared orientation among its members."[9] As such, fields can be thought of as "social microcosms," "operating spaces," or "arenas of struggle" characterized by relative autonomy, each field having its own "distinctive hierarchy, values, struggles, styles of improvising action, and forms of capital."[10]

Following Bourdieu, my approach to Black religious politics as a field of contestation focuses on social fields as sites characterized by competition. As Bourdieu notes, "every field is the site of a more or less overt struggle over the definition of the legitimate principles of the division of the field."[11] Fields are a conceptual tool for thinking about how particular social spaces are understandable in terms of what the sociologist John Levi Martin calls "organized striving."[12] One of the most useful metaphors for thinking about what a social field is and how it works is that of sports or playing games, in which, as Martin argues, "What is at stake in a chess, tennis, or sumo tournament is not simply which individual will be the winner, but what kind of chess, tennis, or sumo (and hence, what kinds of players) will dominate the field in the future."[13] Whether the analogy is chess, tennis, sumo wrestling, or any other organized competitive activity, an analysis of social field dynamics means paying attention not just to the use of an agreed upon set rules or parameters but also to fundamental debates about what the "rules of the game" actually are (or should be).[14] I argue that the concept of social fields provides the best way forward in addressing the paradox we find as we approach the task of understanding Black religious politics in the United

States and its global implications for Israel and Palestine. That paradox is the tension between the strong evidence for a recognition of deep diversity and the persistence of the overarching and contested normative category of "the Black Church" in African American religious spaces.

THE FIELD OF BLACK RELIGIOUS POLITICS

Social meanings are embedded in the real world, they are neither abstract nor detached concepts that exist "out there" somewhere. It is in the dynamic realm of social activity and the relationships between social actors that concepts have meaning. The meaning of "the Black Church" is embedded in the lived world of Black religion, where it is constantly tested and contested. The pastor and politician, Raphael Warnock, describes "the Black Church" as of a "divided mind." For Warnock, this is not simply an observation of the fact of diversity. If there is such a thing as "the Black Church," he is not arguing that it can only be understood as a loose umbrella category covering a wide range of ideas, identities, and lived expressions of religious belief and practice. Warnock states that the identity and purpose of "the Black Church" is contested within the social space of African American religion. We see this in the first line of his book, *The Divided Mind of the Black Church*, which asks: "What is the *true* nature and mission of the [Black] church?"[15]

As I have shown through my attention to African American Christian engagement with Palestine and Israel, there are many competing claims of what this "true nature and mission" should be. The contrasting positions evidenced in this book so far—among Black church clergy and laypeople—point to broad questions about Black churches that participants in and observers of Black religious life have long debated. Is the true nature and mission of "the Black Church" to attend to the spiritual needs of its members, offering salvation and the promise of heaven after the Christian departs this worldly "vale of tears"? Or is its true nature and mission more this-worldly, offering the promise of salvation not in the next life but in this life, through the possibility of improving the lives of marginalized people in this world, people who encounter the harsh realities of racism and discrimination in their everyday lives? And, if the focus is on this world and not just the next, should African American Christians focus on personal prosperity or collective social advancement and empowerment? Perhaps there is a unifying true mission to be found somewhere in between these options. These competing notions of the identity and mission of "the Black Church" are the persistent puzzle of Black religious politics that I address here.

In establishing my approach to Black religious politics as a field of contestation, I return to the work of the sociologist Philip Gorski on *traditions* (see the introduction). For Gorski, a tradition is "a culture that is self-conscious of its past." "To be part of a tradition," he explains, "is to know certain stories, read certain books, admire certain people, and care about certain things. It is to knowingly enter into an ongoing conversation, a conversation that precedes one's birth and continues after one's death."[16] This description of what a tradition is complements what the sociologist Omar McRoberts has written more specifically of Black churches in the United States. He describes them as social and cultural spaces in which "symbols are arranged and presented in ways that motivate human action, inspire emotion, give order to existence and, for the believer, constitute realities in themselves."[17] As both a tradition and a collective identity, "the Black Church" can be seen as a cultural repository, a carrier of meaning, and a driver of collective and individual social action. Like other political traditions and collective identities, the meaning of "the Black Church" is neither static nor fixed in the past. It is, in Gorski's terms, "forged and tested through historical experience and collective debate."[18] It is to that debate that I now turn, distilling the various African American modes of engagement with Israel and Palestine into a direct comparison of their broader outlooks on Black religious politics.

To elaborate this central puzzle of Black religious politics, I look at how these questions are asked, answered, and ultimately contested in my case studies along three related axes:

1. The first is in terms of *hermeneutics*—How do various African American Christians understand, interpret, and apply the Bible as a sacred text and source of identity?

2. The second is in the realm of *political engagement*—What, if any, forms of political engagement are deemed appropriate for African American Christians to engage in collectively?

3. The third axis is the *salience of race*—Where, how, and why does race matter in the theological, social, and political outlooks of African American Christians?

These three axes are closely linked, and the dominant vision for Black religious politics advanced within each of the four case studies is the product of intersections between theological reflection, the possibilities for political participation, and the particular role race plays in both.

The question of the salience of race in Palestine and Israel goes to the heart of the contestation of Black religious politics in the United States because what Black churches are stems from a more fundamental understanding of the significance of race in American society and around the globe. It also stems from long-standing models for understanding the fault lines of Black religious politics, which are oriented around these questions: Are Black churches primarily this-worldly or other-worldly institutions? Should they focus more on the spiritual dimensions of Black religious life with attention to the inner spiritual life on earth and the promise of salvation in the hereafter? Or should they focus more on the here and now and engage in this-worldly social and political work to spur social change? The distinction between these two broad strands of Black religious-political thought has been durable in studies of Black churches, with a range of poles: quietist versus activist, individualistic versus communal, accommodation versus contentious, inward-focused versus outward-focused, and attuned to the sacred versus attuned to the secular.

For each of the four cases, I begin with attention to how social actors formulate theological imperatives with political implications (*hermeneutics*). Then I look at how this theological reflection is manifest in particular preferred modes of *political engagement* (or disengagement). Finally, I discuss how this leads to different conclusions about the *salience of race* in each group's engagement with Israel and Palestine.

THE SAMUEL DEWITT PROCTOR CONFERENCE

Gregory Edwards, the Allentown, Pennsylvania, pastor I met at the Proctor Conference's Howard University Palestine event, described hermeneutics as a core element of Black church identity (see chapter 3). "'Black church' is not just a racial category, it's really a hermeneutic. It's a way of approaching the biblical texts," Edwards said. "It's a way of approaching ministry. It's a way of approaching your neighbor and God. [A way] that sees God very much in the struggle with people who have been dispossessed and marginalized." I also met Rozella White at the Proctor Conference's annual meeting in 2016. She is a theologian and a ministry consultant who was then the program director for the Young Adult Ministry at the Evangelical Lutheran Church in America (ELCA), a predominantly white, American Lutheran denomination. As an affiliate of the Proctor Conference with experience leading trips to Palestine and Israel with her own denomination, she had recently become involved in Proctor's efforts to speak to the question of Palestinian solidarity. She described the uniqueness of the Proctor Conference's voice in Black churches as one that elevates the imperative of an educated Black clergy. "I think in some Black traditions there is a suspicion of formal education, of social and historical critique of the way that we understand the hermeneutical lens of what the Bible says and how the Bible is read. And I think Proctor challenges all of that." She described this outlook on the Bible as "taking scripture seriously but not taking it literally." "The leaders of Proctor do take scripture very seriously," she explained. "[But they] don't necessarily take everything literally, and [they] ask the question of how does this text actually promote justice, point to the person of Jesus Christ . . . and then call us into deeper reflection around themes like love and justice and mercy and compassion and prophetic witness."

Taurean Webb, a former scholar in residence at the Proctor Conference and a leader in the organization's Palestine-focused initiatives, describes the biblical Exodus narrative as "[a] moment that looms large in the Afro-Christian imaginary."[19] Following much discussion of the history of African American religion, Webb acknowledges the biblical Exodus narrative of emancipation from slavery as a focal point of the African American religious imagination—"a rhetorical device used to contextualize, inspire, instruct, and sustain many Black Christians over their long path toward equality." Emphasizing the desired hermeneutic shift Proctor leaders outlined in the roundtable meeting (see chapter 2), Webb links Black church grappling with the Exodus narrative to the politics of dispossession and displacement. "Entry into promised places never comes without conquest and the displacement of the communities that already inhabit them," he writes. "Insofar as the Exodus has operated as a rhetorical device—albeit a very meaningful one—it has also justified tangibly experienced dispossessions of communities." Webb argues that there is a tendency for the issue of Israel and Palestine to provoke African American Christians "to impose the Exodus, metaphorically, on the Black freedom struggle, and/or interpret it literally, to conflate the 'ancient Israelites' with contemporary Israeli Jews physically having the right to inhabit a place that God has allegedly promised." The answer for Webb and his colleagues in the Samuel DeWitt Proctor Conference is an alternative biblical hermeneutic that upholds the Exodus narrative as a blueprint for revolutionary politics.[20]

Returning to Edwards and his attention to the critical role of a Black church hermeneutic that "sees God very much in the struggle with people who have been dispossessed and marginalized," Edwards explained how this connects to Israel and Palestine in his thinking about the biblical text. "Without that critique, I think that folk automatically, specifically the Black church, have been led to be very pro-Israel and not understanding that the Israel that has emerged now is a Eurocentric Israel, which, to a certain extent has been very discriminatory— not only to the Palestinians but even [to] their [Jewish] Ethiopian brothers." For Edwards and other Black clergy who push against what they see as a damaging dominant mode of biblical interpretation, there is hope in appealing to an alternative hermeneutic. "There's been this proclivity to freedom that's in our bones," he insisted, "and we've read the biblical text in a prophetic way. Until recently, that's truly been our foundation."

Based on this interpretive tendency, the Samuel DeWitt Proctor conference represents the most openly and overtly political case of African American Christian engagement with Palestine and Israel in this book. With a mission to "nurture, sustain, and mobilize the African American faith community," the organization's work links theological reflection and ecclesial practices with education, advocacy, and activism. As the SDPC cochair, Frederick Haynes, reminded the 2016 annual meeting of Proctor network members, "this is not just a feel-good gathering, but a *movement*." For the more than 500 clergy, scholars, activists, and lay leaders gathered, Haynes emphasized the need to "put on our prophetic eyeglasses." This statement captures the vision of Black religious politics that the Proctor Conference brings to the issue of Israel and Palestine.

Many of the African American clergy members from the Proctor network I met in my research see themselves as activists as much as pastors; this is a rather fluid boundary for these Black clergy members (see chapter 4). Neichelle Guidry provides one example. When I met her, she had been connecting Black millennial clergy with Black millennial activists in Chicago. Waltrina Middleton, the Proctor-affiliated clergywoman who led the activist-oriented Palestinian solidarity trip I accompanied, reflected on the role of a prophetic, socially and politically engaged Black church throughout the last century. She said that "the church has always been, in my opinion, a very critical, central nucleus of any movement.

When there were movements like the civil rights movement, it was the church that housed the organizers, the activists. That was the place of training, that fed them. That was a safe haven." Looking at the present potential of a politically engaged Black church, she offered, "I think still the church has a role, even if it's not living into it. . . . The church does not always—in this twenty-first century—live into its prophetic calling. But that does not mean that that prophetic calling ceased to exist. . . . It's absolutely integral to the ministry and witness of Christ. And so, if you depart from that, then I would argue that you cease to be the church." For Middleton and her colleagues at the Proctor Conference, "the Black Church" has always been and should always be, in some respect, prophetic *and* political. The church that distances itself from the political work of social justice is not the true church, she contends.

On the issue of Israel and Palestine, the question facing the Proctor Conference is not *should* it venture into politics but rather whether Palestinian solidarity activism is compatible with its broader outlook on Black religious politics and the prophetic mandate of "the Black Church." The answer that SDPC's general secretary, Iva Carruthers, gave to the audience of Proctor affiliates gathered at Howard University to discuss the question of how the Black church should respond to Palestine was an unqualified "yes." With more than a decade of leadership mobilizing African American Christians on domestic social and racial justice issues—such as criminal justice reform and environmental justice—and with a history of attention to transnational racial solidarity-building, it was simply a matter of connecting the dots between the African American experience and the Palestinian experience. As Jasiri X told a gathering of Proctor leaders in 2016: "One of the realest things somebody said to me in Palestine . . . was [from] a professor at a university in Palestine. He said, 'You know why you should care about what's happening in Palestine and why the hood should care?' He said, 'Because the policing that you see here is coming to a hood near you.' And eight months later—August of 2014—I had to go through a checkpoint to get into Ferguson, Missouri!"

The lawyer and activist Timothy Wright described a similar experience of recognizing a pattern of racialized social control in Palestine that was familiar to his experience in the United States. Of his trip to Palestine with a Proctor delegation, Wright commented: "One of the things that really moved me was that we sat down and talked to these little kids who were being arrested by the military, whom they tried to force into confessions. It reminded me so much of what happens in our community, as the kids were forced into confessions.

And they pinned things on them. And they put them in the justice system." He went on to describe his experiences growing up in Compton, California, where "even the nicest kids ended up going to jail." "They took all of us," he continued. "And I never understood why they would do it, and what was happening with that." Describing his reaction to learning about the military court system to which Palestinians in the Occupied Territories are subject, Wright said, "The only ones in that system were the Palestinians. There was no one from Israel." "And then," he added, "I thought about our courtrooms in urban cities—in particular Chicago. . . . If you walk in there, you don't think there are any white people in the world because everybody in there caught up in the justice system is Black. . . . And next to the Cook County Courts, you've got Cook County Jail, brimming to the top with Blacks and Hispanics." With both law and seminary degrees, Wright is typical of the kind of activism-oriented African American Christian engaged with the work of the Proctor Conference. With a background in antiracism legal work and activism in South Africa and in the United States, the resonance of African American and Palestinian experiences came quickly to Wright, as it did to many of the Proctor affiliates I met who have traveled to Palestine.

The politics of race and racial identity are prominent in the work of the Proctor Conference. With their focus on social justice activism, members focus, in particular, on issues where racial difference and racism contribute to social outcomes of concern—from educational attainment to environmental justice, from experiences of police brutality to patterns of incarceration, from poverty to drug policy. When specifically engaging with Palestine and Israel, the focus in the Proctor Conference is on solidarity-building. Here, the organization draws on a history of invoking Black religious politics in global terms, including attending to Pan-African racial identities and transnational racial solidarities. As Guidry put it regarding her visit to Palestine with the Proctor Conference:

> No, we did not go to Palestine on some traditional Christian pilgrimage. Rather, we were sent to survey the land, to open our eyes and our ears and to see the struggle of our Brown brothers and sisters in and through the Holy City of Jerusalem and throughout the West Bank. . . . No, we did not go to the "Holy Land" to walk in the sanctified footsteps of a whitewashed Jesus and lay our hands on the place where he wept in the Garden of Gethsemane. We did not go under the guise of being good Christian Zionist pilgrims, who unquestioningly sow our dollars into the occupation of people who look just like us.

Race and racial solidarity-building were at the forefront as the Proctor Conference began to incorporate Palestine into its portfolio of political and social justice causes. This impetus reflects theological commitments to liberationist principles to act on behalf of the marginalized in society, captured in the often-spoken distinction among Proctor affiliates between the religion *of* Jesus and the religion *about* Jesus. It is also what Bishop Don Williams expressed in his reflection on the significance of his travels in Israel and Palestine for the work of the Proctor Conference. "It felt good to walk where Jesus walked," he noted, "but it felt even better to walk where Jesus is walking today, and that is with those who are undervalued, underestimated, and marginalized."[21] Waltrina Middleton made her purpose in traveling to Palestine clear as well: "We are here to learn about narratives of people of color in the diaspora and compare them to our own."

The clergy, activists, scholars, and professionals who make up the Proctor Conference are guided to Israel and Palestine by a race-focused and liberationist understanding of the Bible and a critique of less politically attuned readings of scripture. Drawing on activism for racial justice issues in the United States, they extend Black religious politics into global spaces by connecting parallel issues of concern in racial justice terms, linking the experiences of African Americans in the United States to Palestinians in Israel and Palestine. Both groups, they contend, are engaged in a racialized anticolonial struggle for dignity, self-determination, and recognition.

THE PERFECTING CHURCH

As a predominantly African American congregation in a more evangelical religious space, The Perfecting Church (TPC) exhibits hermeneutic tendencies that speak to the theological questions and convictions of the broader world of white evangelicalism in which the church operates. In Palestine, late into the evening on the first day of the TPC trip in which I participated, Pastor Kevin Brown spoke to the group of first-time and return visitors to Bethlehem about the kind of theology he saw as dangerous for Christians to let guide them in thinking about the Middle East and Israel and Palestine. He talked about high-profile white Christian Zionist pastors and what he called their "speculative theology." He explained that such "bad theology," as he put it, can lead to a failure to recognize the personhood of anyone but Jews in the region. One member of the group asked him about "blood moons" prophecies—a view of Bible prophecy preached by some Christian pastors, including CUFI founder John Hagee—a series of lunar eclipses that lined up with Jewish holidays from 2014 to 2015 and marked the beginning of the earth's apocalyptic "end-times." The ostensible final "blood moon" of the series had occurred just a few weeks before our trip.[22] "I don't preach it, and I question it when a pastor would use his pulpit for speculation." Brown went on to talk about the perils of Christian pastors who "preach fear."

When we sat down for an interview several weeks after the trip, Brown explained why he thinks "speculative theology" is dangerous and what his alternative way of reading, interpreting, and preaching the Bible looks like. "I think our view on eschatology can get in the way of our view of sanctification, and what it looks like for us to live as followers of Jesus right now," he said. "In too many cases," he continued, "we've exalted what I will call very speculative theology and let that control, and lead, and dictate our actions more than very clear theology." Brown added that he went through a period of reading a lot of Christian books on what he now dismisses as end-times-focused "speculative theology." "And when I finished studying," he said, "I came to the conclusion that nobody knows what the heck they're talking about." His fallback interpretive emphasis in reading the Bible in the face of this uncertainty about the future is two examples of what he called "very clear theology." The first is the Great Commandment, and the second is the Great Commission. "The great commandment is to love the lord your God with all your heart, all your mind, and your strength, and love your neighbor as yourself . . . and the Great Commission is to go and teach all nations as I've commanded you, baptizing them in the name of the Father, Son, and the Holy Spirit," referring to the Gospel of Matthew 22:37–39 and 28:16–20.

Among the African American Christians focusing on connecting with Palestinians, members of TPC were the least likely to wear the activist label as one inextricably linked to their African American Christian identity. Unlike the Black clergy and activists of the Proctor Conference, for example, the leaders and members of TPC are far more ambivalent about mixing religion and politics. In chapter 3, I describe how this ambivalence about political engagement—in the United States and in Israel and Palestine—begins with the leadership of Kevin and Angela Brown. "I've worked on not getting politically involved [in Palestine]. I know that there are some Christians there that are doing an incredible job at being politically involved, but I don't think you can do both well," Kevin Brown told me in conversation I had with him and Angela. "I don't feel that [politics is] our assignment there," he reiterated. But in saying this he looked directly at Angela and laughed, "She's political!" "I try not to be political," Angela responded, "but I absolutely understand that, in doing so, we're choosing a side. She continued to describe how choosing to not take sides is actually a political choice.

This leadership dynamic between Angela and Kevin Brown—toward and away from political engagement—is expressed in some version by virtually all members of TPC I traveled with in Palestine or spoke to in the United States. The lived realities of Palestinians under occupation consistently drew parallels to African American experiences for TPC members, which they voiced freely. Further reflection on what TPC members should do about those connections, however, tended to lead to an aversion to political activism in favor of the kind of "engagement with the domains of society" that forms the core of the church's mandate in Israel and Palestine—areas of civil society such as business development, athletics, social work, the arts, etc. The ultimate rejection of political engagement on behalf of Palestinians is perhaps best captured by the associate pastor who told me his thoughts on the Palestinian BDS movement: "My thing, I'm not an activist. I don't boycott, I don't march, I don't riot, I don't protest." Another TPC leader emphasized the pull toward politics and "choosing sides" as something natural for people to experience—especially for African Americans, who see so many parallels in the lives of Palestinians. The ability to not take sides, however, he described as supernatural:

> I think the way you don't pick sides is divine. I just don't think that—just in our intellect, in our emotions—we have the ability to not pick sides. I think that it has to be a deity. I think it has to be a divine intervention that allows you to go beyond your intellect and beyond your emotions—of just your flesh humanity—to not pick sides.

For the members and leaders of The Perfecting Church, the experience and recognition of racial injustice in Palestine provokes nonpolitical modes of intervention. Instead of focusing on *activism*, they turn toward what they describe as the work of *reconciliation*. This choice stems from core convictions that guide TPC about the theological and political significance of race and racial inequality. Rather than advocating a specific vision for Black religious politics and a unique vision of the role of "the Black Church," they push away from politics in favor of invoking reconciliation as a more universalistic vision of the significance of race.

In the spring of 2015, I first attended TPC on the Sunday that followed the return home of the most recent glocal engagement trip the church had undertaken to Palestine and Israel. During that service, Kevin Brown preached a sermon entitled "The Church: A Reconciling Community." "God calls and uses people," he declared to the congregation. "The church is called to be the reconciler." He went on to explain that this is because God is building something. "He doesn't need us to play church," he said. "He's calling us to become the church. He doesn't need us to tell stories, he needs us to become the story. He doesn't need us to point to scriptures, he needs us to live out the scriptures."

After the short sermon on reconciliation, Brown invited the ten other TPC members who had just returned from Palestine onto the stage to share their own stories of the experience. The group included first-time visitors and members who had traveled to the region on earlier trips. All eleven members were Black. Each one talked about the engagements in which they participated with Palestinians, about the moments of the trip that were most significant and meaningful to them, and about what they had learned. The only time race was mentioned was when one team member laughed about leading an athletic training session with a Palestinian women's soccer team. He described feeling like their reaction to meeting him revealed that they had never seen a Black person before. Race and racial identity were not at the forefront of the team's reports that Sunday morning, but in the following weeks Brown continued to preach a series of sermons specifically focused on the meaning and the significance of race.

That series, entitled "Race, Reconciliation, and the Cross," began with a sermon on the theme of "the changing face of America." In introducing that sermon, Brown told the congregation that this day marked the fiftieth anniversary of the civil rights movement's Bloody Sunday, when hundreds of marchers in Selma, Alabama, were met with a violent police response on the Edmund Pettus Bridge. Brown used the bridge context of Bloody Sunday and the fight for African American civil rights to explain his purpose in the current sermon series being about "tearing down barriers and building bridges." Racism, he explained, is "the lens through which we see others." Brown explained the metaphor using the example of twelve-year-old Tamir Rice, the African American boy who had been killed by police in Cleveland just a few months earlier. He described how the officer who shot and killed Tamir Rice reported seeing "a young thug." "That's a lens that somebody sees through," Brown said. In ending his sermon, he explained its takeaway to his mostly Black congregation. "Examine your preferences and prejudices," he said, "God is calling us together."

In the following weeks, Brown continued to expound on the theological and political significance of race for his congregation. He explained God's vision for what he described as unity in diversity. Across racial, ethnic, and cultural lines, this vision is rooted in the Trinitarian vision of Christianity. He described the need to find common ground as "the place that we come together, and we all feel united." "Too often in America," he added, "[the church] becomes a place of separation." Emphasizing unity, he described a sense of identity within "the kingdom of God" as superseding culture, racial, and ethnic diversity. On the prospect of racial reconciliation, Brown argued, "We can no more reconcile the races than we can reconcile ourselves to God." Racial reconciliation, he claimed, is only possible through God. Taking stock of the racial progress (and lack of racial progress) in U.S. history, Brown concluded that "hatred exists because we can't find value in ourselves without oppressing someone else." "But," he said, "because I'm loved, I can love. Because I've been forgiven, I can forgive."

The outlook on the significance of race that Brown teaches at TPC does not ignore race but channels the salience of race in particular ways. As this chapter and earlier chapters have shown, for members of TPC there is a continuous urge to "take sides"—generally, but not always, in response to the pull to side with the Palestinians. TPC members I met, interviewed, and traveled with perceive the systems of racial profiling and discrimination Palestinians experience, but following the leadership of Kevin and Angela Brown, they push themselves to "choose the cross" rather than "choose sides." This imperative stems from a theology of reconciliation that puts priority on community-building, peacemaking, and unity of purpose—all of which are possible in theological terms of reconciliation. This is not to say that Kevin Brown and his church do not see a unique voice for African American in Palestine. Like the members of his church, he has personally experienced unique points of connection with Palestinians based on being African American. Over lunch with one of their Palestinian partners in the NGO sector, Kevin and Angela Brown described Black Lives Matter as a significant moment for African American and Palestinian connections—even more significant, Kevin Brown said, than the election and presidency of Barack Obama. In specifically Christian spaces, he said that there need to be more African American voices. In spite of their intentions, Brown explained, white Christians "are not always on point" when relating to Palestinians. "The voice of the one who hasn't been oppressed doesn't ring true sometimes," he added. The uniqueness of these points of connection should lead to bridge building—being agents of healing and reconciliation between Jewish Israelis and Palestinians.

Following the lead of Kevin and Angela Brown, the African American Christians at TPC who travel to Israel and Palestine with a glocal mandate to engage with Palestinians are cautious of the kind of end-times-focused theology that often dominates American evangelical thinking about Israel and the Middle East. For them, Palestine is a "hard place in the world" that they feel called to and where they can link a local south New Jersey and Philadelphia area mission to emphasize the biblical commands to "love the lord your God" and "love your neighbor as yourself." This imperative is reinforced with a theology of reconciliation that aims for unity in spite of diversity. Where African American experiences of discrimination in the United States paralleled the experiences of Palestinians, TPC members in Israel and Palestine strive to be agents of reconciliation, building bridges between Jewish Israelis and Palestinians.

CHRISTIANS UNITED FOR ISRAEL

The hermeneutics that drive Black church support for the State of Israel within Christians United for Israel (CUFI) takes a very different starting point. Dumisani Washington, CUFI's diversity outreach coordinator, summarized the typical CUFI outlook on interpreting the Bible when it comes to Israel for an audience of Christian college students in Rochester, New York. His presentation began with a definition: "*Christian Zionism,*" he said, "is the biblical belief that Israel is the homeland of the Jewish people. . . . Just believing that, basically, when God said that, that's exactly what he meant." He went on to show a series of slides with Bible verses from the Old and New Testaments. "God says . . . Israel is my firstborn" (Exodus 4:22). "For the Lord has chosen Jacob to be his own, Israel to be his treasured possession" (Psalm 135:4). He continued with several more verses, emphasizing, "When God says forever, he means forever. That means God's eternal covenant with Israel—being his firstborn and being his chosen—is forever." He ended his whirlwind biblical argument in support of Christian Zionism by saying, "Christian Zionism just basically says, 'I believe that the Bible says what it says and it means what it actually means where the Jewish people are concerned.'"

This literalist "take the Bible at face value" hermeneutic is not unique to African American Christian Zionists. It is shared by white Christian Zionists and others who begin with the Bible as their starting point for making the case that Christians should stand in political solidarity with the Jewish State of Israel. African American Christian Zionists share this interpretive starting point with their white Christian Zionist allies. Jonathan Leath echoed this hermeneutic: "When I read the Bible, it talks about the relationship that God had with the Jewish people. And he chose them—not because there was anything special about them—he just chose them. . . . My mission now is to show our church . . . that there is a relationship that we have with the Jewish nation and it's because God cares for them and God's gonna always care for them."

This biblical hermeneutic extends to what Michael Stevens described to a gathering of African American clergy in 2013 as a complementary "spiritual" logic to Christian Zionism. "I just believe with all my heart—and this is no hype, this is no hustle," he said. "I believe that when we make up our minds to be a blessing to Israel and pray for them and show kindness to them, I believe with all my heart God's gonna bless you and there is a spiritual endowment and blessing that's gonna come your way." The expectation of blessings in return for standing in solidarity with the State of Israel, described in the introduction and chapter 1, is also a hermeneutic outlook widely shared with white American Christian Zionists. But Stevens adds to this what he calls a "moral imperative" for African Americans, specifically, to "stand with Israel." Taking a different interpretation of the Exodus narrative than the prophetic and liberative hermeneutic that the SDPC's Taurean Webb outlined previously, Black CUFI leaders like Stevens deploy an interpretation of the Exodus narrative that specifically links African American Christian identification with that Bible story to contemporary Black Jewish solidarity in pro-Israel activism today.

There are limits, however, to the effectiveness of CUFI's reliance on this hermeneutic of "I believe that Bible says what it says and it means." Following the student event in Rochester, Washington discussed those limits with David Walker, then a campus organizer for CUFI, and another local CUFI regional coordinator. That coordinator described being in a meeting of CUFI leaders who were divided over the question of whether "because the Bible says so" should be enough to equip CUFI's college students to sustain and succeed in pro-Israel activism on their campuses. The three CUFI leaders in Rochester agreed that arguments drawing on biblical interpretation alone were not enough to equip college students to face critiques of their Christian Zionist political positions. Walker later explained this to me:

> For me, what got me involved is, of course, the biblical mandate. Because the Bible is something that touches every part of my life as a Christian and something that I take very seriously. . . . But then you can't stop there. . . . That is the foundation for why we support Israel for a lot of Christian students, but that should not be the end-all. We cannot pigeonhole ourselves into this one argument. We've gotta definitely diversify our argument for supporting Israel.

This impetus to "diversify" the pro-Israel argument is also apparent in the ways CUFI's lobby group activism goes beyond making Bible-based arguments. The final day of CUFI's annual summit in Washington, DC, is dedicated to attendees visiting the offices of their congressional representatives on Capitol Hill. When I went to the summit in 2013, attendees were given a list of talking points for congressional visits that included no mention of the Bible. Instead they focused on (1) the threat of Iran's nuclear program, (2) the situation of Christian populations in the Middle East as minority groups, and (3) strengthening the U.S.-Israel strategic partnership. All of these included specific pieces of legislation tagged for support or opposition.

However, a Bible-based rationale for supporting the State of Israel is only the beginning for CUFI in its Black and white constituencies. Politics is an important axis of contestation among African American churches, and because African American Christians are a small minority of CUFI's members, articulating a uniquely Black vision of Black religious politics is complicated for African American CUFI outreach workers. For the purposes of understanding different hermeneutical positions within Black religious politics more broadly, this strategic biblical-political divide within CUFI gets at the extent to which the political is interwoven with biblical interpretation for more prophetic- and liberationist-oriented African American Christians, such as the Black clergy the Proctor Conference represents. There, the link between "reading the Bible through the eyes of the oppressed" and acting politically is a close one. Whereas for CUFI, the connection can be much more difficult to make, especially when making one argument (a biblical argument) in more traditional Black religious spaces and another (a political argument) on college campuses, for example.

Pro-Israel advocates working for CUFI begin with the Bible in their appeals to African American churches. As white CUFI regional outreach coordinator Victor Styrsky said to a mostly Black church audience at the First Cathedral in Bloomfield, Connecticut: "I've had pastors say, 'Pastor, the Church shouldn't be political.' Now I get whatcha mean on that, yeah absolutely. But Israel's not political, it's *biblical*." CUFI's African American outreach leaders Stevens and Washington similarly begin their appeals to Black Christians with arguments made from the Bible. For CUFI leaders, however, the biblical connection quickly moves into the political realm. The First Cathedral's executive pastor, LeRoy Bailey III, welcomed his congregants to a CUFI presentation by describing the CUFI-led tour of Israel in which he had participated. He first highlighted the religious importance of "having the Bible opened up to you" in the Holy Land but quickly shifted to discussing the privilege of "sharing, witnessing, and experiencing not only the Bible but also the fellowship with the military in Israel." He described getting to meet Israel Defense Forces soldiers on that trip, "thanking them, sharing love for them, and letting them know that we are there for them."

Israel's military and its political role in defending the State of Israel and advancing its policies features prominently in CUFI's messaging. It is one of many overtly political angles of the organization's pro-Israel advocacy. Other political features of its message during my fieldwork in CUFI's African American outreach included criticizing the United Nations and its comparisons of Israel's policies to those of apartheid in South Africa; the threat of Iran's nuclear program; and warnings about the political threat of militant Islamic groups ISIS, Al Qaeda, Hamas, Hezbollah, and Boko Haram. On these issues and others, CUFI pastors and speakers link America's political interests with those of the State of Israel. "You have to realize," Stevens told a Bronx, New York, Black church audience, "in the eyes of jihadist Muslims, every attack against Israel is an attack against the United States of America." "They do consider Israel as the Little Satan," he added, "and they consider you and I, as Americans, the Big Satan." "I'll say that again," he reiterated, "every threat and attack against Israel is a threat and attack against the United States of America."

In some sense, CUFI's vision of Black church politics de-emphasizes the political significance of race, taking the "Black" out of Black religious politics in favor of supporting a political agenda primarily set and advanced by white conservative Christians who often share few other political priorities with their Black partners in pro-Israel activism. My fieldwork in CUFI's African American outreach program took place mostly during Barack Obama's second term in office. During this time, I saw many white CUFI speakers openly and harshly criticize Obama and his policies in no uncertain terms. Black CUFI leaders, however, appeared reluctant to criticize him openly, knowing that even their theologically conservative Black audiences admired Obama and generally supported his presidency. Getting ahead of this issue with the Black church audience in the Bronx, Stevens said:

> What about Barack Obama? Well, I've met the president in my city. I'm praying for my president. . . . We have to continually pray for our president. We know there's been some wonderful achievements he's a part of in our country. But he's also had many areas where he has not been his best at. One of those areas is policy in the Middle East. We would like for him to be a little more stronger, more supportive, of Israel.

In front of this Bronx Black church congregation, Stevens hedged significantly in his critique of Obama, mindful of losing the political interest of his audience. This raises the question, What is the place of African Americans in the world of CUFI's pro-Israel politics? Is there a vision of a uniquely Black religious politics within Christian Zionism that can resonate with African American Christians more broadly? Or are pro-Israel Black pastors consigned to a kind of loneliness that describes the status of many Black political conservatives—shunned in the wider world of Black politics and subordinated among their white partners?[23] The image of African American Christians "taking a seat at the table" helps answer these questions. As outlined in chapter 3, both Stevens and Washington have used this image to spur African American Christians into a particular kind of political engagement, encouraging them to "take a seat at the table" lest they be "on the menu." With this, they carve out a specific kind of Black religious politics that they aim to make compatible with wider African American political sensibilities more broadly—one that gives priority to participation in politics, and the accompanying elevation of status that might entail, over a more issue-centered and justice-focused approach to impelling political action. Again, as I argue in chapter 3, this is a distinctly *brokering* model of Black religious political engagement.

This also relates to another uniquely African American aspect of pro-Israel activism that CUFI's African American outreach pastors put forward as a vision for Black religious politics. That vision looks to the Black-Jewish partnerships of the early part of the U.S. civil rights struggle as their defining feature and cause of success. Within this framework, the salience of race for CUFI's African American Christian Zionists draws lessons from the civil rights era of the 1950s and early 1960s and U.S. foreign policy in the Middle East today. This emphasis on race via Black-Jewish civil rights cooperation has two related consequences for understanding the vision of Black religious politics cultivated by African American pastors in CUFI. First, they argue that it is because of this Jewish support that the movement succeeded at all, and this crucial support motivates the following step of the argument in favor of African American Christian Zionism—now African Americans owe a debt to the Jewish people, which they can repay by lending their political support to the government of the State of Israel. Based on this history-facing logic, all contemporary questions of Black religious politics must pass through the pro-Israel test. For example, the question of the legitimacy of the Movement for Black Lives and whether Black churches should be involved begins with the movement's stance on Palestinian solidarity as a nonstarter. The second consequence of this emphasis on Black-Jewish civil rights partnerships is a tendency toward a deracialized politics of assimilation in the present. In the African American Christian Zionist imagination, American Jews are the model story of assimilation and integration to which Black Americans can aspire. American Jews, they claim, have already taken their place at the table. And the opportunity to join them is available to African Americans through lending political support to the State of Israel.

Within CUFI's African American outreach efforts, a universal biblical argument for supporting the State of Israel is fused with a particularistic argument about the moral responsibility that African Americans bear to support Israel as a Jewish state today because of the contributions of American Jews to the struggle for Black civil rights in the last century. The vision of Black religious politics put forward provides opportunities for pastors to take their seat at the table of a political issue that extends beyond their local communities. Race becomes salient, not so much in terms of building solidarities in specifically racialized terms but in building Black-Jewish solidarities across racial lines while invoking a debt owed for past support in advancing racial progress.

THE INTERNATIONAL FELLOWSHIP OF CHRISTIANS AND JEWS

In many ways, the Black church leaders who work with the International Fellowship of Christians and Jews (IFCJ) invoke a similar hermeneutic approach to the Bible to that of CUFI's Black pastors and outreach leaders. Reverend Deedee Coleman, the member of the IFCJ advisory board for African American church outreach who hosted the IFJC-sponsored Martin Luther King Jr. Jewish-Christian interfaith event at her Detroit church, said of her reasons for supporting Christian Zionist activism, "It is God's choice that we honor the Jewish people. And we don't ask God why." This is the hermeneutic logic she preaches to her Detroit congregation and that she teaches her fellow African American clergy to deploy in their own churches, acting as a speaker for the IFCJ and the American Israel Public Affairs Committee (AIPAC). Coleman was instrumental in connecting the IFCJ to her own 1.5 million member Progressive National Baptist Convention (PNBC) and to the National Baptist Convention of America (NBCA). After taking a delegation of NBCA leaders to Israel with the IFCJ, convention president Samuel Tolbert explained a similar logic to me as guiding his participation in the Fellowship's work, rooted in what he described as "the biblical teachings about the Jews being chosen people." "I believe that," he said. "They are the only people that I can think of off the top of my head that got some sense of deed of property from God for a specific geographic area. And I know it talks about those who bless them shall be blessed and those who curse them shall be cursed. And you know we preach it and we teach it, and we read it." The NBCA pastor and a member of the convention's executive cabinet, Bartholomew Banks, similarly described his interpretive reasoning for pursuing a partnership with the Fellowship and the convention's interest in working in Israel. "I believe that the Land of Israel was promised to Abraham by God," he said. "God chose them to be the people through which his son would be brought into the world. And he said this land would be theirs forever."

When I sat with Edward Branch in the office of his New Hope Baptist Church in Detroit, he explained a similar rationale for partnering with the Fellowship in supporting the State of Israel politically. "You cannot, as a Christian, stand and preach and know nothing about Israel. We learn it because Judaism and the teachings of the Hebrew Bible—or the Old Testament, as it may be referred to—is our underpinning. It's where our roots go in." We had a far-ranging conversation about the politics of the region and how Branch came to become specifically involved in recruiting other Black clergy into the Fellowship's philanthropic work in Israel. "There is a part of me that just identifies with the plight of Israel," he said. "And then," he added, "[it is about] embracing what I believe the Bible says about Israel—Genesis 12:3: *Bless Israel and you get blessed.*" Branch's involvement with the Fellowship had been extensive when I met him in 2016. After having personally organized and led several trips for family, church members, and leaders over the years, he traveled to Israel with AIPAC on a political mission in 2013. Similar to Kristina King, Branch later began working with the Fellowship, looking for an outlet for his affinity for Israel that aligned more with what he described as his interest in helping "everyday people" in their struggles rather than working on high-level global political issues.

When we met, he was preparing to help lead the IFCJ-sponsored delegation of Progressive National Baptist Convention leaders to Israel, and he had recently coauthored a booklet with IFCJ founder Rabbi Yechiel Eckstein entitled *On the Frontlines of Faith: The Historical and Spiritual Bonds Between African-Americans and Jews*. In that booklet, Branch describes his 2013 trip to Israel as an encounter with the everyday struggles of Israelis. "We visited Sderot, the town nearest the Gaza Strip, only to realize that the citizens of this small community live every day under the threat of missiles fired from so close that every home is required to have a bomb shelter. At the northernmost border with Lebanon, we could easily see that Israeli homes were within striking distance from the wire fence that separated their borders."[24] IFCJ-affiliated pastors express a similar biblical hermeneutic impulse to that of CUFI pastors—the simple argument that the Bible requires them to "bless Israel." And they similarly overlay onto that a particular imperative for African American Christians. Branch writes:

> In a thousand ways, the history of African-Americans and that of the Jews parallel. Hardly anything in life ties people closer together than the pain of a common struggle. While the Bible gives us the story of the Hebrew/Jewish record, we are ever mindful of our connection as the people of God. We are inextricably interwoven into the human fabric and our plight is determined by how well we live and work together. Dr. King said it well when he reminded us that "We will either live together as brothers [and sisters], or we will perish together as fools."[25]

Like the African American Christians who partner with CUFI to promote Christian Zionism, the Black clergy and laypeople who work with the International Fellowship of Christians and Jews interweave broadly shared literalist readings of the Bible with particular appeals to a common experience of struggle via the Exodus narrative and the Black experience of slavery. Although they seek less overt political avenues for their Christian Zionism than CUFI or AIPAC, their ostensibly philanthropic outlook on Christian Zionist support of Israel often veers toward politics (see chapter 1). Branch's words here echo this pull as he describes the suffering of Jewish Israeli's in political terms resulting from their proximity to Israel's borders.

I often encountered a strong aversion to politics among the Black church pastors and members that the IFCJ seeks to incorporate into its pro-Israel activism. Kristina King, who left a job in African American outreach at the political lobbying group AIPAC to become the IFCJ's director of African American outreach, did so because of the opportunity it afforded her to engage in a less overtly politicized form of pro-Israel activism. The more spiritual and religiously focused Jewish-Christian partnership for Christian Zionism the Fellowship had long sought to build appealed more to her own motivations for supporting Israel. "My journey into support for Israel came from a place of faith, and my passion comes from a place of faith," she said. The "place of faith" connection to the State of Israel that the Fellowship developed in its African American outreach program identified charitable work as the primary model of Black church social engagement and linked that understanding of Black religious politics to the Fellowship's philanthropic work in Israel. "It's the work that the African-American community does here in the United States," King explained. "And so, it's like a love fest when you see that same work in Israel."

Branch expressed the same sense of a good fit with the IFCJ's approach to attracting African American Christians to the Christian Zionist cause, compared to AIPAC's overtly political approach:

> I think with the International Fellowship of Christians and Jews that speaks more to who I am and to the kind of ministry that I believe God has given more for me. I think it reaches more people. I think it's more about how to help folks, how to service those Jews who are in need and those who are outside of the homeland and desire to get back there. I think the International Fellowship of Christians and Jews have a direct mission that speaks to those kinds of things, and which I could relate to a lot better than the high-level stuff as to what President Obama and Netanyahu want to talk about. I trust that they will take care of their [political] business but it's still those folks who are in need and those people who need shelter, protection, food.

Guided by its African American advisory committee, the Fellowship determined that Black churches, with their long track records of providing social services in Black communities, could be approached with a new global context for extending that work in Israel. This opportunity appealed to denominational leaders like NBCA's Samuel Tolbert, who said:

> This [IFCJ-sponsored Israel] trip opened my eyes to the potential opportunities we have. . . . NBCA does not have to create the infrastructure to do mission in Israel. The infrastructure for us to do mission in Israel is already there through the International Fellowship of Christians and Jews, and we can take advantage of collaborating with them to do what I think biblically we should have been doing all along.

This approach to Black religious politics that emphasizes providing social services opens the possibility of uplifting what Deedee Coleman called "the softer side of Israel." "It's not all about the war," she explained. "It's about people trying to live. It's about children being traumatized. It's about a country striving and wanting to be alive like everybody else. Wanting to be separate but equal and having the relationship." In Israel, as chapter 4 describes, the NBCA delegation focused on IFCJ-sponsored philanthropic projects such as an orphanage, a community center for Ethiopian Jews, a premilitary academy for Ethiopian Jews, and a food pantry facility. NBCA leaders were very comfortable being introduced to philanthropic projects in Israel, even though they were far from their own communities where they typically engage in religiously inspired social service provision.

The salience of race for the African American Christians who get involved in Israel and Palestine is mutable. When envisioning a mode of Black religious politics, the clergy and lay church members who have come into the world of Christian Zionist political engagement largely do so in philanthropic terms, following the IFCJ's lead and well-tested model. And they do so by invoking a vision of Black religious politics that tends to be more inwardly focused than outwardly focused. That vision sees the provision of social services as clearly within the social mandate of Black churches, even when they eschew more overt engagement in politics through protest or policy advocacy work. For several of the Black church denominations and conventions that have worked with the IFCJ, this also aligns with their global outlook on pairing evangelism with providing social services. IFCJ African American outreach leaders make the case that Black churches and Black clergy are naturally positioned to engage and support the Fellowship's philanthropic work in Israel, given their experience doing similar work in their local Black communities in the United States.

The Fellowship also invokes race more directly in their Black-Jewish solidarity-building pro-Israel activism. Here, the stories of Black Ethiopian Jews are brought front and center by the Fellowship's outreach staff and senior leadership. This work happens particularly in Israel because African American delegations on Fellowship-led trips and follow-up visits put connecting with Black Ethiopians in Israel high on their list of priorities. In IFCJ outreach efforts within the United States, on the other hand, race tends to be invoked more in national than in transnational terms, doing the kind of work to bolster Black-Jewish partnerships based on the U.S. civil rights legacy, as the booklet by Branch shows. When I traveled to Israel with the NBCA leadership delegation, sponsored and led by the Fellowship, we visited an Ethiopian Jewish community center; a premilitary leadership training program, where we met Black trainees preparing for their compulsory military service; and an Israeli Border Police outpost near the Palestinian West Bank city of Jericho, where we met a group of border guards that included Black Ethiopian Israelis. On visits like these, the salience of race was mediated variously by white Jewish Fellowship staff and tour guides and by visiting Black pastors.

At the premilitary leadership academy, the NBCA delegation met with three Black teenage trainees. We learned that forty-two of the forty-nine Ethiopian Jewish trainees at the academy were sponsored directly by the Fellowship. We met two of these Ethiopian Jewish trainees and one other Black trainee who was not Ethiopian. That trainee, Ahmadiel, was a nineteen-year-old young man who spoke English fluently and with an American accent. This was in contrast to the two Ethiopian students who spoke little English and had thick accents. Because of his native, American-accented English, the NBCA visitors assumed that Ahmadiel had been born in the United States. He explained that he was born in Israel to parents who immigrated there in 1969 with a group of Black Hebrew Israelites who founded a community in the southern Negev region city of Dimona, which is home to about 3,000 Black Hebrew Israelites.[26] Ahmadiel described his community as believing they are the lost Jewish tribe of Judah and that they practice polygamy. He also explained their sense of feeling discriminated against in Israeli society and how he felt joining the military could help improve their social standing. One visiting NBCA pastor asked Ahmadiel if he had dual U.S.-Israeli citizenship. He answered no, explaining that he has U.S. citizenship but not Israeli citizenship. No further questions were asked about why the two Ethiopian immigrant students were Israeli citizens but the Black Hebrew Israelite born in Israel was not. The group leaders and guides played a significant role in controlling the narrative on race in Israel.

The dominant narrative about Black Jews in Israel on the trip was one of equality, inclusion, and integration. The lower social status of one of the Black trainees we met was a potential moment of rupture that was glossed over. Enlivened by Ahmadiel's story, the visiting African American pastors asked the two Ethiopian trainees to say something about themselves. One of them spoke up, but struggled to find a way to say something defining about himself in English. He eventually offered a concise description of himself as "a normal person" and "not from Dimona or anything." The academy leader, an olive-skinned Israeli Jewish man of perhaps forty sitting next to his three trainees, broke into the conversation to reiterate the equality of races at the academy. Again, a potential moment of rupture in the dominant trip narrative of equality was quickly mended. When our conversation with the Black trainees ended, we walked outside with them and their leaders into an open courtyard, where we posed for a group photograph before boarding the bus to depart for our next destination.

Officials from the Black Pentecostal Church of God in Christ (COGIC) denomination also traveled to Israel on a similar Fellowship-led tour. And I returned with another COGIC delegation of denominational leaders, clergy, and lay members the following year for a follow-up trip. This trip, however, was not directly led by Fellowship staff. The COGIC mandate in Israel developed around a focus on Black Ethiopians, building off the Fellowship's outreach efforts and the denomination's own networking with groups of Ethiopian Jewish "believers."[27] Outside of the direct guidance of Fellowship staff in Israel, the COGIC follow-up trip I participated in presented more opportunities for ruptures in the Fellowship's racial equality narrative. On the trip, Pastor Glenn Plummer, a founding member of the Fellowship's African American advisory board and COGIC's director of Israel missions, explained the perils and potential for COGIC's work with Ethiopian Jewish believers. On the previous IFCJ-led COGIC delegation, one pastor live-streamed a video of the COGIC Ethiopian congregation in Israel, which led to some stress within that community because of the precarious position they occupy as a racial and religious minority. "But," Plummer said, "now is their time to be bold. We are standing with them!" He went on to describe the importance of the U.S.-Israel relationship. "Israel needs U.S. friendship because of their enemies in the region," he said. As an organization of 6.5 million U.S. Christians, he explained that COGIC is an important constituency for the State of Israel to court as a political ally. "Important people in Israel are aware of COGIC's presence," he noted. Plummer went on to discuss the kind of impact this influence could have for Black Israelis, not just in terms of religious freedom for Ethiopian Jewish believers but also in terms of civil rights and social status. Plummer told the group about Black-led protests in Israel in the past year in which protestors accused Israel of racism. He called attention to a *USA Today* cover story from May 2015 that featured parallel images of Black Lives Matter protesters in Baltimore and Ethiopian Jews protesting against the racism, lack of opportunity, poverty, and police harassment they experience in Israel. "Israel doesn't want us to carry the story that Ethiopians are being mistreated," he said. "What's the unemployment rate of the Ethiopian community?" one COGIC missionary asked Plummer. He did not have that information available but by way of a reply he said, "You wanna hear a statistic? 40 percent of all people in Israeli prisons are Ethiopians!" "Well, that sounds familiar," the missionary shot back. Heads around the group nodded with audible sighs of recognition and affirmation. In this instance, outside of the narrative framework of the Fellowship's African American outreach program, race took on additional significance for Black Christians visiting Israel from the United States, as the political salience of race was heightened.

As with CUFI's Black church outreach, the African Americans who have become involved with Christian Zionism through the outreach work of the International Fellowship of Christians and Jews have to define the racial particularities of their Christian Zionism within a predominantly white organization. In the United States, the IFCJ relies on a similar narrative of Black-Jewish civil rights solidarity. In this context, that historical solidarity is evidence of an even older spiritual bond linking African Americans and Jews through the biblical Exodus narrative. In Israel, however, there is an effort to translate that solidarity into contemporary terms through exposure to Black Ethiopian Jewish communities. The IFCJ highlights Ethiopian Jews as integral to Israel's diverse society, emphasizing equality and opportunity. But in spite of dominant narratives about racial equality, African American Christian encounters with Ethiopian Jews in Israel also provoke conversations about racial inequality, linking issues of racial injustice in Israel and in the United States. This highlights the extent to which the salience of race and the corresponding limits of different visions of Black religious politics are mutable and subject to spontaneous change.

Table 5.1 summarizes the orientations to Black religious politics and the identity and mission of "the Black Church" described here.

TABLE 5.1 Black religious politics and the identity and mission of "the Black Church"

Case	Hermeneutics	Political engagement	Salience of race
Samuel DeWitt Proctor Conference (SDPC)	Liberationist theology (God is in the struggle with the oppressed). Prophetic reading of scripture (read the Bible "through the eyes of the oppressed"). "Take scripture seriously, but not literally." The Exodus narrative as a blueprint for revolutionary politics.	Oriented toward activism ("this is a movement") and linking clergy and activists. "The Black Church" needs to live up to its calling as a prophetic, politically engaged institution.	Highlighting global connections across marginalized perspectives and experiences. Recognition of shared struggles and common struggles leads to political solidarity.
The Perfecting Church (TPC)	Avoid "speculative theology" and preaching fear in favor of the "very clear theology" of the Great Commandment and the Great Commission.	Avoid getting involved in politics (instead of "choosing sides," "choose the cross"). Eschew activism in favor of reconciliation and peacebuilding.	Racism is about perception. Unity in the Christian church transcends cultural, racial, and ethnic diversity. Reconciliation between groups of people is rooted in reconciliation with God. A unique voice among those who have been oppressed.
Christians United for Israel (CUFI)	Literalist interpretation of scripture ("When God said that, that's exactly what he meant"). The Bible asserts that Israel is the rightful homeland of the Jewish people. A Christian Zionist reading of the Bible outlines a special relationship between God and the Jewish people. The Bible promises blessings for those who bless Israel.	A moral imperative to "stand with Israel." Political solidarity across racial and religious lines. Jewish-Christian cooperation against the global threat of "radical Islam."	De-emphasizing racial particularity to link Black Christians with all other Americans (and Israelis) in the global fight against "jihadist Muslims." Take a seat at the table. Race is salient in Black-Jewish partnerships (African Americans owe a debt to the Jewish people for their support of civil rights).
The International Fellowship of Christians and Jews (IFCJ)	Literalist interpretation of scripture ("It is God's choice that we honor the Jewish people. And we don't ask God why."). Christian Zionist reading of the Bible (Jewish people have a biblical "deed of property from God for a specific geographic area").	Aversion to politics in favor of approaching Israel "from a place of faith." "Mission" supersedes politics (largely in terms of philanthropy, but also proselytization).	Race is salient for Black-Jewish solidarity based on civil rights partnerships. Racial solidarity with Black Ethiopian Jews as a minority community in Israel. Recognition of inequality in the experiences of Black Ethiopians and other Black Africans in Israel.

RUPTURES AND CROSS-POLLINATION

So far in this chapter, I have presented these case studies as more or less discrete spaces within the social world of Black religious politics, in which visions of the identity and mission of "the Black Church" are constructed and tested in the context of the global issue of Israel and Palestine. Much of the cultural work about the meaning and significance of "the Black Church" and how African American Christians should relate to Palestine and Israel happens within these spaces. It is important to note, however, that these are not strictly isolated or parallel paths of constructing a Black church identity and political mission. They intersect with each other at significant points, highlighting the tensions that exist in advancing competing visions of Black religious politics in particular social spaces, not just between them. I close this chapter with two stories of tensions within the particular Black church spaces I encountered in the field, illustrating how the contestation of competing visions of "the Black Church" and its mandate in Israel and Palestine happen between the networks of organizations represented in these four case studies, but also within them.

The complexity of the field of Black religious politics and the interconnectedness of my cases came into relief for me when I unexpectedly ran into Edward Branch at the annual meeting of the Samuel DeWitt Proctor Conference in Houston in 2016. I had met Branch just a month before, when I visited his Detroit congregation and attended the IFCJ-sponsored Martin Luther King Jr. Interfaith Event at Deedee Coleman's church. The week after our meeting, Branch left for Israel with the Fellowship, where he helped lead a delegation of Progressive National Baptist Convention pastors. Our paths crossed again at the Proctor Conference meeting in Houston, where the dominant narrative on Israel and Palestine was quite different from the one I had learned about from Branch and the Black church advisors who work with the Fellowship. At the Proctor meeting, there were no sessions on Black-Jewish solidarity or the civil rights legacy as an impetus for Christian Zionism. In fact, the 2016 Proctor Conference meeting featured the most sessions ever that focused on Palestine, including Palestine-focused events at a preconference for millennials, two plenary worship services that included discussions of Palestine, one other Palestine-focused plenary session, and three breakout workshops on Palestinian solidarity.

I was initially taken aback at this incongruity. Only having known Branch in his capacity as a proponent of Christian Zionism in his work with AIPAC and the IFCJ, I asked him about his involvement with the Proctor Conference. He said he had been involved with the organization for more than ten years—almost the entirety of its existence. In that time, he had only missed one annual meeting, he said, because it conflicted with an IFCJ speaking engagement in 2015. Being familiar with my research on African American Christian connections to Israel and Palestine, Branch mentioned the recent work of the Proctor Conference on Palestine. I asked him what he thought of the organization's emerging stance on the issue and the increasing profile of its focus on building solidarity with Palestinians. He began by telling me that some of his previous trips to Israel had included meeting with Palestinian leaders. He went on to characterize some at the Proctor Conference, like Jeremiah Wright, as being on the extreme edge of support for Palestinians. "But I enjoy being part of those conversations," he said. "I like being in the room." He went on to caution, however, that "it's important to see the issue in a broader context." That context, he explained, is about the importance of seeing Palestine and Israel in view of Israel's geopolitical situation as a small country in the Middle East surrounded by enemies—something he also spoke about at length in our earlier meeting in Detroit.

We continued our conversation over lunch, as Branch showed me pictures of his most recent IFCJ trip with the Progressive National Baptist Convention. When I asked about the most significant part of the trip for the pastors visiting for the first time, he described how meaningful it was for them to see the Bible sites: the Sea of Galilee and the Jordan River. But he also emphasized the transformative aspect of meeting Jewish Israelis and hearing from them about their lives and experiences. "It's the people who make the place, not the place that makes the people." Branch went on to describe the particular significance of some of the visits that took place during the delegation. From visiting recreational facilities built and sponsored by the IFCJ on military bases in Israel, to touring preparation programs for Ethiopian Jews entering the military, to eating with children in orphanages—the same sites I would visit later that year with the National Baptist Convention of America delegation.

Branch told me that he planned to attend the Palestine workshop the next day on the topic of "The Movement for Justice in Palestine"—perhaps to raise some critical questions, he said. Branch did attend that workshop, which focused on critiquing Christian Zionism, advancing a Palestinian theology of liberation linked with Black theologies of liberation, and sharing Black clergy stories from visits to Palestine. Jeremiah Wright was one of the workshop speakers. Wright spoke specifically to the efforts of what he called "the Zionist lobby's" work to target Black churches and historically Black colleges and universities (HBCUs). On Black clergy preaching Zionism, Wright said, "They're paying $4,000 per speaking engagement, in case you want to defect!" Wright continued to talk about Zionist outreach efforts within the Progressive National Baptist Convention. He emphasized the word *Progressive* in the convention's name, reminding the audience that Martin Luther King Jr. founded the denomination after a split with the National Baptist Convention in 1961 over the latter group's efforts to distance itself from the civil rights movement. And he lamented the role that AIPAC had at the PNBC national meeting. "It's not an easy stream," he said, referring to getting involved in challenging Christian Zionism. "You're gonna be swimming upstream if you try to get Black Christians to understand the State of Israel, created in 1948, has nothing to do with the one in the Bible. Very important and a very tough road for you." Edward Branch did not, in the end, ask a question or voice a comment in response to Wright's invective against Black clergy participation in Christian Zionist outreach.

One NBCA pastor who participated in the Fellowship-led NBCA leadership delegation to Israel also provided a cogent example of the cross-pollination between visions of Black religious politics. His story is also a clear example of both the power and the pitfalls of the IFCJ's approach to Christian Zionist outreach among African American clergy. Keith is an NBCA pastor in Virginia who exhibited a very cautious approach to the politics of Israel and Palestine throughout the trip we shared. Even when Fellowship leaders and the group's Jewish tour guide advanced a more political narrative (during a tour of a British prison used to hold, and even execute, Jewish militants in 1948, or a visit to an Israeli military outpost in the Palestinian West Bank), Keith was reluctant to engage. Outside the former British prison, he told me that a debate had broken out on his personal Facebook page in response to a post he had made about arriving safely in Israel. He described having both pro-Israel and pro-Palestine friends, adding that his own theological orientation made him sympathetic to Israel because he was not guided by liberationist theological thinking. On another day during the trip, we were sitting outside a gift shop where Keith had done some shopping. He showed me a "Jerusalem" baseball cap he had purchased, and I remarked that it looked like a Palestinian design, taking out my phone to look up an image of the iconic black-and-white patterned Palestinian keffiyeh scarf made famous by PLO leader Yasser Arafat, which matched the pattern on his new hat. "I'm gonna have to exchange it," he said abruptly, getting up to walk back into the gift shop. Moments later Keith returned with a new plain blue "Jerusalem" hat. "I'm too far from home to get into a fight," he explained. "I don't want anyone to get the wrong idea." "I just wanted something to keep the sun off my head." Throughout the trip, Keith eschewed the politics of the region, even when IFCJ guides pushed the trip narrative beyond philanthropy into overtly political pro-Israel topics, such as Israeli military operations and the exclusivity of Jewish claims to the land.

Later, I got a glimpse of Pastor Keith's more expansive vision of Black religious politics when he shared a photo of himself on social media, participating in an African American Clergy Advocacy Day in Washington, DC, the following year, where a number of Samuel DeWitt Proctor Conference leaders also took part in the action. The political climate in the United States had shifted since we were in Israel together in the spring of 2016. Donald Trump had been elected president and Black clergy were increasingly mobilizing to protest his administration's cuts to health care, the federal budget more broadly, as well as other issues of civil rights and economic justice. He described the action as "speaking truth to power" and emphasized the need for Black clergy to mobilize and organize ahead of the 2018 midterm elections and the 2020 presidential race. This anecdote from the field highlights the significance of the global dimension of Black religious politics that are at stake when African American clergy and church members venture into the politics of Palestine and Israel. For Black church pastors, denominational leaders, and members, modes of political engagement can vary significantly depending on context. Keith was reluctant to engage politically with regional or global politics related to Israel and Palestine, although he felt more comfortable participating in an African American clergy advocacy day in Washington, DC. Similarly, the possibilities for race-focused political engagement vary by context because the meaning of race may shift from one context to another. For example, African American pastors familiar with the meaning of race and its social/political significance in the United States may find themselves on less familiar ground in the global space of Israel and Palestine. In such spaces, further work becomes necessary to bridge the meaning of race between the United States and Israel and Palestine. This raises questions about the depth of building global solidarity in racial terms on short Christian Zionists tours of the State of Israel—as "familiarization trips" or "missions"—that overlay politics onto religious and touristic experiences. But it also raises questions about the prospects and limits of race-focused solidarity-building between prophetic- and liberationist-minded African American Christians in Palestine. I turn to these questions in the conclusion.

Conclusion

AFRICAN AMERICAN CHRISTIANITY AND GLOBAL BLACK RELIGIOUS POLITICS

Edward Curtis and Sylvester Johnson call for analyses of African American religions in the United States to take an increasingly global and transnational perspective. They point to the many ways that "transnational contact and diasporic consciousness" have affected African American religiosity in the past, how this continues to be the case in the present, and how attention to global connections should animate studies of Black religion in America going forward.[1] For Curtis and Johnson, the relationship between racial and religious identity crosses the boundaries of the nation-state in important ways, including through migration, tourism, and pilgrimage.

> The examination of US Black religions within strictly national borders not only obscures the translocal, often transoceanic nature of religious formation in the modern world, but also silently furthers an exclusively nationalist interpretation of Black religions that underplays political and ethical solidarities that have been abundant in the modern Black experience.[2]

This book on African American Christian engagement with the global political issue of Israel and Palestine is grounded in many of the same theoretical and methodological foundations:

1. African American religious identity is a composite of overlapping racial, religious, and political identities.

2.   Particular expressions of these overlapping identities have always been at least partially formed in global social spaces via transnational connections, networks, and encounters.

Broadly, I discuss how the meaning and the political significance of race shift when political engagement and solidarity-building move from national social spaces into global spaces. In the four case studies, positions regarding Palestine and Israel take shape where racial, religious, and political group identities converge. Furthermore, I have shown how the context of Israel and Palestine, as a global political issue, plays an important role in reworking ideas about Black religious politics in global terms. When the context for creating and deploying trajectories of Black religious politics becomes global, the meaning of *race* and *religion* shift. A fundamental empirical contribution of this work is a partial answer to the question: What global trajectories are possible when Black religious politics are taken out of more familiar territory and brought into new political spaces?

In answering this question through the four case studies—ranging from African American Christian Zionists to Palestinian solidarity activists—I have shown what happens when existing Black religious political orientations are applied to new questions about global solidarities across racial and religious lines. I have argued, in relational sociological terms, for attention to Black religious politics as a dynamic *tradition* and a *field of contestation*, in which competing ideas about the history, identity, and mission of "the Black Church" are put forward and contested. Each of the chapters explores some aspect of how expressions of different groups of African American Christians diverge in their collective interpretations of the Bible, their public theologies, and their modes of political engagement, while simultaneously making universal claims about "the Black Church" and African American Christians collective identity.

WHY LOOK AT ISRAEL AND PALESTINE?

In the introduction, I posed a framing question: Why Black churches? That is, why focus on African American Christianity and Black churches in the service of better understanding the relationship between race, religion, and politics? As a global political issue, framing Israel and Palestine often comes through contradictory lenses, including emphases of that issue as fundamentally a relatively recent regional political contest over land and recognition or, alternatively, as an ancient religious/civilizational struggle between Islam and the guardians of Western "Judeo-Christianity." I argue that these popular alternative perspectives both fail to capture much of the nuance of how Palestine and Israel have become a source for meaningful emerging global solidarities in overlapping racial, religious, and political terms. With this claim, I aim to contribute to wider studies of transnational solidarities with Israel and Palestine, including attention to Zionism as a global Jewish political movement, the transnational scope of the international Boycott, Divestment, and Sanctions (BDS) movement on behalf of Palestinians, and the wider movement linking African Americans with Palestinians in a shared anticolonial struggle animated by resistance to global racialized capitalism. I claim that understanding the complexities of how a category of identity—"the Black Church"—is contested along multiple axes requires attention to global spaces and transnational solidarities in terms of religion and race. In these global spaces and through the transnational solidarities that emerge within them, racial, religious, class, and national identities converge in complex intersections and enmeshments that transcend social boundaries.

In this conclusion, I want to reframe the question first posed in the introduction and ask: If we want to learn something about Black religious politics in the United States and how the normative category of "the Black Church" is contested, why choose to focus on a somewhat empirically narrow section of American Black religious politics where African American Christians engage with Israel and Palestine? This question is particularly relevant because, as I have shown, many Black pastors and leaders describe the challenges they face in convincing their peers in ministry to spend any of their limited attention, time, and resources on an issue that can feel very distant to them, to their congregants, and to their local communities. Beyond the fundamental recognition that global and transnational connections have always been part of American Black religious politics, I also suggest that the politics of Israel and Palestine are particularly salient to understanding trajectories of Black religious politics in the United States. In his history of the ways that the Arab-Israeli conflict became connected to the Black freedom struggle in the United States during the civil rights and Black Power eras, Michael Fischbach notes that "African Americans were keen observers of the Arab-Israeli conflict in the 1960s and 1970s and interpreted it in ways that related to their own lives and priorities at home."[3] He further contends that this attention to Palestine and Israel "was not simply because this particular foreign

policy issue was in the headlines so much but also because it had tremendous resonance with regard to their respective agendas and understandings of how black
identity and black political activity should be expressed in America."[4] Similarly
looking at the same period, the cultural theorist Keith Feldman traces the myr-
iad cultural and political connections linking the post–civil rights United States
with Israel and Palestine. Feldman describes the entanglement of American and
Israeli state-waged battles for hegemony and the parallel emergence of "transnational and translocal liberation struggles" that "crosshatched the globe."[5] Also
in this vein, Alex Lubin's study of linked Afro-Arab political imaginaries begins
in the nineteenth century, tracing the same parallel connections between the
United States and Israel and Palestine involving both state powers and liberationist movements—"the collision between nationalism and colonialism, on one
hand, and subaltern decolonial and liberation politics, on the other."[6] Furthermore, this historical link between African American and Palestinian freedom
struggles rooted in deep resonances of ideas, experiences, and identities also has
contemporary significance. A number of scholars and activists concerned with
Black-Palestinian solidarity have traced the development of what Robin D. G.
Kelley calls a recent period of convergence and catalyzing during and in the wake
of concurrent uprisings in Ferguson, Missouri, and Gaza in 2014.[7] In my fieldwork, one of the clearest expressions of the persistence of the deep connection
these three scholars are making a case for is when hip hop artist Jasiri X told a
plenary gathering of Samuel DeWitt Proctor Conference leaders and members:

> One of the realest things somebody said to me in Palestine . . . was [from] a
> professor at a university in Palestine. He said, "You know why you should care
> about what's happening in Palestine and why the hood should care?" He said,
> "Because the policing that you see here is coming to a hood near you." And
> eight months later—August of 2014—I had to go through a checkpoint to get
> into Ferguson, Missouri!

Part of the answer to the question of *why Palestine and Israel* in studying Black
religious politics in the United States goes back to these deep historical, political connections linking African Americans to the land and the people of
Israel and Palestine—in terms of the persistent pursuit of racial and religious
hegemony by state actors and the mobilization of liberation movements as a
pushback on these battles. The connection between Ferguson and Palestine
for activist-minded African American Christians is a recent manifestation of

a much deeper history of linked anticolonial struggles against militarized state forces policing racial hierarchies.

Another part of the answer lies in the deep vault of spiritual meaning for African American Christians, drawing on the Hebrew Bible, as elaborated in chapters 1 and 2. As religious historian Eddie Glaude notes, "No other story in the Bible has quite captured the imagination of African Americans like that of the Exodus."[8] Although it has this deep religious meaning, for Glaude the Exodus story is also a framework for Black *political* thought—in terms of emancipation, recognition, and even revolution. And this spiritual-political connection to Judaism via the Exodus narrative has had many manifestations in African American religious and political life—from the range of metaphorical and literal associations of African Americans with Judaism in religious terms to Black-Jewish political alliances in civil rights and labor movements. All of this stems from what a national Church of God in Christ (COGIC) worship leader said about how she thinks about her denomination's work in Israel:

> There is an innate sound that comes from those that have endured great duress, great struggle, and triumph. . . . So, Africans and Jews—because of the great atrocities that they have been through—make a sound that is distinct. [It] comes from their music, [it] comes from their writings, it comes from the struggle.

Another reason for *why Israel and Palestine* comes from the extent to which race is increasingly salient in debates about America's foreign policy in the Middle East. In one of the last essays published before his death in 2003, the Palestinian American postcolonial scholar Edward Said wrote, "In America, Palestine and Israel are regarded as local, not foreign policy, matters."[9] Across the political spectrum, the U.S.-Israel relationship is not just a State Department portfolio with little connection to domestic policy and electoral politics. To the contrary, for more than half a century, Israel has loomed large in American domestic politics. Virtually all major party candidates for high political offices in the United States echo the centrality and durability of the U.S.-Israel partnership, but with Donald Trump's rise to the presidency in 2016, American foreign policy in the Middle East increasingly and rapidly shifted away from long-held bipartisan orthodoxies in foreign relations circles about America's position vis-à-vis Israel and Palestine. For example, support for the Jewish state among white American evangelicals came under increased examination in 2017 with the Trump administration's controversial recognition of Jerusalem as the capital of the State of

Israel. The volatile move was widely cast as a quid pro quo arrangement with the conservative evangelical elements of the Republican base of voters who helped propel Trump into office, creating another potential wedge between white and minority political constituencies in the United States.

Another area in which the global issue of Palestine and Israel has seeped into U.S. domestic politics is with regard to the BDS movement, with federal, state, and local laws being proposed and enacted that require government employees and contractors to sign statements pledging not to boycott the State of Israel in any way. As the next section elaborates, race is increasingly salient in American debates over BDS. When Rashida Tlaib and Ilhan Omar became the first Muslim women to serve in the U.S. House of Representatives in 2019, their support for BDS and their criticisms of the State of Israel elevated Israel and Palestine to a higher level of public awareness, with the U.S.-Israel relationship emerging as a wedge issue among Republicans and Democrats leading up to the 2020 election. In the context of the debate over whether Tlaib and Omar should be labeled "anti-Semitic" for their criticism of the State of Israel and their support of BDS, they and their defenders consistently highlighted the racialized nature of the criticism they encountered, especially as their views and positions were cast (by Trump among others) as un-American or foreign. When Republicans gained control of the House of Representatives in 2023, Omar was stripped of her committee assignment by the Republican majority on the grounds that she was biased against the State of Israel. Invoking her racial, religious, and national identities in a response from the House floor, Omar said that she was being targeted as a Black Muslim woman and an immigrant. In other instances, however, the particular salience of race in the politics of Palestine and Israel and the U.S.-Israel relationship is often sublimated in U.S. discourse. In focusing on the link between African American Christians and Israel and Palestine and the centrality of racial identity to outlooks on religious politics, I aim to open a broader, more nuanced conversation about race and politics in America through attention to particular global intersections.

ISRAEL, PALESTINE, AND EMERGING FORMS OF BLACK ACTIVISM

In December 2019, the Christian ecumenical organization Friends of Sabeel North America, in collaboration with Black4Palestine, circulated and published

"A Black Church Call to End Israeli Apartheid."[10] The signatories included Black clergy, activists, and organizations. The Samuel DeWitt Proctor Conference signed as an organization, and several Proctor affiliates—Neichelle Guidry, Frederick Haynes III, Taurean Webb, and Traci Blackmon—signed individually as well. The statement reads, in part:

> The best of the Black Church emerges from a legacy of fighting oppression and speaking truth to power. This prophetic tradition calls us as Black Christians to support the rights, security, and basic human dignity of Palestinian communities. Scripture tells us to "do justice, love mercy and walk humbly with God." Today this means joining the movement for justice in Palestine, a struggle so intimately connected to the Black experience in the United States.

The statement continues, "Black people around the world have built solidarity with the Palestinian people," and explains that "this solidarity is not based on a common experience of oppression, but from a collective commitment to building a world free from oppression." This framing of potential solidarities for African American Christians is a departure from much of the solidarity-building across lines of race, nationality, and religion that involves Black churches looking to the past for groups who have shared their pattern of experiencing oppression. Instead, it looks forward to "building a world free from oppression."

The statement also calls attention to attacks directed at specific Black leaders for their criticisms of the State of Israel and their support of the Palestinian cause—Angela Davis, Marc Lamont Hill, Michelle Alexander, and Ilhan Omar. Indeed, these Black leaders have become polarizing figures within the Black church traditions represented in the case studies of this project. On Omar's 2019 criticism of the State of Israel and the pro-Israel lobby in the United States, Christians United for Israel Black pastors Dumisani Washington and Jonathan Leath voiced criticisms on social media. Leath tweeted, "Rep. Ilhan Omar's comments are very dangerous. . . . I am a Zionist and I stand with Israel. We must condemn hatred in any and all forms." On the same day, Washington went further, specifically labeling Omar's critique as anti-Semitism and an example of "Jew hatred."

On other occasions, Washington similarly voiced criticism of other Black activists and academics who have expressed solidarity with Palestinians—Cornel West, Shaun King, and Marc Lamont Hill. On Twitter, he called Marc Lamont

Hill an anti-Semite and wrote, "Like all anti-Zionists who cloak their Jew-hatred in fake concern for Palestinians, Marc Lamont Hill calls for terrorism against Jews, and the destruction of Israel." He followed this by invoking Martin Luther King Jr.'s phrase from his 1963 book *Strength to Love*: "nothing in the world is more dangerous than sincere ignorance and conscientious stupidity." In contrast, Angela Brown of The Perfecting Church took to Twitter to speak to Hill's firing by CNN, saying that she was sorry to see his message about Palestine "misconstrued as anti-Semitic."

These responses to public position-taking on Israel and Palestine by some of the Black clergy in this study represent a broadening of the political questions at stake for American Black churches, their leaders, and members. Part of the reason for this is that these polarizing figures represent broader visions of Black religious politics that get at emerging cleavages in contemporary African American religious spaces. A significant expression of this broader cleavage includes but goes beyond the issue of Palestine and Israel and can be found in Black clergy responses to Black Lives Matter and the Movement for Black Lives. The response of the African American advisory council of the International Fellowship of Christians and Jews to the Movement for Black Lives is a cogent example. When the Movement for Black Lives, which includes Black Lives Matter and other organizations, released its policy platform in 2016, the Fellowship's advisory council responded in a statement calling the Israel-focused part of the platform "a vitriolic attack against Israel laced with misinformation and anti-Semitism." The statement further contended that those parts of the platform represent "an agenda that is not embraced by the broader African American community." In contrast, within the Samuel DeWitt Proctor Conference network, Black clergy—Neichelle Guidry, Waltrina Middleton, and others—actively seek partnership with millennial Black activists, arguing that the true calling of Black churches is closely connected to supporting activist movements. Middleton described one of the enduring lessons of the civil rights era as establishing a role for Black churches as institutions that house, feed, train, and protect Black activists. "[The Black church] was their fort," she said, adding, "I think, still, the church has a role, even if it's not living into it—it still has that role." Similarly, Guidry told me about her efforts to cultivate a culture of openness and support in Black churches to emerging activism among Chicago's younger millennial activists. "The church is not present," she said. "The church has not shown up in vital ways." As an African American clergywoman, Guidry directs much of her critique at Black churches and Black clergy for failing to show up for young Black activists and for trying to co-opt the movement when they do. "The problem," she said, "is that, at least in Chicago, when Black churches get out into the open, they want to co-opt the whole thing. They want to be at the forefront of everything." Echoing Middleton, she said, "[In] this particular movement, that's not the role of the Black church. The church is called to a supportive role. To a role of providing sanctuary."

This contrast in position-taking on the Movement for Black Lives among African American clergy described in the case studies suggests an important generational component to the contestation of Black religious politics. Black Lives Matter—and the broader Movement for Black Lives as an umbrella for a number of emerging racial justice organizations—is more secular, more democratic, and less male-dominated than many traditional Black churches. The reasons for this are several. They include the incompatibility of the prominent position LGBTQ issues have in contemporary Black secular activism with the gender and sexuality politics of some traditional, theologically conservative Black churches. They also include important differences in organizational structure, with new movements favoring a more radically democratic and less hierarchical authority structure than what is found in most Black churches and denominations.

In the context of this generational cleavage, the Black church clergy and activists described in this book who focus on Palestinian solidarity tend to push Black churches to come alongside emerging secular movements for racial justice in supportive ways. And they do so in ways that, following the logic of the statement of Black4Palestine and Friends of Sabeel North America, emphasize a forward-looking rather than a historically oriented understanding of liberation struggles. In this, the emerging critique forges solidarities based on present experiences of police brutality, militarized policing, mass incarceration, unequal access to resources, economic insecurity, and failing education systems. All of these are linked to broader global trends of the eroding welfare states and neoliberal privatization.[11]

In my fieldwork, at times I found these connections made explicit, as at the Samuel DeWitt Proctor Conference, whose Palestine-focused Black clergy and activists readily invoke explicit critiques of neoliberal capitalism, neoconservative interventionist foreign policy, settler colonialism, and state-level systematic racism as persistent links between Israel and Palestine and the United States. At other times, as with The Perfecting Church, I found these connections acknowledged but less elaborated, such as when Kevin and Angela Brown talked about seeing African Americans in Ferguson, Missouri, and Palestinians in the West Bank connecting on social media. Among the African American Christian Zionists I studied, the distance from new modes of Black activism in the United States was much greater. These pastors tended to be older, more theologically conservative and, as I describe in chapter 3, tend to act as *brokers* more than *mobilizers*. Their emphasis on Black-Jewish solidarities in the last century, via the biblical Exodus narrative, and in U.S.-Israel relations today, is only part of what sets them apart from the Palestinian solidarity-focused African American Christians I studied. For most African American Christian Zionists represented in this book, to the extent that they engage with new movements for racial justice in the United States, they do so in explicit critique and condemnation such as that of CUFI's Dumisani Washington, who has been a vocal critic of Black Lives Matter for its position-taking on Palestine. In 2016, he wrote that Black Lives Matter is "simply a weapon against Israel and the Jews." This, he continued, is "why Israel was brought into a conversation that had nothing to do with Chicago, New Orleans, Baltimore, or Ferguson."

In chapter 1, I describe how a more radical form of Black civil rights activism came to prominence in the 1960s as support for civil rights efforts among some American Jews began to wane. I called attention to Norman Podhoretz's 1963 essay in the Jewish magazine *Commentary* (which Podhoretz edited from 1960 to 1995) entitled, "My Negro Problem—And Ours."[12] Representing the spreading anxiety among some American Jews about the rise and direction of African American political activism, Podhoretz called out "Negro anti-Semitism" and warned that Black and Jewish political interests were diverging. In June 2018, *Commentary* (then edited by Norman Podhoretz's son, John Podhoretz) published an issue with the cover headline, "African Americans vs. American Jews." The lead article in that issue, "My 'Black Lives Matter' Problem," clearly evokes Podhoretz's "My Negro Problem—And Ours." Like many of the African American Christian Zionists in this book, the article's Black author, Jason D. Hill, put the issue of political criticism of the State of Israel front and center in taking stock of contemporary Black-Jewish relations.

> Black Lives Matter is not only being unjust toward Israel; its anti-Israel stance betrays Jews in America, to whom blacks in this country are enormously indebted. If there are any unsung heroes of the civil-rights movement, it is those Jews who played an enormous but largely unacknowledged role in the liberation of blacks from racial oppression.[13]

In 2018 and beyond, as in 1963, the cleavages in American race politics are never far from the issue of Israel and Palestine. As the scholars Edward Said, Keith Feldman, and others argue, persistent congruities exist between the politics of race and racial identity in the United States and in Israel and Palestine. My analysis of African American Christian engagement with Palestine and Israel finds supporting evidence for that conclusion. Although it is beyond the scope of this study to fully explore the significance of generational divides within African American Christianity, attention to these broader trends across time in American politics suggests that what we see within the dynamics of the field of Black religious politics on the issue of Israel and Palestine is suggestive of broader issues where racial, religious, and political identities intersect.

Following the work of Michael Leo Owens, I suggest that African American Christian Zionists tend to engage Black clergy as political *brokers*, whereas Black church Palestinian solidarity-building tends to rely on clergy acting as *mobilizers* (see chapter 3). And the (at least partial) incompatibility of these orientations within the field of Black religious politics is evidenced in the polarization around contemporary racial justice activism that invokes Palestinian solidarity. Black American criticism directed toward the State of Israel on behalf of Palestinians is anathema for many of the African American Christian Zionist pastors who work as brokers in Black communities, representing the predominantly white organizations CUFI and the IFCJ. Owens notes that, in Black religious politics, brokerage does not tend to lead to mobilization. This calls into question the depth of the reach of the African American Christian Zionist message in Black churches via predominantly white organizations. Those organizations have tremendous resources, but the enduring political impact of the application of those resources in Black churches (in paying for clergy and denominational leaders to visit Israel, in sponsoring church-based events, hiring Black clergy speakers, etc.) remains unclear. Part of this, I suggest, follows Owens's point about the disjunction between brokerage and mobilization among Black clergy. Drawing on the work of Adolph Reed Jr., Owens points out that brokerage is indicative of *elite* mobilization—what Reed calls "high-level negotiation," which assumes a monolithic Black political voice.[14] In this kind of elite Black religious political activity, according to Reed, "the 'people' don't get to speak; they are spoken for."[15] Given the diagnoses of a fundamental rupture between Black churches and contemporary Black political activism among the kind of Black clergy who I identify here and in chapter 3 as mobilizers, it raises the question of whether African American

Christian Zionist leaders represent a vocal minority as elite brokers, in Reed and Owens's terms. In contrast, many of this book's mobilizers understand themselves as a part of a remnant within African American Christianity, representing a vision of Black religious politics that they see as increasingly marginalized in more commercialized mainstream Black church spaces. Thus, although this book attends empirically to the context and mechanisms of contestation within Black religious politics, some ambiguity remains about the long-term efficacy of African American Christian Zionist *and* Palestinian solidarity-focused activism in Black churches. In other words, the persistent tension between elite level brokerage and more grassroots mobilization remains unresolved.

CONTESTED LABELS AND CATEGORIES ON A GLOBAL STAGE

I have presented "the Black Church" as a dynamic and multiple category of identity, and as a puzzle best understood through attention to how its core identity is subject to contestation, with specific attention to competing solidarities in Israel and Palestine. The actors and organizations represented in the four cases are all engaged in the work of building two largely antithetical political movements out of the same reference point, discursive tradition, and identity category—namely, "the Black Church." The processes of contesting group identity and purpose—in terms of overlapping religious, racial, and political facets—have parallels in how we understand other contested categories. Other categories at the intersection of religion and politics—such as "Muslim" and "evangelical"—are similarly contested, both from within and from the outside. Beyond religious politics, other politically salient identity categories—"feminist," "disaffected white working class," "LGBTQ+," and "the environmental movement"—pose similar analytical stakes. I suggest a potential for the field analytic approach developed here to be similarly useful in understanding the political salience of other analogous terms and identity categories. Like "the Black Church," all of these categories are underdetermined and subject to contestation over their meaning and political significance. Furthermore, all of these categories and their contested meanings have significance for both electoral politics and policy making in the United States. Digging deeper into such contested and variable identity categories matters for scholarly analysis, journalistic incisiveness, effective policy making, and beyond. Sometimes oversimplified identity categories are uncritically presented as monoliths: "evangelical," "Black," "Muslim American," or "white working class" voters. Finally, I provide a context for further analysis of how field dynamics change when taken out of national political spaces and moved into global spaces, where the mutable meaning and salience of *race* or *religion* shift significantly. Central to my argument here is that part of the importance of understanding African American religion in increasingly global and transnational terms are the emergent connections between national fields and global fields.

A Note on Methods and Cases

In the introduction, I provide a brief account of the research involved in writing this book, including the type and extent of the fieldwork I conducted in the world of Black religious politics in the United States, especially where that world intersects with Israel and Palestine. Across six years of fieldwork among African American Christians who have made Palestine and Israel a core part of their religious and political work, I encountered hundreds of people of different faiths, races, political persuasions, and stations in life. They are pastors, lay church members, academics, theologians, students, journalists, activists, professionals, nonprofit workers, and more. This project is about these people and the organizations and movements in which they work to advocate for the Jewish State of Israel, the people of Palestine, or both. I am grateful to those who took the time to introduce a white Canadian researcher to the world of American Black religious politics from their unique perspectives.

The hallmark of ethnographic fieldwork is participant observation, with varying configurations in the balance between the researcher as *participant* and as *observer*. As a white researcher in predominantly Black spaces, race was a persistent and visible difference between me and most of my research subjects. This difference was always in my mind in the field, and it was, of course, also in the minds of the African American Christians engaging with Palestine and Israel. Much of my learning in the field came from constantly interrogating my own experiences, observations, and reactions with regard to this key visible difference. But I often learned the most from moments when the people of color who live and work within these case studies simultaneously welcomed me into their work and confided in me their own observations and feelings about the racial differences made explicit by my presence in predominantly Black spaces.

Of course, as the chapters show, none of the case studies are exclusively Black spaces. All of them are, to some extent, spaces in which networking, solidarity-building, and fund-raising across racial and religious lines are paramount. I generally found openness, welcoming, and curiosity about my research in all of the spaces I visited in my fieldwork. Whether eager to share their religious convictions, their political causes, or both, most of the people I met in the field welcomed the opportunity to talk with me and invited me into their work. They were confident that their cause is worthy and worth sharing, and we shared a good faith assumption that I was willing to listen and learn with an open mind. In turn, I reciprocated those gestures of good faith, aspiring to understand perspectives that were different from my own (in terms of religious beliefs and practices, political views, and racialized experiences). Another important principle in my approach to this research was committing (and constantly recommitting) to understanding the positions, actions, and beliefs of my research subjects *on their own terms* instead of mine. The question of representation looms large in ethnographic fieldwork and writing. At the end of the day and in the final product that is this book, the primary voice is mine, as I construct the field of Black religious politics around Israel and Palestine as I observed and experienced it as a researcher.

Beyond racial differences, I was younger than most (but not all) of my research subjects. Less obvious in my fieldwork were religious and national differences. I learned quickly that many people I met in the field assumed that I was an American. Some were surprised to learn that I am Canadian and had lived in the United States for fewer than ten years during most of my time in the field. Perceptions of religious similarities and differences also animated my fieldwork. I come from a European Christian background, but my last name is not uncommon among Ashkenazi Jews. This ambiguity led to the real possibility, of which I was keenly aware, that my religious identity could be assumed to be Christian, Jewish, or neither. In both the Christian Zionist and Palestinian solidarity movements I studied, Jewish partners and people of no religious affiliation work closely alongside Christians. I was sometimes asked explicitly about my own religious background (e.g., "Are you Jewish?" or "Are you Christian?"). When asked, I explained that I come from a Christian background. People I met in the field and interviewed were often curious about my own religious background; they wanted to know how much to explain to me about the religious language they used freely in talking about their work and their faith. When speaking with a researcher perceived to be an outsider, it is sometimes the case—and I experienced this often—that people explain their thinking and their actions more explicitly and in greater detail than they typically do among those they perceive as insiders.

The level of personal connection I developed in the field varied depending on how long I spent with certain groups and in certain spaces. Shared trips to Israel and Palestine provided extended contact and afforded the opportunity for the most learning about the lives and stories of African American Christians who, in some way, had prioritized engaging with Palestine and Israel. On these trips, I had longer conversations with some of my fellow travelers about my own identity and experiences with religion and aspects of my political views. I found this to be a good way to build rapport with those I was getting to know as we traveled around "the Holy Land" together. With all the groups I studied, sharing stories and personal narratives was a common way of articulating one's motivations for present work and commitments. In this context and across this range of differences and similarities—some visible and some invisible—I consistently presented myself as an intellectually curious outsider to the movements and organizations I studied. At times my research subjects asked about my own biography, beliefs, experiences, and perspectives, and at other times they did not.

For all of these reasons, I tended to operate in the field more as an observer than as a participant. I did not actively distance myself from personal connections with my subjects or with their work, but it was quite clear to all involved that I was a guest in their spaces—and a short-term one at that. Traditionally, especially in the field of anthropology, ethnographies are based on extended periods of deep immersion in the field. The comparative sociological work of this project called for a different kind of ethnography that is best described as punctuated immersion in African American religious and political social spaces.

I conducted the primary fieldwork for this project from 2013 to 2018, physically sharing the same spaces with my research subjects ranging from a few hours to a few weeks. This included extensive fieldwork within the United States, where political support for the State of Israel and support for the Palestinian cause are initially sought and cultivated among African American Christians. I attended more than thirty events focused on Israel and Palestine in Black church spaces in seven states. These included Sunday morning church services, pastors' briefings, Bible studies, seminars, workshops, conferences, interfaith events, and college campus meetings. At these events, I met pastors, lay leaders, students, activists, and churchgoers of a wide range of ages, social classes, professions, and levels of experience and familiarity with Israel and Palestine. At these events and in many follow-up meetings over meals and cups of coffee, I learned from these African American Christians and their allies how their views on Palestine and Israel have taken shape and how they have acted within their social spheres to bring attention to that issue. I followed up on informal conversations in the field with formal recorded interviews. Sometimes in person and sometimes by phone, I talked with contacts from the field about how they came to attend the events where I met them; how they thought about Israel and Palestine in relation to the broader life and social engagement of their churches; and their formation, unanswered questions, concerns, and challenges related to thinking about the significance of Israel and Palestine for the life of Black churches in the United States. For all of these interviews, I followed an evolving interview schedule, with some questions planned ahead of time, but intentionally leaving space for the conversation to go in unplanned directions. I conducted ninety interviews with seventy-nine individuals who had a stake in the issue of Israel and Palestine in Black churches. I began my fieldwork in the world of Christian Zionism, following the African American outreach efforts of Christians United for Israel (CUFI). I also read and followed the discourse on Palestine and Israel among African American Christians online, including on social media. The contemporary American Black church's engagement with Israel and Palestine had received little scholarly or media attention when I began my fieldwork in 2013, so I relied on word of mouth and suggestions from research participants for whom to talk with and where to find other Black churches talking about Palestine and Israel. My selection of the four cases in this book arose over time as I sought other emerging expressions of African American Christian Zionism beyond CUFI as well as groups of African American Christians focusing on the Palestinian cause. The four cases compared in this book do not represent the totality of African American Christian engagement with Israel and Palestine. But they do represent four of the most active, public, and sustained efforts in Black churches to engage in overlapping religious, political, and racial terms with Israel and Palestine. They also represent a range of types of organizations and theological orientations—from evangelical to more progressive Christian theologies, and from independent churches to historically Black denominations and parachurch organizations.

I also participated in four trips to Palestine and Israel. These trips of ten to fourteen days all included exposure to the State of Israel and the Palestinian Territories (the West Bank), but almost all of the time was spent in one location or the other—focusing either on Jewish Israeli or Palestinian narratives and lived realities in the region. These trips varied in size from eight to forty participants, and I traveled and stayed with groups as a participant and as an observer. The size of these groups permitted me to meet and interact regularly with each member. Because I was invited to participate in each trip as a researcher, trip organizers and sponsors introduced me as such at the beginning of the trip. In some cases, I met trip participants at meetings prior to the trip (either in person or by teleconferences). On one trip, I was the only white participant. On others, I was one of a few white travelers in a majority African American group. As in the United States, in Israel and Palestine I described myself to people we met in the field (tour guides, guest speakers, site experts, etc.) as a researcher studying Christian interest in—and travel to—the region, as well as broader Black church engagement with issues related to Israel and the Middle East. Following each trip, I conducted interviews with participants that provided further participant reflection on various aspects of the trip and their experience as a whole. I also included interviews with participants on many other trips to the region in which I did not personally observe or participate. Thus my interview data adds perspectives from dozens of trips to the Holy Land by African American Christians beyond those in which I took part.

In summary, the multisite, punctuated ethnography I undertook for this project meant that I never fully inhabited the world of those who participated in my research. In describing her multisite ethnography of American Tea Party and religious democratic community organizing groups, the sociologist Ruth Braunstein recounts her experience of being continuously "pulled into one interpretive world or another." She describes this experience in the field as akin to existing perpetually in a liminal space, "embedded in multiple interpretive worlds but immersed fully in none."[1] This description resonates with my own experiences in the field as I reflect on them from a distance. This kind of fieldwork provided the breadth necessary for the comparative analysis I provide in this book, which would not have been possible had I been immersed in just one or two groups for an extended period of time. When doing comparative work, there is a tradeoff between breadth and depth, and I tried to strike the right balance, providing as much comparative leverage as possible without sacrificing the depth necessary to understand each case and its position within the field of Black religious politics.

Notes

INTRODUCTION

1. Throughout, when first and last names are given, they are real names. When only first names are given, they are pseudonyms. Generally, I use real names in reference to speakers at public events and to identify some interview subjects and fieldwork informants who are pastors and public figures, with their consent.

2. This number represents CUFI's claimed membership as of February 2020. Beyond evangelical and pro-Israel circles, Hagee is most widely known for his controversial endorsement of Senator John McCain for president in 2008. Following accusations of anti-Catholicism in Hagee's writing and speaking, as well as attention to Hagee's suggestions that Adolf Hitler and the Holocaust were part of God's plan for the Jewish people and their becoming established in the land of Israel, McCain later rejected Hagee's endorsement because the negative attention it drew far outpaced the intended shoring up of support among conservative evangelicals. For political coverage of McCain's rejection of Hagee's endorsement, see Michael Luo, "McCain Rejects Hagee Backing as Nazi Remarks Surface," *The Caucus* (blog), May 22, 2008, https://thecaucus.blogs.nytimes .com/2008/05/22/mccain-rejects-hagee-backing-as-nazi-remarks-surface/.

3. Michael A. Stevens, *We Too Stand: A Call for the African-American Church to Support the Jewish State* (Lake Mary, FL: FrontLine, 2013).

4. Chapter 1 explores the religious-political phenomenon of Christian Zionism and various perspectives on Christian theological and political support for the State of Israel and its policies. Definitions of the term "Christian Zionism" vary even among those who call themselves Christian Zionists, and certainly among those who study and write about them. As I note briefly in chapter 1, there are a range of views on the sources, motivations, and activities of Christian Zionists—including the question of whether Christian Zionism is *political*, as evidenced in Michael Stevens's insistence to the Bible study group that CUFI is not a political organization. I argue that CUFI and other Christian Zionists groups are, in fact, political, even when they claim not to be. A useful broad starting point is the definition provided by the historian of religion Robert Smith: Christian Zionism is "political action, informed by specifically Christian commitments, to promote or preserve Jewish control over the geographic area now comprising Israel and

Palestine." Robert O. Smith, *More Desired Than Our Owne Salvation: The Roots of Christian Zionism* (New York: Oxford University Press, 2013), 2.

5.   See the appendix for an elaboration of the methods used in the research for this book, the extent of my fieldwork, and a discussion of the challenges and opportunities I discovered as a white researcher in the world of Black religious politics.

6.   Taurean Webb, "Journeys Toward Justice," 2016, http://sdpconference.info/journeys-toward-justice/.

7.   Samuel DeWitt Proctor Conference, "Palestinian Justice Meets the Historic Black Church!," 2015, https://myemail.constantcontact.com/Palestinian-Justice-Meets-the-Historic-Black-Church-.html?soid=1103648503270&aid=JYeWf4Z-JMw.

8.   Treatments of African American Christianity variously label this category as "the Black Church," "the Black church," or "the black church." When I use "the Black Church" (in quotation marks), it refers broadly to reified or ostensibly monolithic applications of the term.

9.   Mark Clatterbuck, "Tribal Alliances: The State of Israel and Native American Christianity," *Journal of Ecumenical Studies* 49, no. 3 (2014): 384–404; John Gee, "Singapore's Expanding Christian Zionist Community," *Washington Report on Middle East Affairs* 28, no. 9 (2009): 36; and Sung-Gun Kim, "Korean Christian Zionism: A Sociological Study of Mission," *International Review of Mission* 100, no. 1 (2011): 85–95, https://doi.org/10.1111/j.1758-6631.2011.00059.x.

10.   Movement for Black Lives, "Invest-Divest," August 2016, https://m4bl.org/policy-platforms/invest-divest/.

11.   On the early twentieth-century roots of Black-Palestinian transnational solidarity, see Maha Nasser, "Palestinian Engagement with the Black Freedom Movement Prior to 1967," *Journal of Palestine Studies* 48, no. 4 (2019): 17–32, https://doi.org/10.1525/jps.2019.48.4.17. Nasser's historical account is part of a special issue of the *Journal of Palestine Studies* that focused on what Robin D. G. Kelley describes as the contemporary *convergence* and *catalyzing* beginning in 2014 in the context of racial justice uprisings in Ferguson, Missouri, and around the United States. See Robin D. G. Kelley, "From the River to the Sea to Every Mountain Top: Solidarity as Worldmaking," *Journal of Palestine Studies* 48, no. 4 (2019): 69–91, https://doi.org/10.1525/jps.2019.48.4.69. Russell Rickford notes that the nascent renewal of 2014 and beyond exists in a long-standing global Black imaginary that includes Palestine. See Russell Rickford, "'To Build a New World': Black American Internationalism and Palestine Solidarity," *Journal of Palestine Studies* 48, no. 4 (2019): 52–68, https://doi.org/10.1525/jps.2019.48.4.52. The convergence and catalyzing exemplified in this special issue of the *Journal of Palestine Studies* reflects several years of interdisciplinary scholarly contributions, as well as journalistic and popular works exploring contemporary Black-Palestinian solidarity in racial terms. See Rabab Ibrahim Abdulhadi, "Framing Resistance Call and Response: Reading Assata Shakur's Black Revolutionary Radicalism in Palestine," *Women's Studies Quarterly* 46, no. 3–4 (2018): 226–31; Sa'Ed Atshan, and Darnell L. Moore, "Reciprocal Solidarity: Where the Black and Palestinian Queer Struggles Meet," *Biography* 37, no. 2 (2014): 680–705; Kristian Davis Bailey, "Black–Palestinian Solidarity in the Ferguson–Gaza Era," *American Quarterly* 67, no. 4 (2015): 1017–26, https://doi.org/10.1353/aq.2015.0060; Andy Clarno, "The Thorns That Exist and Resist: Black-Palestine Solidarity in the Twenty-First Century," *Middle East*

Report 282 (2017): 2–9; Angela Davis, *Freedom Is a Constant Struggle: Ferguson, Palestine, and the Foundations of a Movement* (Chicago: Haymarket, 2016); Fred Moten, "Blackpalestinian Breath," *Social Text* (online), October 25, 2018, https://socialtextjournal.org/periscope _article/blackpalestinian-breath/; and Jasbir K. Puar, *The Right to Maim: Debility, Capacity, Disability* (Durham, NC: Duke University Press, 2017). This literature is also complemented by works analyzing other contemporary expressions of transnational solidarity with Palestine. See, for example, Ruth Sheldon, *Tragic Encounters and Ordinary Ethics: Palestine-Israel in British Universities* (Manchester, UK: Manchester University Press, 2016); and Ather Zia, "'Their Wounds Are Our Wounds': A Case for Affective Solidarity Between Palestine and Kashmir," *Identities* 27, no. 3 (2020): 357–75, https://doi.org/10.1080 /1070289X.2020.1750199.

12.   For analyses of Trump's foreign policy with respect to American evangelicals and Israel, see Kim Sengupta, "The Real Reason Trump Declared Jerusalem the Capital of Israel Was Because He Feared Losing His Evangelical Voter Base," *Independent*, December 8, 2017, https://www.independent.co.uk/voices/jerusalem-donald-trump-israel-capital-decision -reason-why-evangelical-voters-us-fear-a8099321.html; Alana Abramson, "President Trump's Decision on Jerusalem Welcomed by Evangelical Voters, Pro-Israel Groups and Major Donors," *Time*, December 7, 2017, http://time.com/5052363/president-trumps -decision-on-jerusalem-welcomed-by-evangelical-voters-pro-israel-groups-and-major -donors/; and Mark Landler, "Trump Recognizes Jerusalem as Israel's Capital and Orders U.S. Embassy to Move," *New York Times*, January 20, 2018.

13.   Throughout, my use of the term *Black churches* refers primarily to majority African American Protestant congregations. Many such congregations exist in historically Black denominations such as the Church of God in Christ (COGIC) and the African Methodist Episcopal (AME) Church, as well as various Black Baptist conferences such as the National Baptist Convention (NBC), the Progressive National Baptist Convention (PNBC), and the National Baptist Convention of America (NBCA). Others operate independently of these major African American Protestant denominations (even if they have roots in one or more) or are part of smaller networks of churches. This analytical choice is not meant to categorically exclude understudied groups often left out of studies of Black churches—like African American Catholics or African American religious groups that have been, at times, considered "fringe" or "cultlike" among scholars and in African American Protestant contexts. The majority of African American Catholics are part of majority-white parishes. See Pew Research Center, "A Religious Portrait of African-Americans," January 30, 2009, http://www.pewforum.org/2009/01/30/a-religious -portrait-of-african-americans/. However, Black Catholicism is an important religious phenomenon beyond the scope of this study. See, for example, Matthew J. Cressler, *Authentically Black and Truly Catholic: The Rise of Black Catholicism in the Great Migration* (New York: New York University Press, 2017); and Tia Noelle Pratt, "Liturgy as Identity Work in Predominantly African American Parishes," in *American Parishes: Remaking Local Catholicism*, ed. G. J. Adler, T. C. Bruce, and B. Starks (New York: Fordham University Press, 2019), 132–52. So-called fringe movements, historically marginalized in studies of Black religion, are similarly noteworthy, but they too are beyond the scope of the present study. See Judith Weisenfeld, *New World A-Coming: Black Religion and Racial Identity*

During the Great Migration (New York: New York University Press, 2016). Finally, when I talk about "Black religious politics" in the United States, I focus on African American Protestantism. I do this while acknowledging that important contributions have been made by non-Christian Black religious groups—especially African American Muslims, who are discussed in later chapters.

14. Eddie S. Glaude Jr., "What Is African American Religion?," *OUPblog* (blog), October 17, 2014, https://blog.oup.com/2014/10/african-american-religion/.

15. Albert J. Raboteau, *Slave Religion: The "Invisible Institution" in the Antebellum South* (New York: Oxford University Press, 1978).

16. For a broader discussion of efforts to center African and African American experiences in scholarship, see Molefi K. Asante, *Afrocentricity* (Trenton, NJ: Africa World, 1988).

17. On African American churches as an "invisible institution," see E. Franklin Frazier, *The Negro Church in America* (1963; repr., New York: Schocken, 1974). Others have argued that Black religious institutions had never been "invisible," but they had been obfuscated by white historians and similarly needed to be uncovered. See, for example, Mechal Sobel, *Trabelin' On: The Slave Journey to an Afro-Baptist Faith* (Westport, CT: Greenwood, 1979).

18. White scholars, too, engaged questions of Black religion, for example, Gunnar Myrdal, Melville Herskovits, and Hortense Powdermaker.

19. Barbara Dianne Savage, *Your Spirits Walk Beside Us: The Politics of Black Religion* (Cambridge, MA: Belknap Press of Harvard University Press, 2008). Savage gives credit, in particular, to anthropological treatments—such as those of Hurston, Fauset, and Powdermaker—for attending to the diversity of Black religious life, and she praises them for their attention to the nuances of the lived experiences of everyday religious people and not just clergy and other leaders. Their focus on "pews over pulpits," she notes, helped to highlight the kind of diversity that other scholars glossed over (86). For more on the question of whether there has ever been such a thing as "the Black Church" and recent scholarship challenging this long-held assumption, see Clarence E. Hardy, "The End of the 'Black Church': New Directions in African American Religious History," *Church History* 78, no. 3 (2009): 647–51.

20. Frazier, *The Negro Church in America*.

21. Gayraud S. Wilmore, *Black Religion and Black Radicalism* (Garden City, NY: Doubleday, 1972).

22. For discussions of these related binaries, see Obie Clayton, "The Churches and Social Change: Accommodation, Moderation, or Protest," *Daedalus* 124, no. 1 (1995): 101–17; Hans A. Baer and Merrill Singer, *African-American Religion in the Twentieth Century: Varieties of Protest and Accommodation* (Knoxville: University of Tennessee Press, 1992); and Marla Faye Frederick, *Between Sundays: Black Women and Everyday Struggles of Faith* (Berkeley: University of California Press, 2003).

23. See, for example, Frazier, *The Negro Church in America*; Gary T. Marx, *Protest and Prejudice: A Study of Belief in the Black Community* (New York: Harper & Row, 1967); Gunnar Myrdal, *An American Dilemma: The Negro Problem and Modern Democracy* (New York: Harper, 1944), and Adolph L. Reed, *The Jesse Jackson Phenomenon: The Crisis of Purpose in Afro-American Politics* (New Haven, CT: Yale University Press, 1986).

24. See, for example, W. E. B. Du Bois, *The Negro Church* (Atlanta: Atlanta University Press, 1903); C. Eric Lincoln and Lawrence H. Mamiya, *The Black Church in the African American*

Experience (Durham, NC: Duke University Press, 1990); Benjamin E. Mays and Joseph William Nicholson, *The Negro's Church* (New York: Russell & Russell, 1933); Aldon Morris, *Origins of the Civil Rights Movements* (New York: Free Press, 1986); and Carter Woodson, "The Negro Church, an All-Comprehending Institution," *Negro History Bulletin* 3, no. 1 (1939): 7, 15.

25.   C. Eric Lincoln, *The Black Church Since Frazier* (New York: Schocken, 1974), 105-6.

26.   Lincoln and Mamiya, *The Black Church in the African American Experience*.

27.   For a "dialogical" analysis of Black churches, see Evelyn Brooks Higginbotham, *Righteous Discontent: The Women's Movement in the Black Baptist Church, 1880–1920* (Cambridge, MA: Harvard University Press, 1993). For a framework placing various Black churches along a series of "continua," see Tamelyn Tucker-Worgs, *The Black Megachurch: Theology, Gender, and the Politics of Public Engagement* (Waco, TX: Baylor University Press, 2011).

28.   The work of Savage and that of Curtis Evans and Judith Weisenfeld has done much to go beyond assumptions about a unifying scholarly category of "the Black Church" in favor of attention to the essentially contested nature of African American religion. See Savage, *Your Spirits Walk Beside Us*; Curtis J. Evans, *The Burden of Black Religion* (New York: Oxford University Press, 2008); and Weisenfeld, *New World A-Coming*. For an overview of these perspectives, see Hardy, "The End of the 'Black Church.'"

29.   For a discussion of W. E. B. Du Bois's sociological and political analyses of African American Christianity and Black churches, see Roger Baumann, "Race, Religion, and Global Solidarities: W. E. B. Du Bois and 'The Black Church' as a Contested Category," *Journal for the Scientific Study of Religion* 62, no. S1 (2023): 48-67, https://doi.org/10.1111/jssr.12856.

30.   Lincoln, *The Black Church Since Frazier*, 136 (emphasis added).

31.   Nancy Lynne Westfield, Juan M. Floyd-Thomas, Carol B. Duncan, Stacey Floyd-Thomas, and Stephen G. Ray, *Black Church Studies: An Introduction* (Nashville, TN: Abingdon, 2007), xxiii.

32.   Raphael G. Warnock, *The Divided Mind of the Black Church: Theology, Piety, and Public Witness* (New York: New York University Press, 2013).

33.   Josef Sorett, *Black Is a Church: Christianity and the Contours of African American Life* (New York: Oxford University Press, 2023).

34.   Stevens, *We Too Stand*; and Dumisani Washington, *Zionism and the Black Church: Why Standing with Israel Will Be a Defining Issue for Christians of Color in the 21st Century* (Stockton, CA: IBSI, 2014).

35.   Omar M. McRoberts, *Streets of Glory: Church and Community in a Black Urban Neighborhood* (Chicago: University of Chicago Press, 2003).

36.   Nancy Tatom Ammerman, *Congregation & Community* (New Brunswick, NJ: Rutgers University Press, 1997), 355.

37.   McRoberts *Streets of Glory*, 14.

38.   See, for example, Sandra L. Barnes, "Black Church Culture and Community Action," *Social Forces* 84, no. 2 (2005): 967-94, https://doi.org/10.1353/sof.2006.0003; Sandra L. Barnes, *Black Megachurch Culture: Models for Education and Empowerment* (New York: Peter Lang, 2010); Fredrick C. Harris, *Something Within: Religion in African-American Political Activism* (New York: Oxford University Press, 1999); Eric L. McDaniel, *Politics in the Pews: The Political Mobilization of Black Churches* (Ann Arbor: University of

Michigan Press, 2008); Mary Pattillo-McCoy, "Church Culture as a Strategy of Action in the Black Community," *American Sociological Review* 63, no. 6 (1998): 767-84, https://doi .org/10.2307/2657500; and Richard L. Wood, *Faith in Action: Religion, Race, and Democratic Organizing in America* (Chicago: University of Chicago Press, 2002).

39. Weisenfeld, *New World A-Coming.*

40. On attention to the everyday lives of Black church attendees (especially Black women), see, for example, Frederick, *Between Sundays*; Cheryl Townsend Gilkes, "Plenty Good Room: Adaptation in a Changing Black Church," *Annals of the American Academy of Political and Social Science* 558 (1998): 101-21; Higginbotham, *Righteous Discontent*; and Weisenfeld, *New World A-Coming.* On Black church media and televangelism, see, for example, Shayne Lee, *T. D. Jakes: America's New Preacher* (New York: New York University Press, 2007); Carolyn Moxley Rouse, John L. Jackson Jr., and Marla F. Frederick, *Televised Redemption: Black Religious Media and Racial Empowerment* (New York: New York University Press, 2016); and Jonathan L. Walton, *Watch This! The Ethics and Aesthetics of Black Televangelism* (New York: New York University Press, 2009). On Black megachurches, see, for example, Barnes, *Black Megachurch Culture*; and Tucker-Worgs, *The Black Megachurch.*

41. Kate Bowler, *Blessed: A History of the American Prosperity Gospel* (New York: Oxford University Press, 2013), 6. On the relationship between the prosperity gospel and African American Christian Zionism, see Roger Baumann, "Political Engagement Meets the Prosperity Gospel: African American Christian Zionism and Black Church Politics," *Sociology of Religion* 77, no. 4 (2016): 359-85, https://doi.org/10.1093/socrel/srw050.

42. Bowler, *Blessed*, 113.

43. Sociologists Brad Christerson and Richard Flory have similarly described a related and emerging phenomenon they call "network Christianity," within which key pastors operate as independent religious entrepreneurs outside of traditional Christian denominational structures. For Christerson and Flory, network Christianity particularly describes movements within American Pentecostal and charismatic circles, but they also note that its rise is symptomatic of larger macro changes in American society and that the kind of social and cultural shifts that network Christianity has brought to American charismatic spaces are likely to be seen much more broadly within American Christianity. See Brad Christerson and Richard W. Flory, *The Rise of Network Christianity: How Independent Leaders Are Changing the Religious Landscape* (New York: Oxford University Press, 2017).

44. Michael Leo Owens, *God and Government in the Ghetto: The Politics of Church-State Collaboration in Black America* (Chicago: University of Chicago Press, 2007).

45. Pierpaolo Donati, *Relational Sociology: A New Paradigm for the Social Sciences* (London: Routledge, 2010), 4.

46. Mustafa Emirbayer, "Manifesto for a Relational Sociology," *American Journal of Sociology* 103, no. 2 (1997): 281, https://doi.org/10.1086/231209. Emirbayer begins with the fundamental question of whether we conceive of the social world as consisting primarily in *substances* or *processes.* In other words, in static things or in dynamic, unfolding relations. The former, he argues, represents a substantialist outlook on society, which assumes that durable, coherent entities constitute the legitimate starting points of sociological inquiry. The later (relational) approach that he puts forward instead suggests that individuals cannot be understood outside of the "transactional contexts" in which they are embedded.

47. See, for example, Pierre Bourdieu, *The Logic of Practice* (Stanford, CA: Stanford University Press, 1990); and Pierre Bourdieu and Loïc J. D. Wacquant, *An Invitation to Reflexive Sociology* (Chicago: University of Chicago Press, 1992). For more on the many influences on the development of Bourdieu's relational sociology and his use of the concept of *social fields*, see David Swartz, *Culture and Power: The Sociology of Pierre Bourdieu* (Chicago: University of Chicago Press, 1998), especially chaps. 1 and 6.

48. John W. Mohr, "Bourdieu's Relational Method in Theory and in Practice: From Fields and Capitals to Networks and Institutions (and Back Again)," in *Applying Relational Sociology*, ed. F. Dépelteau and C. Powell (New York: Palgrave Macmillan, 2013), 101–2.

49. Again, my focus in identifying and analyzing the field of Black religious politics is on Black Protestants, representing the majority of religious African Americans. This does not exclude other Black religious voices from that field (such as Black Catholics, Black Muslims, and others). But it necessarily brackets them, to some extent. Focusing on the lens of Israel and Palestine takes my analysis deep into African American Protestantism, and only incidentally into African American Islam and religious movements like the Black Hebrew Israelites. For W. E. B. Du Bois, "Black Church" essentially meant Black Methodists and Black Baptists. The same was true for Carter Woodson. As Clarence Hardy impressed on me in the course of this research, there is a tendency in Black Church Studies to make African American religiosity appear more Christian, more Protestant, and more continuous than it actually is. Although my fieldwork took me mostly into Black Protestant religious spaces, this is not to categorically exclude other spaces from consideration within the contentious social dynamics of the field of Black religious politics. Rather, I hope this work will open the door to more analyses of how non-Protestant, non-Christian expressions of African American religiosity contribute to understanding Black religious politics as a field of contestation.

50. Bourdieu's concept of *habitus* refers to "a system of durable, transportable dispositions" that people are socialized into and that correspond to particular social locations. See Pierre Bourdieu, *The Logic of Practice* (Stanford, CA: Stanford University Press, 1990), 53. In other words, a set of deeply ingrained habits, internalized dispositions, or a kind of "structuring structure" that generates social action. For a concise discussion of the evolution of the concept of habitus in Bourdieu's sociology, see Swartz, *Culture and Power*, chap. 5.

51. On the history of the Exodus narrative in the African American religious and political imagination, see Eddie S. Glaude Jr., *Exodus! Religion, Race, and Nation in Early Nineteenth-Century Black America* (Chicago: University of Chicago Press, 2000).

52. Philip Gorski, *American Covenant: A History of Civil Religion from the Puritans to the Present* (Princeton, NJ: Princeton University Press, 2017), 4.

1. STANDING WITH ISRAEL: AFRICAN AMERICAN CHRISTIAN ZIONISM

1. See, for example, Melani McAlister, *Epic Encounters: Culture, Media, and U.S. Interests in the Middle East Since 1945* (Berkeley: University of California Press, 2005); Melani McAlister, *The Kingdom of God Has No Borders: A Global History of American Evangelicals* (New York: Oxford University Press, 2018); Thomas Kidd, *American Christians and Islam: Evangelical*

Culture and Muslims from the Colonial Period to the Age of Terrorism (Princeton, NJ: Princeton University Press, 2009); Michael Oren, *Power, Faith and Fantasy: America in the Middle East: 1776 to the Present* (New York: Norton, 2007); Grace Halsell, *Prophecy and Politics: The Secret Alliance Between Israel and the U.S. Christian Right* (Chicago: Lawrence Hill, 1989); Christine Leigh Heyrman, *American Apostles: When Evangelicals Entered the World of Islam* (New York: Hill and Wang, 2015); and Jonathan Lyons, *Islam Through Western Eyes: From the Crusades to the War on Terrorism* (New York: Columbia University Press, 2012).

2.   Robert O. Smith, *More Desired Than Our Owne Salvation: The Roots of Christian Zionism* (New York: Oxford University Press, 2013), 2.

3.   On Christian Zionism and the Protestant Reformation, see, for example, Smith, *More Desired Than Our Owne Salvation*; on the emergence of dispensationalism as a source for political thinking about the State of Israel, see Donald M. Lewis, *The Origins of Christian Zionism: Lord Shaftesbury and Evangelical Support for a Jewish Homeland* (New York: Cambridge University Press, 2009); and on the subsequent transplanting and thriving of dispensationalist theology within American evangelicalism, see Timothy P. Weber, *On the Road to Armageddon: How Evangelicals Became Israel's Best Friend* (Grand Rapids, MI: Baker Academic, 2004). Some contemporary Christian Zionists seek to shed the association of Christian Zionism with dispensational premillennialism and its apocalyptic theologies focused on the cataclysmic "end-times" of the earth. They argue for a rehabilitated version based on historical, political, and theological grounds that predate the advent of dispensationalism. See, for example, Gerald R. McDermott, ed., *The New Christian Zionism: Fresh Perspectives on Israel and the Land* (Downers Grove, IL: IVP Academic, 2016).

4.   See Hal Lindsey, *The Late Great Planet Earth* (Grand Rapids, MI: Zondervan, 1970). In this best-selling dispensationalist Bible prophecy book, Lindsey discusses the Jewish repossession of Jerusalem and the expected mass conversion of Jews to Christianity as events that must take place before the Second Coming. Pointing to the 1967 Six-Day War and the Israeli army's occupation of Jerusalem, Lindsey writes, "against incredible odds, the Jews had unwittingly further set up the stage for their final hour of trial and conversion" (55). For more on the impact of the Six-Day War on American Protestant politics and culture, see Jason M. Olson, *America's Road to Jerusalem: The Impact of the Six-Day War on Protestant Politics* (Lanham, MD: Lexington, 2018). This is not to say that Christian Zionism did not have political implications for British and American Protestants before 1948. As Paul Merkley notes, Christian Zionists in both countries played a political part in the success of the Zionist movement from the late nineteenth century to the founding of the State of Israel. See Paul C. Merkley, *The Politics of Christian Zionism 1891–1948* (Portland, OR: Routledge, 1998).

5.   For more on the origins of Hagee's Christian Zionism and CUFI as an organization, see Sean Durbin, *Righteous Gentiles: Religion, Identity, and Myth in John Hagee's Christians United for Israel* (Boston: Brill, 2018). On Falwell and the Moral Majority, see Halsell, *Prophecy and Politics*; and Susan Friend Harding, *The Book of Jerry Falwell: Fundamentalist Language and Politics* (Princeton, NJ: Princeton University Press, 2000).

6.   Both critics and defenders of Christian Zionism include Jews and Christians. Jewish authors who have written in defense of Christian Zionism include David Brog, *Standing with Israel: Why Christians Support the Jewish State* (Lake Mary, FL: Charisma House,

2006); Zev Chafets, *A Match Made in Heaven: American Jews, Christian Zionists, and One Man's Exploration of the Weird and Wonderful Judeo-Evangelical Alliance* (New York: Harper Perennial, 2008); Paul Charles Merkley, *Christian Attitudes Towards the State of Israel* (Montreal, Canada: McGill Queens University Press, 2007); Faydra L. Shapiro, "The Messiah and Rabbi Jesus: Policing the Jewish-Christian Border in Christian Zionism," *Culture and Religion* 12, no. 4 (2011): 463-77, https://doi.org/10.1080/14755610.2011.633537; and Stephen Spector, *Evangelicals and Israel: The Story of American Christian Zionism* (New York: Oxford University Press, 2008). Christian authors who have written in defense of Christian Zionism include John Hagee, *In Defense of Israel*, rev. ed. (Lake Mary, FL: Front-Line, 2007); Thomas Ice, *The Case for Zionism* (Green Forest, AR: New Leaf, 2005); Paul R. Wilkinson, *For Zion's Sake: Christian Zionism and the Role of John Nelson Darby* (Colorado Springs, CO: Paternoster, 2007); and Paul R. Wilkinson, *Understanding Christian Zionism: Israel's Place in the Purposes of God* (Bend, OR: Berean Call, 2013). Jews are also among the critics of Christian Zionism; see Mark Braverman, *Fatal Embrace: Christians, Jews, and the Search for Peace in the Holy Land* (New York: Beaufort, 2012); and Gershom Gorenberg, *The End of Days: Fundamentalism and the Struggle for the Temple Mount* (New York: Oxford University Press, 2002). Critics of Christian Zionism also include many Christians; see Naim Ateek, Cedar Duaybis, and Maurine Tobin, eds., *Challenging Christian Zionism: Theology, Politics and the Israel-Palestine Conflict* (London: Melisende, 2005); Gary M. Burge, *Whose Land? Whose Promise? What Christians Are Not Being Told About Israel and the Palestinians* (Cleveland, OH: Pilgrim, 2004); Rosemary Radford and Herman J. Ruether, *The Wrath of Jonah: The Crisis of Religious Nationalism in the Israeli-Palestinian Conflict* (Minneapolis, MN: Fortress, 2002); Stephen Sizer, *Christian Zionism: Road-Map to Armageddon?* (Downers Grove, IL: IVP Academic, 2006); Donald Wagner, "Evangelicals and Israel: Theological Roots of a Political Alliance," *Christian Century* 115, no. 30 (1998): 1020; and Weber, *On the Road to Armageddon*. Christian Zionism has also featured prominently in scholarly works on Evangelical-Jewish relations, see Yaakov S. Ariel, *An Unusual Relationship: Evangelical Christians and Jews* (New York: New York University Press, 2013); and Alan Mittleman, Byron Johnson, and Nancy Isserman, *Uneasy Allies? Evangelical and Jewish Relations* (Lanham, MD: Lexington, 2007). On Christian travel/pilgrimage to Israel, see Jackie Feldman, "Constructing a Shared Bible Land: Jewish Israeli Guiding Performances for Protestant Pilgrims," *American Ethnologist* 34, no. 2 (2007): 351-74; Halsell, *Prophecy and Politics*; Hillary Kaell, *Walking Where Jesus Walked: American Christians and Holy Land Pilgrimage* (New York: New York University Press, 2014); and Stephanie Stidham Rogers, *Inventing the Holy Land: American Protestant Pilgrimage to Palestine, 1865–1941* (Lanham, MD: Lexington, 2011). On the influence of Evangelicals on U.S. foreign policy in the Middle East, see Mark R. Amstutz, *Evangelicals and American Foreign Policy* (New York: Oxford University Press, 2014); Irvine H. Anderson, *Biblical Interpretation and Middle East Policy: The Promised Land, America, and Israel, 1917–2002* (Gainesville, FL: University Press of Florida, 2005); John J. Mearsheimer and Stephen M. Walt, *The Israel Lobby and U.S. Foreign Policy* (New York: Farrar, Straus and Giroux, 2007); and Nilay Saiya, "Onward Christian Soldiers: American Dispensationalists, George W. Bush and the Middle East," *Holy Land Studies: A Multidisciplinary Journal (Edinburgh University Press)* 11, no. 2 (2012): 175-204, https://doi.org/10.3366/hls.2012.0044. On American Christian attitudes toward Muslims and the Arab world, see Sean Durbin, "Mediating the Past Through the Present and the Present Through the Past," *Political Theology* 15, no. 2 (2014): 110–31, https://doi.org/10.1179/1462317X13Z.00000000070; Kidd, *American Christians and Islam*; and Fuad Sha'ban, *For Zion's Sake: The Judeo-Christian Tradition in American Culture* (Ann Arbor, MI: Pluto, 2005).

7.   There are a few notable exceptions to the overwhelming focus on white American Christians in studies of Christian Zionism. For example, see Smith, *More Desired Than Our Owne Salvation*, 40–45, who argues that support for U.S. policy that favors Israel among American Christians cannot be predicted by adherence to conservative doctrine alone. Instead, noting differences in attitudes on Israel and Palestine captured by survey research between Black and white Protestants in the United States, he suggests attention to a combination of religious traditionalism, American nationalist exceptionalism, and *whiteness* as predictors of Christian Zionist political positions on American-Israeli relations. Other treatments of Christian Zionism have shifted the empirical focus from white evangelicals to expressions of Christian Zionism among other groups. On Native Americans, see Mark Clatterbuck, "Tribal Alliances: The State of Israel and Native American Christianity," *Journal of Ecumenical Studies* 49, no. 3 (2014): 384–404; on Singaporeans, see John Gee, "Singapore's Expanding Christian Zionist Community," *Washington Report on Middle East Affairs* 28, no. 9 (2009): 36; on South Koreans, see Sung-Gun Kim, "Korean Christian Zionism: A Sociological Study of Mission," *International Review of Mission* 100, no. 1 (2011): 85–95, https://doi.org/10.1111/j.1758-6631.2011.00059.x; and on Hondurans, see William Girard, "Christian Zionism at Jerusalén Church in Copán Ruinas, Honduras, an 'Out-of-the-Way' Place," in *Comprehending Christian Zionism: Perspectives in Comparison*, ed. G. Gunner and R. O. Smith (Minneapolis, MN: Fortress, 2014), 125–35. Attention to Black voices within the Christian Zionist movement and among its critics has been limited. See Damu Smith, "The African-American Experience," in *Challenging Christian Zionism: Theology, Politics and the Israel-Palestine Conflict*, ed. N. Ateek, C. Duaybis, and M. Tobin (London: Melisende, 2005), 215–25. African American defenses of Christian Zionism have come from Black pastors Michael Stevens and Dumisani Washington, both of whom are part of the focus of this book. See Michael Stevens, *We Too Stand: A Call for the African-American Church to Support the Jewish State* (Lake Mary, FL: FrontLine, 2013); and Dumisani Washington, *Zionism and the Black Church: Why Standing with Israel Will Be a Defining Issue for Christians of Color in the 21st Century* (Stockton, CA: IBSI, 2014).

8.   A number of scholars have developed aspects of this story in far greater depth and with more attention to detail than my necessarily brief overview. In particular, on the connection between Israel and Palestine and post-Cold War racial formations in the United States, see Keith P. Feldman, *A Shadow Over Palestine: The Imperial Life of Race in America* (Minneapolis: University of Minnesota Press, 2015). Similarly, on the emergence and development of Palestinian solidarity among American African Americans and globalizing racial concerns (especially post-1967), see Michael R. Fischbach, *Black Power and Palestine: Transnational Communities of Color* (Stanford, CA: Stanford University Press, 2018). For an overview of African American encounters with Jews and Judaism in religious terms, see Yvonne Patricia Chireau and Nathaniel Deutsch, eds., *Black Zion: African American Religious Encounters with Judaism* (New York: Oxford University Press,

2000). And for a wide-ranging volume on both religious and political relations between African Americans and Jews in the United States, see Jack Salzman and Cornel West, eds., *Struggles in the Promised Land: Towards a History of Black-Jewish Relations in the United States* (New York: Oxford University Press, 1997).

9.   In the 1990s, many American Jews and African Americans took stock of the state of Black-Jewish relations, with efforts to explain the development (or the undoing) of Black-Jewish partnerships for civil rights and the common good in America. Such efforts included efforts to expose and explain Black antisemitism; see, for example, Henry Louis Gates Jr., "Black Demagogues and Pseudo-Scholars," *New York Times*, July 20, 1992, http://www.nytimes.com/1992/07/20/opinion/black-demagogues-and-pseudo-scholars.html; and Joshua Muravchik, "Facing Up to Black Anti-Semitism," *Commentary* 100, no. 6 (1995): 26. On attempts to engage in constructive dialogue, see, for example, Michael Lerner and Cornel West, *Jews & Blacks: A Dialogue on Race, Religion, and Culture in America* (New York: Plume, 1996). To generally explain what went wrong, see, for example, Murray Friedman, *What Went Wrong? The Creation and Collapse of the Black-Jewish Alliance* (New York: Free Press, 1995); and Jonathan Kaufman, *Broken Alliance: The Turbulent Times Between Blacks and Jews in America* (New York: Scribner, 1995). Concerned with the apparent lack of a historical account of Black-Jewish relations in America, scholars also intervened with volumes to fill the void from historical, political, and theological perspectives. See, for example, Maurianne Adams and John H. Bracey, eds., "Go Down, Moses," in *Strangers & Neighbors: Relations Between Blacks & Jews in the United States* (Amherst: University of Massachusetts Press, 1999), 53–54; Paul Berman, ed., *Blacks and Jews: Alliances and Arguments* (New York: Delacorte, 1994); Chireau and Deutsch, *Black Zion*; V. P. Franklin, Nancy L. Grant, Harold M. Kletnick, and Genna Rae McNeil, eds., *African Americans and Jews in the Twentieth Century: Studies in Convergence and Conflict* (Columbia: University of Missouri Press, 1998); Gates, "Black Demagogues and Pseudo-Scholars"; Muravchik, "Facing Up to Black Anti-Semitism"; and Salzman and West, *Struggles in the Promised Land*. In these accounts, the goal is generally not to answer *what went wrong* but rather to begin with the more fundamental question of *what happened*? The authors of several of these treatments of Black-Jewish relations in America have argued that the relationship should not be viewed entirely through the lens of conflict; neither should recent tensions be sharply contrasted with an earlier period of positive relations free from problems. See Clayborne Carson, "The Politics of Relations Between African-Americans and Jews," in *Blacks and Jews: Alliances and Arguments*, ed. P. Berman (New York: Delacorte, 1994), 131–43; Chireau and Deutsch, *Black Zion*; and Salzman and West, *Struggles in the Promised Land*. In doing so, they challenge both the notion of a golden age of Black-Jewish relations and its later total collapse. This kind of nuanced approach provides clarity through attention to complexity. It also reaches the more tenable and ambivalent conclusion that relations between African Americans and Jews, as Jack Salzman puts it, "at times provided an important impetus for social justice in the United States and, at other times, have been the cause of great tension." See Jack Salzman, introduction to *Struggles in the Promised Land: Towards a History of Black-Jewish Relations in the United States*, ed. J. Salzman and C. West (New York: Oxford University Press, 1997), 1–19 at 5. For accounts of the wide range of uses of the civil rights legacy

through divergent cultural and collective memories of the movement, see Renee C. Romano and Leigh Raiford, eds., *The Civil Rights Movement in American Memory* (Athens: University of Georgia Press, 2006); and Hajar Yazdiha, *The Struggle for the People's King: How Politics Transforms the Memory of the Civil Rights Movement* (Princeton, NJ: Princeton University Press, 2023).

10.   Jonathan Kaufman, "Blacks and Jews: The Struggle in the Cities," in *Struggles in the Promised Land: Towards a History of Black-Jewish Relations in the United States*, ed. Jack Salzman and Cornel West (New York: Oxford University Press, 1997), 107–21, at 107.

11.   Kaufman claims that as many as three quarters of the white volunteers who went south to take part in the civil rights movement in the 1960s were Jews, whereas Clayborne Carson acknowledges substantial Jewish participation in these organizations but questions the existence of sources upon which to base specific claims about the extent of this participation. Carson also highlights the difficulty in identifying the motivations (religious, political, etc.) of those Jews who actively participated in the civil rights movement. See Kaufman, "Blacks and Jews: The Struggle in the Cities"; and Clayborne Carson, "Black-Jewish Universalism in the Era of Identity Politics," in *Struggles in the Promised Land: Towards a History of Black-Jewish Relations in the United States*, ed. Jack Salzman and Cornel West (New York: Oxford University Press, 1997), 177–96.

12.   On reconciling the organizational cooperation of African Americans and Jews within the civil rights movement with broader tensions experienced across the cities of the northern United States, Paul Buhle and Robin Kelley suggest that the tensions between Black and Jewish communities in many of the cities of the North demonstrates that cooperation between Blacks and Jews in the civil rights movement might best be described as one between leaders and not between average citizens. See Paul Buhle and Robin Kelly, "Allies of a Different Sort: Jews and Blacks in the American Left," in *Struggles in the Promised Land: Towards a History of Black-Jewish Relations in the United States*, ed. Jack Salzman and Cornel West (New York: Oxford University Press, 1997), 197–229.

13.   Norman Podhoretz, "My Negro Problem–And Ours," *Commentary*, February 1963, 93–101.

14.   Yvonne Patricia Chireau, "Black Culture and Black Zion: African American Religious Encounters with Judaism, 1790–1930, an Overview," in *Black Zion: African American Religious Encounters with Judaism*, ed. N. Deutsch and Y. P. Chireau (New York: Oxford University Press, 2000), 15–32.

15.   Attention to the formative role of the biblical Exodus narrative in African American religious and political identity formation goes from early commentaries on African American religion through recent analyses. W. E. B. Du Bois analyzed the figure of Booker T. Washington as potential biblical Joshua figure. See W. E. B. Du Bois, *The Souls of Black Folk*, ed. B. H. Edwards (1903; repr. New York: Oxford University Press, 2007). In the mid-twentieth century, E. Franklin Frazier described Bible stories like the Exodus narrative as a source of rich imagery for African American religious identity— what Howard Thurman calls a "deep river" of spiritual meaning. See E. Franklin Frazier, *The Negro Church in America* (1963; repr. New York: Schocken, 1974); and Howard Thurman, *Deep River: An Interpretation of Negro Spirituals* (Mills College, CA: Eucalyptus, 1945). More recently, historians of Black religion such as Albert Raboteau and Eddie

Glaude have shown how the Exodus narrative appropriations of the Exodus story tran-
scended African American religious identity and spiritual formation and contributed
to *this-worldly* liberative collective political identity as a people. See Albert J. Raboteau,
Slave Religion: The "Invisible Institution" in the Antebellum South (New York: Oxford University Press, 1978); and Eddie S. Glaude Jr., *Exodus! Religion, Race, and Nation in Early
Nineteenth-Century Black America* (Chicago: University of Chicago Press, 2000).

16. Albert J. Raboteau, "African-Americans, Exodus, and the American Israel," in *Strangers
& Neighbors: Relations Between Blacks & Jews in the United States*, ed. M. Adams and J. H.
Bracey (Amherst: University of Massachusetts Press, 1999), 57–58.

17. See Jacob S. Dorman, *Chosen People: The Rise of American Black Israelite Religions* (New
York: Oxford University Press, 2013). This is a comprehensive study of Black Israelite
religions in the United States. Dorman traces the historical development among African
Americans of the belief that the true ancient Hebrew Israelites were Black and that
African Americans are their descendants. In surveying Black Israelite history and theology from the nineteenth century into the Great Migration, Dorman pays particular
attention to what he calls the transnational "polycultural" identity formation of the
movement.

18. As Black Hebrew congregations grew in the urban North, a racialized religious identity
emerged wherein "the 'real' Jews were Black people, while Jews of European descent were
said to be 'offshoots' of the original lineage of Black Jews or converts who had received
the religion secondhand from Africans." See Chireau, "Black Culture and Black Zion," 24.
For another look at Black Hebrew groups and their role in advancing new conceptions
of "religio-racial identity" during the Great Migration, see Judith Weisenfeld, *New World
A-Coming: Black Religion and Racial Identity During the Great Migration* (New York: New
York University Press, 2016).

19. On the Black Hebrew Israelites, their history, migration, and community in Israel, see
Merrill Singer, "Symbolic Identity Formation in an African American Religious Sect:
The Black Hebrew Israelites," in *Black Zion: African American Religious Encounters with
Judaism*, ed. N. Deutsch and Y. P. Chireau (New York: Oxford University Press, 2000),
55–72.

20. Dorman, *Chosen People*.

21. For example, see E. U. Essien-Udom, *Black Nationalism: The Search for Identity in America*
(Chicago: University of Chicago Press, 1962), who discusses Black Muslim American
exodus and nationhood movements under the rubric of "Zionism." On the connection
between African Americans and Jews in white racial classification categories and gene-
alogies, see, for example, Arthur Talmage Abernethy, *The Jew a Negro: Being a Study of the
Jewish Ancestry from an Impartial Standpoint* (Moravian Falls, NC: Dixie, 1910).

22. John Hagee, "Understanding Christian Zionism," OnFaith, September 19, 2012, http://
www.faithstreet.com/onfaith/2012/09/19/understanding-christian-zionism/10779.

23. John Hagee, "How a Night to Honor Israel Was Born," Christians United for Israel, 2011,
Accessed July 19, 2017, http://www.cufi.org/site/PageServer?pagename=events_Night_to
_Honor_Israel_History.

24. All Hagee quotes in this paragraph are from Hagee, "How a Night to Honor Israel
Was Born."

25. Lauren Blair Aronson, "CUFI Surpasses 5 Million Member Mark," CUFI press release, 2018.

26. Stevens, *We Too Stand*, xvii.

27. Messianic Jews believe in and worship Jesus (Yeshua) as the Jewish Messiah. They see themselves as living an authentic, fulfilled expression of Judaism, whereas their critics (most notably Orthodox Jews) see them as converts to evangelical Christianity. See Dan Cohn-Sherbok, *Messianic Judaism: A Critical Anthology* (New York: Continuum, 2000). Dumisani Washington does not consider himself a Messianic Jew, or any other kind of Jew. For him, there is a clear distinction between his "Hebrew roots" Christianity and Judaism itself. The line between identification *with* Israel and identity *as* Israel is one that Washington addresses in his pro-Israel advocacy work, speaking against groups such as the Black Hebrew Israelites, whom he criticizes for claiming to be the "true Israel."

28. The history and origins of BASIC are discussed further in chapter 2.

29. Quoted in Frank J. Prial, "Blacks Organize Pro-Israel Group," *New York Times*, September 12, 1975.

30. The historian Gayle Plummer describes BASIC's position-taking on Israel as part of "a fragile alliance between civil rights 'moderates' and supporters of Israel [that] tried to connect Israel with themes of domestic freedom." See Brenda Gayle Plummer, *In Search of Power: African Americans in the Era of Decolonization, 1956–1974* (New York: Cambridge University Press, 2012), 294. Plummer shows how Israel's diplomatic, economic, and military relations with apartheid South Africa were a significant wedge that challenged the strength of this fragile alliance between moderate African American civil rights leaders and the State of Israel. The Committee of Black Americans for the Truth About the Middle East, another Black organization formed to criticize Israel's policies, and the Student Nonviolent Coordinating Committee (SNCC) called attention to Israel's treatment of Palestinians, comparing discrimination against Arabs in Israel to Jim Crow segregation. But Rustin, called "Israel's man in Harlem" by some, was the most reliably pro-Israel of his generation of civil rights leaders; see Fischbach, *Black Power and Palestine*, 181. For an overview of Bayard Rustin's views on Israel and the founding of BASIC, see Fischbach, *Black Power and Palestine*, chap. 9.

31. Christians United for Israel, "CUFI in Action," CUFI newsletter, 2016.

32. Israel Collective, "The Truth About Israel and South African Apartheid" (video), December 14, 2015, https://www.youtube.com/watch?v=KdEAMa6CT5I.

33. Christians United for Israel, "Mission and Vision," accessed May 31, 2018, https://www.cufi.org/impact/about-us/mission-and-vision/.

34. Zev Chafets, "The Rabbi Who Loved Evangelicals (and Vice Versa)," *New York Times*, July 24, 2005; Zev Chafets, *The Bridge Builder: The Life and Continuing Legacy of Rabbi Yechiel Eckstein* (New York: Sentinel, 2015), x.

35. Biographical details on Yechiel Eckstein in this section draw on conversations with IFCJ staff, Eckstein's authorized biography (Chafets, *The Bridge Builder*), and the Fellowship's website at IFCJ.org.

36. Chafets, *The Bridge Builder*, 52.

37. Chafets, *The Bridge Builder*, 59–60.

38. Chafets, *The Bridge Builder*, 66.

39. Chafets, *The Bridge Builder*, 67.

40. Fund-raising figures are from International Fellowship of Christians and Jews, "Report on Impact: IFCJ Projects in Israel and Around the World 2017," *2017 Annual Report*; and Loveday Morris, Michelle Boorstein, and Ruth Eglash, "Long, Uneasy Love Affair of Israel and U.S. Evangelicals May Have Peaked," *Washington Post*, January 28, 2018.

41. Deedee Coleman, "Q & A with Rev. Dr. Deedee M. Coleman," *CT Jewish Ledger*, January 2011.

42. Edward L. Branch and Yechiel Eckstein, "On the Frontlines of Faith: The Historical and Spiritual Bonds Between African-Americans and Jews" (Chicago: International Fellowship of Christian and Jews, 2016), 14.

43. Branch and Eckstein, "On the Frontlines of Faith," 21–22.

44. Branch and Eckstein, "On the Frontlines of Faith," 26.

45. Branch and Eckstein, "On the Frontlines of Faith," 41.

46. International Fellowship of Christians and Jews, "Our Programs," accessed February 13, 2019, http://www.ifcj.org/who-we-are/programs/.

47. Mike Pence, "Remarks by Vice President Mike Pence in Special Session of the Knesset," *The White House*, January 22, 2018.

48. Quoted in Morris, Boorstein, and Eglash, "Long, Uneasy Love Affair of Israel and U.S. Evangelicals May Have Peaked."

49. International Fellowship of Christians and Jews, "African-American Leaders Reject Anti-Israel Stance of Movement for Black Lives," *Baltimore Jewish Life*, August 22, 2016.

2. JOURNEYS TO JUSTICE: AFRICAN AMERICAN CHRISTIAN PALESTINIAN SOLIDARITY

1. Michael R. Fischbach, *Black Power and Palestine: Transnational Countries of Color* (Stanford, CA: Stanford University Press, 2018), 3.

2. See Alexander Crummell, "'The Regeneration of Africa,'"in *African American Religious History: A Documentary Witness*, ed. M. C. Sernett (1891; repr. Durham, NC: Duke University Press, 1999), 282–88; and Henry McNeal Turner, "Emigration to Africa," in *African American Religious History: A Documentary Witness*, ed. M. C. Sernett (1883; repr. Durham, NC: Duke University Press, 1999), 289–95.

3. Thierno Thiam and Gilbert Rochon elaborate the connection between Black churches and the Pan-African movements of the late nineteenth and into the twentieth century, suggesting that the Black church is part of a "triatic hub" of institutions undergirding the growth of the Pan-African movement, alongside the Black press and Black academic institutions. Thierno Thiam and Gilbert Rochon, *Sustainability, Emerging Technologies, and Pan-Africanism* (New York: Palgrave Macmillan, 2020).

4. Barbara Dianne Savage, "Benjamin Mays, Global Ecumenism, and Local Religious Segregation," *American Quarterly* 59, no. 3 (2007): 785–806, https://doi.org/10.1353/aq.2007.0068.

5. Lilian Calles Barger, *The World Come of Age: An Intellectual History of Liberation Theology* (New York: Oxford University Press, 2018), 210.

6.   Waldo E. Martin Jr., "'Nation Time!': Black Nationalism, the Third World, and Jews," in *Struggles in the Promised Land: Towards a History of Black-Jewish Relations in the United States*, ed. Jack Salzman and Cornel West (New York: Oxford University Press, 1997), 341–55.

7.   A 1967 SNCC newsletter contained a "Third World" feature titled "The Palestine Problem" that characterized the 1967 war as a war of dispossession, cast the State of Israel as a colonial state backed by U.S. imperialism, and identified Palestinians as victims of racial subjugation. SNCC Newsletter, "The Palestine Problem," June–July 1967, https://www.crmvet.org/docs/sv/6707_sncc_news-r.pdf; compare with Robin D. G. Kelley, "Another Freedom Summer," *Journal of Palestine Studies* 44, no. 1 (2014): 29–41, https://doi.org/10.1525/jps.2014.44.1.29.

8.   For a detailed account of the emerging anti-Zionism of Stokely Carmichael and SNCC in 1967 and the central part that Black Nationalist position-taking on Israel played in severing existing Black-Jewish relations in the United States, see Paul Buhle and Robin D. G. Kelley, "Allies of a Different Sort: Jews and Blacks in the American Left," in *Struggles in the Promised Land: Towards a History of Black-Jewish Relations in the United States*, ed. Jack Salzman and Cornel West (New York: Oxford University Press, 1997), 214–17; Keith P. Feldman, *A Shadow Over Palestine: The Imperial Life of Race in America* (Minneapolis: University of Minnesota Press, 2015), chap. 2; Fischbach, *Black Power and Palestine*, chap. 2; and Alex Lubin, *Geographies of Liberation: The Making of an Afro-Arab Political Imaginary* (Chapel Hill: University of North Carolina Press, 2014), chap. 4.

9.   On the history of Black-Jewish relations within the American political left, see Buhle and Kelley, "Allies of a Different Sort."

10.   Clayborne Carson, "Black-Jewish Universalism in the Era of Identity Politics," in *Struggles in the Promised Land: Towards a History of Black-Jewish Relations in the United States*, ed. Jack Salzman and Cornel West (New York: Oxford University Press, 1997), 190.

11.   Quoted in Robert G. Weisbord and Richard Kazarian, *Israel in the Black American Perspective* (Westport, CT: Greenwood, 1985), 94.

12.   The meeting ended with Jackson and the group linking arms with Arafat and singing the civil rights anthem, "We Shall Overcome." See Karin L. Stanford, *Beyond the Boundaries: Reverend Jesse Jackson in International Affairs* (Albany: State University of New York Press, 1997). After returning to the United States, Jackson gave a speech in which he called Zionism a "poisonous weed" choking Judaism. See Gary E. Rubin, "African Americans and Israel," in *Struggles in the Promised Land: Towards a History of Black-Jewish Relations in the United States*, ed. Jack Salzman and Cornel West (New York: Oxford University Press, 1997), 360.

13.   Thomas A. Johnson, "Black Leaders Air Grievances on Jews," *New York Times*, August 23, 1979.

14.   Rubin, "African Americans and Israel."

15.   A leadership debate developed within SNCC over the merits of the Christian ideals that continued to guide the SCLC. Savage describes the respective views on Black religion between John Lewis, who led SNCC from 1963–1966, and Stokely Carmichael, who took over the organization's chairmanship when Lewis and other leaders were asked to leave to make way for new leadership more committed to Black radicalism and less inclined

toward nonviolence. Although Carmichael's own motivations derived in part from Black religion as a repository for Black history and identity, as well as an imperative for justice, Savage shows that he rejected the explicitly Christian outlook of Lewis and others, and he also rejected pacifism outright. See Barbara Dianne Savage, *Your Spirits Walk Beside Us: The Politics of Black Religion* (Cambridge, MA: Belknap Press of Harvard University Press, 2008), chap. 6.

16. On the broader debate about the relationship between Black religion and political participation and the question of whether Black religion impels or impedes political engagement, see the relevant summary and discussion of that debate in the introduction and chapter 3 of Savage, *Your Spirits Walk Beside Us*. Since the civil rights movement, scholars of Black religion and Black politics have tended to recognize, at some level, the political significance of Black churches. For example, the historian, theologian, and ethicist Gayraud Wilmore traces a liberationist core in Black religion as beginning during slavery and continuing into the twentieth century, which he connects directly to this-worldly political concerns. Wilmore argues that "Black pride and power, Black nationalism and Pan-Africanism have no past without the Black church and Black religion." Gayraud Wilmore, *Black Religion and Black Radicalism* (Garden City, NY: Doubleday, 1972), xiii. In this same vein, C. Eric Lincoln and Lawrence Mamiya outline a post–civil rights era critique of what they call a long-standing "Myth of the Black Church and Politics." That myth, they explain, posits that Black religion and politics are fundamentally incompatible. Following Wilmore, Lincoln and Mamiya trace a liberationist core throughout the history of Black religion in America that finds Black religion and Black politics essentially fused. Thus they argue against what they see as the exclamation point on the view that Black religion suppresses political activism—Gary Marx's conclusion that Black religion is essentially an opiate in the Black community. See C. Eric Lincoln and Lawrence Mamiya, *The Black Church in the African American Experience* (Durham, NC: Duke University Press, 1990); and Gary Marx, *Protest and Prejudice: A Study of Belief in the Black Community* (New York: Harper & Row, 1967). For a detailed discussion of the relationship between Black religion and African American political engagement, see Frederick C. Harris, *Something Within: Religion in African-American Political Activism* (New York: Oxford University Press, 1999).

17. Savage, *Your Spirits Walk Beside Us*, 241.

18. Aldon Morris, *Origins of the Civil Rights Movements* (New York: Free Press, 1986), 5.

19. Savage, *Your Spirits Walk Beside Us*. Anthony B. Pinn argues similarly that not only did Black churches provide material resources—bodies, building space, information dissemination networks, funding, etc.—they also provided the ideological and theological underpinnings of the movement. Pinn notes that clergy active in the movement served as examples and role models to their members and, more broadly, to laypeople outside of their churches who still looked to Black clergy as leaders of African American communities. Anthony B. Pinn, *The Black Church in the Post-Civil Rights Era* (Maryknoll, NY: Orbis, 2002).

20. Savage, *Your Spirits Walk Beside Us*, 270.

21. Quoted in Savage, *Your Spirits Walk Beside Us*, 247. Savage elaborates on the (often unsung) role of women as organizers and activists in the civil rights movement as

being parallel to the underappreciated role women play as the "backbone" in Black churches. Across generations, she highlights connections between religious beliefs and political activism among Black women Christian activists Ella Baker, Mary McLeod Bethune, Nannie Helen Burroughs, Septima Clark, Marian Wright Edelman, and Fannie Lou Hamer.

22. Vincent Harding, "Black Power and the American Christ," *Christian Century* 84, no. 1 (1967): 10–13.

23. Edward J. Blum and Paul Harvey, *The Color of Christ: The Son of God and the Saga of Race in America* (Chapel Hill: University of North Carolina Press, 2014), 218–19.

24. Wilmore, *Black Religion and Black Radicalism*, 269.

25. Historians of the development of Black Liberation Theology trace its sources in what Blum and Harvey call "long" and "short" histories. The long history of Black Liberation Theology goes back to the Black religion of African American slaves and images of Jesus as a liberator. Here, the Black identification with the biblical Exodus narrative (discussed in chapter 1) extends its implications beyond identification with the people and the land of Israel in the Bible to a broader emancipatory religious impulse rooted in the Exodus narrative. This long history develops as Black Christians in successive generations (including clergy and laity, elite and popular voices)—from emancipation, to reconstruction, to Jim Crow segregation, and into the civil rights era—developed Christian theologies in opposition to white supremacist Christian hegemony in America. The short history of Black Liberation Theology focuses on the 1950s and 1960s, as a number of pastors, theologians, and seminarians began to more systematically interrogate and reevaluate biblical texts with attention to humanizing and elevating Blackness in the face of dehumanizing white supremacy. On the history of the development and articulation of Black liberation theologies, See Blum and Harvey, *The Color of Christ*, 218–24; Wilmore, *Black Religion and Black Radicalism*, chap. 8; Anthony B. Pinn, "Black Theology," in *Black Liberation Theologies in the United States: An Introduction*, ed. S. M. Floyd-Thomas and A. B. Pinn (New York: New York University Press, 2010), 15–36; Kelly Brown Douglas, *The Black Christ* (Maryknoll, NY: Orbis, 1994), 53–77; and C. Eric Lincoln, *The Black Church Since Frazier* (New York: Schocken, 1974), chap. 3.

26. Pinn, "Black Theology," 18.

27. James H. Cone, *Black Theology and Black Power* (1969; repr. Maryknoll, NY: Orbis, 1997). See collaborative statements such as "Black Power" (1966), "The Black Manifesto" (1969), "Black Theology" (1969), and "The Black Paper" (1968). All reprinted in Lincoln, *The Black Church Since Frazier*, appendices A–D.

28. Cone, *Black Theology and Black Power*, viii.

29. James H. Cone, *A Black Theology of Liberation* (Philadelphia: Lippincott, 1970), 28. On these and other intellectual and political precursors to Black Theology, see Barger, *The World Come of Age*, 206–16.

30. See Wilmore, *Black Religion and Black Radicalism*; Cornel West, *Prophesy Deliverance! An Afro-American Revolutionary Christianity* (Philadelphia: Westminster, 1982); Katie Geneva Cannon, *Black Womanist Ethics* (Atlanta: Scholars, 1988); Jacquelyn Grant, *White Women's Christ and Black Women's Jesus: Feminist Christology and Womanist Response* (Atlanta: Scholars, 1989); Jacquelyn Grant, "Black Theology and the Black Woman," in *African American*

Religious Thought: An Anthology, ed. C. West and E. S. Glaude (Louisville, KY: Westminster John Knox, 2003), 831–48; Delores S. Williams, *Sisters in the Wilderness: The Challenge of Womanist God-Talk* (Maryknoll, NY: Orbis, 1993); and Evelyn Brooks Higginbotham, *Righteous Discontent: The Women's Movement in the Black Baptist Church, 1880–1920* (Cambridge, MA: Harvard University Press, 1993).

31. Samuel DeWitt Proctor Conference, "About Us," accessed February 14, 2019, http://sdpconference.info/about-us/.

32. Today Wright is perhaps best known as the former pastor of Barack and Michelle Obama. As the Obamas' pastor at Trinity, Wright presided over their wedding and baptized their two daughters. The title of Obama's keynote speech at the Democratic National Convention in 2004 and later his second book, "The Audacity of Hope," comes from a phrase in one of Wright's sermons on "the audacity *to* hope." However, controversy erupted in 2008 following Wright's disinvitation to participate in Obama's presidential campaign announcement. This disinvitation came after media attention to Wright's past sermons highlighted a selection of remarks about the United States and its treatment of African Americans. In a 2003 sermon, for example, Wright said: "The government gives [African Americans] the drugs, builds bigger prisons, passes a three-strike law and then wants us to sing 'God Bless America.' No, no, no, God damn America. . . . God damn America for treating our citizens as less than human. God damn America for as long as she acts like she is God and she is supreme." This kind of incendiary language was shocking to many who had never heard of Jeremiah Wright before the controversy over his pastoral relationship to Barack Obama became national news. Critics questioned Obama's patriotism and the appropriateness of a presidential candidate being associated with ostensibly unpatriotic views. Many of Wright's fellow Black clergy and scholars of American religion came to his defense, however, chiding Wright's (mostly white) critics for their own unfamiliarity with African American preaching and the legacy of Black religious political engagement—including the activism of Martin Luther King Jr. They pointed to the long tradition of "jeremiad" preaching in the United States (in reference to the biblical prophet Jeremiah) broadly, and to the Black prophetic religious tradition more specifically, putting Wright firmly within that tradition among other Black preachers such as King and Wyatt Tee Walker. For a discussion of this episode with reference to the African American jeremiad tradition, see Bernard W. Bell, "President Barack Obama, the Rev. Dr. Jeremiah Wright, and the African American Jeremiadic Tradition," *Massachusetts Review* 50, no. 3 (2009): 332–43.

33. Quoted in Samuel DeWitt Proctor Conference, "About Us."

34. The play, *Passages of Martin Luther King*, was written by the professor and King scholar Clayborne Carson. The West Bank production and tour was led by Carson and was the subject of the documentary film *Al Helm ("the dream"): Martin Luther King in Palestine*. It explores parallels between the African American civil rights struggles in the United States and Palestinian struggles in the occupied territories. See http://www.clarityfilms.org/mlk/.

35. Don Williams, "Walking Where Jesus Walked Led to the Proctor Conference," Kairos USA, March 11, 2015, https://kairosusa.org/walking-where-jesus-walked-led-to-the-proctor-conference/.

36. Black for Palestine, "2015 Black Solidarity Statement with Palestine," 2015, http://www
.blackforpalestine.com/read-the-statement.html; and Taurean Webb, "Journeys Toward
Justice," 2016, http://sdpconference.info/journeys-toward-justice.

37. Samuel DeWitt Proctor Conference, "Journey to Justice: From Black America to Palestine," accessed May 17, 2018, https://www.youtube.com/watch?v=9VFpz3YWGkg&feature
=youtu.be.

38. For the 1985 South African Kairos document, see The Kairos Document, "The Kairos
Document," 1985, https://www.sahistory.org.za/archive/challenge-church-theological
-comment-political-crisis-south-africa-kairos-document-1985. For the 2009 Kairos Palestine document, see Kairos Palestine, "Kairos Document," 2009, https://www.kairospales-
tine.ps/index.php/about-kairos/kairos-palestine-document.

39. A pseudonym. In all places where only a first name is given, these are pseudonyms.

40. Webb, "Journeys Toward Justice." All quotes are from the curriculum's student and facilitator guides. Available at http://sdpconference.info/journeys-toward-justice/.

41. For the full statement that Carruthers read an excerpt from, see Black for Palestine, "2015
Black Solidarity Statement with Palestine."

42. Recognition of sovereignty over the city of Jerusalem has long been a central issue in the
context of Israel and Palestine, with the State of Israel consistently maintaining the city as
its "eternal and indivisible capital" and Palestinians claiming East Jerusalem as the capital
of a future Palestinian state. The decision (before 2018) to maintain its embassy in Tel Aviv
rather than Jerusalem put U.S. foreign policy in line with the United Nations, which has
long identified East Jerusalem as occupied territory and considers the status of Jerusalem
as "disputed" and subject to negotiations between the State of Israel and the Palestinians.

43. Samuel DeWitt Proctor Conference, "Prayers for Gaza!," 2018.

44. Taurean Webb, "On Gaza and the U.S. Embassy Opening," 2018, http://files.constant
contact.com/6e5b396f001/d057aec0-2b17-46ea-a27b-414017c8174e.pdf.

45. Bob Roberts Jr., "Bob Roberts Jr.: Going Glocal," 2014, http://208.106.253.109/premier
-only/going-glocal.aspx.

46. Bob Roberts Jr., *Transformation: How Glocal Churches Transform Lives and the World* (Grand
Rapids, MI: Zondervan, 2006), 75.

47. Glocal.net, "Multifaith," accessed February 15, 2019, https://web.archive.org/web/2015
0709002302/http://www.glocal.net/multifaith/.

48. See Michelle Boorstein, "How the National Prayer Breakfast Sparked an Unusual Meeting Between Muslims and Evangelicals," *Washington Post*, February 8, 2018. For more on
the National Prayer Breakfast and its sponsoring organization, The Fellowship (not affiliated with the International Fellowship of Christians and Jews), see Jeff Sharlet, *The Family: The Secret Fundamentalism at the Heart of American Power* (New York: Harper, 2008).

49. Christ at the Checkpoint (CATC) is an initiative of the small evangelical Bethlehem
Bible College in the West Bank. Together with its Palestinian and international partner
organizations, CATC aims to bring together Palestinian and international evangelical
Christians to talk about theologies of the land held and the issue of Palestine and Israel
from a Palestinian Christian perspective. Information is available at https://christatthe
checkpoint.bethbc.edu/.

50. Roberts, "Bob Roberts Jr.: Going Glocal."

3. "MY PASTOR IS WHERE? HE'S IN ISRAEL?!": BLACK PASTORS AS BROKERS AND MOBILIZERS

1. Early studies that take up the question of the social significance of Black churches include W. E. B. Du Bois, *The Negro Church* (Atlanta: Atlanta University Press, 1903); Carter Godwin Woodson, *The History of the Negro Church* (Washington, DC: Associated, 1921); Benjamin E. Mays and Joseph William Nicholson, *The Negro's Church* (New York: Russell & Russell, 1933); St. Clair Drake and Horace R. Cayton, *Black Metropolis: A Study of Negro Life in a Northern City* (1945; repr. Chicago: University of Chicago Press, 1993); and E. Franklin Frazier, *The Negro Church in America* (1963; repr. New York: Schocken, 1974).

2. Frazier, *The Negro Church in America.*

3. Carter Woodson, "The Negro Church, an All-Comprehending Institution," *Negro History Bulletin* 3, no. 1 (1939): 7, 15.

4. Mays and Nicholson, *The Negro's Church.*

5. On the pioneering social scientific work of W. E. B. Du Bois on the liberative potential of Black churches, see Roger Baumann, "Race, Religion, and Global Solidarities: W. E. B. Du Bois and 'The Black Church' as a Contested Category," *Journal for the Scientific Study of Religion* 62, no. S1 (2023): 48–67, https://doi.org/10.1111/jssr.12856.

6. On these critiques, see Barbara Diane Savage, *Your Spirits Walk Beside Us: The Politics of Black Religion* (Cambridge, MA: Belknap Press of Harvard University Press, 2008), 65, 29.

7. Zora Neale Hurston as quoted in Savage, *Your Spirits Walk Beside Us*, 84.

8. C. Eric Lincoln and Lawrence H. Mamiya, *The Black Church in the African American Experience* (Durham, NC: Duke University Press, 1990), 167.

9. William M. Berenson, Kirk W. Elifson, and Tandy Tollerson, "Preachers in Politics: A Study of Political Activism Among the Black Ministry," *Journal of Black Studies* 6, no. 4 (1976): 373–92; and Charles V. Hamilton, *The Black Preacher in America* (New York: Morrow, 1972).

10. Aldon Morris, *Origins of the Civil Rights Movement* (New York: Free Press, 1986), 5. Some scholars of Black religious politics have argued for paying attention primarily to clergy and denominational leaders, see, for example, Frazier, *The Negro Church in America*; and Adolph L. Reed, *The Jesse Jackson Phenomenon: The Crisis of Purpose in Afro-American Politics* (New Haven, CT: Yale University Press, 1986). Others have emphasized the need to balance attention to clergy priorities with the political interests and attitudes of Black church laity, see, for example, Eric L. McDaniel, "Black Clergy in the 2000 Elections," *Journal for the Scientific Study of Religion* 42, no. 4 (2003): 533–46, https://doi.org/10.1046/j .1468-5906.2003.00201.x. In challenging this narrow focus on clergy, some scholars of Black churches have argued for a wider understanding of African American religious leadership that includes more attention to laypeople, who often are more educated than their pastors. See Eric L. McDaniel, *Politics in the Pews: The Political Mobilization of Black Churches* (Ann Arbor: University of Michigan Press, 2008); and Anthony B. Pinn, *The Black Church in the Post-Civil Rights Era* (Maryknoll, NY: Orbis, 2002). In Lincoln and Mamiya, *The Black Church in the African American Experience*, they emphasize the central role clergy play in Black churches and focus almost exclusively on male senior leadership in Black churches and not on the rank and file of the laity, where women represent the majority, as drivers of congregational activity and interests on a range of issues. On this

blind spot, several scholars have pointed out the de facto leadership role women have always played in Black churches, even when they are held out of formal senior leadership positions. See Marla Faye Frederick, *Between Sundays: Black Women and Everyday Struggles of Faith* (Berkeley: University of California Press, 2003); Evelyn Brooks Higginbotham, *Righteous Discontent: The Women's Movement in the Black Baptist Church, 1880–1920* (Cambridge, MA: Harvard University Press, 1993); and Savage, *Your Spirits Walk Beside Us.*

11.   Allison Calhoun-Brown, "African American Churches and Political Mobilization: The Psychological Impact of Organizational Resources," *Journal of Politics* 58, no. 4 (1996): 935-53, at 936, https://doi.org/10.2307/2960144.

12.   Reed, *The Jesse Jackson Phenomenon*, 42.

13.   McDaniel, "Black Clergy in the 2000 Elections," 543.

14.   R. Khari Brown and Ronald E. Brown, "Faith and Works: Church-Based Social Capital Resources and African American Political Activism," *Social Forces* 82, no. 2 (2003): 617-41, at 622.

15.   Omar M. McRoberts, *Streets of Glory: Church and Community in a Black Urban Neighborhood* (Chicago: University of Chicago Press, 2003), 59.

16.   Tamelyn Tucker-Worgs defines *megachurches* as congregations that attract two thousand or more weekly attendees and own their own facilities (as opposed to renting a space such as a school or an auditorium). "Black" megachurches are majority Black congregations—whether independent/nondenominational within historically Black Protestant denominations or majority Black congregations within predominantly white denominations. See Tamelyn Tucker-Worgs, *The Black Megachurch: Theology, Gender, and the Politics of Public Engagement* (Waco, TX: Baylor University Press, 2011). On Black megachurches, see also Sandra L. Barnes, *Black Megachurch Culture: Models for Education and Empowerment* (New York: Peter Lang, 2010).

17.   Barnes, *Black Megachurch Culture*.

18.   Shayne Lee, *T. D. Jakes: America's New Preacher* (New York: New York Uuniversity Press, 2007).

19.   Paula L. McGee, *Brand New Theology: The Wal-Martization of T. D. Jakes and the New Black Church* (Maryknoll, NY: Orbis, 2017).

20.   Jonathan L. Walton, *Watch This! The Ethics and Aesthetics of Black Televangelism* (New York: New York University Press, 2009).

21.   Melissa Victoria Harris-Lacewell, *Barbershops, Bibles, and BET: Everyday Talk and Black Political Thought* (Princeton, NJ: Princeton University Press, 2004).

22.   W. E. B. Du Bois, *The Souls of Black Folk*, ed. B. H. Edwards (1903; repr. New York: Oxford University Press, 2007), 129.

23.   See, for example, Brown and Brown, "Faith and Works"; Calhoun-Brown, "African American Churches and Political Mobilization"; Fredrick C. Harris, "Something Within: Religion as a Mobilizer of African-American Political Activism," *Journal of Politics* 56, no. 1 (1994): 42–68, https://doi.org/10.2307/2132345; Harwood K. McClerking and Eric L. McDaniel, "Belonging and Doing: Political Churches and Black Political Participation," *Political Psychology* 26, no. 5 (2005): 721–34, https://doi.org/10.1111/j.1467-9221.2005.00441.x; and McDaniel, *Politics in the Pews*.

24. As the introduction outlines, this distinction has been variously framed as whether churches have a "this-worldly versus an other-worldly" orientation, or a "liberator versus an opiate" function. This has been a durable typology, reaching from early debates over whether Black churches could better the social conditions of Black Americans, see Du Bois, *The Souls of Black Folk*; and Woodson, "The Negro Church, an All-Comprehending Institution." From these early debates and into the height of the civil rights era and beyond, some observers of Black churches have concluded that they tend to retreat from politics in favor of focusing on the other-worldly, spiritual, and religious needs of African Americans. See Frazier, *The Negro Church in America*; Gary T. Marx, *Protest and Prejudice: A Study of Belief in the Black Community* (New York: Harper & Row, 1967); Gunnar Myrdal, *An American Dilemma: The Negro Problem and Modern Democracy* (New York: Harper, 1944); and Reed, *The Jesse Jackson Phenomenon*. Others have made the case that Black churches tend to transcend the spiritual concerns of their members to speak to this-worldly aspects of community and social life, including politics. See James H. Cone, *A Black Theology of Liberation* (Philadelphia: Lippincott, 1970); Lincoln and Mamiya, *The Black Church in the African American Experience*; Doug McAdam, *Political Process and the Development of Black Insurgency 1930–1970* (Chicago: University of Chicago Press, 1982); Morris, *Origins of the Civil Rights Movement*; Gayraud S. Wilmore, *Black Religion and Black Radicalism* (Garden City, NY: Doubleday, 1972); and Woodson, "The Negro Church, an All-Comprehending Institution." Taking stock of this historical debate, analyses of the political significance of Black churches in the United States since the civil rights movement tend to balance these emphases, pointing to the dual nature of Black religion in America and describing the relationship between Black religion and Black politics variously as "contradictory" (Hans A. Baer and Merrill Singer, *African-American Religion in the Twentieth Century: Varieties of Protest and Accommodation* [Knoxville: University of Tennessee Press, 1992]), "dialectical" (Lincoln and Mamiya, *The Black Church in the African American Experience*), "dialogical" (Higginbotham, *Righteous Discontent*), "multidimensional" (Harris, *Something Within*), "divided" (Raphael G. Warnock, *The Divided Mind of the Black Church: Theology, Piety, and Public Witness* [New York: New York University Press, 2013]), or as defined by their position on a series of "continua" (Tucker-Worgs, *The Black Megachurch*).

25. Fredrick C. Harris, *Something Within: Religion in African-American Political Activism* (New York: Oxford University Press, 1999), 8.

26. McDaniel, *Politics in the Pews*, 3.

27. Calhoun-Brown, "African American Churches and Political Mobilization," 941.

28. McClerking and McDaniel, "Belonging and Doing," 722.

29. Calhoun-Brown, "African American Churches and Political Mobilization"; McDaniel, *Politics in the Pews*; and Katherine Tate, *From Protest to Politics: The New Black Voters in American Elections* (Cambridge, MA: Harvard University Press, 1993).

30. Tucker-Worgs, *The Black Megachurch*.

31. Angelique Harris, *AIDS, Sexuality, and the Black Church: Making the Wounded Whole* (New York: Peter Lang, 2010).

32. Christian Smith, ed., *Disruptive Religion: The Force of Faith in Social Movement Activism* (New York: Routledge, 1996).

33. Aldon D. Morris, Shirley J. Hatchett, and Ronald E. Brown, "The Civil Rights Movement and Black Political Socialization," in *Political Learning in Adulthood: A Sourcebook of Theory and Research*, ed. Roberta S. Sigel (Chicago: University of Chicago Press, 1989), chap. 7.

34. Michael Leo Owens, *God and Government in the Ghetto: The Politics of Church-State Collaboration in Black America* (Chicago: University of Chicago Press, 2007).

35. Allison Calhoun-Brown, "What a Fellowship: Civil Society, African American Churches, and Public Life," in *New Day Begun: African American Churches and Civic Culture in Post–Civil Rights America, The Public Influences of African American Churches*, ed. R. D. Smith (Durham, NC: Duke University Press, 2003), 39-57, at 46.

36. Owens, *God and Government in the Ghetto*, 28.

37. Owens, *God and Government in the Ghetto*, 3.

38. Berenson, Elifson, and Tollerson, "Preachers in Politics," 374.

39. See Reed, *The Jesse Jackson Phenomenon*.

40. Kate Bowler, *Blessed: A History of the American Prosperity Gospel* (New York: Oxford University Press, 2013), 6.

41. Bowler (in *Blessed*) highlights the importance of these kinds of informal networks, which she calls pastoral "fellowships." Fellowships do not ordain ministers or oversee their ministries directly, but they provide symbolic "badges of belonging" among high-profile pastors and those who aspire to reach their levels of success in ministry. Brad Christerson and Richard Flory have similarly described the emergence of a kind of "network Christianity," in which pastors connect outside of traditional denominational structures. See Brad Christerson and Richard Flory, *The Rise of Network Christianity: How Independent Leaders Are Changing the Religious Landscape* (New York: Oxford University Press, 2017).

42. Owens, *God and Government in the Ghetto*, 26.

43. Chapter 4 focuses on how travel to "the Holy Land" generates, shapes, and sustains Black church engagement with Israel and Palestine. There I elaborate on tensions between ostensibly apolitical religious purposes and the ubiquitous politics of the region, and how the perceived salience of race for African American Christians in the land shapes their outlooks on regional and global politics.

44. Jackie Feldman, an anthropologist with decades of experience as a professional tour guide in Israel, writes about the political, commercial, and religious roles Israeli tour guides play. See Jackie Feldman, *A Jewish Guide in the Holy Land: How Christian Pilgrims Made Me Israeli* (Bloomington: Indiana University Press, 2016). During his training as a guide through the Israeli Ministry of Tourism, he was told that guides are "Israel's best ambassadors" (11). Feldman describes the mediating relationship of a professional tour guide as "a seduction"—a social process spanning ritual, belief, experience, and consumption, whereby the professional Holy Land tour guide seeks to manage and gratify pilgrim-tourists to "win their confidence, engage their emotions, satisfy their expectations, and yield compliments, requests for future services, and generous tips" (116).

45. When I spoke to Gregory Edwards in 2014, Raphael Warnock was well known in Black Christian circles as the pastor of Martin Luther King Jr.'s church and as an author (see Warnock, *The Divided Mind of the Black Church*). In 2020 and 2021, Warnock became nationally recognized as a candidate for the U.S. Senate in the much watched and closely contested Georgia senate races.

46. Warnock, *The Divided Mind of the Black Church*, 13.

47. Warnock, *The Divided Mind of the Black Church*, 13–14.

4. WALKING IN THE FOOTSTEPS OF A WHITEWASHED JESUS?

1. Simon Coleman and John Elsner, *Pilgrimage: Past and Present: Sacred Travel and Sacred Space in the World Religions* (London: British Museum, 1995); and John Eade and Michael J. Sallnow, eds., *Contesting the Sacred: The Anthropology of Christian Pilgrimage* (New York: Routledge, 1991).

2. Kobi Cohen-Hattab and Noam Shoval, *Tourism, Religion and Pilgrimage in Jerusalem* (New York: Routledge, 2014).

3. Israel Ministry of Tourism Statistics Department, "3.3 Million Visitors to Israel in 2014," May 1, 2015, https://embassies.gov.il/la/NewsAndEvents/Pages/3-3-million-visitors-to-Israel -in-2014.aspx.

4. Victor Turner, "The Center Out There: Pilgrim's Goal," *History of Religions* 12, no. 3 (1973): 191–230, https://doi.org/10.1086/462677; and Victor Turner and Edith Turner, *Image and Pilgrimage in Christian Culture: Anthropological Perspectives* (New York: Columbia University Press, 1978).

5. Jerry D. Moore, *Visions of Culture: An Introduction to Anthropological Theories and Theorists*, 4th ed. (Lanham, MD: AltaMira, 2012).

6. Victor and Edith Turner argue that it is necessary to study the nonritualized factors surrounding pilgrimage in a context because, to some extent, "comfortable travel has replaced penitential travel." Modern pilgrimages, they suggest, are best understood not only in terms of the universal and obligatory liminal rites of passage found in traditional societies but also as voluntary liminoid phenomena—something resembling tourism as we know it today. Turner and Turner, *Image and Pilgrimage in Christian Culture*, 39.

7. Eade and Sallnow show how the Turners' work on pilgrimage provides an important course correction to earlier functionalist outlooks that, drawing on studies of small-scale non-Western societies, stressed organizational coherence and treated pilgrimages as "local cults writ large"—that is, as simply reinforcing the pilgrim's existing social structures. They emphasize the need to avoid imposing a homogeneity on pilgrimage that masks an observable heterogeneity in various pilgrimage processes around the world. See Eade and Sallnow, *Contesting the Sacred*, 3. Subsequent studies of various kinds of religious pilgrimage systems have echoed this conclusion, suggesting that pilgrimage is never purely religious but rather the site of competing secular and religious discourses. See Vida Bajc, "For a Sociology of Pilgrimage," *Sociological Forum* 27, no. 4 (2012): 1052–55; Toni Huber, *The Holy Land Reborn: Pilgrimage & the Tibetan Reinvention of Buddhist India* (Chicago: University of Chicago Press, 2008); Shaul Kelner, *Tours That Bind: Diaspora, Pilgrimage, and Israeli Birthright Tourism* (New York: New York University Press, 2010); and Sarah Thal, *Rearranging the Landscape of the Gods: The Politics of a Pilgrimage Site in Japan, 1573–1912* (Chicago: University of Chicago Press, 2005).

8. See Baumann for a discussion of how pilgrimage functions as a site where religion, politics, economy, and cultural production converge. I argue there that pilgrimage can best be understood as a social context characterized by the negotiation of priorities across

several overlapping *fields*, each representing a unique set of goals and priorities that are subject to negotiation and contestation with respect to the overall meaning and purpose of the trip. Roger Baumann, "A Social Fields Theory of Pilgrimage: African American Christians in Israel and Palestine," *Sociological Forum* 34, no. 3 (2019): 685–704, https://doi .org/10.1111/socf.12520.

9. On the political implications of Holy Land pilgrimage, see Yaniv Belhassen and Jonathan Ebel, "Tourism, Faith and Politics in the Holy Land: An Ideological Analysis of Evangelical Pilgrimage," *Current Issues in Tourism* 12, no. 4 (2009): 359–78, https://doi.org /10.1080/13683500802469342; Cohen-Hattab and Shoval, *Tourism, Religion and Pilgrimage in Jerusalem*; Dan Cohn-Sherbok, *The Politics of Apocalypse: The History and Influence of Christian Zionism* (Oxford: Oneworld, 2006); Jackie Feldman, *A Jewish Guide in the Holy Land: How Christian Pilgrims Made Me Israeli* (Bloomington: Indiana University Press, 2016); Curtis Hutt, "Christian Zionist Pilgrimage in the Twenty-First Century," in *Comprehending Christian Zionism: Perspectives in Comparison*, ed. G. Gunner and R. O. Smith (Minneapolis, MN: Fortress, 2014), 137–60; Hillary Kaell, *Walking Where Jesus Walked: American Christians and Holy Land Pilgrimage* (New York: New York University Press, 2014); and Robert O. Smith, *More Desired Than Our Owne Salvation: The Roots of Christian Zionism* (New York: Oxford University Press, 2013). At the extreme end of politicized travel, political engagement in Israel and Palestine by visitors invokes notions of "activist" or "political" tourism, where travelers seek opportunities for political solidarity-building, educational experiences, engagement on humanitarian issues, and cultural exchanges. See Maureen Moynagh, *Political Tourism and Its Texts* (Toronto, Canada: University of Toronto Press, 2008); and Felicia Gobba Shinnamon, "Activist Tourism: Perceptions of Ecotourism and Sustainability in Costa Rica" (PhD diss., California Institute of Integral Studies, San Francisco, 2010). On "volunteer" tourism, see Angela M. Benson, ed., *Volunteer Tourism: Theoretical Frameworks and Practical Applications* (New York: Routledge, 2010). And on "ecotourism," see David A. Fennell, *Ecotourism* (New York: Routledge, 2008).

10. Kelner, *Tours That Bind*, xv.

11. Kaell, *Walking Where Jesus Walked.*

12. For attention to the production side of the production-consumption dynamic within tourism economies, see Defne Över, "Cultural Tourism and Complex Histories: The Armenian Akhtamar Church, the Turkish State and National Identity," *Qualitative Sociology* 39, no. 2 (2016): 173–94, https://doi.org/10.1007/s11133-016-9323-x; Lauren A. Rivera, "Managing 'Spoiled' National Identity: War, Tourism, and Memory in Croatia," *American Sociological Review* 73, no. 4 (2008): 613–34; and Jonathan R. Wynn, *The Tour Guide: Walking and Talking New York* (Chicago: University of Chicago Press, 2011).

13. Sara A. Williams, "Moral Commodities and the Practice of Freedom," *Journal of Religious Ethics* 48, no. 4 (2020): 642–63, https://doi.org/https://doi.org/10.1111/jore.12333.

14. Kaell, *Walking Where Jesus Walked*; Thomas S. Kidd, *American Christians and Islam: Evangelical Culture and Muslims from the Colonial Period to the Age of Terrorism* (Princeton, NJ: Princeton University Press, 2009); Ussama Makdisi, "Reclaiming the Land of the Bible: Missionaries, Secularism, and Evangelical Modernity," *American Historical Review* 102, no. 3 (1997): 680–713, https://doi.org/10.2307/2171506; and Lester Irwin Vogel, *To See a*

Promised Land: Americans and the Holy Land in the Nineteenth Century (University Park: Pennsylvania State University Press, 1993).

15.   Examples of attention to so-called secular pilgrimages include studies of travel to polit-ical/national sites such as battlefields. See David William Lloyd, *Battlefield Tourism: Pilgrimage and the Commemoration of the Great War in Britain, Australia and Canada, 1919–1939* (New York: Bloomsbury Academic, 1998); Richard West Sellars, "Pilgrim Places: Civil War Battlefields, Historic Preservation, and America's First National Military Parks, 1863–1900," *CRM: Journal of Heritage Stewardship* 2, no. 1 (2005): 23–52; Catherine Switzer, *Ulster, Ireland and the Somme: War Memorials and Battlefield Pilgrimages* (Dublin: History Press, 2013); and Brad West, "Enchanting Pasts: The Role of International Civil Religious Pilgrimage in Reimagining National Collective Memory," *Sociological Theory* 26, no. 3 (2008): 258–70. On the site of the 9/11 World Trade Center attacks, see Thomas Conran, "Solemn Witness: A Pilgrimage to Ground Zero at the World Trade Center," *Journal of Systemic Therapies* 21, no. 3 (2002): 39–47, https://doi.org/10.1521/jsyt.21.3.39.23329. For geno-cide sites like Auschwitz in Poland, see Jackie Feldman, "Israeli Youth Voyages to Holo-caust Poland: Through the Prism of Pilgrimage," in *Redefining Pilgrimage: New Perspectives on Historical and Contemporary Pilgrimages*, ed. A. M. Pazos (New York: Routledge, 2014), chap. 5. For the Killing Fields of Cambodia, see Brent Crane, "Beyond the Killing Fields," *New Republic* 247, no. 10 (2016): 6–8. Pilgrimage has also been used to describe political travel of a more ideological—rather than national—kind, including Western intellectual travels to Communist countries. See Paul Hollander, *Political Pilgrims: Western Intellec-tuals in Search of the Good Society* (New Brunswick, NJ: Transaction, 1997). For political and educational delegations to civil rights era protest sights, see Jonathan Capehart, "Walking with Giants of the Civil Rights Movement," *Washington Post*, March 12, 2017. For personal and communal travel to the homes of notable literary icons, see Amy L. Montz, "The Personal Is Pilgrimage: Literary Tourism Through and with Ms Austen and Mrs Gaskell," *Gaskell Journal* 30 (2016): 57. For Elvis Presley's Graceland home in Mem-phis, see Christine King, "His Truth Goes Marching On: Elvis Presley and the Pilgrimage to Graceland," in *Pilgrimage in Popular Culture*, ed. I. Reader and T. Walter (London: Macmillan, 1993), 92–104. These have also been described as forms of secular pilgrimage. Pilgrimage has also been used to analyze participation in sports. See Daniel J. Corcoran, "Golf's Pilgrimage," *Incentive* 182, no. 9 (2008): 102–3; Horace G. Hutchinson, *The Golfing Pilgrim on Many Links* (London: Methuen, 1898); Jeffrey Scholes and Raphael Sassower, *Religion and Sports in American Culture* (New York: Routledge, 2013); and Daniel Wojcik, "Pre's Rock: Pilgrimage, Ritual, and Runners' Traditions at the Roadside Shrine for Steve Prefontaine," in *Shrines and Pilgrimage in the Modern World: New Itineraries Into the Sacred*, ed. P. J. Margry (Amsterdam: Amsterdam University Press, 2008), 201–37. For annual festivals like Burning Man, see Lee Gilmore, "Desert Pilgrimage: Liminality, Transfor-mation, and the Other at the Burning Man Festival," in *On the Road to Being There: Stud-ies in Pilgrimage and Tourism in Late Modernity*, ed. William H. Swatos Jr. (Boston: Brill, 2006), 125–58. Finally, sites of ancient traditional religious pilgrimages have also taken on new secular significance as hikers, tourists, and other nonspiritual travelers have recently begun to follow and broaden well-worn pilgrimage routes for novel nonreligious reasons—examples include the Camino de Santiago in Spain. See Taylor M. James, Rory

J. Siegel, Meredith P. Crizer, Martha C. Bland, and M. Brennan Harris, "Exercise Self-Efficacy Among Pilgrims on the Camino de Santiago," *Medicine & Science in Sports & Exercise* 47, no. 5S (2015): 727-28, https://doi.org/10.1249/01.mss.0000478713.77391.65; Kyung-Mi Im and JuSung Jun, "The Meaning of Learning on the Camino de Santiago Pilgrimage," *Australian Journal of Adult Learning* 55, no. 2 (2015): 331-51; and Michael Murray, "The Cultural Heritage of Pilgrim Itineraries: The Camino de Santiago," *Journeys* 15, no. 2 (2014): 65-85, https://doi.org/10.3167/jys.2014.150204. On Saint Olav's Way in Norway, see Mari Kollandsrud, "Saint Olav of Norway: Reviving Pilgrim Ways to Trondheim," in *In Search of Heritage: As Pilgrims or Tourist?*, ed. J. M. Fladmark and T. Heyerdahl (Dorset, England: Donhead, 1998), 91-103. All of these suggest that what might simply be thought of as examples of nonreligious travel or tourism actually share structural similarities with the ostensibly distinct category of more overt religious travel.

16. Simon Coleman and John Eade, eds., *Reframing Pilgrimage: Cultures in Motion* (New York: Routledge, 2004); Simon Coleman and John Eade, eds., *Pilgrimage and Political Economy: Translating the Sacred* (New York: Berghahn, 2018); Dionigi Albera and John Eade, eds., *New Pathways in Pilgrimage Studies: Global Perspectives* (New York: Routledge, 2016); and Antón M. Pazos, ed., *Redefining Pilgrimage: New Perspectives on Historical and Contemporary Pilgrimages* (New York: Routledge, 2014).

17. Maurice Halbwachs, *On Collective Memory*, trans. Lewis A. Coser (Chicago: University of Chicago Press, 1992).

18. Vida Bajc, "Christian Pilgrimage Groups in Jerusalem: Framing the Experience Through Linear Meta-Narrative," *Journeys* 7, no. 2 (2006): 101-28, at 102, https://doi.org/10.3167/jys .2006.070206.

19. Turner and Turner, *Image and Pilgrimage in Christian Culture*, 33.

20. Kaell, *Walking Where Jesus Walked*, 74.

21. See, for example, Nancy Tatom Ammerman, *Bible Believers: Fundamentalists in the Modern World* (New Brunswick, NJ: Rutgers University Press, 1987); James S. Bielo, *Words Upon the Word: An Ethnography of Evangelical Group Bible Study* (New York: New York University Press, 2009); Susan Friend Harding, *The Book of Jerry Falwell: Fundamentalist Language and Politics* (Princeton, NJ: Princeton University Press, 2000); and Webb Keane, *Christian Moderns: Freedom and Fetish in the Mission Encounter* (Berkeley: University of California Press, 2007).

22. Eddie S. Glaude Jr., *Exodus! Religion, Race, and Nation in Early Nineteenth-Century Black America* (Chicago: University of Chicago Press, 2000).

23. Yvonne Patricia Chireau and Nathaniel Deutsch, eds., *Black Zion: African American Religious Encounters with Judaism* (New York: Oxford University Press, 2000); and Jacob S. Dorman, *Chosen People: The Rise of American Black Israelite Religions* (New York: Oxford University Press, 2013).

24. Keith P. Feldman, *A Shadow Over Palestine: The Imperial Life of Race in America* (Minneapolis: University of Minnesota Press, 2015); and Alex Lubin, *Geographies of Liberation: The Making of an Afro-Arab Political Imaginary* (Chapel Hill: University of North Carolina Press, 2014).

25. Don Williams, "Walking Where Jesus Walked Led to the Proctor Conference," Kairos USA, March 11, 2015, https://kairosusa.org/walking-where-jesus-walked-led-to-the-proctor -conference/.

26. David Brog and John Hagee, "CUFI in Action," CUFI newsletter, 2018.

27. Christians United For Israel, "Mission and Vision," accessed May 31, 2018, https://www
.cufi.org/impact/about-us/mission-and-vision/.

28. These are Ethiopian Jews who were brought to Israel from Ethiopia by the State of
Israel as Jewish immigrants. They maintain their Jewish identity but confess Jesus as
their Messiah. Because they see Messianic Judaism as a stigmatized form of conversion
to Christianity, they do not identify as Messianic Jews. "Ethiopian Jewish believers"
is the most common label they assume, and it is how COGIC leaders typically refer
to them.

29. Kaell, *Walking Where Jesus Walked*; Thomas S. Kidd, "Evangelicals, the End Times, and
Islam," *Historically Speaking* 10, no. 1 (2009): 16–18, https://doi.org/10.1353/hsp.0.0004;
Makdisi, "Reclaiming the Land of the Bible"; and Vogel, *To See a Promised Land*.

30. Williams, "Walking Where Jesus Walked Led to the Proctor Conference."

31. Williams, "Walking Where Jesus Walked Led to the Proctor Conference."

32. The trope of "living stones" (a reference to 1 Peter 2:4–5) is frequently used among Palestinian Christians to underscore that community's authority and spiritual connection to
the earliest Christian church and to the land of the Bible. See Sara A. Williams, "Moral
Apprentices at the Margins: Come and See Tours and the Making of the Ethical Self"
(PhD diss., Emory University, Atlanta, GA, 2021).

33. Sabeel Ecumenical Liberation Theology Center, "Sabeel Ecumenical Liberation Theology Center," accessed March 1, 2020, https://sabeel.org/.

34. On the relationship between Israeli security agencies and American law enforcement
organizations, see Sari Horwitz, "Israeli Experts Teach Police on Terrorism," *Washington
Post*, June 12, 2005.

35. Brog and Hagee, "CUFI in Action."

5. THE FIELD OF BLACK RELIGIOUS POLITICS

1. Michael A. Stevens, *We Too Stand: A Call for the African-American Church to Support the
Jewish State* (Lake Mary, FL: FrontLine, 2013); and Dumisani Washington, *Zionism and
the Black Church: Why Standing with Israel Will Be a Defining Issue for Christians of Color in
the 21st Century* (Stockton, CA: IBSI, 2014).

2. Brubaker and Cooper introduced "categories of identity" and "categories of practice" as
useful concepts in the service of evaluating the sometimes slippery notion of "identity."
Noting the proliferation of the term *identity* in contemporary politics, they aimed to
chart a path between constructivist approaches to identity (constructed, fluid, and multiple) and essentialist approaches (fixed and unchanging). As use of the term proliferates,
they argue that it loses its analytical purchase—"if identity is everywhere, it is nowhere."
See Rogers Brubaker and Frederick Cooper, "Beyond 'Identity,'" *Theory and Society* 29,
no. 1 (2000): 1–47, at 1.

3. Brubaker and Cooper, "Beyond 'Identity,'" 4; and Pierre Bourdieu, *Outline of a Theory of
Practice* (New York: Cambridge University Press, 1977).

4. Brubaker and Cooper further argue that we should seek to explain the processes and
mechanisms through which categories "can crystallize, at certain moments, as a powerful,

compelling reality." "But," they caution, "we should avoid unintentionally *reproducing* or *reinforcing* such reification by uncritically adopting categories of practice as categories of analysis." See Brubaker and Cooper, "Beyond 'Identity,'" 5. The kind of observable links and evident slippages between analytical and practice-oriented usages of many categories of identity that Brubaker and Cooper describe have a wide application. On race and racial identity, for example, Loïc Wacquant points out "the continual barter between folk and analytic notions, the uncontrolled conflation of social and sociological understandings." See Loïc J. D. Wacquant, "For an Analytic of Racial Domination," *Political Power and Social Theory* 11 (1997): 221–34, at 222.

5. Rogers Brubaker, *Ethnicity Without Groups* (Cambridge, MA: Harvard University Press, 2004), 44. This relates to other sociological work on shared group cultural understandings. See, for example, Kathleen M. Blee, *Democracy in the Making: How Activist Groups Form* (New York: Oxford University Press, 2012); Nina Eliasoph and Paul Lichterman, "Culture in Interaction," *American Journal of Sociology* 108, no. 4 (2003): 735–94, https://doi.org/10.1086/367920; Betsy Leondar-Wright, *Missing Class: Strengthening Social Movement Groups by Seeing Class Cultures* (Ithaca, NY: ILR, 2014); Andrew J. Perrin, *Citizen Speak: The Democratic Imagination in American Life* (Chicago: University of Chicago Press, 2006); Melissa J. Wilde, "How Culture Mattered at Vatican II: Collegiality Trumps Authority in the Council's Social Movement Organizations," *American Sociological Review* 69, no. 4 (2004): 576–602, https://doi.org/10.1177/000312240406900406; and Richard L. Wood, *Faith in Action: Religion, Race, and Democratic Organizing in America* (Chicago: University of Chicago Press, 2002). Furthermore, although collective identities are sometimes viewed as static or preexisting categories, research on the culture of groups has shown that collective identities are actually constructed through group practices, sometimes called "identity work." Related research on "boundary work" has also contributed to inter- and intragroup identity formation. See Michèle Lamont, *The Dignity of Working Men: Morality and the Boundaries of Race, Class, and Immigration* (Cambridge, MA: Harvard University Press, 2000); and Michèle Lamont, Graziella Moraes Silva, Jessica Welburn, Joshua Guetzkow, Nissim Mizrachi, Hanna Herzog, and Elisa Reis, *Getting Respect: Responding to Stigma and Discrimination in the United States, Brazil, and Israel* (Princeton, NJ: Princeton University Press, 2016).

6. On the narrative construction of identity, see Scott A. Hunt and Robert D. Benford, "Identity Talk in the Peace and Justice Movement," *Journal of Contemporary Ethnography* 22, no. 4 (1994): 488–517, https://doi.org/10.1177/089124194022004004; Francesca Polletta, *It Was Like a Fever: Storytelling in Protest and Politics* (Chicago: University of Chicago Press, 2006); Margaret R. Somers, "Narrativity, Narrative Identity, and Social Action: Rethinking English Working-Class Formation," *Social Science History* 16, no. 4 (1992): 591–630, https://doi.org/10.2307/1171314; and Charles Tilly, *Stories, Identities, and Political Change* (Lanham, MD: Rowman & Littlefield, 2002).

7. See Ruth Braunstein, *Prophets and Patriots: Faith in Democracy Across the Political Divide* (Oakland: University of California Press, 2017), 24. This also gets at an ontological dimension of group cultural narratives that Braunstein calls *situated intersubjectivity*: "a collective sense of what kind of group it is, how it relates to other groups, and how (given the first two) it is prepared to collectively act" (74).

8. Pierre Bourdieu and Loïc J. D. Wacquant, *An Invitation to Reflexive Sociology* (Chicago: University of Chicago Press, 1992), 97. I will not elaborate at length on the context or theoretical foundation of Bourdieu's field analysis here. Interested readers can find that basis in a number of Bourdieu's later works: see Pierre Bourdieu, *In Other Words: Essays Toward a Reflexive Sociology* (Stanford, CA: Stanford University Press, 1990); Pierre Bourdieu, *The Logic of Practice* (Stanford, CA: Stanford University Press, 1990); Pierre Bourdieu, *Sociology in Question* (London: Sage, 1993); Pierre Bourdieu, *The Rules of Art: Genesis and Structure of the Literary Field* (Stanford, CA: Stanford University Press, 1996); and Bourdieu and Wacquant, *An Invitation to Reflexive Sociology*. David Swartz also provides a concise overview. See David Swartz, *Culture and Power: The Sociology of Pierre Bourdieu* (Chicago: University of Chicago Press, 1998), chap. 5. Bourdieu is best known for studies of the fields of literature and art in France, but he also applied his theory of social fields to studies of religion, law, science, and philosophy. See Pierre Bourdieu, *The Field of Cultural Production* (New York: Columbia University Press, 1993); and Bourdieu, *The Rules of Art*. Drawing on Bourdieu, successive approaches to field analysis have focused on organizations and institutional constraints within fields. See Walter W. Powell and Paul J. DiMaggio, eds., *The New Institutionalism in Organizational Analysis* (Chicago: University of Chicago Press, 1991). On strategic collective action, see Neil Fligstein and Doug McAdam, *A Theory of Fields* (New York: Oxford University Press, 2012). Various approaches to field analysis have been used to study a range of empirical phenomena, including art. See Larissa Buchholz, "What Is a Global Field? Theorizing Fields Beyond the Nation-State," *Sociological Review Monographs* 64, no. 2 (2016): 31–60, https://doi.org/10.1002/2059-7932.12001. On journalism, see Rodney Benson and Erik Neveu, *Bourdieu and the Journalistic Field* (Malden, MA: Polity, 2005). On think tanks, see Thomas Medvetz, *Think Tanks in America* (Chicago: University of Chicago Press, 2012). On state power and bureaucracies, see Loïc J. D. Wacquant, "Crafting the Neoliberal State: Workfare and Prisonfare in the Bureaucratic Field," in *Bourdieu's Theory of Social Fields: Concepts and Applications*, ed. M. Hilgers and E. Mangez (New York: Routledge, 2014), 238–56. On humanitarianism, see Shai M. Dromi, *Above the Fray: The Red Cross and the Making of the Humanitarian NGO Sector* (Chicago: University of Chicago Press, 2020); and Monika Krause, *The Good Project: Humanitarian Relief NGOs and the Fragmentation of Reason* (Chicago: University of Chicago Press, 2014). On social movements, see Damon Mayrl, *Secular Conversions: Political Institutions and Religious Education in the United States and Australia, 1800–2000* (New York: Cambridge University Press, 2016). On American evangelicalism, see Wes Markofski, *New Monasticism and the Transformation of American Evangelicalism* (New York: Oxford University Press, 2015); and Brad Vermurlen, *Reformed Resurgence: The New Calvinist Movement and the Battle Over American Evangelicalism* (New York: Oxford University Press, 2020).
9. Emily Barman, "Varieties of Field Theory and the Sociology of the Non-Profit Sector," *Sociology Compass* 10, no. 6 (2016): 442–58, at 442, https://doi.org/10.1111/soc4.12377.
10. Craig Calhoun, "For the Social History of the Present: Bourdieu as a Historical Sociologist," in *Bourdieu and Historical Analysis*, ed. P. S. Gorski (Durham, NC: Duke University Press, 2013), 36–66, at 49, 37.

11.   Pierre Bourdieu, "The Social Space and the Genesis of Groups," *Theory and Society* 14, no. 6 (1985): 723-44, at 734, https://doi.org/10.1007/BF00174048. Here "principles of division" refers to Bourdieu's focus on understanding the social world through attention to classification, differentiation, and distinction. The social dynamics of fields, in other words, are in part about "organizing the image of the social world." See Pierre Bourdieu, *Distinction: A Social Critique of the Judgement of Taste* (London: Routledge, 1986), 471.

12.   John Levi Martin, "What Is Field Theory?," *American Journal of Sociology* 109, no. 1 (2003): 1-49, https://doi.org/10.1086/375201.

13.   Martin, "What Is Field Theory?," 23.

14.   For an extended explanation and analysis of social field dynamics in terms of contesting "rules of the game," see Julian Go, "Global Fields and Imperial Forms: Field Theory and the British and American Empires," *Sociological Theory* 26, no. 3 (2008): 201-29, https://doi.org/10.1111/j.1467-9558.2008.00326.x.

15.   Raphael G. Warnock, *The Divided Mind of the Black Church: Theology, Piety, and Public Witness* (New York: New York University Press, 2013), 1 (emphasis added).

16.   Philip Gorski, *American Covenant: A History of Civil Religion from the Puritans to the Present* (Princeton, NJ: Princeton University Press, 2017), 4.

17.   Omar M. McRoberts, *Streets of Glory: Church and Community in a Black Urban Neighborhood* (Chicago: University of Chicago Press, 2003), 14.

18.   Gorski, *American Covenant*, 4.

19.   Taurean J. Webb, "Troubling Idols: Black-Palestinian Solidarity in U.S. Afro-Christian Spaces," *Journal of Palestine Studies* 48, no. 4 (2019): 33-51, at 34, https://doi.org/10.1525/jps.2019.48.4.33.

20.   The quotes in this paragraph are all from Webb, "Troubling Idols," 35-38.

21.   Don Williams, "Walking Where Jesus Walked Led to the Proctor Conference," Kairos USA, March 11, 2015, https://kairosusa.org/walking-where-jesus-walked-led-to-the-proctor-conference/.

22.   The blood moon prophecies are a series of prophecies in the Bible preached by John Hagee and Mark Biltz who state a tetrad—a series of four consecutive lunar eclipses coinciding with Jewish holidays and with six full moons in between and no intervening partial lunar eclipses—that began with the April 2014 lunar eclipse is the beginning of the end-times as described in the Bible in the Book of Joel, Acts 2:20, and Revelation 6:12. The tetrad ended with the lunar eclipse on September 27-28, 2015. See John Hagee, *Four Blood Moons: Something Is About to Change* (Brentwood, TN: Worthy, 2013); and Mark Biltz, *Blood Moons: Decoding the Imminent Heavenly Signs* (Washington, DC: WND, 2014).

23.   On the "loneliness" of African American conservatives and their political position-taking, see Leah Wright Rigueur, *The Loneliness of the Black Republican: Pragmatic Politics and the Pursuit of Power* (Princeton, NJ: Princeton University Press, 2016).

24.   Edward L. Branch and Yechiel Eckstein, *On the Frontlines of Faith: The Historical and Spiritual Bonds Between African-Americans and Jews* (Chicago: International Fellowship of Christian and Jews, 2016), 26.

25.   Branch and Eckstein, *On the Frontlines of Faith*, 26.

26.   See the discussion of the Black Hebrew Israelites in chapter 1.

27.   See the discussion of "Ethiopian Jewish believers" in chapter 3.

CONCLUSION

1. Edward E. Curtis and Sylvester A. Johnson, "The Transnational and Diasporic Future of African American Religions in the United States," *Journal of the American Academy of Religion* 87, no. 2 (2019): 333–65, at 333, https://doi.org/10.1093/jaarel/lfz018.
2. Curtis and Johnson, "The Transnational and Diasporic Future," 334.
3. Michael R. Fischbach, *Black Power and Palestine: Transnational Countries of Color* (Stanford, CA: Stanford University Press, 2018), 2.
4. Fischbach, *Black Power and Palestine*, 2–3.
5. Keith P. Feldman, *A Shadow Over Palestine: The Imperial Life of Race in America* (Minneapolis: University of Minnesota Press, 2015), 3.
6. Alex Lubin, *Geographies of Liberation: The Making of an Afro-Arab Political Imaginary* (Chapel Hill: University of North Carolina Press, 2014), 7.
7. Robin D. G. Kelley, "From the River to the Sea to Every Mountain Top: Solidarity as Worldmaking," *Journal of Palestine Studies* 48, no. 4 (2019): 69–91, https://doi.org/10.1525/jps .2019.48.4.69. For other analyses of Black-Palestinian solidarity in the context of transnational links between Ferguson and Gaza, see Kristian Davis Bailey, "Black–Palestinian Solidarity in the Ferguson–Gaza Era," *American Quarterly* 67, no. 4 (2015): 1017–26, https:// doi.org/10.1353/aq.2015.0060; Andy Clarno, "The Thorns That Exist and Resist: Black-Palestine Solidarity in the Twenty-First Century," *Middle East Report* 282 (2017): 2–9; Angela Davis, *Freedom Is a Constant Struggle: Ferguson, Palestine, and the Foundations of a Movement* (Chicago: Haymarket, 2016); and Noura Erakat and Marc Lamont Hill, "Black-Palestinian Transnational Solidarity: Renewals, Returns, and Practice," *Journal of Palestine Studies* 48, no. 4 (2019): 7–16, https://doi.org/10.1525/jps.2019.48.4.7.
8. Eddie S. Glaude Jr., *Exodus! Religion, Race, and Nation in Early Nineteenth-Century Black America* (Chicago: University of Chicago Press, 2000), 3.
9. Edward Said, "The Imperial Bluster of Tom Delay," CounterPunch.org, August 20, 2003, https://www.counterpunch.org/2003/08/20/the-imperial-bluster-of-tom-delay/.
10. Friends of Sabeel North America, "A Black Church Call to End Israeli Apartheid," 2020, https://fosna.nationbuilder.com/black_church_statement.
11. On these connections, the Black4Palestine/Friends of Sabeel North America statement refers specifically to the work of Robin D. G. Kelley on Palestinian national liberation movements. See Robin D. G. Kelley, "Yes, I Said 'National Liberation,'" CounterPunch.org, February 24, 2016, https://www.counterpunch.org/2016/02/24/yes-i-said-national-liberation/.
12. Norman Podhoretz, "My Negro Problem—And Ours," *Commentary*, February 1963, 93–101.
13. Jason D. Hill, "My 'Black Lives Matter' Problem," *Commentary*, June 14–18, 2018, 15.
14. Michael Leo Owens, *God and Government in the Ghetto: The Politics of Church-State Collaboration in Black America* (Chicago: University of Chicago Press, 2007), 4.
15. Adolph L. Reed, *Class Notes: Posing as Politics and Other Thoughts on the American Scene* (New York: New Press, 2000), 5.

APPENDIX: A NOTE ON METHODS AND CASES

1. Ruth Braunstein, *Prophets and Patriots: Faith in Democracy Across the Political Divide* (Oakland: University of California Press, 2017), 199.

Bibliography

Abdulhadi, Rabab Ibrahim. "Framing Resistance Call and Response: Reading Assata Shakur's Black Revolutionary Radicalism in Palestine." *Women's Studies Quarterly* 46, no. 3-4 (2018): 226-31.

Abernethy, Arthur Talmage. *The Jew a Negro: Being a Study of the Jewish Ancestry from an Impartial Standpoint.* Moravian Falls, NC: Dixie, 1910.

Abramson, Alana. "President Trump's Decision on Jerusalem Welcomed by Evangelical Voters, Pro-Israel Groups and Major Donors." *Time,* December 7, 2017. http://time.com/5052363 /president-trumps-decision-on-jerusalem-welcomed-by-evangelical-voters-pro-israel -groups-and-major-donors/.

Adams, Maurianne, and John H. Bracey, eds. "Go Down, Moses." In *Strangers & Neighbors: Relations Between Blacks & Jews in the United States,* 53-54. Amherst: University of Massachusetts Press, 1999.

Albera, Dionigi, and John Eade, eds. *New Pathways in Pilgrimage Studies: Global Perspectives.* New York: Routledge, 2016.

Ammerman, Nancy Tatom. *Bible Believers: Fundamentalists in the Modern World.* New Brunswick, NJ: Rutgers University Press, 1987.

——. *Congregation & Community.* New Brunswick, NJ: Rutgers University Press, 1997.

Amstutz, Mark R. *Evangelicals and American Foreign Policy.* New York: Oxford University Press, 2014.

Anderson, Irvine H. *Biblical Interpretation and Middle East Policy: The Promised Land, America, and Israel, 1917–2002.* Gainesville: University Press of Florida, 2005.

Ariel, Yaakov S. *An Unusual Relationship: Evangelical Christians and Jews.* New York: New York University Press, 2013.

Aronson, Lauren Blair. "CUFI Surpasses 5 Million Member Mark." CUFI press release. 2018.

Asante, Molefi K. *Afrocentricity.* Trenton, NJ: Africa World, 1988.

Ateek, Naim, Cedar Duaybis, and Maurine Tobin, eds. *Challenging Christian Zionism: Theology, Politics and the Israel-Palestine Conflict.* London: Melisende, 2005.

Atshan, Sa'Ed, and Darnell L. Moore. "Reciprocal Solidarity: Where the Black and Palestinian Queer Struggles Meet." *Biography* 37, no. 2 (2014): 680-705.

Baer, Hans A., and Merrill Singer. *African-American Religion in the Twentieth Century: Varieties of Protest and Accommodation.* Knoxville: University of Tennessee Press, 1992.

Bailey, Kristian Davis. "Black–Palestinian Solidarity in the Ferguson-Gaza Era." *American Quarterly* 67, no. 4 (2015): 1017-26. https://doi.org/10.1353/aq.2015.0060.

Bajc, Vida. "Christian Pilgrimage Groups in Jerusalem: Framing the Experience Through Linear Meta-Narrative." *Journeys* 7, no. 2 (2006): 101-28. https://doi.org/10.3167/jys.2006.070206.

——. "For a Sociology of Pilgrimage." *Sociological Forum* 27, no. 4 (2012): 1052-55.

Barger, Lilian Calles. *The World Come of Age: An Intellectual History of Liberation Theology.* New York: Oxford University Press, 2018.

Barman, Emily. "Varieties of Field Theory and the Sociology of the Non-Profit Sector." *Sociology Compass* 10, no. 6 (2016): 442-58. https://doi.org/10.1111/soc4.12377.

Barnes, Sandra L. "Black Church Culture and Community Action." *Social Forces* 84, no. 2 (2005): 967-94. https://doi.org/10.1353/sof.2006.0003.

——. *Black Megachurch Culture: Models for Education and Empowerment.* New York: Peter Lang, 2010.

Baumann, Roger. "Political Engagement Meets the Prosperity Gospel: African American Christian Zionism and Black Church Politics." *Sociology of Religion* 77, no. 4 (2016): 359-85. https://doi.org/10.1093/socrel/srw050.

——. "Race, Religion, and Global Solidarities: W. E. B. Du Bois and 'The Black Church' as a Contested Category." *Journal for the Scientific Study of Religion* 62, no. S1 (2023): 48-67. https://doi.org/10.1111/jssr.12856.

——. "A Social Fields Theory of Pilgrimage: African American Christians in Israel and Palestine." *Sociological Forum* 34, no. 3 (2019): 685-704. https://doi.org/10.1111/socf.12520.

Belhassen, Yaniv, and Jonathan Ebel. "Tourism, Faith and Politics in the Holy Land: An Ideological Analysis of Evangelical Pilgrimage." *Current Issues in Tourism* 12, no. 4 (2009): 359-78. https://doi.org/10.1080/13683500802469342.

Bell, Bernard W. "President Barack Obama, the Rev. Dr. Jeremiah Wright, and the African American Jeremiadic Tradition." *Massachusetts Review* 50, no. 3 (2009): 332-43.

Benson, Angela M., ed. *Volunteer Tourism: Theoretical Frameworks and Practical Applications.* New York: Routledge, 2010.

Benson, Rodney, and Erik Neveu. *Bourdieu and the Journalistic Field.* Malden, MA: Polity, 2005.

Berenson, William M., Kirk W. Elifson, and Tandy Tollerson. "Preachers in Politics: A Study of Political Activism Among the Black Ministry." *Journal of Black Studies* 6, no. 4 (1976): 373-92.

Berman, Paul, ed. *Blacks and Jews: Alliances and Arguments.* New York: Delacorte, 1994.

Bielo, James S. *Words Upon the Word: An Ethnography of Evangelical Group Bible Study.* New York: New York University Press, 2009.

Biltz, Mark. *Blood Moons: Decoding the Imminent Heavenly Signs.* Washington, DC: WND, 2014.

Black for Palestine. "2015 Black Solidarity Statement with Palestine." Black for Palestine, 2015. http://www.blackforpalestine.com/read-the-statement.html.

Blee, Kathleen M. *Democracy in the Making: How Activist Groups Form.* New York: Oxford University Press, 2012.

Blum, Edward J., and Paul Harvey. *The Color of Christ: The Son of God and the Saga of Race in America.* Chapel Hill: University of North Carolina Press, 2014.

Boorstein, Michelle. "How the National Prayer Breakfast Sparked an Unusual Meeting Between Muslims and Evangelicals." *Washington Post*, February 8, 2018.

Bourdieu, Pierre. *Distinction: A Social Critique of the Judgement of Taste.* London: Routledge, 1986.

——. *The Field of Cultural Production.* New York: Columbia University Press, 1993.

—. *The Logic of Practice*. Stanford, CA: Stanford University Press, 1990.

—. *The Rules of Art: Genesis and Structure of the Literary Field*. Stanford, CA: Stanford University Press, 1996.

—. "The Social Space and the Genesis of Groups." *Theory and Society* 14, no. 6 (1985): 723–44. https://doi.org/10.1007/BF00174048.

—. *Sociology in Question*. London: Sage, 1993.

—. *In Other Words: Essays Toward a Reflexive Sociology*. Stanford, CA: Stanford University Press, 1990.

—. *Outline of a Theory of Practice*. New York: Cambridge University Press, 1977.

Bourdieu, Pierre, and Loïc J. D. Wacquant. *An Invitation to Reflexive Sociology*. Chicago: University of Chicago Press, 1992.

Bowler, Kate. *Blessed: A History of the American Prosperity Gospel*. New York: Oxford University Press, 2013.

Branch, Edward L., and Yechiel Eckstein. *On the Frontlines of Faith: The Historical and Spiritual Bonds Between African-Americans and Jews*. Chicago: International Fellowship of Christian and Jews, 2016.

Braunstein, Ruth. *Prophets and Patriots: Faith in Democracy Across the Political Divide*. Oakland: University of California Press, 2017.

Braverman, Mark. *Fatal Embrace: Christians, Jews, and the Search for Peace in the Holy Land*. New York: Beaufort, 2012.

Brog, David. *Standing with Israel: Why Christians Support the Jewish State*. Lake Mary, FL: Charisma House, 2006.

Brog, David, and John Hagee. "CUFI in Action." CUFI newsletter. 2018.

Brown, R. Khari, and Ronald E. Brown. "Faith and Works: Church-Based Social Capital Resources and African American Political Activism." *Social Forces* 82, no. 2 (2003): 617–41.

Brubaker, Rogers. *Ethnicity Without Groups*. Cambridge, MA: Harvard University Press, 2004.

Brubaker, Rogers, and Frederick Cooper. "Beyond 'Identity.'" *Theory and Society* 29, no. 1 (2000): 1–47.

Buchholz, Larissa. "What Is a Global Field? Theorizing Fields Beyond the Nation-State." *Sociological Review Monographs* 64, no. 2 (2016): 31–60. https://doi.org/10.1002/2059-7932.12001.

Buhle, Paul, and Robin D. G. Kelley. "Allies of a Different Sort: Jews and Blacks in the American Left." In *Struggles in the Promised Land: Towards a History of Black-Jewish Relations in the United States*, ed. J. Salzman and C. West, 197–229. New York: Oxford University Press, 1997.

Burge, Gary M. *Whose Land? Whose Promise? What Christians Are Not Being Told About Israel and the Palestinians*. Cleveland, OH: Pilgrim, 2004.

Calhoun, Craig. "For the Social History of the Present: Bourdieu as a Historical Sociologist." In *Bourdieu and Historical Analysis*, ed. P. S. Gorski, 36–66. Durham, NC: Duke University Press, 2013.

Calhoun-Brown, Allison. "African American Churches and Political Mobilization: The Psychological Impact of Organizational Resources." *Journal of Politics* 58, no. 4 (1996): 935–53. https://doi.org/10.2307/2960144.

—. "What a Fellowship: Civil Society, African American Churches, and Public Life." In *New Day Begun: African American Churches and Civic Culture in Post-Civil Rights America, the Public Influences of African American Churches*, ed. R. D. Smith, 39–57. Durham, NC: Duke University Press, 2003.

Cannon, Katie Geneva. *Black Womanist Ethics*. Atlanta: Scholars, 1988.

Capehart, Jonathan. "Walking with Giants of the Civil Rights Movement." *Washington Post*, March 12, 2017.

Carson, Clayborne. "Black-Jewish Universalism in the Era of Identity Politics." In *Struggles in the Promised Land: Towards a History of Black-Jewish Relations in the United States*, ed. J. Salzman and C. West, 177–96. New York: Oxford University Press, 1997.

—. "The Politics of Relations Between African-Americans and Jews." In *Blacks and Jews: Alliances and Arguments*, ed. P. Berman, 131–43. New York: Delacorte, 1994.

Chafets, Zev. *The Bridge Builder: The Life and Continuing Legacy of Rabbi Yechiel Eckstein*. New York: Sentinel, 2015.

—. *A Match Made in Heaven: American Jews, Christian Zionists, and One Man's Exploration of the Weird and Wonderful Judeo-Evangelical Alliance*. New York: Harper Perennial, 2008.

—. "The Rabbi Who Loved Evangelicals (and Vice Versa)." *New York Times*, July 24, 2005.

Chireau, Yvonne Patricia. "Black Culture and Black Zion: African American Religious Encounters with Judaism, 1790–1930, an Overview." In *Black Zion: African American Religious Encounters with Judaism*, ed. N. Deutsch and Y. P. Chireau, 15–32. New York: Oxford University Press, 2000.

Chireau, Yvonne Patricia, and Nathaniel Deutsch, eds. *Black Zion: African American Religious Encounters with Judaism*. New York: Oxford University Press, 2000.

Christerson, Brad, and Richard W. Flory. *The Rise of Network Christianity: How Independent Leaders Are Changing the Religious Landscape*. New York: Oxford University Press, 2017.

Christians United for Israel. "CUFI in Action." CUFI newsletter. 2016.

Christians United for Israel. "Mission and Vision." Accessed May 31, 2018. https://www.cufi.org/impact/about-us/mission-and-vision/.

Clarno, Andy. "The Thorns That Exist and Resist: Black-Palestine Solidarity in the Twenty-First Century." *Middle East Report* 282 (2017): 2–9.

Clatterbuck, Mark. "Tribal Alliances: The State of Israel and Native American Christianity." *Journal of Ecumenical Studies* 49, no. 3 (2014): 384–404.

Clayton, Obie. "The Churches and Social Change: Accommodation, Moderation, or Protest." *Daedalus* 124, no. 1 (1995): 101–17.

Cohen-Hattab, Kobi, and Noam Shoval. *Tourism, Religion and Pilgrimage in Jerusalem*. New York: Routledge, 2014.

Cohn-Sherbok, Dan. *Messianic Judaism: A Critical Anthology*. New York: Continuum, 2000.

—. *The Politics of Apocalypse: The History and Influence of Christian Zionism*. Oxford: Oneworld, 2006.

Coleman, DeeDee. "Q & A with Rev. Dr. DeeDee M. Coleman." *Southern New England Jewish Ledger*, January 5, 2011. http://www.jewishledger.com/2011/01/q-a-with-rev-dr-deedee-m-coleman/.

Coleman, Simon, and John Eade, eds. *Pilgrimage and Political Economy: Translating the Sacred*. New York: Berghahn, 2018.

—, eds. *Reframing Pilgrimage: Cultures in Motion*. New York: Routledge, 2004.

Coleman, Simon, and John Elsner. *Pilgrimage: Past and Present: Sacred Travel and Sacred Space in the World Religions*. London: British Museum, 1995.

Cone, James H. *Black Theology and Black Power*. Maryknoll, NY: Orbis, 1997.

—. *A Black Theology of Liberation*. Philadelphia: Lippincott, 1970.

Conran, Thomas. "Solemn Witness: A Pilgrimage to Ground Zero at the World Trade Center." *Journal of Systemic Therapies* 21, no. 3 (2002): 39–47. https://doi.org/10.1521/jsyt.21.3.39.23329.

Corcoran, Daniel J. "Golf's Pilgrimage." *Incentive* 182, no. 9 (2008): 102–3.

Crane, Brent. "Beyond the Killing Fields." *New Republic* 247, no. 10 (2016): 6–8.

Cressler, Matthew J. *Authentically Black and Truly Catholic: The Rise of Black Catholicism in the Great Migration*. New York: New York University Press, 2017.

Crummell, Alexander. "'The Regeneration of Africa.'" In *African American Religious History: A Documentary Witness*, ed. M. C. Sernett, 282–88. Durham, NC: Duke University Press, 1999. First published in 1891.

Curtis, Edward E., and Sylvester A. Johnson. "The Transnational and Diasporic Future of African American Religions in the United States." *Journal of the American Academy of Religion* 87, no. 2 (2019): 333–65. https://doi.org/10.1093/jaarel/lfz018.

Davis, Angela. *Freedom Is a Constant Struggle: Ferguson, Palestine, and the Foundations of a Movement*. Chicago: Haymarket, 2016.

Donati, Pierpaolo. *Relational Sociology: A New Paradigm for the Social Sciences*. London: Routledge, 2010.

Dorman, Jacob S. *Chosen People: The Rise of American Black Israelite Religions*. New York: Oxford University Press, 2013.

Douglas, Kelly Brown. *The Black Christ*. Maryknoll, NY: Orbis, 1994.

Drake, St. Clair, and Horace R. Cayton. *Black Metropolis: A Study of Negro Life in a Northern City*. Chicago: University of Chicago Press, 1993. First published in 1945.

Dromi, Shai M. *Above the Fray: The Red Cross and the Making of the Humanitarian NGO Sector*. Chicago: University of Chicago Press, 2020.

Du Bois, W. E. B. *The Negro Church*. Atlanta: Atlanta University Press, 1903.

——. *The Souls of Black Folk*, ed. B. H. Edwards. New York: Oxford University Press, 2007. First published in 1903.

Durbin, Sean. "Mediating the Past Through the Present and the Present Through the Past." *Political Theology* 15, no. 2 (2014): 110–31. https://doi.org/10.1179/1462317X13Z.00000000070.

——. *Righteous Gentiles: Religion, Identity, and Myth in John Hagee's Christians United for Israel*. Boston: Brill, 2018.

Eade, John, and Michael J. Sallnow, eds. *Contesting the Sacred: The Anthropology of Christian Pilgrimage*. New York: Routledge, 1991.

Eliasoph, Nina, and Paul Lichterman. "Culture in Interaction." *American Journal of Sociology* 108, no. 4 (2003): 735–94. https://doi.org/10.1086/367920.

Emirbayer, Mustafa. "Manifesto for a Relational Sociology." *American Journal of Sociology* 103, no. 2 (1997): 281–317. https://doi.org/10.1086/231209.

Erakat, Noura, and Marc Lamont Hill. "Black-Palestinian Transnational Solidarity: Renewals, Returns, and Practice." *Journal of Palestine Studies* 48, no. 4 (2019): 7–16. https://doi.org/10.1525/jps.2019.48.4.7.

Essien-Udom, E. U. *Black Nationalism: The Search for Identity in America*. Chicago: University of Chicago Press, 1962.

Evans, Curtis J. *The Burden of Black Religion*. New York: Oxford University Press, 2008.

Feldman, Jackie. "Constructing a Shared Bible Land: Jewish Israeli Guiding Performances for Protestant Pilgrims." *American Ethnologist* 34, no. 2 (2007): 351–74.

—. "Israeli Youth Voyages to Holocaust Poland: Through the Prism of Pilgrimage." In *Redefining Pilgrimage: New Perspectives on Historical and Contemporary Pilgrimages*, ed. A. M. Pazos, chap. 5. New York: Routledge, 2014.

—. *A Jewish Guide in the Holy Land: How Christian Pilgrims Made Me Israeli*. Bloomington: Indiana University Press, 2016.

Feldman, Keith P. *A Shadow Over Palestine: The Imperial Life of Race in America*. Minneapolis: University of Minnesota Press, 2015.

Fennell, David A. *Ecotourism*. New York: Routledge, 2008.

Fischbach, Michael R. *Black Power and Palestine: Transnational Countries of Color*. Stanford, CA: Stanford University Press, 2018.

Fligstein, Neil, and Doug McAdam. *A Theory of Fields*. New York: Oxford University Press, 2012.

Floyd-Thomas, Stacey M., and Anthony B. Pinn, eds. *Liberation Theologies in the United States: An Introduction*. New York: New York University Press, 2010.

Franklin, V. P., Nancy L. Grant, Harold M. Kletnick, and Genna Rae McNeil, eds. *African Americans and Jews in the Twentieth Century: Studies in Convergence and Conflict*. Columbia: University of Missouri Press, 1998.

Frazier, E. Franklin. *The Negro Church in America*. New York: Schocken, 1974. First published in 1963.

Frederick, Marla Faye. *Between Sundays: Black Women and Everyday Struggles of Faith*. Berkeley: University of California Press, 2003.

Friedman, Murray. *What Went Wrong? The Creation and Collapse of the Black-Jewish Alliance*. New York: Free Press, 1995.

Friends of Sabeel North America. "A Black Church Call to End Israeli Apartheid." 2020. https://fosna.nationbuilder.com/black_church_statement.

Gates, Henry Louis, Jr. "Black Demagogues and Pseudo-Scholars." *New York Times*, July 20, 1992. http://www.nytimes.com/1992/07/20/opinion/black-demagogues-and-pseudo-scholars.html.

Gee, John. "Singapore's Expanding Christian Zionist Community." *Washington Report on Middle East Affairs* 28, no. 9 (2009): 36.

Gilkes, Cheryl Townsend. "Plenty Good Room: Adaptation in a Changing Black Church." *Annals of the American Academy of Political and Social Science* 558 (1998): 101–21.

Gilmore, Lee. "Desert Pilgrimage: Liminality, Transformation, and the Other at the Burning Man Festival." In *On the Road to Being There: Studies in Pilgrimage and Tourism in Late Modernity*, ed. William H. Swatos Jr., 125–58. Boston: Brill, 2006.

Girard, William. "Christian Zionism at Jerusalén Church in Copán Ruinas, Honduras, an 'Out-of-the-Way' Place." In *Comprehending Christian Zionism: Perspectives in Comparison*, ed. G. Gunner and R. O. Smith, 125–35. Minneapolis, MN: Fortress, 2014.

Glaude, Eddie S., Jr. *Exodus! Religion, Race, and Nation in Early Nineteenth-Century Black America*. Chicago: University of Chicago Press, 2000.

—. "What Is African American Religion?" *OUPblog* (blog). October 17, 2014. https://blog.oup.com/2014/10/african-american-religion/.

Glocal.net. "Multifaith." Accessed February 15, 2019. https://web.archive.org/web/20150709002302/http://www.glocal.net/multifaith/.

Go, Julian. "Global Fields and Imperial Forms: Field Theory and the British and American Empires." *Sociological Theory* 26, no. 3 (2008): 201–29. https://doi.org/10.1111/j.1467-9558.2008.00326.x.

Gorenberg, Gershom. *The End of Days: Fundamentalism and the Struggle for the Temple Mount.* New York: Oxford University Press, 2002.

Gorski, Philip. *American Covenant: A History of Civil Religion from the Puritans to the Present.* Princeton, NJ: Princeton University Press, 2017.

Grant, Jacquelyn. "Black Theology and the Black Woman." In *African American Religious Thought: An Anthology,* ed. C. West and E. S. Glaude, 831–48. Louisville, KY: Westminster John Knox, 2003.

—. *White Women's Christ and Black Women's Jesus: Feminist Christology and Womanist Response.* Atlanta: Scholars, 1989.

Hagee, John. *In Defense of Israel,* rev. ed. Lake Mary, FL: FrontLine, 2007.

—. *Four Blood Moons: Something Is About to Change.* Brentwood, TN: Worthy, 2013.

—. "How a Night to Honor Israel Was Born." Christians United for Israel. 2011. Accessed July 19, 2017. http://www.cufi.org/site/PageServer?pagename=events_Night_to_Honor_Israel_History.

—. "Understanding Christian Zionism." OnFaith. September 19, 2012. http://www.faithstreet .com/onfaith/2012/09/19/understanding-christian-zionism/10779.

Halbwachs, Maurice. *On Collective Memory,* trans. Lewis A. Coser. Chicago: University of Chicago Press, 1992.

Halsell, Grace. *Prophecy and Politics: The Secret Alliance Between Israel and the U.S. Christian Right.* Chicago: Lawrence Hill, 1989.

Hamilton, Charles V. *The Black Preacher in America.* New York: Morrow, 1972.

Harding, Susan Friend. *The Book of Jerry Falwell: Fundamentalist Language and Politics.* Princeton, NJ: Princeton University Press, 2000.

Harding, Vincent. "Black Power and the American Christ." *Christian Century* 84, no. 1 (1967): 10–13.

Hardy, Clarence E. "The End of the 'Black Church': New Directions in African American Religious History." *Church History* 78, no. 3 (2009): 647–51.

Harris, Angelique. *AIDS, Sexuality, and the Black Church: Making the Wounded Whole.* New York: Peter Lang, 2010.

Harris, Fredrick C. *Something Within: Religion in African-American Political Activism.* New York: Oxford University Press, 1999.

—. "Something Within: Religion as a Mobilizer of African-American Political Activism." *Journal of Politics* 56, no. 1 (1994): 42–68. https://doi.org/10.2307/2132345.

Harris-Lacewell, Melissa Victoria. *Barbershops, Bibles, and BET: Everyday Talk and Black Political Thought.* Princeton, NJ: Princeton University Press, 2004.

Heyrman, Christine Leigh. *American Apostles: When Evangelicals Entered the World of Islam.* New York: Hill and Wang, 2015.

Higginbotham, Evelyn Brooks. *Righteous Discontent: The Women's Movement in the Black Baptist Church, 1880–1920.* Cambridge, MA: Harvard University Press, 1993.

Hill, Jason D. "My 'Black Lives Matter' Problem." *Commentary,* June 14–18, 2018.

Hollander, Paul. *Political Pilgrims: Western Intellectuals in Search of the Good Society.* New Brunswick, NJ: Transaction, 1997.

Horwitz, Sari. "Israeli Experts Teach Police on Terrorism." *Washington Post,* June 12, 2005.

Huber, Toni. *The Holy Land Reborn: Pilgrimage & the Tibetan Reinvention of Buddhist India.* Chicago: University of Chicago Press, 2008.

Hunt, Scott A., and Robert D. Benford. "Identity Talk in the Peace and Justice Movement." *Journal of Contemporary Ethnography* 22, no. 4 (1994): 488–517. https://doi.org/10.1177/08912419022004004.

Hutchinson, Horace G. *The Golfing Pilgrim on Many Links.* London: Methuen, 1898.

Hutt, Curtis. "Christian Zionist Pilgrimage in the Twenty-First Century." In *Comprehending Christian Zionism: Perspectives in Comparison,* ed. G. Gunner and R. O. Smith, 137–60. Minneapolis, MN: Fortress, 2014.

Ice, Thomas. *The Case for Zionism.* Green Forest, AR: New Leaf, 2005.

International Fellowship of Christians and Jews. "African-American Leaders Reject Anti-Israel Stance of Movement for Black Lives." August 22, 2016. https://web.archive.org/web/20170224160640/http://www.ifcj.org/who-we-are/press-room/african-american-leaders.html.

—. "Our Programs." Accessed February 13, 2019. http://www.ifcj.org/who-we-are/programs/.

—. "Report on Impact: IFCJ Projects in Israel and Around the World 2017." 2017 Annual Report.

Israel Collective. "The Truth About Israel and South African Apartheid" (video). December 14, 2015. https://www.youtube.com/watch?v=KdEAMa6CT5I.

Israel Ministry of Tourism Statistics Department. "3.3 Million Visitors to Israel in 2014." May 1, 2015. https://embassies.gov.il/la/NewsAndEvents/Pages/3-3-million-visitors-to-Israel-in-2014.aspx.

James, Taylor M., Rory J. Siegel, Meredith P. Crizer, Martha C. Bland, and M. Brennan Harris. "Exercise Self-Efficacy Among Pilgrims on the Camino de Santiago." *Medicine & Science in Sports & Exercise* 47, no. 5S (2015): 727–28. https://doi.org/10.1249/01.mss.0000478713.77391.65.

Johnson, Thomas A. "Black Leaders Air Grievances on Jews." *New York Times,* August 23, 1979.

Kaell, Hillary. *Walking Where Jesus Walked: American Christians and Holy Land Pilgrimage.* New York: New York University Press, 2014.

Kairos Palestine. "Kairos Document." 2009. https://www.kairospalestine.ps/index.php/about-kairos/kairos-palestine-document.

Kaufman, Jonathan. "Blacks and Jews: The Struggle in the Cities." In *Struggles in the Promised Land: Towards a History of Black-Jewish Relations in the United States,* ed. J. Salzman and C. West, 107–21. New York: Oxford University Press, 1997.

—. *Broken Alliance: The Turbulent Times Between Blacks and Jews in America.* New York: Scribner, 1995.

Keane, Webb. *Christian Moderns: Freedom and Fetish in the Mission Encounter.* Berkeley: University of California Press, 2007.

Kelley, Robin D. G. "Another Freedom Summer." *Journal of Palestine Studies* 44, no. 1 (2014): 29–41. https://doi.org/10.1525/jps.2014.44.1.29.

—. "From the River to the Sea to Every Mountain Top: Solidarity as Worldmaking." *Journal of Palestine Studies* 48, no. 4 (2019): 69–91. https://doi.org/10.1525/jps.2019.48.4.69.

—. "Yes, I Said 'National Liberation.'" CounterPunch.org. February 24, 2016. https://www.counterpunch.org/2016/02/24/yes-i-said-national-liberation/.

Kelner, Shaul. *Tours That Bind: Diaspora, Pilgrimage, and Israeli Birthright Tourism.* New York: New York University Press, 2010.

Kidd, Thomas S. *American Christians and Islam: Evangelical Culture and Muslims from the Colonial Period to the Age of Terrorism.* Princeton, NJ: Princeton University Press, 2009.

——. "Evangelicals, the End Times, and Islam." *Historically Speaking* 10, no. 1 (2009): 16–18. https://doi.org/10.1353/hsp.0.0004.

Kim, Sung-Gun. "Korean Christian Zionism: A Sociological Study of Mission." *International Review of Mission* 100, no. 1 (2011): 85–95. https://doi.org/10.1111/j.1758-6631.2011.00059.x.

King, Christine. "His Truth Goes Marching On: Elvis Presley and the Pilgrimage to Graceland." In *Pilgrimage in Popular Culture*, ed. I. Reader and T. Walter, 92–104. London: Macmillan, 1993.

Kollandsrud, Mari. "Saint Olav of Norway: Reviving Pilgrim Ways to Trondheim." In *In Search of Heritage: As Pilgrims or Tourist?*, ed. J. M. Fladmark and T. Heyerdahl, 91–103. Dorset, England: Donhead, 1998.

Krause, Monika. *The Good Project: Humanitarian Relief NGOs and the Fragmentation of Reason.* Chicago: University of Chicago Press, 2014.

Kyung-Mi Im and JuSung Jun. "The Meaning of Learning on the Camino de Santiago Pilgrimage." *Australian Journal of Adult Learning* 55, no. 2 (2015): 331–51.

Lamont, Michèle. *The Dignity of Working Men: Morality and the Boundaries of Race, Class, and Immigration.* Cambridge, MA: Harvard University Press, 2000.

Lamont, Michèle, Graziella Moraes Silva, Jessica Welburn, Joshua Guetzkow, Nissim Mizrachi, Hanna Herzog, and Elisa Reis. *Getting Respect: Responding to Stigma and Discrimination in the United States, Brazil, and Israel.* Princeton, NJ: Princeton University Press, 2016.

Landler, Mark. "Trump Recognizes Jerusalem as Israel's Capital and Orders U.S. Embassy to Move." *New York Times*, January 20, 2018.

Lee, Shayne. *T. D. Jakes: America's New Preacher.* New York: New York University Press, 2007.

Leondar-Wright, Betsy. *Missing Class: Strengthening Social Movement Groups by Seeing Class Cultures.* Ithaca, NY: ILR, 2014.

Lerner, Michael, and Cornel West. *Jews & Blacks: A Dialogue on Race, Religion, and Culture in America.* New York: Plume, 1996.

Lewis, Donald M. *The Origins of Christian Zionism: Lord Shaftesbury and Evangelical Support for a Jewish Homeland.* New York: Cambridge University Press, 2009.

Lincoln, C. Eric. *The Black Church Since Frazier.* New York: Schocken, 1974.

Lincoln, C. Eric, and Lawrence H. Mamiya. *The Black Church in the African American Experience.* Durham, NC: Duke University Press, 1990.

Lindsey, Hal. *The Late Great Planet Earth.* Grand Rapids, MI: Zondervan, 1970.

Lloyd, David William. *Battlefield Tourism: Pilgrimage and the Commemoration of the Great War in Britain, Australia and Canada, 1919–1939.* New York: Bloomsbury Academic, 1998.

Lubin, Alex. *Geographies of Liberation: The Making of an Afro-Arab Political Imaginary.* Chapel Hill: University of North Carolina Press, 2014.

Luo, Michael. "McCain Rejects Hagee Backing as Nazi Remarks Surface." *The Caucus* (blog). May 22, 2008. https://thecaucus.blogs.nytimes.com/2008/05/22/mccain-rejects-hagee-backing-as-nazi-remarks-surface/.

Lyons, Jonathan. *Islam Through Western Eyes: From the Crusades to the War on Terrorism.* New York: Columbia University Press, 2012.

Makdisi, Ussama. "Reclaiming the Land of the Bible: Missionaries, Secularism, and Evangelical Modernity." *American Historical Review* 102, no. 3 (1997): 680–713. https://doi.org/10.2307/2171506.

Markofski, Wes. *New Monasticism and the Transformation of American Evangelicalism.* New York: Oxford University Press, 2015.

Martin, John Levi. "What Is Field Theory?" *American Journal of Sociology* 109, no. 1 (2003): 1–49. https://doi.org/10.1086/375201.

Martin, Waldo E., Jr. " 'Nation Time!': Black Nationalism, the Third World, and Jews." In *Struggles in the Promised Land: Towards a History of Black-Jewish Relations in the United States,* ed. J. Salzman and C. West, 341–55. New York: Oxford University Press, 1997.

Marx, Gary T. *Protest and Prejudice: A Study of Belief in the Black Community.* New York: Harper & Row, 1967.

Mayrl, Damon. *Secular Conversions: Political Institutions and Religious Education in the United States and Australia, 1800–2000.* New York: Cambridge University Press, 2016.

Mays, Benjamin E., and Joseph William Nicholson. *The Negro's Church.* New York: Russell & Russell, 1933.

McAdam, Doug. *Political Process and the Development of Black Insurgency 1930–1970.* Chicago: University of Chicago Press, 1982.

McAlister, Melani. *Epic Encounters: Culture, Media, and U.S. Interests in the Middle East Since 1945.* Berkeley: University of California Press, 2005.

——. *The Kingdom of God Has No Borders: A Global History of American Evangelicals.* New York: Oxford University Press, 2018.

McClerking, Harwood K., and Eric L. McDaniel. "Belonging and Doing: Political Churches and Black Political Participation." *Political Psychology* 26, no. 5 (2005): 721–34. https://doi.org/10.1111/j.1467-9221.2005.00441.x.

McDaniel, Eric L. "Black Clergy in the 2000 Elections." *Journal for the Scientific Study of Religion* 42, no. 4 (2003): 533–46. https://doi.org/10.1046/j.1468-5906.2003.00201.x.

——. *Politics in the Pews: The Political Mobilization of Black Churches.* Ann Arbor: University of Michigan Press, 2008.

McDermott, Gerald R., ed. *The New Christian Zionism: Fresh Perspectives on Israel and the Land.* Downers Grove, IL: IVP Academic, 2016.

McGee, Paula L. *Brand New Theology: The Wal-Martization of T. D. Jakes and the New Black Church.* Maryknoll, NY: Orbis, 2017.

McRoberts, Omar M. *Streets of Glory: Church and Community in a Black Urban Neighborhood.* Chicago: University of Chicago Press, 2003.

Mearsheimer, John J., and Stephen M. Walt. *The Israel Lobby and U.S. Foreign Policy.* New York: Farrar, Straus and Giroux, 2007.

Medvetz, Thomas. *Think Tanks in America.* Chicago: University of Chicago Press, 2012.

Merkley, Paul Charles. *Christian Attitudes Towards the State of Israel.* Montreal, Canada: McGill Queens University Press, 2007.

——. *The Politics of Christian Zionism 1891–1948.* Portland, OR: Routledge, 1998.

Mittleman, Alan, Byron Johnson, and Nancy Isserman. *Uneasy Allies? Evangelical and Jewish Relations.* Lanham, MD: Lexington, 2007.

Mohr, John W. "Bourdieu's Relational Method in Theory and in Practice: From Fields and Capitals to Networks and Institutions (and Back Again)." In *Applying Relational Sociology,* ed. F. Dépelteau and C. Powell, 101–35. New York: Palgrave Macmillan, 2013.

Montz, Amy L. "The Personal Is Pilgrimage: Literary Tourism Through and with Ms Austen and Mrs Gaskell." *Gaskell Journal* 30 (2016): 57.

Moore, Jerry D. *Visions of Culture: An Introduction to Anthropological Theories and Theorists*. 4th ed. Lanham, MD: AltaMira, 2012.

Morris, Aldon. *Origins of the Civil Rights Movements*. New York: Free Press, 1986.

Morris, Aldon D., Shirley J. Hatchett, and Ronald E. Brown. "The Civil Rights Movement and Black Political Socialization." In *Political Learning in Adulthood: A Sourcebook of Theory and Research*, ed. Roberta S. Sigel, chap. 7. Chicago: University of Chicago Press, 1989.

Morris, Loveday, Michelle Boorstein, and Ruth Eglash. "Long, Uneasy Love Affair of Israel and U.S. Evangelicals May Have Peaked." *Washington Post*, January 28, 2018.

Moten, Fred. "Blackpalestinian Breath." *Social Text* (online). October 25, 2018. https://socialtextjournal.org/periscope_article/blackpalestinian-breath/.

Movement for Black Lives. "Invest-Divest." August 2016. https://m4bl.org/policy-platforms/invest-divest/.

Moynagh, Maureen. *Political Tourism and Its Texts*. Toronto, Canada: University of Toronto Press, 2008.

Muravchik, Joshua. "Facing Up to Black Anti-Semitism." *Commentary* 100, no. 6 (1995): 26.

Murray, Michael. "The Cultural Heritage of Pilgrim Itineraries: The Camino de Santiago." *Journeys* 15, no. 2 (2014): 65–85. https://doi.org/10.3167/jys.2014.150204.

Myrdal, Gunnar. *An American Dilemma: The Negro Problem and Modern Democracy*. New York: Harper, 1944.

Nassar, Maha. "Palestinian Engagement with the Black Freedom Movement Prior to 1967." *Journal of Palestine Studies* 48, no. 4 (2019): 17–32. https://doi.org/10.1525/jps.2019.48.4.17.

Olson, Jason M. *America's Road to Jerusalem: The Impact of the Six-Day War on Protestant Politics*. Lanham, MD: Lexington, 2018.

Oren, Michael B. *Power, Faith, and Fantasy: America in the Middle East: 1776 to the Present*. New York: Norton, 2007.

Över, Defne. "Cultural Tourism and Complex Histories: The Armenian Akhtamar Church, the Turkish State and National Identity." *Qualitative Sociology* 39, no. 2 (2016): 173–94. https://doi.org/10.1007/s11133-016-9323-x.

Owens, Michael Leo. *God and Government in the Ghetto: The Politics of Church-State Collaboration in Black America*. Chicago: University of Chicago Press, 2007.

Pattillo-McCoy, Mary. "Church Culture as a Strategy of Action in the Black Community." *American Sociological Review* 63, no. 6 (1998): 767–84. https://doi.org/10.2307/2657500.

Pazos, Antón M., ed. *Redefining Pilgrimage: New Perspectives on Historical and Contemporary Pilgrimages*. New York: Routledge, 2014.

Pence, Mike. "Remarks by Vice President Mike Pence in Special Session of the Knesset." *The White House*. January 22, 2018. https://www.whitehouse.gov/briefings-statements/remarks-vice-president-mike-pence-special-session-knesset/.

Perrin, Andrew J. *Citizen Speak: The Democratic Imagination in American Life*. Chicago: University of Chicago Press, 2006.

Pew Research Center. "A Religious Portrait of African-Americans." January 30, 2009. http://www.pewforum.org/2009/01/30/a-religious-portrait-of-african-americans/.

Pinn, Anthony B. *The Black Church in the Post-Civil Rights Era*. Maryknoll, NY: Orbis, 2002.

——. "Black Theology." In *Liberation Theologies in the United States: An Introduction*, ed. S. M. Floyd-Thomas and A. B. Pinn, 15–36. New York: New York University Press, 2010.

Plummer, Brenda Gayle. *In Search of Power: African Americans in the Era of Decolonization, 1956–1974.* New York: Cambridge University Press, 2012.

Podhoretz, Norman. "My Negro Problem–And Ours." *Commentary*, February 1963, 93-101.

Polletta, Francesca. *It Was Like a Fever: Storytelling in Protest and Politics.* Chicago: University of Chicago Press, 2006.

Powell, Walter W., and Paul J. DiMaggio, eds. *The New Institutionalism in Organizational Analysis.* Chicago: University of Chicago Press, 1991.

Pratt, Tia Noelle. "Liturgy as Identity Work in Predominantly African American Parishes." In *American Parishes: Remaking Local Catholicism*, ed. G. J. Adler, T. C. Bruce, and B. Starks, 132-52. New York: Fordham University Press, 2019.

Prial, Frank J. "Blacks Organize Pro-Israel Group." *New York Times*, September 12, 1975.

Puar, Jasbir K. *The Right to Maim: Debility, Capacity, Disability.* Durham, NC: Duke University Press, 2017.

Raboteau, Albert J. "African-Americans, Exodus, and the American Israel." In *Strangers & Neighbors: Relations Between Blacks & Jews in the United States*, ed. M. Adams and J. H. Bracey, 57-63. Amherst: University of Massachusetts Press, 1999.

—. *Slave Religion: The "Invisible Institution" in the Antebellum South.* New York: Oxford University Press, 1978.

Reed, Adolph L. *Class Notes: Posing as Politics and Other Thoughts on the American Scene.* New York: New Press, 2000.

—. *The Jesse Jackson Phenomenon: The Crisis of Purpose in Afro-American Politics.* New Haven, CT: Yale University Press, 1986.

Rickford, Russell. "'To Build a New World': Black American Internationalism and Palestine Solidarity." *Journal of Palestine Studies* 48, no. 4 (2019): 52-68. https://doi.org/10.1525/jps.2019.48.4.52.

Rigueur, Leah Wright. *The Loneliness of the Black Republican: Pragmatic Politics and the Pursuit of Power.* Princeton, NJ: Princeton University Press, 2016.

Rivera, Lauren A. "Managing 'Spoiled' National Identity: War, Tourism, and Memory in Croatia." *American Sociological Review* 73, no. 4 (2008): 613-34.

Roberts, Bob, Jr. "Bob Roberts Jr.: Going Glocal." 2014. http://208.106.253.109/premier-only/going-glocal.aspx.

—. *Transformation: How Glocal Churches Transform Lives and the World.* Grand Rapids, MI: Zondervan, 2006.

Rogers, Stephanie Stidham. *Inventing the Holy Land: American Protestant Pilgrimage to Palestine, 1865–1941.* Lanham, MD: Lexington, 2011.

Romano, Renee C., and Leigh Raiford, eds. *The Civil Rights Movement in American Memory.* Athens: University of Georgia Press, 2006.

Rouse, Carolyn Moxley, John L. Jackson Jr., and Marla F. Frederick. *Televised Redemption: Black Religious Media and Racial Empowerment.* New York: New York University Press, 2016.

Rubin, Gary E. "African Americans and Israel." In *Struggles in the Promised Land: Towards a History of Black-Jewish Relations in the United States*, ed. J. Salzman and C. West, 357-70. New York: Oxford University Press, 1997.

Ruether, Rosemary Radford, and Herman J. Ruether. *The Wrath of Jonah: The Crisis of Religious Nationalism in the Israeli-Palestinian Conflict.* Minneapolis, MN: Fortress, 2002.

Sabeel Ecumenical Liberation Theology Center. "Sabeel Ecumenical Liberation Theology Center." Accessed March 1, 2020. https://sabeel.org/.

Said, Edward. "The Imperial Bluster of Tom Delay." CounterPunch.org. August 20, 2003. https://www.counterpunch.org/2003/08/20/the-imperial-bluster-of-tom-delay/.

Saiya, Nilay. "Onward Christian Soldiers: American Dispensationalists, George W. Bush and the Middle East." *Holy Land Studies: A Multidisciplinary Journal (Edinburgh University Press)* 11, no. 2 (2012): 175–204. https://doi.org/10.3366/hls.2012.0044.

Salzman, Jack. Introduction to *Struggles in the Promised Land: Towards a History of Black-Jewish Relations in the United States*, ed. J. Salzman and C. West, 1–19. New York: Oxford University Press, 1997.

Salzman, Jack, and Cornel West, eds. *Struggles in the Promised Land: Towards a History of Black-Jewish Relations in the United States*. New York: Oxford University Press, 1997.

Samuel DeWitt Proctor Conference. "About Us." Accessed February 14, 2019. http://sdpconference.info/about-us/.

——. "Journey to Justice: From Black America to Palestine." Accessed May 17, 2018. https://www.youtube.com/watch?v=9VFpz3YWGkg&feature=youtu.be.

——. "Palestinian Justice Meets the Historic Black Church!" 2015. https://myemail.constantcontact.com/Palestinian-Justice-Meets-the-Historic-Black-Church-.html?soid=1103648503270&aid=JYeWf4Z-JMw.

——. "Prayers for Gaza!" 2018.

Savage, Barbara Dianne. "Benjamin Mays, Global Ecumenism, and Local Religious Segregation." *American Quarterly* 59, no. 3 (2007): 785–806. https://doi.org/10.1353/aq.2007.0068.

——. *Your Spirits Walk Beside Us: The Politics of Black Religion*. Cambridge, MA: Belknap Press of Harvard University Press, 2008.

Scholes, Jeffrey, and Raphael Sassower. *Religion and Sports in American Culture*. New York: Routledge, 2013.

Sellars, Richard West. "Pilgrim Places: Civil War Battlefields, Historic Preservation, and America's First National Military Parks, 1863–1900." *CRM: Journal of Heritage Stewardship* 2, no. 1 (2005): 23–52.

Sengupta, Kim. "The Real Reason Trump Declared Jerusalem the Capital of Israel Was Because He Feared Losing His Evangelical Voter Base." *Independent*, December 8, 2017. https://www.independent.co.uk/voices/jerusalem-donald-trump-israel-capital-decision-reason-why-evangelical-voters-us-fear-a8099321.html.

Sha'ban, Fuad. *For Zion's Sake: The Judeo-Christian Tradition in American Culture*. Ann Arbor, MI: Pluto, 2005.

Shapiro, Faydra L. "The Messiah and Rabbi Jesus: Policing the Jewish–Christian Border in Christian Zionism." *Culture and Religion* 12, no. 4 (2011): 463–77. https://doi.org/10.1080/14755610.2011.633537.

Sharlet, Jeff. *The Family: The Secret Fundamentalism at the Heart of American Power*. New York: Harper, 2008.

Sheldon, Ruth. *Tragic Encounters and Ordinary Ethics: Palestine-Israel in British Universities*. Manchester, UK: Manchester University Press, 2016.

Shinnamon, Felicia Gobba. "Activist Tourism: Perceptions of Ecotourism and Sustainability in Costa Rica." PhD diss., California Institute of Integral Studies, San Francisco, 2010.

Singer, Merrill. "Symbolic Identity Formation in an African American Religious Sect: The Black Hebrew Israelites." In *Black Zion: African American Religious Encounters with Judaism*, ed. N. Deutsch and Y. P. Chireau, 55–72. New York: Oxford University Press, 2000.

Sizer, Stephen. *Christian Zionism: Road-Map to Armageddon?* Downers Grove, IL: IVP Academic, 2006.

Smith, Christian, ed. *Disruptive Religion: The Force of Faith in Social Movement Activism*. New York: Routledge, 1996.

Smith, Damu. "The African-American Experience." In *Challenging Christian Zionism: Theology, Politics and the Israel-Palestine Conflict*, ed. N. Ateek, C. Duaybis, and M. Tobin, 215-25. London: Melisende, 2005.

Smith, Robert O. *More Desired Than Our Owne Salvation: The Roots of Christian Zionism*. New York: Oxford University Press, 2013.

SNCC Newsletter. "The Palestine Problem." June–July 1967. https://www.crmvet.org/docs/sv/6707_sncc_news-r.pdf.

Sobel, Mechal. *Trabelin' On: The Slave Journey to an Afro-Baptist Faith*. Westport, CT: Greenwood, 1979.

Somers, Margaret R. "Narrativity, Narrative Identity, and Social Action: Rethinking English Working-Class Formation." *Social Science History* 16, no. 4 (1992): 591–630. https://doi.org/10.2307/1171314.

Sorett, Josef. *Black Is a Church: Christianity and the Contours of African American Life*. New York: Oxford University Press, 2023.

Spector, Stephen. *Evangelicals and Israel: The Story of American Christian Zionism*. New York: Oxford University Press, 2008.

Stanford, Karin L. *Beyond the Boundaries: Reverend Jesse Jackson in International Affairs*. Albany: State University of New York Press, 1997.

Stevens, Michael A. *We Too Stand: A Call for the African-American Church to Support the Jewish State*. Lake Mary, FL: FrontLine, 2013.

Swartz, David. *Culture and Power: The Sociology of Pierre Bourdieu*. Chicago: University of Chicago Press, 1998.

Switzer, Catherine. *Ulster, Ireland and the Somme: War Memorials and Battlefield Pilgrimages*. Dublin: History Press, 2013.

Tate, Katherine. *From Protest to Politics: The New Black Voters in American Elections*. Cambridge, MA: Harvard University Press, 1993.

Thal, Sarah. *Rearranging the Landscape of the Gods: The Politics of a Pilgrimage Site in Japan, 1573–1912*. Chicago: University of Chicago Press, 2005.

The Kairos Document. "The Kairos Document." 1985. https://www.sahistory.org.za/archive/challenge-church-theological-comment-political-crisis-south-africa-kairos-document-1985.

Thiam, Thierno, and Gilbert Rochon. *Sustainability, Emerging Technologies, and Pan-Africanism*. New York: Palgrave Macmillan, 2020.

Thurman, Howard. *Deep River: An Interpretation of Negro Spirituals*. Mills College, CA: Eucalyptus, 1945.

Tilly, Charles. *Stories, Identities, and Political Change*. Lanham, MD: Rowman & Littlefield, 2002.

Tucker-Worgs, Tamelyn. *The Black Megachurch: Theology, Gender, and the Politics of Public Engagement*. Waco, TX: Baylor University Press, 2011.

Turner, Henry McNeal. "Emigration to Africa." In *African American Religious History: A Documentary Witness*, ed. M. C. Sernett, 289–95. Durham, NC: Duke University Press, 1999. First published in 1883.

Turner, Victor. "The Center Out There: Pilgrim's Goal." *History of Religions* 12, no. 3 (1973): 191–230. https://doi.org/10.1086/462677.

Turner, Victor, and Edith Turner. *Image and Pilgrimage in Christian Culture: Anthropological Perspectives.* New York: Columbia University Press, 1978.

Vermurlen, Brad. *Reformed Resurgence: The New Calvinist Movement and the Battle Over American Evangelicalism.* New York: Oxford University Press, 2020.

Vogel, Lester Irwin. *To See a Promised Land: Americans and the Holy Land in the Nineteenth Century.* University Park: Pennsylvania State University Press, 1993.

Wacquant, Loïc J. D. "Crafting the Neoliberal State: Workfare and Prisonfare in the Bureaucratic Field." In *Bourdieu's Theory of Social Fields: Concepts and Applications*, ed. M. Hilgers and E. Mangez, 238–56. New York: Routledge, 2014.

——. "For an Analytic of Racial Domination." *Political Power and Social Theory* 11 (1997): 221–34.

Wagner, Donald. "Evangelicals and Israel: Theological Roots of a Political Alliance." *Christian Century* 115, no. 30 (1998): 1020.

Walton, Jonathan L. *Watch This! The Ethics and Aesthetics of Black Televangelism.* New York: New York University Press, 2009.

Warnock, Raphael G. *The Divided Mind of the Black Church: Theology, Piety, and Public Witness.* New York: New York University Press, 2013.

Washington, Dumisani. *Zionism and the Black Church: Why Standing with Israel Will Be a Defining Issue for Christians of Color in the 21st Century.* Stockton, CA: IBSI, 2014.

Webb, Taurean. "Journeys Toward Justice." 2016. http://sdpconference.info/journeys-toward-justice/.

——. "On Gaza and the U.S. Embassy Opening." 2018. http://files.constantcontact.com/6e5b396f001/d057aec0-2b17-46ea-a27b-414017c8174e.pdf.

——. "Troubling Idols: Black-Palestinian Solidarity in U.S. Afro-Christian Spaces." *Journal of Palestine Studies* 48, no. 4 (2019): 33–51. https://doi.org/10.1525/jps.2019.48.4.33.

Weber, Timothy P. *On the Road to Armageddon: How Evangelicals Became Israel's Best Friend.* Grand Rapids, MI: Baker Academic, 2004.

Weisbord, Robert G., and Richard Kazarian. *Israel in the Black American Perspective.* Westport, CT: Greenwood, 1985.

Weisenfeld, Judith. *New World A-Coming: Black Religion and Racial Identity During the Great Migration.* New York: New York University Press, 2016.

West, Brad. "Enchanting Pasts: The Role of International Civil Religious Pilgrimage in Reimagining National Collective Memory." *Sociological Theory* 26, no. 3 (2008): 258–70.

West, Cornel. *Prophesy Deliverance! An Afro-American Revolutionary Christianity.* Philadelphia: Westminster, 1982.

Westfield, Nancy Lynne, Juan M. Floyd-Thomas, Carol B. Duncan, Stacey Floyd-Thomas, and Stephen G. Ray. *Black Church Studies: An Introduction.* Nashville, TN: Abingdon, 2007.

Wilde, Melissa J. "How Culture Mattered at Vatican II: Collegiality Trumps Authority in the Council's Social Movement Organizations." *American Sociological Review* 69, no. 4 (2004): 576–602. https://doi.org/10.1177/000312240406900406.

Wilkinson, Paul R. *For Zion's Sake: Christian Zionism and the Role of John Nelson Darby.* Colorado Springs, CO: Paternoster, 2007.

—. *Understanding Christian Zionism: Israel's Place in the Purposes of God.* Bend, OR: Berean Call, 2013.

Williams, Delores S. *Sisters in the Wilderness: The Challenge of Womanist God-Talk.* Maryknoll, NY: Orbis, 1993.

Williams, Don. "Walking Where Jesus Walked Led to the Proctor Conference." Kairos USA, March 11, 2015. https://kairosusa.org/walking-where-jesus-walked-led-to-the-proctor-conference/.

Williams, Sara A. "Moral Apprentices at the Margins: Come and See Tours and the Making of the Ethical Self." PhD diss., Emory University, Atlanta, GA, 2021.

—. "Moral Commodities and the Practice of Freedom." *Journal of Religious Ethics* 48, no. 4 (2020): 642–63. https://doi.org/https://doi.org/10.1111/jore.12333.

Wilmore, Gayraud S. *Black Religion and Black Radicalism.* Garden City, NY: Doubleday, 1972.

Wojcik, Daniel. "Pre's Rock: Pilgrimage, Ritual, and Runners' Traditions at the Roadside Shrine for Steve Prefontaine." In *Shrines and Pilgrimage in the Modern World: New Itineraries Into the Sacred*, ed. P. J. Margry, 201–37. Amsterdam: Amsterdam University Press, 2008.

Wood, Richard L. *Faith in Action: Religion, Race, and Democratic Organizing in America.* Chicago: University of Chicago Press, 2002.

Woodson, Carter Godwin. *The History of the Negro Church.* Washington, DC: Associated, 1921.

—. "The Negro Church, an All-Comprehending Institution." *Negro History Bulletin* 3, no. 1 (1939): 7, 15.

Wynn, Jonathan R. *The Tour Guide: Walking and Talking New York.* Chicago: University of Chicago Press, 2011.

Yazdiha, Hajar. *The Struggle for the People's King: How Politics Transforms the Memory of the Civil Rights Movement.* Princeton, NJ: Princeton University Press, 2023.

Zia, Ather. "'Their Wounds Are Our Wounds': A Case for Affective Solidarity Between Palestine and Kashmir." *Identities* 27, no. 3 (2020): 357–75. https://doi.org/10.1080/1070289X.2020.1750199.

Index